## Also by Meredith Tax

NONFICTION

*The Rising of the Women: Feminist Solidarity and Class Conflict 1880–1917*

*Double Bind: The Muslim Right, the Anglo-American Left, and Universal Human Rights*

FICTION

*Rivington Street*

*Union Square*

# A Road Unforeseen

## Women Fight
## the Islamic State

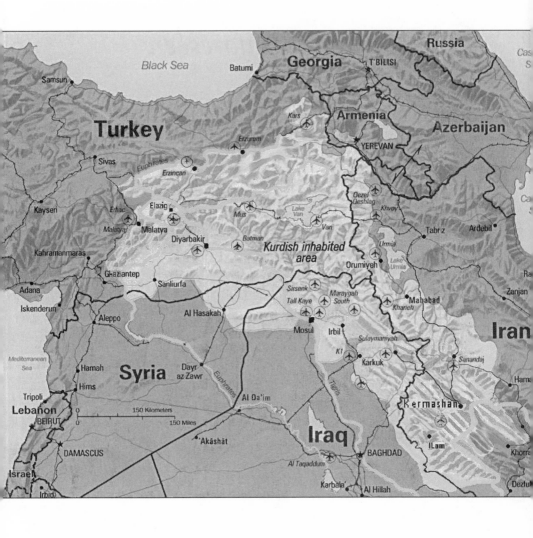

# A Road Unforeseen

## Women Fight
## the Islamic State

*Meredith Tax*

PHOTOGRAPHS BY
*Joey L.*

Bellevue Literary Press
NEW YORK

First published in the United States in 2016 by
Bellevue Literary Press, New York

For information, contact:
Bellevue Literary Press
NYU School of Medicine
550 First Avenue
OBV A612
New York, NY 10016

**Library of Congress Cataloging-in-Publication Data**
is available from the publisher upon request

Bellevue Literary Press would like to thank all its generous
donors—individuals and foundations—for their support.

 The New York State Council on the Arts
with the support of Governor Andrew
NYSCA  Cuomo and the New York State Legislature

ART WORKS.

**National
Endowment
for the Arts**
arts.gov

This project is supported in part
by an award from the National
Endowment for the Arts.

Book design and composition by Mulberry Tree Press, Inc.

Manufactured in the United States of America.
First Edition

1 3 5 7 9 8 6 4 2

paperback ISBN: 978-1-942658-10-8

ebook ISBN: 978-1-942658-11-5

*To Myra Malkin,*
*My steadfast friend and support for over fifty years*

"We must take a hard road, a road unforeseen.
There lies our hope, if hope it be."

—J.R.R. Tolkien, *The Lord of the Rings*

# Contents

*Glossary of Organizational Names*   13

Introduction: A Road Unforeseen   17

1: The Kurds   37

2: Separated at Birth   59

3: Insurrection and Genocide   79

4: The People Take Up the Struggle   105

5: Kurdish Women Rising   133

6: Democratic Autonomy in Turkey and Syria   155

7: The Battle of Kobane and Its Backlash   179

8: The Birth of Daesh   201

9: Daesh vs. Kobane   225

10: War and Peace in Turkey   243

Coda: Some Questions Remain   259

*Notes*   265

*Suggestions for Further Reading*   318

*Acknowledgments*   320

*Index*   322

# Glossary of Organizational Names

## GEOGRAPHY OF KURDISTAN

Iran = East Kurdistan/Rojhilat

Iraq = South Kurdistan/Bashur

Syria = West Kurdistan/Rojava

Turkey = North Kurdistan/Bakur

## IRAQI KURDISH PARTIES

KRG: Kurdistan Regional Government (coalition)

KDP: Kurdistan Democratic Party, led by Masoud Barzani

PUK: Patriotic Union of Kurdistan, led by Jalal Talabani

Gorran (Movement for Change): third party breakaway from
   PUK in 2009

## THE KURDISH LIBERATION MOVEMENT (PKK) NETWORK

KCK: Association of Communities in Kurdistan

KJK: Kurdistan Women's Liberation Movement

PJAK: Party for a Free Life in Kurdistan (Iran)

   YRK-HPJ: Eastern Kurdistan Protection Units and
      Women's Protection Units

PYD: Democratic Union Party (Syria)

   YPG-YPJ: People's Protection Units and Women's
      Protection Units (Syria)

   TEV-DEM (multi-party civil society coalition)

PKK: Kurdistan Workers Party (Turkey)

   TAJK: Free Women's Movement of Kurdistan

> HPG-YJA-Star: People's Defense Forces and Free Women's Forces
>
> YDG-H and YDG-K: Patriotic Revolutionary Youth Movement and Union of Patriotic Revolutionary Young Women
>
> DTK: Democratic Society Congress (multi-party civil society coalition)

## GENEALOGY OF KURDISH PARLIAMENTARY PARTIES IN TURKEY

HEP 1990–1993

DEP 1993–1994

HADEP 1994–2003

DEHAP 2003–2006, merged with another Kurdish party to form the DTP

DTP Democratic Society Party 2006–2009

BDP Successor party to DTP 2008–2014, merged with HDP

HDP Kurdish and Gezi feminist-LGBT-Left Party, 2014–present

## AL QAEDA AND DAESH

Al Qaeda in Iraq (IQI) is founded 2002

Changes name to Islamic State in Iraq (ISI) 2006

Sends infiltrators into Syria 2011 who found Jabhat al-Nusra

ISI announces merger with Jabhat al-Nusra 2013 under a name translated either as ISIS (Islamic State in Iraq and Syria/Iraq and al-Sham) or ISIL (Islamic State in Iraq and the Levant)

Jabhat al-Nusra refuses to merge so al Qaeda and ISIS split 2013

ISIS declares itself a caliphate under the name Islamic State (IS) 2014

Daesh is the Arabic name for Islamic State, used by its opponents

# A Road Unforeseen

Women Fight
the Islamic State

*Didar, a soldier with the Women's Protection Units (YPJ).*

# A Road Unforeseen

N AUGUST 2014, DAESH—the Arabic acronym for the terrorist group that has been variously called ISIS, ISIL, and the Islamic State[1]—attacked the city of Kobane in Northern Syria, and I started seeing pictures of smiling rifle-toting girls in uniform defending the city. Who were these girls? After hours of searching the web, I realized that they belonged to a revolutionary organization of which I had never heard, the Democratic Union Party (PYD) of the Syrian Kurds, which had liberated three areas, Cizire, Afrin, and Kobane, on the Syria-Turkey border, setting up cantons where people make decisions through local councils and women hold 40 percent of all leadership positions. As an entity, the cantons are called Rojava.

That such a liberated area even existed was big news to me. On that summer's maps, Rojava—the Kurdish word for "west"—looked like three unconnected yellow blobs making up an area slightly smaller than Connecticut, surrounded by a vast and menacing gray field representing territory controlled by Daesh. In the summer of 2014, the ski-masked jihadis of Daesh seemed invincible as they swept down on the terrified towns and cities of Iraq, while the Iraqi army and the vaunted Iraqi Kurdish militia, the *peshmerga,* fled before them. Not until Daesh reached Kobane did they meet guerrillas who had built something they were willing to fight for. Since then, the Rojava forces have captured Tal Abyad, linking two of the three yellow blobs to make a larger contiguous unit; Daesh has also lost other territory.

The Obama administration had named Daesh an "imminent threat to every interest we have," so the media were ecstatic to discover the photogenic young female guerrillas.[2] The press tended, however, to avoid discussing what they stood for, and no wonder, for these girls did not fit into any acceptable Western narrative: They were feminists, socialists, if not

17

indeed anarchists or communists, and led by a group linked to Turkey's Kurdistan Workers' Party (PKK), which is listed as a terrorist organization by NATO, the UK, and the US.

Fascinated, I searched for more information and found it mainly on anarchist websites, for the anarchist movement has been following the PKK ever since its leader, Abdullah Ocalan, said American radical Murray Bookchin was a major influence on his thinking. But in October 2014, nobody else seemed to be paying much attention to Rojava or the PKK, as the anthropologist and activist David Graeber wrote in a *Guardian* op-ed. Comparing the struggle against Daesh to that of the Spanish Republic in 1937, when his father had joined the International Brigade to fight fascism, Graeber called for similar solidarity with Rojava, saying it is "a remarkable democratic experiment. Popular assemblies have been created as the ultimate decision-making bodies . . . and, in a remarkable echo of the armed Mujeres Libres (Free Women) of Spain, a feminist army . . . has carried out a large proportion of the combat operations against the forces of Islamic State. How can something like this happen and still be almost entirely ignored by the international community, even, largely, by the international Left?"[3]

In December 2014, when the Kurds in Kobane had been fighting Daesh for over two months with no help from anybody, the monthly news magazine *In These Times* organized a panel that framed the issues purely in terms of US military intervention. One of the panelists, Richard Falk, a human rights expert, said, "The plight of the Kurds in Kobani and their courage in resisting ISIS poses a tragic predicament that does challenge the kind of anti-interventionism that I feel is justified overall, particularly in the Middle East. But to overcome the presumption against military intervention, especially from the air, one needs very powerful evidence. . . . [T]he ISIS intervention doesn't seem designed to actually deal with the problem. Rather, it looks like a projection of US power in the region."[4]

To Falk, the only important question was one of US power, not whether Kobane needed help or had asked for it or even what other kinds of help besides bombing might be available. To me, this single-minded focus on the US smacks of imperial narcissism. Like the neocons they hate, some on the Left see the US as all powerful—in their view, any popular movement that is not fighting the US is being manipulated by it, and the only thing Americans have to worry about is opposing their own government. Personally, I think the world has more than one "Evil Empire," and agree with David Graeber that anti-imperialist critique is insufficient without solidarity. That means supporting people who stand for the same things progressives elsewhere support—human rights, a strong labor movement, separation between religion and politics, equality for all, racial justice, women's liberation, an end to discrimination on the basis of sexuality or belief—and coming through when they ask for help.

The more I learned about the Rojava cantons, the more I heard echoes in my mind of *The Lord of the Rings*, Tolkien's saga of a lust for power gone mad and a handful of people pitted against it in a battle that will decide the fate of the world. As their strategy council decides, "We must take a hard road, a road unforeseen. There lies our hope, if hope it be."[5] Only by destroying the ring of power, rather than trying to use it themselves, can Tolkien's heroes defeat evil; only by destroying that metaphorical ring of power called the state, built on domination and ruled by force, do members of the Syrian and Turkish Kurdish liberation movement believe they can create societies based on equality, democracy, ecology, and mutual respect.

Note that I am careful to say Syrian and Turkish Kurds, rather than just talk about "the Kurds," as Western media often do in what sometimes looks like deliberate obfuscation. Because Americans have been hearing about the Iraqi Kurds since the Gulf War, many assume all Kurds are in Iraq. That is a misconception. Kurdistan was divided between Iran, Iraq, Syria, and Turkey after World War I. Today the dominant party in the Kurdistan Regional Government of Iraq, led by Masoud Barzani, is competing with the Kurdish liberation movement of Rojava and the Turkish Kurds for ideological leadership. Like the little ethnic states that emerged in Eastern Europe at the end of the Cold War, the Iraqi Kurds want their own nation. In contrast, the Kurdish liberation movement thinks the nation-state is old-fashioned in an age of globalization; they want something more democratic, feminist, and ethnically inclusive, and are trying to build it in Rojava.

On New Year's Day, 2015, I decided it was my responsibility to tell my friends about Rojava and sent out an email with a map and some links, saying, "At the end of such a dark and difficult year, one searches for light. It can sometimes be found in unexpected places." Then I wrote an article for *Dissent* magazine, which was published in April 2015 and resulted in an invitation to write this book.[6]

I agreed because I thought the matter was so urgent. But I had another reason: to answer my own questions about the Kurdish women's movement and its militias. Because in all my years as a feminist on the Left, I had never seen an armed liberation struggle with women so clearly in front. They reminded me of the immigrant women of the Lawrence textile strike of 1912, of whom I wrote in my first book, *The Rising of the Women*. The strike was organized by a militant syndicalist union, the Industrial Workers of the World, usually called the Wobblies; the local workforce was mostly immigrant; and since everybody—men, women, and children—worked in the mills, the strike involved the whole community.

The employers mobilized anti-immigrant feeling to break the strike, students came out from Harvard to beat up strikers, and the governor of Massachusetts called out the National Guard. Thinking they had a better chance than men of facing armed police without getting shot, the women strikers used to march at the front of the IWW demonstrations. When reporters asked Elizabeth Gurley Flynn, a Wobbly organizer, why the IWW was pushing women to the front, she said, "We don't push women to the front—we're the only organization that doesn't hold them back and they go to the front!"[7]

The leading role of Kurdish women in the war against Daesh, and what that implies about the kind of society they are trying to build, demands our attention. It is a crux, marking the stirrings of a new historical period. As Kurdish writer Memed Aksoy put it, "The Kurds and their country Kurdistan is the site of a great battle now, between freedom and enslavement, the womb from where a new civilisation has the opportunity to grow."[8]

I have lived through two such moments before: the sixties and the end of the Cold War.

When I was growing up, the world was divided into two warring systems, called the "Free World" and "the Socialist Camp." Each had its own narrative. The Free World narrative promised that an ever-expanding capitalist market would bring democratic rights, freedom, and prosperity to all. The US had come out of World War II in better shape than anybody else, with an economy so strong it could handle an enormously expensive arms and nuclear race and still have enough left over to fuel domestic consumption at unheard-of levels. The Free World narrative acknowledged that some would become richer than others, but promised that there would be enough refrigerators, cars, and Happy Meals for everyone. By the late sixties, the civil rights movement and

youth rebellion had poked holes in US assertions of equality and democratic bliss, but the narrative still had a lot of power internationally.

To this dream of democratic consumerism, the Soviet bloc counter-
posed a narrative in which power and wealth were shared, everyone
had free healthcare and education, and there was no gulf between rich
and poor. The goal was "from each according to his ability, to each
according to his needs."[9] But there was a large gap between this promise and reality. The Soviet Union had lost huge numbers of people and
most of its industrial base in World War II. By the sixties, it had managed to pull nearly equal in the arms race but only at enormous cost
to its people, many of whom had to live three families to an apartment
and line up to get basic subsistence needs. They longed for the consumer comforts of the West. And while they had jobs and health care,
they lacked the freedoms that might have made them feel they had
some control over their lives, for in practice communist parties were
top-down authoritarian elites, and their people unwilling subjects.

In the eighties, when the USSR got stuck in the quagmire of a war
in Afghanistan, its whole edifice became economically and politically unsustainable. In 1989, it withdrew its troops from Afghanistan.
Shortly thereafter the Communist Party dissolved and the USSR itself
fell to bits. The former Soviet empire became a collection of nationalist
states, many run by demagogues and oligarchs, distinguished mainly
for corruption and authoritarianism.

During the Cold War, people in the communist-influenced Left used
to refer to the Soviet Union and its allies as "really-existing socialism"—
meaning, okay, it wasn't perfect, but it was the best people had come up
with so far. Their whole world crumbled when the Soviet Union did.
They lost their political bearings and also lost their language, not knowing what words to use anymore for the aspirations of social justice they
still cherished. Many fell into a reactive anti-US stand that shaped their
view of the entire world: Anything the US supported must be bad; anything that opposed the US must be good, including Islamist jihadis who
said they were anti-imperialist.[10] Their thinking was frozen in Cold War
dichotomies and, if they no longer had anything to defend, at least they
could still criticize the triumph of capital.

And capital had triumphed with a vengeance. With no ideological
opponent to restrain them, US and European financial and business
interests went on the offensive. Working through the World Bank and

the International Monetary Fund, and inspired by the gospel of free trade, they pushed open the markets of the world. Capital had always been mobile, but now it broke down national boundaries as never before. As American companies moved their work and resources from country to country in search of the cheapest labor and raw materials, labor unions in the US began to crumble and the living standards of most Americans declined.

The triumph of the capitalist narrative after 1989 fast-forwarded the world into a state of revolutionary transformation in economics, politics, and technology. In the name of free trade, Western financial institutions, led by the US, imposed "shock therapy" on the former Soviet bloc, creating a new ruling elite of thieves in which public goods were looted by government-connected oligarchs, and vast numbers lost the social benefits they once had without getting any richer. This cataclysm discredited democracy to the point that Vladimir Putin, a former KGB director, was elected president.

In much of the Global South, the offensive took the form of "structural adjustment," opening countries up to world trade, forcing government-owned industries to privatize, and devastating fragile local economies. In exchange, the countries' leaders were given loans, the repayment of which could eat up their entire social service budgets.

In this "new world order," labor too became globalized, as huge numbers of migrants flooded Europe and the US in search of work that would enable them to support their families back home—families who could no longer feed themselves because competition from subsidized American crops, war, climate change, or predatory landowners had made farming unsustainable, or because they had switched from growing their own food to growing export crops for an international market whose prices fluctuated wildly because of speculation by traders in faraway world capitals.

In response to these changes, the international Left developed a critique centered on the concepts of "neoliberalism" and "globalization." What both terms really mean is an unrestrained global free market based on an unproven economic theory that says any benefits gained by the rich will trickle down to the poor. And indeed, in some places, particularly China and India, while people at the low end of the economy remain profoundly poor, the middle class has expanded through the emergence of new industries and opportunities. But in many other places, this theory has led to unbelievable wealth for a few—the one percent—and declining standards of living for most. Workers in Italy, Greece, Spain, and the United States, for instance, have seen their liveli-hoods grow increasingly precarious, their government services disap-pear, and their labor unions and social benefits shrink.[11]

In the Middle East, despite the fabulous wealth of oil-dependent elites, most countries are cursed with stagnant economies and very high levels of poverty and illiteracy. For many years their politics, too, were stagnant, the life crushed out of them by entrenched military dictatorships which had long since wiped out their left-wing opponents and were now threat-ened only by Islamists, whom they did their best to accommodate.

When the "Arab Spring" revolts began in 2011, their initial demands were economic—the poor simply could not survive. These uprisings were transformed within weeks by massive demands for democracy as well as economic reform. But, except in Tunisia, the social forces were not organized enough to develop a democratic alternative to dictator-ships. Instead, the rewards of insurrection were scooped up by Islamists or the military—or in Egypt, first one and then the other. The autono-mous Kurdish region of Iraq, for all its tribalism and corruption, is a shining exception to this pattern.

Particularly in Egypt and Tunisia, women were active in the Arab Spring uprisings despite extreme sexual harassment from police, thugs, and Islamists—harassment that was especially violent in Egypt, where female protestors were assaulted by mobs in the public square and by police. Some were stripped and beaten, like the hijab-wearing "woman in a blue bra," whose picture, being dragged off by police, went viral; others were subjected to forced virginity tests.[12] The mes-sage of these attacks was a familiar one to women all over the world: Stay home if you want to be safe.

These assaults took place in a region feminist sociologists some-times call "the patriarchal belt," which stretches from the Middle East and North Africa to South Asia and is described thus by Handan Caglayan, a political scientist at the University of Ankara: "The patri-archal family in this geography is the main social unit, and the oldest men have rights over all the other family members. The main charac-teristic of the social structures under the patriarchal belt is the strict control over women's behavior. In question is a strong ideology which relates the honor of the family to women's chastity."[13]

I deliberately do not use the term "the Muslim world" for this region.

"The patriarchal belt" is a geographical designation, not a religious one, for the region also contains Christians, Jews, Zoroastrians, Parsees, Sikhs, Hindus, and many smaller religious groups, while Muslims themselves have a great range of doctrinal variations and cultural practices. And throughout the region, living alongside people who live by the old rules, are others who passionately rebel against these rules and think the defense of secularism and defeat of patriarchy are essential to real democracy.

As feminist sociologist Deniz Kandiyoti explains, the increased level of violence against women in this region is not a sign of the old patriarchal order's strength but of its weakness: "The fact is that the provisions that underwrite the positional superiority of men over women in Islam are, sociologically speaking, in tatters. The male provider image jars with the multitudes of unemployed male youth who are unable to provide for themselves, much less protect women from bread-winning roles and the rigours of exposure to public spaces. We are witnessing a profound crisis of masculinity leading to more violent and coercive assertions of male prerogatives where the abuse of women can become a blood sport."[14]

This violence is intimately tied up with the rise of fundamentalist and other right-wing identity movements since the end of the Cold War, movements that invoke a dream of homogeneous ancient communities ruled by male elders. As these movements become more powerful, their capacity for violence grows and can lead to war with neighboring ethnic or religious groups. Control of women as the symbols and carriers of a "pure" national, ethnic, or religious identity is central to the programs of such movements, and when they go to war, rape is the weapon by which they demonstrate their victory over "the other," by defiling "his" women and making them give birth to enemy aliens.

In a 2006 talk before the American Society of International Law, Gita Sahgal, a founder of Women Against Fundamentalism in the UK, defined fundamentalist movements as existing both within and outside the state, sometimes simultaneously. "While some of these movements may be represented by traditional power structures, such as the Catholic Church, many fundamentalist political formations are modern, frequently global, political movements, which draw their strength from large diaspora support and while insisting on 'purity' and 'authenticity' have little relation to traditional religious formations (which may be patriarchal and oppressive but are not necessarily fundamentalist). They recreate 'tradition' to provide new meanings to older practices, and in doing so invent traditions just as nineteenth-century European nationalism did."[15]

The year 1989 is notable for a great worldwide upsurge of fundamentalism. In Afghanistan, the Taliban moved into the vacuum left by departing Soviet troops and began to impose their brutal version of sharia law. In an alliance between the South Asian Sunni fundamentalists of Jamaat e Islami and the Shia fundamentalists who follow Iran's leadership, Islamists mobilized globally against Salman Rushdie's novel *The Satanic Verses*, burning books, staging riots in Islamabad, Bombay, and Dhaka, and bombing the British embassy in Karachi. The campaign culminated in a fatwa by Iran's Ayatollah Khomeini that forced Rushdie underground for many years. In Yugoslavia, Serbian nationalist Slobodan Milosevic consolidated his rise to power with a speech in Kosovo that looked back to the Ottoman Empire's conquest of the region six centuries earlier and called on Serbs to go into battle to defend Christian civilization. In India, the Hindu extremists of Shiv Sena began their long climb to political power by winning local office in the state of Maharashtra. In the United States, Pat Robertson formed the Christian Coalition to serve as the organizational center of a drive by Protestant evangelicals to transform the Republican Party into the defender of Christian "family values" against the globalizing elites of the Northeast and the West Coast and their degenerate ways.

Why did these fundamentalist movements become so strong after 1989? Two reasons are usually given. First, with the removal of Soviet state control, nationalist and religious identity movements that had been building up steam for decades blew the lid off the pressure cooker. Second, with globalization, capitalist forms of organization and notions of individual liberty—wrongly defined as Western—penetrated to the most remote areas, bringing their values and media to threaten traditional male elites, who reacted violently. While the US interventions in the Middle East and South Asia—from the overthrow and murder of Iran's Mossadegh in 1953 to the support of Afghan jihadis against the Soviets to the 2003 invasion of Iraq—have certainly destabilized the region, the seductions of Western media and the freedom offered by the internet have been equally upsetting to supporters of ancient traditions and power arrangements.

But I believe there is a third reason for the rise of fundamentalism around the world: the success of the global women's movement, which has been growing in strength, despite numerous setbacks and massive cooptation. Its legal achievements peaked at UN conferences in the early nineties, setting off alarm bells in traditionalist enclaves from the Vatican to Saudi Arabia.

The backlash had already begun in the US, where the gay rights movement and *Roe v. Wade*, the Supreme Court decision that legalized abortion, had been galvanizing conservative opposition since the late seventies. But in many parts of the world, the women's movement did not make substantial gains until the nineties, when new information technologies enabled organizers to coordinate their activities across borders. Linked by a blizzard of faxes, women worked together transnationally at the 1992 UN Conference on the Environment in Rio; the 1993 UN Conference on Human Rights in Vienna; the 1994 UN Conference on Population and Development in Cairo; and the 1995 UN Conference on Women in Beijing.

The transnational feminists in this movement defined themselves in terms of universal human rights, but insisted that the human rights framework had to be applied to women's lives in ways not previously imagined, ways that challenged the long-established distinction between public and private spheres. Why, for instance, was it murder when a man killed a woman he didn't know but an "honor crime" if he killed his wife or sister or daughter?

By insisting that human rights are indivisible and apply in the home as well as in the public square, the women's movement brought violations like forced marriage, mistreatment of widows, and "honor killings" into the open, not to mention the widespread practice of female genital mutilation (FGM).[16] Since the family is the last bastion of traditional male authority, right-wing identity movements have been enormously threatened by attempts to give women equal rights and protection under the law, which they see as an invasion of privacy. They fiercely resist such change in the name of tradition, religious dogma, or defense of the family. They also criticize these innovations as Western, although in fact, like the Universal Declaration of Human Rights itself, the framework of women's human rights has been profoundly shaped by women of the Global South.

While Eleanor Roosevelt may have chaired the drafting committee for the Universal Declaration of Human Rights, in fact, the UDHR was drafted and redrafted by people from former colonies all around the world, as human rights expert Susan Waltz has documented. Their concerns went far beyond the US emphasis on civil and political rights to include social and economic rights, female autonomy, national liberation, and freedom from discrimination by race and ethnicity—issues that were not on the minds of the US political class in 1948. In Waltz's words:

> The most ardent champions of socioeconomic rights, for example, came from Latin America (rather than Soviet bloc countries, as often supposed). The Soviet bloc delegations resisted encroachments on sovereignty but tenaciously pressed the issue of nondiscrimination, and it is thanks in large part to their persistence that every article of the Declaration applies to everyone. Egypt is responsible for the strong statement of universality at the opening of the Declaration, its delegate having pushed to make the Declaration's provisions applicable "both among peoples of the Member States and among peoples of territories under their jurisdiction."
>
> Anticipating concerns of our own times, delegates from India, the Dominican Republic, and Denmark fought to have rights expressed in gender-neutral language and for explicit recognition of the rights of women. The delegate from Poland called attention to the issue of human trafficking, and the draft was amended to prohibit slavery "in all its forms." A young woman delegate from Pakistan, herself raised in purdah (the custom of keeping women fully covered with clothing and apart from the rest of society), spoke out strongly against child marriage.[17]

One of the most influential drafters was Hansa Mehta, an Indian feminist activist, who insisted that Article I be worded "All human beings are equal in dignity and rights," arguing that if the usual language of "All men are created equal" were used, it would not be applied universally but be taken to exclude women. Indeed, Mehta was "the key figure who ensured gender equality in the document."[18]

Still, decades after the adoption of the UDHR, forced and child marriages remained common in many parts of the Middle East, North Africa, and South Asia, while domestic violence was still epidemic throughout the world. For this reason, a global coalition of feminists mobilized for the 1993 UN Conference on Human Rights in Vienna, organizing a special Tribunal on Violence Against Women, which they saw as a human rights violation. Forcing violence against women onto the agenda of the UN Conference, they persuaded participants to redefine rape, formerly considered a minor and inevitable part of conflict, as a war crime. The next year, the same coalition defeated an alliance between the Vatican and conservative Islamic states at the UN Conference on Population and Development in Cairo, and succeeded in reframing population issues in terms of women's health and reproductive rights. This campaign culminated in the 1995 Beijing Conference on Women, which gave a new breadth of vision and authority to the idea of women's human rights.

The organizing efforts behind these UN conferences led to rising expectations and increasing assertiveness in women all over the world, and created a cadre of activists who were able to push for change in their own countries on matters as various as domestic violence, equal pay, and female genital mutilation (FGM). Real progress resulted. Some countries (India, France, Sweden) passed rules mandating quotas for women in their legislatures. Women moved into jobs previously reserved for men and, with increased income, were more able to leave brutal or unsatisfactory marriages. Naturally this progress was resented, particularly when new laws affected land ownership—still reserved for men in many parts of the world. Tribal leaders and traditionalists thought the world was coming to an end, and became part of the social base for the fundamentalist movements that are such a threat today, the most violent being Daesh.

By taking up arms to oppose Daesh, Kurdish feminists have set a new standard for the next wave of feminist action, saying that it must incorporate armed self-defense when necessary along with social and economic rights. But, as in the nineties, the international Left has failed to grasp the importance of these epic developments in women's consciousness and mobilization, and has been unable to develop a coherent and principled response to the rise of fundamentalism. Instead, it got stuck in the middle of a paradigm shift.

Unable to find a new theoretical footing after the disappearance of "really-existing socialism," left-wing thinkers of the nineties called for resistance to neoliberalism and globalization. But they rarely noticed how central female labor was to these economic and social changes, or understood their relationship to Kandiyoti's "crisis of masculinity" and the growth of fundamentalist movements.

In the US, thanks to stagnant wages, out-of-control health care costs, and minimal social benefits, women's unpaid work caring for children and the elderly props up the whole economy. In the Global South, women do most of the work involved in agriculture and food production; make up the basic labor force in the textile, electronics, and garment industries;

and are the main commodity in the global sex trade. Some countries import women for these purposes; others, like the Philippines, export them. All the kinds of labor traditionally belonging to women, including childcare and care of the aged, have become items that are bought and sold in a global market. Women are thus central to the whole project of global economic integration and modernization.

For these economic reasons, if for no other, the international Left should have made women's liberation central to its program. But that didn't happen. Starting in Rio in 2001, a succession of World Social Forums became the central gathering place for the international anti-globalization Left under the slogan, "Another world is possible." But even though women worked hard organizing for these events, feminist issues were usually relegated to a separate space rather than integrated into any overall program.[19] In fact, fundamentalist movements that appropriated the language of national liberation were more easily accepted than feminists who opposed them in the language of universal human rights.

In 2005, the pioneering network Women Living Under Muslim Laws wrote the World Social Forum a letter accusing its leaders of ignoring the dangers presented by fundamentalism. It said,

"We are now facing a new challenge: what seemed to be clear politically when we were talking of far off countries loses its clarity when fundamentalist policies come closer to Europe and the USA in the guise of 'authentic' cultural identity, and the worldwide support once given to both victims and resisters of fundamentalism vanishes under the weight of considerations of right to 'difference' and cultural relativism. . . . We have already witnessed prominent Left intellectuals and activists publicly share the view that they could not care less if fundamentalist theocratic regimes come to power in Palestine or Iraq, provided that the USA and Israel get booted out. We have witnessed representatives of fundamentalist organizations and their ideologists be invited and cheered in Social Fora. We have witnessed prominent feminists defend the 'right to veil'— and this sadly reminds us of the defense of the 'cultural right' to female genital mutilation, some decades ago."[20]

Feminist sociologist Nadje Al-Ali made a similar critique of the anti-imperialist Left's valorization of "the Iraqi resistance," which amounted to endorsing attacks upon Shia civilians by jihadis linked to al Qaeda. She wrote: "At the World Tribunal on Iraq in Istanbul in 2005, for example, almost every speaker either began or finished his or her talk with a similar statement: 'We have to support the Iraqi resistance!' Many speakers added that this was not just a matter of fighting the occupation inside Iraq but part of a wider struggle against encroaching neocolonialism, neoliberalism and imperialism. But none of the speakers explained to the jury of conscience, the audience and their fellow speakers what they actually meant by 'the resistance.' No one felt it was necessary to differentiate between, on the one hand, the right of self-defence and the patriotic attempt to resist foreign occupation and, on the other, the unlawful indiscriminate killings of noncombatants. Neither did anyone question the motivations and goals of many of the numerous groups, networks, individuals and gangs grouped all too casually under 'the resistance'—a term that through lack of clear definition has been used to encompass various forms of non-violent political oppositions, armed resistance, guerrilla combat and mafia-type criminality."[21]

In recent years, feminists have sometimes seemed to be the only people at such left-wing events pointing to the dangers of fundamentalism. We knew fundamentalism was a threat because we were the ones being attacked. In the US, the Catholic Right and Protestant evangelicals have been campaigning against LGBTI rights and women's reproductive freedom since the seventies. Latin American feminists are locked in struggle with the Church over birth control and abortion; Indian feminists have had to fight both Hindu and Muslim fundamentalists to win a uniform code of family law; women's movements in the Middle East and South Asia are battling Islamists to gain basic human rights. And in most of these places, the Left has not been listening.

In 1995, the year of the UN Conference on Women in Beijing, I became founding President of a transnational free speech network of feminist writers called Women's WORLD (Women's World Organization for Rights, Literature and Development), which drafted a manifesto for Beijing called *The Power of the Word: Culture, Censorship and Voice.*[22]

We began by describing a world crisis, symptoms of which included the accelerating destruction of the environment, vast movements of population fleeing war and famine, the growing dominance of transnational corporations accountable to nobody but their shareholders, the triumph of free market policies that were impoverishing people all over the world, and the rise of various forms of religious fundamentalism as political movements targeting women and ethnic minorities. "The increasing internationalization and collusion of these movements," we said, "raises the possibility of a worldwide reactionary movement similar to fascism in the 1920s and 30s."

Strategically, we could see only one source of hope: an alliance between feminists and other progressive social movements: "All our movements face the same oppressive forces: a New World Order that props up modern dictatorships, and a reactionary traditionalism that represents the worst form of patriarchal control. We have a common vision of a future in which extremes of wealth and poverty will vanish; in which human rights, sustainable livelihoods, universal literacy, and cultural diversity will become the norm; and in which decisions will be made and social conflicts resolved by negotiation, rather than force or domination."

But were our brothers on the Left willing to commit to such feminist principles?

"Again and again," we said, "women have fought beside men in movements for social change, only to see them set up new ruling elites that left gender and family hierarchies intact, continued to practice the power politics of dominance and submission, and resolved social and personal conflicts through violence or repression.

"Today, women, particularly women of the South," we went on, "make up the vast majority of the poor and politically disenfranchised people of the world, the true 'prisoners of starvation' and 'wretched of the earth.' Thus, any movement for real transformation must make the demands of women central. And, because so many of the chains that bind women are located in the realm of tradition rather than pure politics or economics, a thorough transformation must involve struggles over culture."

We had no idea that, while we were writing these words, Abdullah Ocalan and Kurdish women activists were wrestling with similar questions and beginning to build a movement that would eventually be able to test its ideas about women's liberation in practice, using southeastern Turkey and northern Syria as a social laboratory. We can all learn from their experiments. For, with all our freedoms, Western feminists have seldom had the opportunity to test our ideas on a large scale and gain experience in strategic thinking.

By strategic thinking, I do not mean what goes by that name in corporate seminars or NGO training sessions. I mean a way of thinking that moves between the big picture and one's own situation to chart out a principled path to liberation and power. As Archimedes, inventor of the lever, said, "Give me a place to stand and I will move the world." Moving the world involves having a clear view of present conditions, grasping their potential for transformation, and seeing how to utilize one's own meager strength as a lever for change. How do people learn to think this way?

Over the centuries, men have learned strategy, tactics, and long-range planning by running countries, building businesses, serving in military campaigns, even leading sports teams. But, until very recently, women were barred from these fields. We did not accumulate capital or command armies. In most societies, our work was concentrated in subsistence agriculture and handicrafts, caring for children, managing the survival needs of our families, and engaging in low-level mercantile activity or small-scale garment or food production. Centuries of that kind of work have shaped women's habits of thinking in ways that tend to emphasize cultural transmission, frugality, the value of life, and the importance of human relations.

Abdullah Ocalan, ideological leader of the Kurdistan Workers' Party (PKK), has suggested that women's habits of mind can be symbolized by the ancient Mesopotamian goddess Ishtar, symbol of sexuality and war in the Neolithic period, when people first began to live in villages. "Production developed with the unity of land and woman. . . . Animals were domesticated, seeded plants were cultivated, and women did the majority of these jobs. Ishtar was the goddess of this culture," he says. Elsewhere, he has argued that "What underlies sacredness is food. . . . What underlies food is mothers' labor. She is the creator, the inventor, and the nurturer. . . . [S]he works solely on production; she knows it; she sustains humanity through it. That is how she understands humanity."[23]

To Ocalan, the Neolithic village was an Eden where women had power and status equal to or possibly greater than that of men; only when males began to dominate did our species turn to war, empire, and slavery. In this part of Ocalan's thought, he is a classical Marxist, following in the tradition of Engels' *Origin of the Family, Private Property and the State*: "The overthrow of mother-right was the world historical defeat of the female sex. The man took command in the home also; the woman was degraded and reduced to servitude, she became the slave of his lust and a mere instrument for the production of children."[24]

This theory of human development may be based on very little solid evidence, but it has great and enduring power as a myth of The Fall. Like a number of feminist theorists, including Maria Gimbutas and Riane

Eisler, Ocalan has been constructing a mythic version of prehistory to assert that patriarchy was not inevitable and gender arrangements could still be revised. Few Marxists have pursued this approach in recent years. As David Graeber says, "One of Öcalan's most radical moves is to revive the notion of Neolithic matriarchy. This notion was very common in the 19th and early 20th century but has recently been cast aside. . . . [and] once it went out it just was gone. It became like a taboo, no one can touch it, you're considered crazy if you talk about it."[25] Instead of invoking Ishtar, the dominant Western political and philosophical traditions, including Marxism, have favored Athena, the Greek virgin goddess of war and abstract thought. Athena was not born of woman but sprang directly from the forehead of her father Zeus. Dissenting from this narrative in her novel *Cassandra*, Christa Wolf asked, what would "the history of thought" have been like if it had come from some place other than the head of a male god? What would it have been like if women had helped to shape it?[26]

The Kurdish women's movement has asked the same question and called for a new sociology of women's thought. Its word for this is *Jineology—jin* means "women" in Kurdish. In a speech at the first world conference on Jineology in Cologne, Kurdish writer Gonul Kaya explained the need for the "creation of a women's paradigm" in the social sciences:

> As an extension of the patriarchal system, a field of social sciences has been created, which is male, class-specific, and sexist in character. This field is in turn broken up into different parts that are torn apart from each other. The implementation of the interpretations of these sciences has led to devastating results for nature, society, and human beings: The normalization of militarism and violence, the deepening of sexism and nationalism, the unrestrained development of technology, especially weapon technology for the control of society and individuals, the destruction of nature, nuclear energy, cancerous urbanization, demographic problems, anti-ecological industrialism, Gordian knots of social issues, extreme individualization, the rise of sexist policies and practices against women, rights and freedoms that only exist on paper.
>
> At this point, we propose Jineology. It was observed that it is necessary to overcome the system of the dominating field of science and to construct an alternative system of science. In addition,

we understood that the existing fields of the social sciences must
be freed from sexism.[27]

This speech points to errors that run like a thread through the history of left-wing thought: male repression, exclusion, devaluation, and
just not getting the point when it comes to real life issues that concern
women. With few important exceptions, left-wing movements have been
overwhelmingly led by men and served by women: men making speeches,
women making coffee. As a result, the history of the Left is lopsided,
reflecting the ideas, history, and experience of only half the species. Its
theory does not accurately describe the world, and its practice does not
prefigure any future society most of us would want to belong to. No wonder it has reached an impasse. How could a theory and practice based—at
best—on the experience of only half the human race possibly be adequate?
The famous Zen riddle asks, "What is the sound of one hand clapping?" It
is the sound we have been hearing for the last hundred years, the sound of
left-wing feminists beating their heads against the wall.[28]

So what makes the Kurdish women's movement different? Considering that it evolved as part of the PKK, which began as a classic Marxist-
Leninist party, how did women members avoid being stopped in their
tracks and go on to form militias and become 40 percent of leadership
on all levels? Have human beings finally been able to create a political
culture that is not divided by gender? And how does that work with being
constantly at war? Why were the left-wing militias of Rojava, despite their
lack of sophisticated equipment and before they had any air support, the
only ground forces able to resist Daesh? Does their military success have
something to do with their ability to draw on the strength of women? Or
with their commitment to bottom-up democracy?

This book is an attempt to address these questions. Like a gyroscope, it
revolves on two axes. One is the collision of three visions of social organization, all reflections of larger global paradigms but particularly intense
in Kurdistan: the Islamism of Daesh, the "capitalist modernity" (Ocalan's
phrase) of the Kurdish Regional Government in Iraq, and the new kind
of left-wing, nonstate, democratic formation developing in the liberated
cantons of Syria. The other axis is the role of women in these paradigms.

Ocalan's dream is that human domination, slavery, and empire will be
undone in Kurdistan, by a people so oppressed they had almost lost any
sense of their own worth. As Ocalan sees it, "Kurdistan is the place where

humanity itself fades away in its most solid form. It is humankind's oldest cradle. A magnificent victory for humanity may be gained in the place where it has been most 'deformed'. Such magnificence will be in proportion to the debasement."[29]

In other words, by disdaining the "ring of power" that we call the state—power that, like Tolkien's ring, is of no use to people who want to build an egalitarian society rather than one based on dominance and submission—the Kurds may become able to defeat Daesh and al Qaeda, the most vicious enemies of freedom. At the same time, they hope to bring democracy to Syria and Turkey, converting their brothers and sisters who still worship at the shrines of power and consumerism to more humane values. It's a tall order, but they have already done the impossible just by continuing to exist.

This book is an overview of the history of the Kurdish region, which is essential for understanding the painful, convoluted path that led to the experiment that is the Rojava Cantons. The cantons are an experiment in motion, a living, breathing entity, constantly evolving, offering a vision of social relations that many of us would have thought impossible. Whatever lies ahead, they have shown the world new ways to dream about democracy, equality, and living together.

*Cars abandoned on the Yazidi flight up Sinjar Mountain in August 2014.*

CHAPTER I

# The Kurds

N 1976, A DUTCH ANTHROPOLOGY STUDENT named Martin van Bruin-essen went to Kurdistan to do field work, and described its geography in his thesis: "The heart of Kurdistan consists of forbidding mountains that have always deterred invading armies and provided a refuge to the persecuted and to bandits. The eastern or Kurdish Taurus and the Zagros chain form its backbone, having a northwest-southeastern direction. On the southwestern flank a large number of parallel, often very high and steep folds gradually lower toward the Mesopotamian plains. To the north and northeast the landscape changes into a steppe-like plateau and highlands."[1]

Today these mountains and the ancient fertile crescent they protect are the focal point of an epic three-way struggle between the violent Islamist jihadis of Daesh and al Qaeda, the *peshmerga* of the autonomous Kurdish region in Iraq, and the left-wing Syrian Kurdish militias with their liberated territory in Rojava, as well as the main regional and global powers aiding one or the other. This struggle will not only determine the future of the Kurds; it is an illustration of three possible futures for the entire region, if not the world—futures that were rehearsed on Sinjar Mountain in Iraq in 2014.

## The Battle of Sinjar Mountain

In June 2014, the leaders of Daesh decided it was firmly enough established to declare itself a caliphate—the Islamic State—and did so, claiming territory from Aleppo in Syria to Diyala in eastern Iraq in pursuit of its goal of erasing the borders in the region.[2] Its armies began a blitzkrieg south into Iraq along the Tigris River. They did not expect to meet much opposition from the army of Iraq—local humorists say its name is an acronym for I Ran Away Quickly—and they didn't. In

37

fact, as they neared Mosul, Iraq's second-largest city, the Iraqi Army and police force—52,000 men—fell apart. Their commanders fled, while soldiers stripped off their uniforms and threw away their guns, some even running through the streets in their underwear.[3] In the next two days, Daesh fighters traveled over a hundred miles south and surrounded the oil refinery at Baji. By June 11, they had already captured Samarra with no difficulty and moved on to Tikrit.

Daesh military strategy involves attacking several places at the same time. That June, besides threatening Baghdad, they moved into positions to attack two Kurdish targets: Kirkuk, at the edge of the autonomous region controlled by the Iraqi Kurds, and Kobane, the autonomous Kurdish canton in Syria.

The Iraqi Kurds have been US allies since the Gulf War of 1990. Though technically citizens of Iraq, they are self-governed, for most practical purposes, by the Kurdistan Regional Government (KRG). Closely allied with Turkey, which controls much of its economy, the KRG is progressive in the context of the Middle East as a whole but troubled by tribalism and corruption. It is controlled by two feuding political parties: the Kurdish Democratic Party (KDP), led by Masoud Barzani, and the Patriotic Union of Kurdistan (PUK), led by Jalal Talabani. Barzani is currently President of the Kurdish Regional Government and, though his last term ended in August 2015, seems determined to remain in office.[4]

The great goal of the KDP since its formation has been to gain control over the city of Kirkuk and the large and immensely profitable oil fields surrounding it. Iraq was never willing to cede this control. But on June 12, 2014, with Daesh poised to attack and the Iraqi army in flight, the city was left to the Kurds. The KDP quickly moved its *peshmerga* into Kirkuk and fortified the city.

Strangely enough, despite its love of annexing oil fields, Daesh did not attempt to capture this prize. Instead it moved on to other targets in Iraq and, on July 2, attacked Kobane, the central canton of the three run by the revolutionary Syrian Kurdish Democratic Union Party (PYD).

This time, Daesh had a tough opponent. The Syrian Kurds have two militias, the YPG (People's Protection Units), made up of both men and women, and the YPJ (Women's Protection Units), the autonomous women's army. Though separate, they work together and are usually referred to as the YPG-YPJ. By the summer of 2014, the YPG-YPJ had been successfully fighting Daesh for eighteen months and was calling for Kurdish unity across borders and a coalition of all ethnic groups to fight the jihadis.[5] They particularly hoped to forge a joint military strategy with the Iraqi Kurds.

But KDP leader Masoud Barzani was not interested in such an alliance: Coooperating with revolutionary Kurds would have alienated Turkey. He was more interested in capturing Kirkuk and laying the basis for an independent Kurdish nation in Iraq.[6] So when Daesh began a major offensive against Kobane in July, the YPG-YPJ got no help.

On August 3, Daesh opened a second front against the Kurds by attacking Sinjar (also called Shingal), a town on the border between Iraq and Syria, populated largely by the Yazidis, a long-persecuted Iraqi Kurdish minority who practice an ancient religion that predates Islam and involves the worship of seven angels. Sunni fundamentalists call the Yazidis pagans and Daesh considers them devil-worshippers who should be exterminated.[7]

Daesh had been attacking Yazidi villages since June and, certain that a major offensive was coming, the Yazidis had appealed for help to both the Iraqi government in Baghdad and Barzani's KDP.[8] The Iraqi Army had fled the area, but the KDP said its *peshmerga* were fully prepared to defend Sinjar, which was, after all, only twenty-five miles away from their capital in Erbil.[9]

But when Daesh fighters neared Sinjar on August 3, the 17,000 *peshmerga* who were supposed to defend the Yazidis melted away, saying they had no instructions to fight Daesh.[10] Only a handful of fighters stayed on their own to defend the otherwise unprotected civilians. They managed to hold Daesh back long enough to allow thousands of Yazidis to flee into the mountains, climbing higher and higher to keep ahead of Daesh. Then Daesh cut off the roads behind them and they were marooned without food, warm clothing, or water.[11]

Naima Faris, a woman in her forties who lived in a village on the outskirts of Sinjar, was recovering from a hysterectomy when the attack began. She could barely walk but her children insisted they had to leave at once. Her daughter-in-law didn't even take the time to locate her shoes so the two shared a pair of slippers and wrapped their feet in Naima's keffiyeh throughout the next weeks. "I ran away, dragging myself over the rocks. My clothes were destroyed. We didn't eat for twelve days," Naima said. They caught goats and milked them to feed the children. Her younger brother, his wife, and their children were captured and she has not heard from them since. She says of the Iraqi *peshmerga*, "How were we supposed to know that they were leaving us to the wolves?"[12]

What happened to those who did not escape was genocide pure and simple, reminiscent of the worst horrors of the Bosnian war. According to a UN report, at least 5,000 men were gunned down, while thousands of women and children were captured and held in pens to be sold into sexual slavery or used as prizes to reward jihadis.[13]

As soon as Daesh took over a Yazidi village, they sorted the victims. First they separated the males and females. They told all the boys to lift up their shirts; those who had armpit hair were herded together with their older male relatives, driven or marched to a nearby field, forced to lie down, and killed with a barrage of machine gun fire. The little boys would be forced to convert and sent to training camps to be indoctrinated and taught to fight their own people.[14]

Matthew Barber, who researches Yazidi culture and was in Sinjar in the summer of 2014, says the real purpose of the offensive was to capture Yazidi women. Daesh even brought flatbed trucks for the purpose.[15] The captives were taken to the nearest town, where Daesh separated the young unmarried girls from their mothers, forced them into buses that had been prepared in advance, with curtains over the windows, and drove them to their destined point of sale, where they were stripped naked and examined for breast size and good looks. The prettiest virgins, who fetched the highest prices, were auctioned off at the Daesh slave market in Raqqa, where buyers haggle furiously to drive the prices down.

"There is a hierarchy: sheikhs get first choice, then emirs, then fighters," according to a reporter for the *Washington Post*. "They often take three or four girls each and keep them for a month or so, until they grow tired of a girl, when she goes back to market."[16]

By 2016, though at least 2,500 Yazidi women were still held captive, some had escaped by themselves, and others had been rescued by an underground railway run by Yazidi men.[17] One of the rescuers, Khaleel, described what the women told him:

"They beat the women, they gang rape them, they make them have forced marriage with many men. Some women have their infant babies taken away by force. . . . They take them to a slave market and give women to each other like a gift." The vast majority are raped, including young children, since Daesh doctrine says it is okay to marry nine-year-old girls. Women who try to resist are killed, or put out in the sun until they die of heat prostration. Khaleel tells of a nine-year-old girl who was brutally raped by a middle-aged fighter, who tore her vagina; she was then made to have FGM surgery, after which he tried to rape her again.[18]

A prepubescent twelve-year-old Yazidi girl who escaped after eleven months in captivity told *The New York Times* of repeated rapes by her "owner:" "Because the preteen girl practiced a religion other than Islam, the Quran not only gave him the right to rape her—it condoned and encouraged it, he insisted. He bound her hands and gagged her. Then he knelt beside the bed and prostrated himself in prayer before getting on top of her. When it was over, he knelt to pray again, book-ending the rape with acts of religious devotion." When she told him he hurt her and asked him to stop, he said that by raping her he was drawing closer to God.[19]

As part of its recruitment drive for foreign fighters, Daesh published a guide to sex slavery in December 2014. This guide explains that it is perfectly permissible to take people such as Christians and Jews as slaves, but not Muslim apostates—all apostates, male and female, must be killed for leaving the faith. Other unbelievers are fine; they should be raped immediately "after taking possession;" this includes girls who haven't yet reached puberty, as long as they are "fit for intercourse." Since the Daesh interpretation of Muslim law says it is forbidden to have intercourse with pregnant slaves, captives are fed birth control pills to ensure they don't conceive.[20]

Knowing that the KDP had promised to defend the Yazidi, Kurds in Rojava and Turkey were stunned when they heard that the *peshmerga* had withdrawn from Sinjar. The YPG-YPJ forces in Rojava were already stretched very thin because of heavy fighting going on in Kobane and Qamishli; they had also sent fighters to Rabiah in Iraq to help KDP *peshmerga* hold a border crossing there. But they could see that if they didn't help, nobody would. The women guerrillas had a special motivation, knowing what happened to women captured by Daesh.

The commanders asked for volunteers in Cizire canton and a group of women trainees who had not yet seen combat put up their hands, as did fighters from the YPG, and even local policewomen in the asayish, who normally handle only civil crimes. They were joined by more experienced PKK troops, including the women's unit, YJA-Star.[21] The entire force set out immediately. To reach the Yazidis, they had to go many miles across the border into Iraq, and then make their way through the mountains. They arrived above the town of Sinjar on August 4, the day after it fell to Daesh.

In the mountains, they found tens of thousands of stranded refugees, including elderly people and children who were sick or starving. Many were not strong enough to travel the long distance through Iraq to get to Syria. That meant the rescuers would have to create a shortcut through the mountains, fighting Daesh as they did so, and evacuate the Yazidis directly into Rojava.

By now the attention of the world media was riveted upon the Sinjar mountains, but nobody in the West seemed to notice the arrival of the YPG-YPJ and PKK troops. On August 6, Reuters reported that thousands of Yazidis, including 25,000 children, were in danger of imminent starvation.[22] The next day, President Obama authorized limited air strikes against Daesh in Iraq and air drops of supplies to the Yazidis.[23] Beyond that, there was nothing but talk and hand wringing. The United States continued to "weigh its options," the UK and Germany talked about sending aid, and the Pope condemned the jihadis.[24]

Daesh seemed invincible at that point. On August 9, *The Guardian* reported, "In the last two weeks alone, Isis has fought on five fronts: against the Iraqi army, the Kurdish *peshmerga*, the Syrian regime, the Syrian opposition and the Lebanese army. In Syria the group has all but consolidated control of the eastern provinces of Raqqa and Deir Ezzor, as it made advances against government forces in Raqqa and subdued most of the rebel forces in Deir Ezzor. It is also advancing into Aleppo, reaching the city's eastern outskirts, and in Hasaka, and is battling the Kurdish militias in the north-east. In Iraq it has advanced to a point only half an hour's drive from Irbil, the Kurdish capital."[25]

Meanwhile, though nobody was looking, the YPG-YPJ and PKK militias, without heavy weapons or air cover, cut a path of roughly 100 kilometers (64 miles) through the mountains to Cizire canton, battling Daesh all the way. On August 10, they got the last of the Yazidis out and were able to report that they had brought an estimated 100,000 refugees to safety.[26]

As one of the few success stories of the Syrian civil war, the battle of

Sinjar and rescue of the Yazidis deserve close examination. The story raises many questions. Why did Daesh leave the oil-rich city of Kirkuk alone and instead attack Kobane and Sinjar? Why did the KDP *peshmerga* fail to help the Yazidis as they had promised? Why were the PKK-linked militias the only ones who rose to the challenge?

When Daesh reached Kirkuk on June 12, 2014, its fighters paused on the road, and then, instead of attacking, proceeded on to Mosul. During the whole summer offensive in 2014, with the exception of one suicide bomb attack in early June, Daesh left the Iraqi Kurds alone. And the Kurdistan Democratic Party did nothing to help the Yazidi until KDP *peshmerga* retook Sinjar Mountain with much fanfare in December—although most of it had actually been liberated a month earlier by a combination of *peshmerga*, YPG-YPJ, and Yazidi forces.[27]

Were the KDP leaders willing to sacrifice the Yazidis to their dream of an independent state with its capital in Kirkuk? Journalist Dexter Filkins, who was in Erbil, the capital of the KRG, three months later, related, "With the newly acquired land, the political climate for independence seemed promising. The region was also finding new economic strength; vast reserves of oil have been discovered there in the past decade." Indeed, that July, while Kobane was being pounded, President Barzani asked the KRG parliament to begin preparations for a vote on self-rule. "The time has come to decide our fate, and we should not wait for other people to decide it for us," Barzani said.[28]

Najat Ali Saleh, who was in command of the KDP *peshmerga* at the time of the attack on Sinjar, claimed they intended to fight. In fact, he seemed ashamed and embarrassed by their failure to battle Daesh. He told Filkins, "We were totally unprepared for what happened," adding that party leaders were so incensed by the capitulation that they relieved five commanders of duty and held them for interrogation.[29]

But other sources tell a different story. Dutch-Palestinian analyst Mouin Rabbani refers to an "informal non-aggression pact between the IS and Iraq's Kurdish Regional Government, which allowed the latter to seize Kirkuk and expand its territory by some 40 percent while the IS consolidated its hold on Iraq's Arab Sunni heartland."[30]

A week after the attack on Sinjar, Rudaw, a press agency based in Erbil, said Daesh had proposed a truce: If the *peshmerga* did not attack them, they would leave Kirkuk alone. "According to information provided by the *peshmerga* forces, the ISIS checkpoint is only half a kilometer away from the Kurdish forces and that via taxi drivers on the road, the militants have asked for reassurance that they will not be attacked from the north."[31]

Christoph Reuter of *Der Speigel* refers to the same truce to support his contention that the leaders of Daesh are practitioners of *realpolitik*, willing to make deals: "This is not a jihadist outlet of believers. They have no problem to have deals with the KRG, with Barzani's government, like: 'we take Mosul and we don't touch Kirkuk.' So you had no clashes or conflict from June to August 2014, then suddenly they felt powerful enough and they took a lot of the Kurdish areas."[32]

In August 2015, *Ezidi Press*, a Yazidi paper published in Germany, ran an extremely detailed investigative piece called "The Betrayal of Shingal," not only indicting the KDP *peshmerga* for having failed to defend them, but accusing them of taking away their weapons, thus making it impossible for them to defend themselves, and of actually turning back Yazidis who tried to flee villages marked for attack. The article named names and published pictures of the four *peshmerga* commanders involved. It noted that, despite Barzani's announcement that he would bring all those responsible to justice, in the year that had passed since the attack, there had not yet been a serious investigation of what had happened.

"Why was the genocide not prevented by the *peshmerga*, which was supposed to be committed to it, why was the IS not stopped or at least held back until the civilian population was able to get to safety? Even one year after the disaster, the cause that allowed this genocide to happen is either not being addressed or only brought to the agenda in a political battle ... We are speaking of a genocide that has claimed thousands of Yezidi's lives and has brought slavery to thousands of women and children."[33]

In June 2014, two weeks after Barzani's forces captured Kirkuk, Asya Abdullah, co-president of Rojava's Democratic Union Party (PYD) was asked about a statement by Barzani that the flight of the Iraqi troops had presented an opportunity for the Kurds to move into Kirkuk and the KDP had taken advantage of it—not mentioning the price paid by the Yazidis. She answered by saying it was essential that everyone fighting Daesh unite: "It is legitimate to defend Kurdistan, but also it is a must to defend Turkmens, Arabs, and Assyrians and to include them in the administration. With the recent attacks of ISIS, a common defence force of the Kurds is an imperative. Defending both the national gains and the gains of all the people with whom we live is possible by developing a common strategy and a defence force."[34]

But Barzani and the PDK have repeatedly been torn between their desire to fight alongside other Kurds and their economic relationship with Turkey, which is determined to divide Iraqi Kurds from the PKK and PYD. Such attempts by regional powers to play one group of Kurds against another, and the Kurds' own oscillations between rivalry and cooperation, are themes that go back a long way. To understand what is going on today, some history of the region is helpful.

## The Kurds

The Kurds are often called the world's largest nation without a state.[35] Though most are Sunni Muslims, some belong to religious minorities like the Yazidi and Alevi. Under the Ottoman Empire, most were either peasants or pastoral herders who moved around from place to place. Land was concentrated in the hands of *aghas* (village chiefs), who collected taxes for the sultan and were often predatory. A layer of religious leaders, shaikhs, had the job of keeping order and resolving disputes between tribes. By the 19th century, however, the Ottoman empire was no longer isolated; the Russians and British were making promises to various tribal rulers in exchange for political or military help. The *aghas* in turn played the empires off against the sultan, sometimes siding with one and sometimes with the other, but not uniting against either.[36]

This pattern—small groups playing their enemies off against one another instead of uniting against them—is characteristic of tribalism. Former US Secretary of Labor Robert Reich once offered a "tribalism for dummies" definition: "Before the rise of the nation-state, between the eighteenth and twentieth centuries, the world was mostly tribal. Tribes were united by language, religion, blood, and belief. They feared other tribes and often warred against them. Kings and emperors imposed temporary truces, at most. But in the past three hundred years the idea of nationhood took root in most of the world. Members of tribes started to become citizens, viewing themselves as a single people with patriotic sentiments and duties toward their homeland. Although nationalism never fully supplanted tribalism in some former colonial territories, the transition from tribe to nation was mostly completed by the mid twentieth century."[37] But tribalism has remained an important factor in key locations of the US "war on terror," including Iraq, Syria, Afghanistan, and Pakistan.

By 1914, when World War I began and Turkey came in on the side of Germany and Austro-Hungary, the Ottoman Empire had shrunken considerably from its greatest size, but it still covered substantial territory, including the countries that are now Syria, Lebanon, Iraq, Turkey, Palestine, Israel, Jordan, Saudi Arabia, Yemen, and the other Persian Gulf states. Most of the Kurds were concentrated in Turkey and Iraq.

To get Kurdish help against the Turks, the British and French allies made the Kurds many promises, offering them assurances of independence or at least autonomy. Despite these pledges, Britain and France made a secret treaty during the war, the Sykes-Picot agreement, which carved the Ottoman Empire into "protectorates" that they would control: England got Jordan, Palestine, and southern Iraq; France got Lebanon, Syria, and northern Iraq. Sowing the seeds of future conflict, Britain also secretly promised Palestine to both the Jordanian Arabs and the Zionist movement. Another ally, Russia, was given pieces of Turkey but after the revolution of 1917 the Bolsheviks gave up all claim to the territory and made the Sykes-Picot treaty public.

The Kurds had no reason to suspect they were being lied to. After all, the French and British had said the main reason they got into the war was "the complete and final liberation of the peoples who have for so long been oppressed by the Turks," and Woodrow Wilson's Fourteen Points said "nationalities which are now under Turkish rule should be assured an undoubted security of life and an absolutely unmolested opportunity of autonomous development."[38]

But talk is cheap. After all the treaties were signed, the Kurds found they had been divided up between four different states: Iran, Iraq, Syria, and Turkey. Over the following decades, they frequently revolted against these states but were always defeated and often savagely repressed, a minority people, as they always say, with "no friend but the mountains."

And what part did women play in this tormented story? It is difficult to know, because there is so little about them in most histories of the Kurds. In fact, one cannot even find "women" in the index of most of the authoritative English-language books on Kurdistan (which is considered to encompass the Kurdish areas of Iran, Iraq, Syria, and Turkey). Turkish social scientist Ali Kemal Ozcan is one of the few to acknowledge women's role in the introduction to his book on the PKK, although he goes no further than an acknowledgement:

"An interesting point about the Kurdish movement is the remarkable participation of women. In the sphere of both civilian (mass protests, marches, celebrations, festivals) and military (guerrilla) activities the noteworthy presence of women appeared to me to be an important phenomenon. Considering the unusually high percentage of women in Kurdish guerrilla forces, set against the fanatically religious and largely pre-feudal state of Kurdish society—and also in view of the fact that the party persists in identifying itself as Marxist-socialist—this issue cannot be ignored. However, it necessitates an additional study in itself. Furthermore, as a man, I felt discouraged from examining an issue that I might not fully understand."[39]

According to activist and researcher Shahrzad Mojab, scholarly neglect of Kurdish women is partly an artifact of the way academic fields are set up and their work financed: "Kurdish studies is shaped by the status of the Kurds as a non-state nation. . . . Middle Eastern studies programs are predominantly focused on Turkish, Arab, Persian and Hebrew studies, some of them with close ties to the Middle Eastern states. . . . The Kurds are excluded from Middle Eastern studies establishments and Kurdish women are excluded from studies of Middle Eastern women."[40]

While nationalist writers may contend that Kurdish women have always been more equal than others in the Middle East, they have not done the work necessary to back up these claims, of which Martin van Bruinessen says: "In some parts of Kurdistan women have a certain freedom of movement, perhaps more than in many other parts of the Middle East. This is certainly not characteristic, however, of all Kurdistan, and the nature and degree of this freedom moreover depend much on their families' social status."[41]

In fact, violations of women's human rights such as forced marriage, child marriage, "honor crimes," and seclusion can be found in Kurdistan as elsewhere in the region, and female genital mutilation (FGM) in particular is extremely common among Iraqi Kurds, though not in other parts of Iraq. Iraqi Kurdistan has an FGM rate of 72 percent according to a survey done by WADI, a small German-Iraqi women's NGO. In 2011, the practice was made illegal but the ban is seldom enforced.[42] Rates of FGM in other parts of Kurdistan are not known.

Today the Kurds number between thirty and forty million world-wide. While they are dispersed in many countries, including a dias-pora of at least two million in Europe, their main concentration of population, some fifteen million, is still in historic Kurdistan. In each of these countries, Kurds have a great smorgasbord of organizations, open and secret, nationalist, left-wing, and Islamist, which battle each other and the government and try to get help from other Kurds and neighboring states. Because of this proliferation of organizations, each one with its three-letter abbreviation, discussions of Kurdish politics can sound like alphabet soup.

Over eight million Kurds live in Iran. Because they have not been a strong factor in the recent regional struggle, they do not figure promi-nently in this story. The Iranian Kurds live mostly in the mountain area bordering Turkey and Iraq. Unlike Turkey, Iran allows its many minorities cultural rights like the use of their own languages, but all separate Kurdish parties are banned and, in 2015, a number of Kurdish political prisoners were executed.[43]

### Iraq

Iraq has about five and a half million Kurds, who make up 17.5 percent of the country's population; they were the first group of Kurds to mobi-lize on a nationalist basis, and rebelled against the government fairly frequently from the time it was taken over by the British after World War I. At the end of the war, Iraq had become a British protectorate under the nominal rule of King Faisal I. The monarchy remained in power until 1958, when it was overthrown by a left-wing military coup. A succession of rulers followed, until the Baath Party, with CIA help, staged its own coups in 1963 and again in 1968.[44] By that time Saddam Hussein was already running the party's security apparatus and gradu-ally took control of the country.

Saddam became President in 1979 and immediately declared war on the new Islamic Republic of Iran, which had called for a similar Islamic revolution to take place in Iraq. The war went on for eight years with no one the victor. During the struggle the KDP, the Kurdish nationalist party in northern Iraq, helped Iran seize the Iraqi border town of Hajj Umran.[45] In revenge, Saddam Hussein waged a genocidal campaign against the Kurds, which included the use of chemical weapons. Hun-dreds of thousands of Kurds were murdered and thousands of villages destroyed during the campaign, which is known as the Anfal after a Koranic chapter on the spoils of war.

In 1991, to recoup his losses from the war with Iran, Saddam invaded and annexed Kuwait. This time, in what became known as the Gulf War, the US put together a coalition to stop him, with allies that included Saudi Arabia, Egypt, the UK, and many others. During the war, Saddam again started bombing the Kurds. Kurdish refugees flooded into Iran, which let them in, but when they tried to get into Turkey, they found the borders closed. Hoping to avoid another Kurdish genocide, the US and UK set up a no-fly zone in northern Iraq, which not only prevented further air attacks by Saddam, but also gave the Kurds the opportunity to establish an unofficial autonomy.

The UN put severe economic sanctions on Iraq after the Gulf War, resulting in general malnutrition and a high level of infant mortality. For the next four years, the Kurds suffered heavily from these sanctions, since all postwar aid went through Baghdad, and Saddam would not give them even their reduced share. Northern Iraqi Kurdistan could get food via Turkey, but the cities further south suffered severely; by January 1993, residents were getting no more than 10 percent of the UN rations provided for other Iraqis.[46] For the next twelve years, Iraqi Kurds were subject to severe economic sanctions, punished by both the UN and Saddam's regime, but their leaders continued to look to the US.

In 2003, when the US invaded Iraq, the Kurds rose up again and this time were rewarded with official status as the Kurdistan Regional Government (KRG), an autonomous region of Iraq under the terms of the 2005 constitution. In subsequent years, they have had a contentious relationship with the central government in Baghdad, which cut off all their funds when they bypassed it to sign their own oil contracts with Turkey and Western oil companies. But in the middle of fighting a war with Daesh, the Baghdad government has had problems bigger than the Kurds.

Iraqi Kurdistan has two main political parties, the KDP and the PUK, both based on dynastic and tribal politics. A third party, Gorran, founded in 2009, quickly turned into the largest opposition party. The government is extremely corrupt and, in the fall of 2015, there were large demonstrations and a one-week strike by civil servants who had not been paid for three months.[47] Even with these problems, however, the Kurdish Regional Government, as social scientist Hamit Bozarslan says, "represents one of the most dynamic, politically pluralistic and peaceful spaces in the Middle East."[48]

## Syria

Established as a French protectorate after World War I, Syria gained its independence in 1946. Its first years were rocky, with numerous coups. A climate of rising Arab nationalism led to ethnic tensions, notably an arson attack in 1957 in which 250 Kurdish schoolboys perished.[49] When Syria and Egypt formed the United Arab Republic 1958, publications in Kurdish were banned. The UAR was ended by a Syrian military coup in 1961 and the next year, the Arab Republic of Syria was founded. Because Syria is a mosaic of many peoples; defining the country as Arab excluded a number of ethnic groups. In 1963, a Baath Party military coup made Syria a dictatorship, ruled under a permanent state of emergency decree by Hafez al Assad (1970–2000) and then by his son Bashar.

Syria has only 1.7 million Kurds, around 10 percent of its population, who live mostly in the northeastern part of the country. In 1962, when Syria declared itself an Arab republic, 120,000 Kurds were stripped of citizenship on the claim that their ancestors had infiltrated into Syria from Turkey.[50] This made it impossible for them to get an education, jobs, or public benefits. Their land was given to Arabs who were strategically placed in an "Arab Belt" to break up the contiguous Kurdish area near the Turkish border.[51]

Abdullah Ocalan, founder of the Turkish Kurdistan Workers' Party (PKK), lived in exile in Damascus from 1980 to 1998. He and the Baath Party government had a more or less acknowledged agreement that the PKK could recruit Syrian Kurds as long as they didn't fight in Syria. Thus the PKK had Syrian members from the beginning; recent estimates of the percentage of Syrians within its ranks range from 20 to 30 percent.[52] Syria's arrangement with the PKK ended in 1998, when Turkey threatened to invade Syria unless Ocalan was handed over and he fled the country. After that, the government heavily suppressed Kurdish political activity.

In 2003, Syrian members of the PKK founded the Democratic Union Party (PYD) and in 2010 Salih Muslim, a chemical engineer, was elected as chair. The PYD was involved in organizing the first major uprising of Syrian Kurds the next year, after police violence at a soccer match in Qamishli in which nine people were killed. Police also fired on the Kurdish funeral march the next day, killing another eight. Demonstrations and street fighting broke out in Cizire, Afrin, Aleppo, and Damascus. Two thousand Kurds were arrested, with PYD leaders particularly targeted.[53] Salih Muslim was arrested so many times he finally went into exile in Iraq.

When the Arab Spring uprising in Syria began in 2011, many young urban Kurds were involved, but the Kurdish political parties were unsure about participating, nervous about Arab nationalism and suspicious of the strong Muslim Brotherhood influence within the Syrian opposition. When the opposition Syrian National Council refused to discuss their desire for autonomy at a meeting, all the Kurdish parties walked out.[54]

Salih Muslim returned to Syria in April 2011, and the PYD soon became "the best organized, best armed, and single biggest Kurdish party inside Syria," leading the struggle to declare self-rule and establish an autonomous region in the Rojava cantons on Turkey's border.[55]

### Turkey

Like other countries in the region, the Republic of Turkey was established after World War I, in a process that involved the overthrow of the Sultanate by an army led by General Mustapha Kemal Pasha, later called Ataturk or "father of his country," who became the republic's first president. Ataturk's vision of nationhood involved an extremely strong and centralized state, secularism, and cultural and linguistic homogeneity. In practice, Kemalism, or "Turkification" has come to mean forced assimilation.

In 1947, as part of an effort to prevent a Communist revolution in Greece, the US proclaimed the "Truman Doctrine," which included massive military and security-related aid to both Greece and Turkey. This policy inaugurated what is now called the "deep state," a hidden array of security operatives and secret government groups allied with right-wing paramilitaries and fascists.[56] Nevertheless, Turkey progressed toward becoming a multiparty republic, though this advance was disrupted by coups and states of emergency in 1960, 1971, and 1980.

Although most of the country's population is Turkish and Sunni, Turkey has numerous ethnic minorities—Armenians, Arabs, Circassians, Greeks, and many others—as well as minority religions: Orthodox Christians, Jews, and Alevis (a minority branch of Shia Islam, often considered heretical by Sunnis and mainstream Shia), among others. Kurds, at about 20 percent of the population, are the largest minority. Because there are so many of them, Turkey has always suspected them of separatist tendencies.

The virulence of Turkish ethnic nationalism was evident even before the formation of the republic, in the Armenian genocide during World War I. Since then, Turkey has pursued Kemalist policies towards the Kurds that include forced population transfers; mass random killings; a ban on use of the Kurdish language, costume, music, festivals. and names; and extreme political repression.[57]

The policy of repression escalated after the formation of the PKK, which initiated armed struggle in 1984. The guerrilla war that resulted lasted until 1999, when PKK leader Abdullah Ocalan was captured and imprisoned. For much of this time, southeastern Turkey was under martial law and Kurds were subject to arbitrary arrest, torture, and death. There have been alternating periods of ceasefire and renewed warfare since.

In 1990, Turkish Kurds attempted to gain some political space by forming a legal political party, HEP, and running candidates for Parliament, but, as historian David McDowall says, "The state was determined to stifle any Kurdish voice."[58] HEP was banned in 1993 and its deputies prosecuted for alleged ties to the PKK. What followed was a twenty-five-year long game of political musical chairs, in which the Kurds attempted to have a legal political voice by starting first one party, then another, with each declared illegal in turn.

But the game changed in 2013 with the occupation of Taksim Square in Istanbul, which became the Turkish version of Occupy Wall Street. The occupation began in response to President Recep Tayyip Erdogan's plan to destroy Gezi Park, one of the few green spaces left in Istanbul, and hand the land over to developers, combined with his increasing authoritarianism, restrictions on freedom of expression, and imposition of Islamist ideas. A loose coalition of Leftists, secularists, feminists, greens, the LGBTI movement, and Kurds, occupied the Square and sparked a national protest movement. The Erdogan government responded with a harsh crackdown. The Turkish Left had already suffered from repression, arbitrary arrest, and censorship. Now, faced with even greater police brutality, they began to work in coalition with the Kurds to contest the next national elections.[59] The People's

Democratic Party (HDP), previously the party of the urban Left, feminists, and gays, merged with the Kurdish Peace and Democracy Party (BDP), and formed a new social-democratic, secular, and minority-rights party which kept the name of the HDP but adopted much of the program of the radical Kurds. Journalist Adam Barnett described this program in February 2015:

"A social-democratic bloc of Kurds, secularists, feminists, LGBT activists, and greens with twenty-eight seats in the Turkish national assembly (making it the fourth-largest party), the HDP . . . advocates equal rights for all minorities (including Alevis and Armenians) and state neutrality on matters of religion, as well as mandating at least one female co-chair at every administrative level and applying a sort of 'affirmative action' for LGBT candidates. . . . But what truly distinguishes the HDP, and could have wider resonance across an ever more fragmented Middle East, is its call for a radical decentralization of powers from Ankara to regional assemblies, along the lines of the democratic experiment being conducted in the area of northern Syria known to Kurds as Rojava."[60]

## Revolution from the Bottom Up

Since 2005, revolutionary Kurds associated with the HDP had been trying to build a structure of local democratic autonomy in cities across southeastern Turkey, but meeting with government harassment and arrest at every turn. The Syrian civil war gave the Kurdish liberation movement a stage where they could freely test out Ocalan's ideas about democratic self-rule in practice.

In the summer of 2012, as opposition to Bashar al-Assad grew and Saudi- and Qatari-sponsored jihadis flocked into Syria, followed by Daesh, Assad withdrew most of his troops from Northern Syria to protect his home base in Damascus and on the coast. The Syrian Kurdish Democratic Union Party (PYD) moved into the vacuum with its own militias, the People's Protection Units (YPG ) and Women's Protection Units (YPJ), and set up three independent cantons—Afrin, Cizire, and Kobane.

By January 2014, they had established a system of participatory democracy in each canton, with political decisions made by local councils, and social service and legal questions administered by civil society structures under the umbrella of a coalition called TEV-DEM

(Democratic Society Movement). While most of TEV-DEM's ideological leadership came from the PYD, it included people from all the ethnic groups and political parties in the cantons, including a party affiliated with the KDP in Iraq.

The feminism of the Rojava cantons, and their ability to resist Daesh, grew out of changes in the political line of the PKK in the 1990s, as it evolved from a disciplined Marxist-Leninist party to something a lot more complicated. By 2016, the Kurdish liberation movement was more like a network of groups united by common ideas than like a Leninist party, although elements of the latter were still strong in the PKK itself. Social scientists who study the Kurdish liberation movement have described it as "a formation of parties and organizations comprising several parties (including the PKK as a party), a co-party which separately organizes women, sister parties in Iraq (PCDK), Iran (PJAK), and Syria (PYD), and guerilla forces related to these parties." The network also contained mass organizations and coalitions led by the PKK, including the Association of Communities in Kurdistan (KCK), made up of elected local and regional councils, and the National Congress of Kurdistan, which brought together representatives of various parties, religious organizations, and the Kurdish diaspora.[61]

All these associations were shaped by the ideas of Abdullah Ocalan, leader of the PKK since its inception, who had been imprisoned on the Turkish island of Imrali since 1999. Turkey and the CIA thought that removing Ocalan from circulation would kill the PKK but instead of dying, the party evolved into the much more mass-based and diffuse organizational network described above.

Though his critics say Ocalan did not rethink PKK strategy until after he was captured, the organizational evolution of the PKK actually began well before his arrest, and went together with a change in political line from a classic guerrilla war strategy to an emphasis on negotiations. Along with that change came a revolution in the role of women in the party.

The PKK's ideological transformation was a function not only of the collapse of the Soviet bloc and "really-existing socialism" but a reflection of the ways the organization's base was expanding. The PKK was started by students and ex-students and had a cadre of women from its beginning, but the guerrilla war in the eighties brought an influx of rural Kurds whose villages had been attacked by Turkey. Struggling to deal with the feudal and nationalistic ideas of these new recruits, the women's cadre realized they needed their own organizations.

These autonomous women's organizations came into existence in the nineties with Ocalan's backing. His prestige shielded them from attacks by men who wanted to hold on to their traditional privileges, and in return, as law professor Necla Acik said, the women "supported him most during the turbulent years following his arrest and the declaration of his new political, and at that time, controversial line."[62]

Kept in almost total isolation after he was captured, Ocalan did a lot of reading. He was particularly influenced by anarchist theorist Murray Bookchin, world systems theorists Immanuel Wallerstein and Fernand Braudel, and theorist of nationalism Benedict Anderson. He wrote several volumes of prison essays, selections of which have been translated, with some released as downloadable pamphlets.[63]

Publicly disowning his previous beliefs in democratic centralism and armed struggle, he wrote in 2008 that a top-down, centralist party structure was in contradiction to "principles of democracy, freedom and equality." He also distanced himself from the old militaristic PKK culture in which "war was understood as the continuation of politics by different means and romanticized as a strategic instrument."[64]

He sharply criticized nationalism and the goal of a Kurdish state, arguing that nation-states were intrinsically hierarchical and ethnically based, and that the goal instead should be to develop democratic economies and local methods of self-governance—anti-capitalist, anti-statist, and environmentally sound.

Ocalan distinguished between what he called a democratic nation and a nation-state, by which he meant, for the latter, the European or Kemalist model of a nation with a culture so homogeneous that it experienced difference as an existential threat, rather than one where citizenship could be combined with cultural diversity. "A nation-state requires the homogeneity of citizens with a single language and single ethnicity. . . . Adherence to this belief is not patriotism; rather, it is chauvinistic nationalism and religionism. The nation-state disapproves of social differences, insisting on their sameness, as fascist ideology did. By contrast, a democratic nation is multilingual, multireligious, multiethnic, and multicultural, encompassing groups and individuals with different interests. . . . It rejects the equation between state and nation, viewing each as different formations."[65]

The idea was that the state should have a democratic constitution, become decentralized, and concentrate on its relations with other states while letting the people themselves run society at the local level. "Civil society, democratized, will aim to become neither a state nor an extension of it. . . . Democracy does not need to eliminate the state; nor should the state dissolve democracy for its benefit. The extreme intertwinement of the two within the Western system transforms democracy into a showcase institution."[66]

Ocalan called this political philosophy democratic confederalism. While it has much in common with anarchism, participatory democracy, and libertarian socialism, no other major left-wing movement, with the possible exception of the Zapatistas in Mexico and the Gandhian movement in India, had put women's liberation so squarely at the center of its revolutionary project. In fact, despite slogans like the Chinese "Women hold up half the sky," Marxist revolutions have—at best—seen women as support troops for the working class, not as a submerged and dominated majority whose liberation is fundamental to everyone else's.

Similarly, in national liberation movements, women are often encouraged to be politically active and even to serve as soldiers during the struggle, but, once the battle is won, patriarchal norms tend to be reasserted in the name of religion or indigenous tradition. Ocalan's views in his book, *Liberating Life: Woman's Revolution,* were a startling departure from this tendency: "The solutions for all social problems in the Middle East should have woman's position as focus. . . . The role the working class have once played, must now be taken over by the sisterhood of women."

Such statements may seem surprising coming from a former Marxist-Leninist guerrilla, let alone one in the Middle East. But the Arab Spring uprisings demonstrated that the days of the old Middle Eastern regimes were over and people were searching for alternatives. In the battle of Sinjar Mountain, Kurdish women guerrillas enacted a new model of feminist authority. Rojava is a further demonstration that the region could become a laboratory for fresh ways of thinking and alternative modes of political and economic development.

But more than one kind of social revolution has emerged from the wars in Iraq, Syria, and Turkey. Daesh has offered an opposing model: a violent totalitarian and theocratic state, based on Sunni exclusivity.

The Kurds themselves have developed two alternative paradigms: the oil-based conservative semi-state of the Iraqi Kurds, and the non-statist democratic autonomy of Rojava. Like twins separated at birth, they are related and yet totally different.

*Yazidi volunteer fighter, Sinjar Mountain.*

# CHAPTER 2

# Separated at Birth

A T THE END OF WORLD WAR I, Kurds in Turkey and Iraq were at roughly the same stage of social and economic development. A small class of rich absentee landlords and middle class Kurds had moved into cities, especially in Iraq, but most Kurds were still peasants who grew subsistence crops: wheat, barley, and lentils; tomatoes, onions, cucumbers, melons. Their cash crops were tobacco in Iraq and cotton, which had recently been introduced, in Turkey.

In the mountains, the majority of peasants owned their own land but made a poor living from it because of harsh conditions and a low level of technology. As late as 1976, they were still using wooden plows and iron plowshares drawn by oxen or the occasional mule, and reaping with sickles and scythes. In the plains, most were sharecroppers who paid their landlords a percentage of their yield ranging from 10 to 80 percent, though some were agricultural laborers who earned a small wage. In both places, they were ruled over by the shaikhs and *aghas*.

The year 1976 was a time of revolutions all over the world, so when Dutch anthropology student Martin van Bruinessen went to Iraq to do fieldwork, he assumed that the Kurdish movement there would be as class-conscious and anti-imperialist as the national liberation movements of China, Cuba, Mozambique, and Vietnam. To his surprise, "The Kurdish leadership seemed to wish for more imperialist interference in the region rather than less; Mela Mistefa Barzani [Mullah Mustafa Barzani, the father of the leader of the Kurdistan Regional Government] repeatedly expressed his warm feelings for the United States, whom he wanted to join as the fifty-first state and to whom he wanted to give control of the oil in Kurdistan (in exchange for aid)."[1]

Van Bruinessen concluded that Kurdish leaders sought Western intervention because "the first Kurdish nationalists were from the ranks of the traditional authorities, shaikhs and *aghas.*" This tribal authority structure led to perpetual rivalries between leaders, which made Kurdish unity difficult.[2]

But tribalism did not sustain itself naturally; it was re-inscribed upon Iraqi Kurdish society repeatedly, first by the British colonialists and later by Baghdad. "Divide and rule" was a major tactic of British colonialists, perfected in Africa and India, where they governed by playing one unruly tribal chief or local prince off against the next. Since many in the southern part of Iraqi Kurdistan now lived in cities and were largely detribalized, the British had to reinvent and impose a tribal system on them. One of their administrators described the process: "Every man who could be labeled a tribesman was placed under a tribal leader. The idea was to divide South Kurdistan into tribal areas under tribal leaders. Petty village headmen were unearthed and discovered as leaders of long dead tribes."[3]

One problem with such tribalism is that it encourages war. According to van Bruinessen: "In periods of peace the function of the tribal chief does not amount to much, and the unity of his tribe exists in name only. Often therefore, ambitious chieftains actively seek conflicts, in order to re-affirm their leadership and the unity of their tribe and to enlarge the scope of both. It is no exaggeration to say that quarrelling and mediating in other people's quarrels are the most important activities by which one can establish, consolidate and extend one's authority—if we exclude seeking help from outside." For, along with military prowess, a leader's charisma is shown by his ability to get help from powerful neighbors.[4]

With tribalism come blood feuds, family against family, tribe against tribe.[5] Since North Kurdistan's most important and prestigious tribe was the Barzanis, the British needed to ally with them—but that meant tribes who hated the Barzanis would oppose the British. And even tribes that supported the British would not put all their eggs in one basket; a powerful clan would place a family member in every political party. According to van Bruinessen, "When the monarchy was overthrown and the communist party emerged from illegality some of those families suddenly appeared to have someone there too, which was very useful during the campaigns against landlords. They could direct peasant anger against landowning families other than their own."[6]

The Kurdish nationalist movements in both Iraq and Turkey developed in this kind of society, but soon diverged politically. One reason was a variation in the speed of urbanization and class formation, but the biggest difference was government policy. In Iraq, successive governments alternated between offering the carrot or the stick, holding out the hope of autonomy, then dashing it, making war on the Kurds, then pulling back. In the context of the Cold War, in which Iran and Turkey were lined up with the West and Iraq and Syria with Moscow, Iraqi Kurds had considerable room to maneuver between placating Baghdad, soliciting help from its regional rivals, and taking up arms. There was no such room for maneuver in Turkey, where government policy towards the Kurds was no carrot and all stick. To survive at all, they had to become revolutionaries.

## Iraq: The Carrot and the Stick 1946–1975

The political advantages and disadvantages of tribalism are illustrated by the life of Mullah Mustafa Barzani, father of Mousad Barzani, President of the Kurdistan Regional Government. (To avoid confusion, I will call the father Mullah Mustafa and the son Barzani.)

In 1945, after a failed rebellion against the monarchy, Mullah Mustafa, with his brother and about a thousand followers, fled across the border to Iran. There, with other Kurdish Leftists and the help of the Soviet Union, they set up the first attempt at a Kurdish nation, the Republic of Mahabad. It lasted a year before it was shut down by Tehran and the Barzanis had to flee again, fighting their way through the mountains to get to the Soviet Union—a dramatic journey that reinvented Mullah Mustafa as the sort of legendary charismatic military hero required by tribal politics.[7]

This was the middle of the Cold War, when most national liberation movements were financed at least in part by the Soviet Union, and the Iraqi Left was busy trying to figure out if Kurds were an oppressed people who needed their own liberation struggle or a national minority who belonged in the Iraqi Communist Party. In 1946 Mullah Mustafa proposed a third solution: the creation of a new broad-based nationalist party to be called the Kurdish Democratic Party (KDP), which would incorporate both Kurdish communists and the *aghas* and shaikhs.[8]

The KDP was founded later that year, and Mullah Mustafa, still in the USSR, became its president in exile. Its politics were fuzzy at first, but by its Third Congress in 1956 it had come under the leadership of left-wing urban intellectuals, including Jalal Talabani, a member of the powerful Talabani tribe. They wanted land reform.

Mechanization was changing the agricultural economy in Iraqi Kurdistan. As the big landlords got access to tractors and harvesters, their need for labor decreased. As a result, many landless peasants could no longer earn a living and were migrating to the cities. At its Third Congress, the KDP adopted a left-wing program calling not only for land reform, but also for the recognition of peasants' and workers' rights and the formation of labor unions.

Two years later, the Iraqi monarchy was overthrown in a military coup led by Brigadier Abdal Karim Qasim, who pledged to form a democratic republic. He invited Mullah Mustafa to return home, named him official head of the KDP, and gave him a house in Baghdad, a car, and a monthly stipend. Working with the Iraqi Communist Party, Mullah Mustafa helped Qasim put down a 1959 revolt by Baathists who wanted pan-Arab unity and rejected class politics.

After that, like any good tribal leader, Mullah Mustafa went back home to the north, where he began to settle old scores and consolidate his hold on Kurdish politics. He may have been the titular head of the KDP, but his base was among the tribes, not in the cities in the southern part of Iraqi Kurdistan, like the left-wing intellectuals who had pushed for land reform.[9]

Qasim didn't want Mullah Mustafa to become too powerful so he began to criticize him publically, made it clear that he did not support Kurdish autonomy, and armed the northern tribes that were enemies of the Barzanis. So Mullah Mustafa attacked these tribes.

The old ruling class of Iraqi Kurdistan did not like all this turmoil. They had not welcomed the end of the monarchy and were appalled by the idea of land reform. Now they revolted, staging a tax strike. Mullah Mustafa, despite his Leftist credentials, formed an alliance with the rebel *aghas* and landlords, and when Qasim hit them with indiscriminate airstrikes, most of the tribes in the north joined the revolt—unemployment was high and there were plenty of landless peasants willing to fight for money to feed their families.

Left-wing members of the KDP had been appalled by the revolt against land reform, but there was disagreement within the party on how to respond. The question became moot in September 1961, when Qasim declared the KDP illegal. This brought everyone in the party into the rebellion and the KDP began to build its own army, known as the *peshmerga*, meaning "those who face death." (From the beginning the Kurdish *peshmerga* were party militias, taking their orders from party leaders, not from any government.)

Baghdad's response was to build its own Kurdish fighting force, made up of tribes hostile to the Barzanis, unemployed peasants who needed the money, and villagers who joined under government pressure or coercion. Kurds willing to work for Baghdad were called *jash* (children of donkeys, in other words, idiots) by everyone else. They were to become a major element in the politics of Iraqi Kurdistan.[10]

By creating the *jash* in the sixties, says van Bruinessen, the Iraq government again re-imposed and reinvented tribalism; it "provided the occasion for very considerable government subsidies to tribes (or rather, to tribal chieftains) and gave these tribes a new relevance as forms of social and political organisation. . . . These militia regiments were treated as collectivities; all arms, money, and commands were communicated through the chieftain. This had the effect of reinforcing the chieftains' control over their tribes, strengthening the hierarchical and centripetal rather than the egalitarian, segmentary aspects of tribal organisation." Even so, as urbanization continued, the number of Iraqi Kurds whose primary identification was tribal steadily shrank; in 1960, it was probably sixty percent but by the late 1980s only twenty.[11]

In February 1963, two years after Qasim made the KDP illegal, he was overthrown by a combination of the military and the Baath party, which made vague promises to the KDP about Kurdish autonomy in order to keep them quiet. The promises proved illusory, possibly because Mullah Mustafa had a way of upping the ante. When the new government sent a delegation to see him, he demanded not only Kurdish autonomy but also an independent standing army and two-thirds of all the income from Iraq's oil industry, which was located in territory he claimed as part of Kurdistan, notably Kirkuk. In the end, his demands didn't matter because there was another coup by a different faction of the Baath party nine months later.

Under the leadership of Abd el-Salam Arif, the new military government signed a peace agreement with Mullah Mustafa, but this agreement left out any mention of Kurdish self-government or autonomy. When Talabani and other KDP left-wingers objected, the KDP split; historian David McDowall describes the conflict as a "contest between the religious and the secular, the primordial and the nationalist, tradition versus atheistic Marxism."[12] The Left wing of the KDP didn't stand a chance. Not only was Mullah Mustafa the poster boy for Kurdish nationalism, he was backed by the *aghas* and shaikhs, with their conservative agendas. Before long, Talabani and his allies had to flee the country for Iran.

Once he had a free hand, Mullah Mustafa reasserted the old KDP demand for autonomy and started another war with Baghdad in 1965. That ended when President Arif was killed in a helicopter accident in 1966. A struggle for power between the military and civilians broke out in the capital, a drama cut short in July 1968 by yet another Baath Party coup, this one led by Ahmed Hassan al-Bakr, who became President. Saddam Hussein began his rise to power as al-Bakr's deputy; he was also the head of security and the man in charge of the Revolutionary Command Council, the leading body of the Baath Party.

The Kurds still wanted autonomy. The Baathists did not want to give it to them but they also wanted to avoid another war in Kurdistan while they consolidated power. They were willing to grant Barzani some of what he wanted, even agree to allow the Kurdish language to be taught in schools throughout Iraq. But they would not relinquish control of Kirkuk and its oil.[13]

Saddam's project was to make the Baath Party secure and the country stable: This depended on oil. In 1972, he nationalized Iraq's oil industry, which meant the profits from then on flowed to the state rather than to British and US oil companies. He also signed a fifteen-year friendship agreement with the Soviet Union. In the Cold War context, these moves were a repudiation of the West.

In 1973, a world energy crisis sent oil prices sky-high. With Iraq's oil income, Saddam was able to set up the strongest welfare state in the region, with compulsory free education, free hospital care, land reform, and farm subsidies. He created an impressive security apparatus with help provided by the Soviet Union and East Germany. In a 2000 interview, Palestinian journalist Said Aburish described this as the basis of Saddam's hold on power: "Saddam Hussein borrowed from Stalinism. He had his security people trained in Eastern Europe, particularly East Germany. Then he brought them back to Iraq and he taught them how to use the tribal linkage to eliminate people. So whereas they used Stalinist methods to discover people who were opposed to the regime, after that came the tribal factor, when Saddam said 'Don't get rid of Abdullah, get rid of his whole family, because one member of his family might assassinate us.' And that made it a perfect system for Iraq. . . . Family and tribal connections are supreme. They come ahead of ideology. They come ahead of commitment to the nation-state, they come ahead of all commitments. Saddam Hussein realizes that. This is why, at a certain point, he transferred power from the Ba'ath Party, which put him in power, to his family, because he decided that the family can be trusted, but the party cannot be trusted."[14]

Mullah Mustafa also understood tribal politics and he too was building a secret police force, the Parastin, trained by the Shah's dreaded SAVAK. Determined to permanently sideline the KDP Left, Mullah Mustafa not only sought aid from the Shah, but also turned to the US and Israel, a pariah state in the Arab world since the Six-Day War of 1967. To the Baath Party, these alliances were enough to make him look like a traitor. The alliance with the US and Israel also infuriated left-wing members of the KDP, but anyone who protested was expelled.[15]

Mullah Mustafa trusted the West. In July 1972, his representatives met with Richard Helms, head of the CIA, and Alexander Haig, Under-Secretary of State for Henry Kissinger, who said they were willing to give him military aid at the request of the Shah. On the CIA's recommendation, the Nixon administration funded the KDP *peshmerga*. With additional funds contributed by Israel and Iran, the military aid package came to $18 million.[16]

Mullah Mustafa told the *Washington Post* in June 1973, "We are ready to act according to US policy, if the US will protect us from the wolves. In the event of sufficient support we should be able to control the Kirkuk oilfields and confer exploitation rights on an American company."[17]

This was not the smartest thing to say to an international newspaper. Saddam responded by bombing Kurdish positions. He had been biding his time while secretly negotiating with the Shah, who was willing to dump the Kurds in exchange for the Shatt al Arab, a disputed waterway between Iran and Iraq leading into the Persian Gulf. In early 1974, Saddam offered Mullah Mustafa a new autonomy law, which gave him much of what he had been asking for, though not Kirkuk. Mullah Mustafa not only rejected the law but sent his secret police to arrest and murder Kurdish members of the Iraqi Communist Party, allies of the

Baath. Left-wing members of the KDP, including his oldest son, were so outraged that they left the KDP to join a "national front" with Saddam.

War between the KDP and the central government in Baghdad broke out in spring 1974. Mullah Mustafa was confident of victory; he had military aid, 50,000 regular troops and 50,000 more irregulars, support from Iran, and a distinguished record of defeating Baghdad. But the Iraqi Army had heavy weapons, almost the same number of troops as the Kurds, and more professional leadership than in the past. By the fall they had moved into Iraqi Kurdistan, captured substantial territory, and were threatening the KDP supply route from Iran—and this time they didn't go home for the winter as they always had before.

By early 1975, it was clear that the Kurds faced defeat unless they got more help from Iran. At that point Saddam said he would give Iran the disputed Shatt al Arab waterway if Iran would stop helping the Kurds and seal the border. In March 1975, he and the Shah signed an agreement; within hours, Iran withdrew its forces and Iraq cut the KDP supply lines.[18]

The KDP *peshmerga* could only flee or surrender. About 100,000 refugees, including Mullah Mustafa and his family, managed to cross the border into Iran before it was closed, but had no food or supplies. When they pleaded for refugee assistance from the US, Secretary of State Henry Kissinger ruled that they were not eligible, and when the Senate's Pike Committee questioned Kissinger about US responsibility for creating hundreds of thousands of Kurdish refugees, he said, "Covert action should not be confused with missionary work."[19]

The war of 1974–1975 was a disaster for the Iraqi Kurds. Saddam created a "security belt" along the Iranian and Turkish borders, which involved razing as many as 1,400 Kurdish villages. The inhabitants of these villages, at least 600,000 people, were deported to internment camps elsewhere in the country, and Arabs were resettled in their place.[20] Completely disgusted with Mullah Mustafa's leadership, the Left wing of the KDP formed a new party, the Patriotic Union of Kurdistan (PUK), led by Jalal Talabani, who was still at its head in 2016.

Mullah Mustafa Barzani died in a US hospital in 1979. But his son Masoud, who had spent most of his life at war, was ready to carry on the Barzani tradition of tribal patronage, war, and an often-betrayed love affair with the US.

## Turkey: Implacable Kemalism 1924–1980

Unlike the Iraqi carrot and stick, Turkish policy towards the Kurds was shaped by what historians call "implacable Kemalism," named after Kemal Ataturk. Although Ataturk introduced progressive policies in some areas, particularly women's rights, his idea of complete cultural uniformity allowed for no minority deviations. Since at least a quarter of the Turkish population is made up of ethnic or religious minorities, this was a major problem.[21] One of Ataturk's first acts was to make it illegal to use any language but Turkish. Other rules enforced secularism, abolished religious schools, and forbade any discussion of religion in public life. These methods of cultural suppression were supposed to unite the Turkish people.

But religious schools were practically the only schools that existed in the country's southeast. Despite the fact that Kurds make up perhaps 20 percent of Turkey's population, there were only 215 government schools in the Kurdish region, out of 4,873 in the whole country. Very few people in southeastern Turkey spoke anything but Kurdish. By neglecting public schools and forbidding religious ones, Kemalist policy kept southeastern Turkey in a perpetual state of underdevelopment and illiteracy.[22]

The new rules prompted two Kurdish revolts, one by a nationalist group called Azadi, another led by a religious leader, Shaikh Said. Neither had much support, but they gave the government an excuse to declare a state of emergency that lasted two years and involved human rights violations that were to become routine in Turkey's treatment of the Kurds: deportation of vast numbers of people to other parts of the country; destruction of their villages; widespread rape, brutality, and murder; massive press censorship; and martial law.

Turkey wanted nothing less than the total obliteration of Kurdish culture. No one was even allowed to acknowledge the existence of a people called the Kurds; they were supposed to be called "mountain Turks." Their language was illegal, their publications were illegal, even celebrations of their traditional spring holiday, Newroz, were illegal. The Turkish army's main function was control of Kurdistan. With the exception of the Korean War and the 1974 invasion of Cyprus, the military fought all its battles in southeastern Turkey.

All this was excused by fairly naked racism. A shocked British diplomat wrote home in 1927 to relay the Turkish foreign minister's prescription for the Kurds: "their cultural level is so low, their mentality so backward, that they cannot be simply in the general Turkish body politic. . . . they will die out, economically unfitted for the struggle for life in competition with the more advanced and cultured Turks. . . . as many as can will emigrate into Persia and Iraq, while the rest will simply undergo the elimination of the unfit."[23]

In 1934, Turkey passed what was known as the "Resettlement Law," which divided the country into three zones: Turkish zones, zones where minorities with "non-Turkish culture" were to be moved for the purpose of assimilation, and zones that were to be completely evacuated. All the property in the evacuated zones was to be confiscated. As described by David McDowall, the law "was intended to disperse the Kurdish population, to areas where it would constitute no more than 5 percent of the population, thus extinguishing Kurdish identity. It was even proposed that village children should be sent to boarding establishments where they would be obliged to speak only in Turkish and thus lose their Kurdish identity entirely."[24]

McDowall compared the Resettlement Law to social engineering policies then current among the Nazis, but comparisons with the history of indigenous people in Canada, the United States, New Zealand, and Australia also come to mind.

The Resettlement Law was never enforced in more than piecemeal fashion because there were simply too many Kurds to resettle. But it was enforced in Dersim, an area in Eastern Turkey noted for uprisings even under the Ottomans, where the people were predominantly Alevi. Dersim was given a new Turkish name, Tunceli, made into a vilayet, or official government province, and placed under military rule.

In 1937, Dersim rebelled. The government invaded the province with thousands of soldiers, who proceeded to raze villages and attack their inhabitants with bombs, gas, and artillery. When the people of Dersim sent emissaries to Ankara, their emissaries were killed; when they fought, they were exterminated; and when they appealed to British Foreign Secretary Anthony Eden, they were stonewalled.

In 1938, a junior diplomat wrote Sir Percy Lorraine, the British ambassador to Turkey, that the military was doing to the Kurds what they had done to the Armenians in World War I: "Thousands of Kurds including women and children were slain; others, mostly children, were thrown into the Euphrates, while thousands of others in less hostile areas, who had first been deprived of their cattle and other belongings, were deported to vilayets in Central Anatolia." But Sir Percy Lorraine was a personal friend of Ataturk's and did not believe these rumors.[25]

Once the lands of Dersim were empty of Kurds, ethnic Turks were settled there.

Villagers who survived the massacres drifted towards the cities, where they were gradually joined by economic migrants. In the fifties, as in Iraq, mechanization made the old sharecropping system unsustainable and hundreds of thousands more landless Kurds came to the cities, first to those in the southeast, then to centers of population in Western Turkey. There they became a new urban proletariat, as described by sociologist Erdem Yoruk: "Internally displaced Kurds who left villages that had been destroyed by the army or an economy generally ruined by war were desperate, and willing to do even the worst jobs, without social security or job security, often on a temporary basis, in what came to be known as the informal sector. These people swelled into the big cities, which were on every level—in terms of housing, infrastructure, health—barely able to accommodate them, and everything in their daily lives became a matter of makeshift solutions and negotiation."[26]

The first wave of openly nationalist politics among Turkish Kurds developed in these urban ghettos after the adoption of a more liberal constitution in 1961. The constitution contained no mention of Kurds, but it did allow for the formation of a legal socialist party, the Turkish Workers' Party. Unlike right-wing parties, the TWP had Kurdish members, who eventually convinced other party members to take up the "Kurdish question."

In 1967, radical students and young workers began to organize in groups loosely affiliated with an umbrella organization, the Federation of Revolutionary Youth. Some of these left-wing students were Kurds, who began to shape Kurdish nationalism in Turkey into something resembling other left-wing national liberation movements of the period. In 1969, they formed a network of cultural clubs called Revolutionary Eastern Cultural Hearths (DDKO), with centers in the southeastern cities of Diyarkabir, Ergani, Silvan, Kozluk, and Batman. These clubs also organized Kurdish language educational programs in the countryside.

Any attempt to use the Kurdish language awakened Kemalist paranoia and in October 1970, DDKO was closed down by the military.

Commandos were stationed in the southeast to watch for signs of separatism and a number of DDKO activists were arrested, among them Abdullah Ocalan, a kid from the country in his early twenties who was picked up at a protest demonstration in Ankara. He spent seven months in jail, where he met other students more sophisticated than he, and did a lot of listening.[27]

Radical student fervor was also high in western Turkey; in fact, there was so much unrest among left-wing students that the military became nervous and, in 1971, staged another coup. The Turkish Workers Party was declared illegal; martial law was imposed on university towns; and thousands were arrested in Kurdistan. The government accused Mullah Mustafa, across the border in Iraq, of trying to foment rebellion among Turkish Kurds, and began another reign of terror in the countryside.

After two years of repression, the military loosened the reins again in 1973 and permitted a civilian election. The new president, Bulent Ecevit, amnestied most of the students who had been in jail and they immediately started organizing again. Islamist student associations also formed, and right-wing students created a fascist group, the Gray Wolves, who wanted to exterminate everyone not of Turkish blood. Left- and right-wing student factions fought each other in the streets of university towns.

During this period, Abdullah Ocalan and six friends formed a group to study Marxism-Leninism. Such study circles were forming everywhere in the seventies, when the international distribution of radical literature exploded with the works of Frantz Fanon, Fidel Castro, Che Guevera, and Mao Zedong, among others. In China's economic mixture of feudalism, local capitalism, and imperialism, Ocalan's study circle found much that resembled Turkey. They also studied Fanon and Castro, and agreed that the only hope for systemic change lay in revolutionary violence and people's war.

In this they resembled other student groups of the period, such as India's Naxalite movement, the Peruvian groups Tupac Amaru and Sendero Luminoso, and Sri Lanka's LTTI or Tamil Tigers. These groups were to take different paths in years to come. Some, like the PKK, the Indian Naxalites, and, later, Nepal's Maoists, developed strategies beyond armed struggle and began to build mass organizations and do electoral work. Others, like the LTTI and Sendero Luminoso, became gangs of killers preying on a terrified population. Within the international Left, these two models of revolutionary strategy—an exclusive emphasis on armed struggle and terror, leading to "the dictatorship of the proletariat," versus a more flexible view of strategy that included armed struggle but also popular education, civil resistance, and electoral work—continued to compete throughout the nineties.

Ocalan's study group decided there was no point in trying to form a legal organization or even thinking about publishing in Kurdish; they would only be arrested. Instead, the group, which had grown to fifteen members, decided the main task was to send cadres to the countryside to work directly with the peasants, one on one. By now the study group was calling itself the "Kurdistan Revolutionaries."

Most of the radical Kurdish students in Turkey looked up to the more advanced movement in Iraq, which had already begun armed struggle. They were very disappointed when Mullah Mustafa had to flee the country in 1975. In speeches and meetings with other Kurdish groups in Ankara, Ocalan analyzed the failure of Mullah Mustafa, arguing that he had been defeated because he wasn't radical enough. His mistake, according to Ocalan, was that he had sought autonomy rather than an independent Kurdish nation, and, instead of siding with the workers and peasants, had stood with the big landlords and depended on support from the Shah and the US.[28]

Ocalan's group had to fight for their analysis. Marxist-Leninist politics in the seventies was nothing if not sectarian, and, like other student groups around the world, the Kurdistan Revolutionaries concentrated most of their energy upon their immediate rivals—other student Leftists. But the Kurdistan Revolutionaries were a little different from most groups, according to sociologist Joost Jongerden, because they "did not consider any of the 'really-existing socialist' countries to be a guiding light—not China, not Cuba, not Albania, nor the Soviet Union. . . . [They] observed that the reality in the countries where national liberation movements, or 'really-existing socialism', took hold was very different from the promises for which people had fought."[29]

By the spring of 1977, the Kurdistan Revolutionaries had recruited two to three hundred cadre and were ready to go public. By all accounts a compelling if lengthy speaker, Ocalan embarked on a six-week tour of country villages and towns to introduce core supporters to the group's basic program, which held that Kurdistan was an internal colony of Turkey, oppressed by both imperialism and the local capitalist class, and the solution was armed struggle leading to an independent socialist nation. Anybody who disagreed was an enemy—right-wing nationalists were wrong because they did not want to overthrow capitalism; Turkish socialists and communists were wrong because they did not recognize the national liberation struggle of the Kurds; and other Kurdish Leftists were wrong because they had a different political line.

The Kurdistan Revolutionaries were determined to clear the field of rival groups who might mislead the people, not only by ideological struggle but by fighting with fists or guns over who had the right to hang out in a specific coffeehouse or patrol certain streets.[30] This "revolutionary violence" was part of the spirit of the times. Everyone admired the way the Vietnamese were battling the US military, and one of Mao Zedong's most quoted proverbs was "Political power grows out of the barrel of a gun." In the international Left, where Frantz Fanon and Sartre's introduction to Fanon's book *The Wretched of the Earth* were extremely influential, the cleansing effect of violence was almost a truism. In Turkey this tendency was surely magnified by the violence visited by the state upon the Kurds, making it virtually impossible for them to do anything except fight back.

Ocalan's group decided their first targets—beyond other Leftist groups—should be the big Kurdish landlords whom they called the comprador bourgeoisie, a Marxist term meaning a native elite that acts on behalf of foreign imperialists and gets its position and money from them. Economic relations in the Kurdish countryside were certainly highly exploitative. In 1983, *Le Monde* described a cotton-growing village in Mardin Province where the *agha* was an absentee landlord: All the peasants except those who were too old or young worked eleven hours a day in the cotton fields for a daily wage that was the equivalent of $1 per child, $1.50 per woman, and $2 per man. Children in the area had a thirty percent mortality rate.[31]

In November 1978, the study group became a political party, the Kurdistan Workers Party (PKK). The PKK's first public action was a killing to avenge the murder of one of its cadre by conservatives. Battles between the PKK and conservative Kurds raged until the spring of 1979, when the Turkish government started arresting party activists.

That July, the PKK made a failed attempt to assassinate Mehmet Celal Bucak, a prominent conservative politician and landlord who owned thousands of hectares of land and collected the votes of more than 20 villages. Bucak was an aggressive anticommunist who bragged that he had a blacklist of Leftists who were to be killed, making him an ideal target. And attacking a man whom Mullah Mustafa would have considered a comrade enabled the PKK to show how different it was from the bourgeois nationalists of Iraq's KDP. With its attack on Bucak, it began to win the support of peasants who had never had anybody to defend them before.[32]

By that time, there were so many signs that another Turkish military coup was coming that Ocalan fled the country for Syria. He was to remain there for the next eighteen years. His plan was to make contact with Palestinian revolutionary groups in Syria and ask them for military training. After six months of trying, he was introduced to leaders of the Democratic Front for the Liberation of Palestine (DFLP) in Beirut and succeeded in convincing them to train a small number of PKK members in guerrilla warfare; they had already done this with fighters from Iran, Nicaragua, and Greece. In the summer of 1980, the likelihood of a military coup in Turkey was so great that Ocalan told his people to get out of the country and join him as soon as possible.

That year, the first group of about forty to fifty PKK fighters began to train at various camps in Lebanon's Bekaa Valley, which was controlled by Syria. In addition to the DFLP, Ocalan organized training arrangements with other Palestinian factions and the Lebanese Communist Party.[33]

While PKK members trained for armed struggle, other Kurdish activists sought ways to bring about democratic change through civic resistance and political organizing—legal in most democracies, but off limits for Turkish Kurds. One of the most prominent leaders to emerge from the struggle for democracy was Leyla Zana, who was born in 1961 in the village of Silvan in Diyarbakir Province. Her father, who worked for the local water authority, was a man of very traditional views, and the family was poor, with five daughters and only one son. In a 1991 interview, Zana described her family environment: "Everywhere in the world women are ill-treated by men but amongst the Kurds it is especially bad. A woman is not even treated as a servant, she is a thing, almost an animal. At home, for example, my father slept from the morning through to the evening when he would wake, eat, and go out to see his friends to chat with them. Meanwhile, my mother spent the whole day working, taking care of the animals. When she returned home in the evening to prepare food and take care of the family he would regularly beat her. He believed she should do everything he wanted, just like a slave.

"For the first 12 years of their married life my mother did not bear children. Then she had four daughters, in quick succession. Nobody talked to her, especially my father's family. If one of my little sisters would awake and cry in the night and disturb my father, he would take my mother and the child and throw them outside, whatever the weather. She would stay there until she felt he was asleep and it was safe to creep back inside. For a Kurd the birth of a girl is nothing."[34]

Her father didn't believe in female education and pulled Leyla out of school after a year and a half, but this only made her more rebellious about the way women were treated; she even refused to wear a headscarf as was normal in the Kurdish countryside. "I have never accepted the idea that I should be a slave, be passive. When I was only nine-years-old I attacked my 45 year-old uncle for beating my aunt. I have always been a combatant."[35]

In 1975, when she was fifteen, her father married her off to the thirty-five-year-old son of a cousin. Mehdi Zana was a tailor and communist activist who had just spent three years in prison, but this did not seem to have bothered her father. She did not want to get married, especially to someone she didn't know who was so much older, but she couldn't do anything about it. A year after she was married, Leyla Zana gave birth to a son. The next year, Mehdi was elected mayor of Diyarbakir. Though he was a man of the Left, he did nothing to educate his wife politically.

"Until 1980," she said, referring to the military coup that year, "the politicians of Mehdi's generation did not mix their family life with their political life; afterwards that changed." She was one of the people who changed it, but that didn't happen right away. During the first years of her marriage she was submissive, unhappy, and confused. "When I married Mehdi I was full of contradictions; until then I had no say in choosing my own life, somebody else had done the choosing for me. For the next five years it was the same, it was still not my own life, it was controlled by Mehdi. I was somebody to please Mehdi. I was not brave enough to scream and shout, the age difference was too big. But inside myself I was screaming and shouting as I have always been."[36]

During those years, the political climate in Turkey degenerated and the country became increasingly unstable. There was a severe economic depression, with inflation at 90 percent. Armed left- and right-wing Turkish students fought on campus and in the streets. The fascists of the Gray Wolves organized pogroms against minority groups. When the long-predicted military coup finally came about in September 1980, Parliament was abolished and martial law imposed throughout the country. Along with many other Kurdish politicians, Mehdi Zana was arrested. He was sentenced to thirty years in prison.

Leyla Zana was by then pregnant with her second child, a daughter. Twenty years old, with no education and no way to support herself and her children, she did nothing but cry for the first year. She gradually grew more politically conscious, starting with the issue of torture. "I had known it was going on since 1979 but when Mehdi was imprisoned they began to torture him and his friends, I saw it as a personal thing then. I began reading political books. . . . I didn't understand all the words. For six months I was not allowed to see Mehdi, during this time they were torturing him and beating him. Every week I would go to the prison to see him to be told 'no visit.' About that time I began reading the books." She had trouble reading because she knew so little Turkish, but her language skills began to improve when her son started school; she learned Turkish by doing his lessons with him.[37]

The government moved Mehdi around from prison to prison: from Diyarbakir to Aydin, from Afyon to Eskisehir. She and the children moved with him so she could visit, waiting at the prison gates with other women who came to visit their own arrested husbands, brothers, and sons. Some of them were highly politicized.

"Little by little I began to change," she said. "To question my own identity and to wonder exactly who I was. Until then I had no interest in the fact that I was a Kurd. The ideal was to be a Turk. The Turks were openly saying 'the Kurds are bullshit' or 'the Kurds have tails' (like the animals), and we put up with it, it was the official ideology, to be a Kurd was a disgrace."

In 1984, having learned Turkish, she decided to try to get a certificate indicating that she had graduated from primary school. She was successful and then went on to get a high school diploma, all without ever having attended any actual school. Soon she began to lead other women at the prison gates in protests and strikes. "I saw oppression. I saw brutality. I had to do something against that injustice," she said. One protest was sparked when an officer threw an old woman waiting outside the jail to the ground because she was speaking Kurdish, that forbidden language.[38]

Before long, Zana became a spokeswoman for the wives and families of political prisoners. Next she helped start a women's support group that eventually opened offices in Diyarbakir and even Istanbul. She worked for the Diyarbakir office of the Human Rights Association, founded in 1986 by relatives of political prisoners and then moved on to a job on a Kurdish paper, *Yeni Ulke,* where she was an editor until it was closed down by the government.[39]

Mehdi didn't like what she was doing. "There continued to be conflict between Mehdi and myself. He wanted me to be politically involved, to do things, but for him. He was not happy when I did something for me." But all this self-education and political activity felt wonderful to a woman who had seen her mother worked to death like a mule. "It was tremendous. I had changed, become different, I had an identity. It was terrific. In 1984 I was able to tell myself, 'Here I am. I do exist.'"[40]

*Portrait of Abdullah Ocalan at PKK base in Makhmour, Iraq, captured by Daesh in August 2014, and liberated by the PKK.*

# CHAPTER 3

# Insurrection and Genocide

THE YEAR 1979 WAS A TURNING POINT for both Iran and Iraq. The corrupt and repressive Shah of Iran, who had been propped up by the US, was overthrown by a popular revolution. Islamists, led by the Ayatollah Khomeini, took power, killed, imprisoned, or drove into exile most of the Iranian Left, and imposed a rigid Shia theocracy on the entire population. The new Iranian government also affronted the US when it allowed students to take over the American Embassy in November 1979 and hold the employees hostage. As all this was going on, Iranian Kurds rebelled, but without success.[1]

## Saddam Hussein vs. the Kurds

In July of that same year, Saddam Hussein finally seized total power in Iraq, becoming simultaneously Secretary General of the Baath Party, Commander in Chief of the armed forces, and President. To make sure no rivals would arise in the future, he purged anyone who could conceivably challenge him. At the Baath Party Congress that month, he read out the names of 68 men, who were then dragged out to be executed, some on the spot. He congratulated those who remained on their present and future loyalty.[2]

Hoping the Iranian revolution would spark a pan-Islamic movement throughout the region, Ayatollah Khomeini called for an Islamic revolution in Iraq, which is majority Shia, while Saddam's government was largely Sunni. In response, Saddam Hussein invaded Iran in September 1980. He expected a lightning victory, but the war lasted for eight years.

During the war, the Reagan administration did everything in its power to help Saddam, whom they considered the lesser of two evils. Saddam's onetime employee Said Aburish recalled, "He got blueprints to help make chemical warfare plans from the United States.

Everybody accused the Europeans of that. It was actually an American company and writers in New York would supply him with this [sic] blueprints. The US government knew about it. He got offers for fighter bombers from both the UK and France. For helicopters, for an atomic reactor from France. For suits against atomic, biological, and chemical warfare from the UK."[3]

When the war with Iran began, the Iraqi Kurds were busy fighting each other. The Left wing of Barzani's KDP had split in 1975 and formed the PUK under Jalal Talabani. The two parties had spent most of their time since skirmishing and trying to assassinate each other's leaders. The KDP spied on the PUK for Iran, and the PUK spied on the KDP for Saddam.

Hoping to stave off any more Kurdish attacks, Saddam had beefed up the *jash*—the Kurdish tribal militias paid by the government. By the summer of 1986, there were three times as many *jash* as *peshmerga*. Some people joined the *jash* because they were forced to, some to avoid being drafted and sent to the front, and some because they had no other income—the war had made farming impossible. Others cooperated to avoid having their villages burned.[4]

But years of war with Iran had so weakened Saddam's forces that the Kurds could again consider rebelling. In February 1987, Barzani and Talabani, having finally agreed to a ceasefire, announced they were forming a Kurdistan National Front and would unite their *peshmerga* in a joint command. The time seemed right; Saddam's forces were concentrated on the border with Iran farther south, leaving Kurdistan largely alone.

According to Middle East Watch, in the course of the war with Iran, "the Iraqi regime's authority over the North had dwindled to control of the cities, towns, complexes, and main highways. Elsewhere, the *peshmerga* forces could rely on a deep-rooted base of local support. Seeking refuge from the army, thousands of Kurdish draft-dodgers and deserters found new homes in the countryside. Villagers learned to live with a harsh economic blockade and stringent food rationing, punctuated by artillery shelling, aerial bombardment and punitive forays by the Army and the paramilitary *jahsh*. In response, the rural Kurds built air-raid shelters in front of their homes and spent much of their time in hiding in the caves and ravines that honeycomb the northern Iraqi countryside. For all the grimness of this existence, by 1987 the mountainous interior of Iraqi Kurdistan was effectively liberated territory. This the Ba'ath Party regarded as an intolerable situation."[5]

## The Anfal

In March 1987, Saddam appointed his cousin, Ali Hasan al Majid, as governor of northern Iraq, giving him absolute powers. Al Majid, later known as "Chemical Ali," decided on a scorched earth policy: He would empty and destroy the villages that supported the *peshmerga*, beginning with those in the Balisan valley, where the PUK command was located. He used the chemical bombs whose blueprints he had gotten from the US under Reagan.

A survivor told Middle East Watch what happened next: "It was all dark, covered with darkness, we could not see anything. . . . It was like fog. And then everyone became blind. Some vomited. Faces turned black; people experienced painful swellings under the arm, and women under their breasts. Later, a yellow watery discharge would ooze from the eyes and nose. Many of those who survived suffered severe vision disturbances, or total blindness for up to a month. . . . Some villagers ran into the mountains and died there. Others who had been closer to the place of impact of the bombs, died where they stood."[6]

Having tested his new weapons, in 1988 Chemical Ali initiated Operation Anfal, a year of total destruction wreaked on Iraqi Kurdistan, during which he used chemical weapons as well as bombs to decimate and depopulate the region and prepare for a ground assault.

After the war, Middle East Watch did extensive research in the area and published a report formally accusing Saddam's government of genocide. They compared the actions of the Iraqi government to those of Nazi Germany, saying "the Iraqi regime became the first in history to attack its own civilian population with chemical weapons." Estimates of the number of civilians killed range from Middle East Watch's fifty to a hundred thousand to 182,000 by Kurdish count.[7] The Middle East Watch report cites gross violations of human rights including:

- mass summary executions and mass disappearance of many tens of thousands of non-combatants, including large numbers of women and children, and sometimes the entire population of villages;

- the widespread use of chemical weapons, including mustard gas and the nerve agent GB, or Sarin, against the town of Halabja as well as dozens of Kurdish villages, killing many thousands of people, mainly women and children;
- the wholesale destruction of some 2,000 villages, which are described in government documents as having been "burned," "destroyed," "demolished" and "purified," as well as at least a dozen larger towns;
- the wholesale destruction by Army engineers of schools, mosques, wells and other non-residential structures in the targeted villages, and a number of electricity substations;
- the looting of civilian property and farm animals on a vast scale by army troops and pro-government militias;
- the arbitrary arrest of all villagers captured in designated "prohibited areas" despite the fact that these were their own homes and lands;
- arbitrary jailing and warehousing for months, in conditions of extreme deprivation, of tens of thousands of women, children and elderly people, without judicial order or any cause other than their presumed sympathies for the Kurdish opposition. Many hundreds of them were allowed to die of malnutrition and disease;
- forced displacement of hundreds of thousands of villagers upon the demolition of their homes, their release from jail or return from exile; these civilians were trucked into areas of Kurdistan far from their homes and dumped there by the army with only minimal governmental compensation or none at all for their destroyed property, or any provision for relief, housing, clothing or food, and forbidden to return to their villages of origin on pain of death. In these conditions, many died within a year of their forced displacement;
- destruction of the rural Kurdish economy and infrastructure.[8]

Masses of Kurdish refugees poured across the borders of Iraq into Iran and Turkey. But despite extensive press coverage of the crisis, appeals by the Kurds, and documentation of genocide by human rights organizations, absolutely nothing was done by the West either to stop the attacks or to punish the Iraqi government for its human rights violations. Everyone, including the US, was too worried about Iran becoming dominant in the region, not to mention eager to sell arms to Saddam Hussein after the war.[9]

Saddam drew the lesson that he could get away with war crimes. The Iran-Iraq war had ended with no gains for either side, only huge losses, and, betting his shirt on winning, he had borrowed $14 billion from Kuwait to finance his troops. Now oil prices were falling and he did not want to pay the money back. He had gotten away with murder before; why shouldn't he now? As Saddam's onetime employee Said Aburish described the situation, "All of a sudden he was sitting on top of a million-man tested army, unconventional weapons and he was broke, and restless. He became dangerous. He had to do something in order to survive."[10]

In August 1990, he invaded Kuwait and easily overran it. The royal family and half the population fled and Iraq installed a puppet government. The invasion was universally condemned, leading the UN to impose sanctions and demand that Saddam leave Kuwait. When he didn't, the US and others formed a UN-backed coalition and invaded Iraq in January 1991.

The Kurds had been holding their collective breath, waiting to see what would happen. Both the KDP and the PUK had moved their bases to Iran after the Anfal, waging a low-level guerrilla war against the Iraqi government, hitting and running, but not attempting to hold territory for fear of another chemical attack. Now, as Coalition forces advanced, Saddam warned the Kurds to stay out of it. To further discourage their participation, Turkey, a Coalition member, vowed that no autonomous Kurdish entity would be allowed to emerge in Iraq.

But other Coalition members were singing a different song. In February 1991, President George Bush broadcast a message over Voice of America, saying "there's another way for the bloodshed to stop, and that is for the Iraqi military and the Iraqi people to take matters into their own hands to force Saddam Hussein, the dictator, to step aside."[11] This certainly sounded like an invitation, particularly since the message was broadcast in both Arabic and Kurdish. Still the KDP and PUK waited, too afraid of a new Anfal to revolt again.

The Shia in southern Iraq beat them to it, rising up against Saddam's government the minute Coalition forces defeated the Iraqi Army, in

February 1991. Then a popular uprising exploded in Kurdistan, orga-nized by the *jash*, of all people. They suddenly decided they were not going to support Baghdad any longer and told local Iraqi army com-manders to withdraw their troops from Kurdistan. As David McDow-all put it, "The majority of *jash* leaders were thus transformed from embarrassed collaborators with Baghdad into champions of the upris-ing." In return for their support, the KDP and PUK promised them amnesty for their previous collaboration with Saddam, and the *jash* rushed to join both parties' *peshmerga*. Kurdish forces expanded from 11,000 to over 100,000 in just a few days. Thus strengthened, the united Kurdish force advanced on Kirkuk, long the desired capital of a future Kurdish state.[12]

Saddam Hussein was not ready to give up Kirkuk's oil. As the threat to Kirkuk increased, he took five thousand women and children hos-tage. Rushing his most high tech weapons and best troops to the area in March 1991, he forced the Kurds from Kirkuk, then from Erbil and other towns. Soon atrocity stories began to spread. Human Rights Watch reported, "In their attempts to retake cities, and after consoli-dating control, loyalist forces killed thousands of unarmed civilians by firing indiscriminately into residential areas; executing young people on the streets, in homes and in hospitals; rounding up suspects, espe-cially young men, during house-to-house searches, and arresting them without charge or shooting them *en masse*; and using helicopters to attack unarmed civilians as they fled the cities."[13]

Panic seized the Kurds; over a million and a half stampeded to the borders, trying to get to safety in Turkey or Iran. It was winter in the mountains and bitterly cold. Iran set up refugee camps on its side of the Iraq border, but Turkish soldiers used their rifle butts to beat back refugees, even invalids and mothers with babies. The Bush adminis-tration did nothing. As *The Independent* said scornfully, "The man who reportedly told the CIA in January to provoke the Kurds into insurrection and preached rebellion during the Gulf War, now acts like someone with a nasty bout of amnesia."[14]

Turkey's behavior was a major embarrassment for the Coalition, especially since Turkey was being considered for membership in the European Union at the time. Finally, under international pressure to do something, the Coalition announced a safe haven inside Iraq, including a no-fly zone, and pledged to keep Iraqi planes from flying above the 36th parallel. A green line was established around Iraqi Kurdistan, giving the Kurds control of Suleimaniya, Erbil, and Dohuk but not Kirkuk—the US feared that, if the Kurds had access to that much oil, they would become economically self-sufficient and secede from Iraq. Keeping Iraq in one piece has been a consistent point of State Department policy.[15]

Iraqi Kurdistan was now more or less free of Saddam, more or less at peace. But it would continue to suffer from what Kurdish writer Choman Hardi called "a legacy of violence."

## Armed Struggle in Turkey: 1984–1990

In 1980, the Turkish military once again overthrew the government. Turkish journalist Ismet G. Imset described the outcome: "By the morning of September 12, 1980, when tanks moved into [the] capital, Ankara, and a nation-wide curfew was imposed by the junta, Turkey's martial law-based system had already banned most legal left-wing, radical Marxist activities as well as propaganda and had jailed thousands of Turks under the US-indoctrinated concept of 'preventing the spread of Communism.' Hundreds of Turks and Kurds were facing systematic torture sessions throughout the country. . . . the very fact that a group of generals, using their force and weaponry had ousted an elected civilian regime and abolished the country's constitution, spoke for itself in [the] way of legitimacy for any form of resistance. The generals had taken over the country, closing down parliament, banning all political parties and placing their leaders, including the prime minister, under 'protective custody.'"

According to Imset, during the period of the coup, 650,000 people were arrested and most were tortured; 500 died as a result; and 85,000 were put on trial for thought crimes or because of guilt by association. "114 thousand books were seized and burned," Imset also reported. "937 films were banned; 2,729 writers, translators, journalists and actors were put on trial for expressing their opinions. One can hardly argue, as we enter the 21st century, that such a regime had any legitimacy other than to conform with the financial and political expectations of its foreign supporters."[16]

In 1983, after three years of this, the Turkish military allowed the country to return to civilian rule, convinced they had either killed, jailed, or driven into exile all the radicals, and destroyed the Kurdish liberation movement. They could not have been more wrong.[17]

The PKK's Second Congress took place in August 1982, before the end of the military dictatorship and in the middle of the Iran-Iraq war, at a Palestinian camp on the border of Jordan and Syria. By then about 300 guerrillas had been trained by the Palestinians and others. The party decided on a strategy of armed propaganda.[18] While they did not have a large enough force to seriously threaten the Turkish army, military victory was not the point of armed propaganda, as Che Guevara said in his message to the Tricontinental Conference, a meeting of revolutionary movements in Havana in 1967. The point was to inspire the peasants: "We shall follow the perennial example of the guerrilla, carrying out armed propaganda (in the Vietnamese sense, that is, the bullets of propaganda, of the battles won or lost — but fought — against the enemy). The great lesson of the invincibility of the guerrillas taking root in the dispossessed masses. The galvanizing of the national spirit, the preparation for harder tasks, for resisting even more violent repressions."[19] In other words, survival itself would be a victory. Or, as Henry Kissinger once put it, "the guerrilla wins if he does not lose. The conventional army loses if it does not win."[20]

The KDP agreed to let the PKK set up bases in the Qandil Mountains of Iraq, where they built their main camp in Lolan, a border area between Iran, Iraq, and Turkey. Then the PKK began to call in its cadres, who had to cross the border by foot. Over the next two years, PKK guerrillas went back and forth from Turkey in small groups of three to five, reconnoitering and mapping, figuring out where Turkish troops were concentrated and finding places to hide.[21]

On August 15, 1984, they staged their first two armed propaganda actions. In the early evening, thirty guerrillas entered Eruh, a mountain town of about 4,000, and opened fire on its military barracks, killing a soldier. While some PKK members guarded the barracks to make sure none of the soldiers got out, others occupied the mosque, using its loudspeakers to announce themselves to the town. Still others distributed leaflets in the coffee shops in the main street, saying this was the beginning of the Kurdish liberation war. When it became clear the soldiers were not going to do anything, the PKK raided another building for weapons, then left in a truck belonging to the Turkish water administration.

They used similar tactics in Semdinli, an even smaller mountain town: Eighteen cadre swept in, firing warning shots; then, while some guarded the officers' club and barracks, others went to the city square and read a prepared statement saying they had formed a liberation army and the war was about to start. Sari Baran, the commander of the attack, later explained, "Our goal really wasn't to kill a lot of soldiers. The attack was more to gain people's support and get them to join us. . . . We wanted to make an attack that would give people trust in us."

The PKK conducted other actions that month, killing three soldiers accompanying a presidential tour, and eight more near the Iraqi border. The Turkish military couldn't seem to find them, and young men from the villages started joining up. Over the course of 1984, Baran's team went from eighteen to fifty.[22]

In PKK historiography, according to social scientists Ahmet Hamdi Akkaya and Joost Jongerden, the two August 15 actions marked a turning point, a "day of awakening. It is believed that through the dual attack, which marked the start of the armed struggle, the chains of submission and assimilation were broken and Kurds rediscovered themselves." Prior to August 15, the story goes, Kurds were ashamed of their Kurdishness, and were forgetting their culture and language. The first shot fired on 15 August thus hit two enemies—Turkish colonialism and Kurdish self-hatred—with one bullet. This echoes Sartre's argument in his preface to Fanon's *The Wretched of the Earth*, a romanticization of the curative powers of violence, which is a common theme in revolutionary literature of the sixties and seventies. Martin van Bruinessen refers to the PKK's "almost religious belief in violence as a means of salvation" in this period.[23]

But soon the Turkish military began to catch up with the PKK. Winter in the mountains is very hard. The guerrillas were inexperienced, outnumbered, and outgunned. A number were captured and sent to prison. Some talked under torture and gave up the names and locations of others. Turkey poured troops into the region: Five divisions were stationed in the southeast, military installations were beefed up, and new outposts were established near areas where the PKK relied on villages for food and intelligence.[24]

Then, following the model of the Iraqi *jash*, Turkey began to develop an army of locally based Kurdish irregulars to fight the PKK, a system of village guards. As in Iraq, the plan re-inscribed tribalism on the Kurds. Village guards were paid so well—the equivalent of $70 a month—that 13,000 men enlisted before the end of 1985. As van Bruinessen described the system, "Village guards (korucu) received arms and attractive payment, in exchange for which they were expected to hunt down any PKK partisans coming near their villages (and later, to take part in anti-PKK operations further away as well). They received a bounty for each killed guerrilla, and soon there were reports that for the sake of bounty or private revenge many people were killed who had no relation to the PKK but were posthumously declared guerrillas. The village guard system reinforced the old tribal structures that had been gradually loosening during the preceding half century, and brought back some of the worst features of traditional Kurdish society. . . . Moreover amnesty was offered to criminals who joined the village guard system; the effect was that former bandits henceforth could with impunity harass their neighbours in the name of the struggle against the PKK."[25]

Faced with these new enemies, the PKK found it impossible to expand, though it managed to hold onto the bases it already had. But this was not good enough for Ocalan, who had no military experience himself—he later said he had never shot a gun in his life—and tended to overestimate what was possible. If the PKK wasn't winning, that had to mean people were not trying hard enough, or their commanders were making mistakes or were ideologically unsound. Over the next two years, the cadre who had planned and led the August 15 actions were targeted for internal discipline, made to look ridiculous or incompetent, or even arrested by their comrades.[26]

The PKK held its Third Congress in October 1986. Historians speak of this congress as the one where Ocalan consolidated his power, establishing a cult of personality that could not be questioned. Cemil Bayak, a founder of the PKK who later became head of the Association of Communities in Kurdistan (KCK), called it "the congress at which internal accounts were settled."[27] A practice had already begun of executing people who were considered disruptive, on the theory that they were police agents or working against the party in some way.

Cetin Gungor (party name Semir) had dared to question the plan to begin the armed struggle at the Second Congress; he was threatened and fled to Sweden, where he was assassinated. At least eleven other high level cadre were killed between 1983 and 1985, gunned down in Europe or at the PKK's camp in northern Iraq.[28]

The Third Congress made other serious decisions: In order to strengthen their numbers and treasury, the party decided the PKK should start forcibly conscripting peasants and make them pay taxes as well.[29] They addressed the need for training by setting up the Mahsum Korkmaz Academy, named after the first commander of the PKK militia forces, who had been killed by the Turks. The Academy was a three-week immersion program held every year at the PKK camp in Lebanon's Bekaa valley.

Because there were so many new recruits, the need for training was acute. Peasants were joining from villages in the southeast, and, increasingly, students were joining from cities in western Turkey, where probably half of the country's Kurdish population lived by then. There were even recruits from Europe, where the PKK was actively organizing among Kurdish exiles. Most of those who joined, according to van Bruinessen, were "drawn almost exclusively from the lowest social classes—the uprooted, half-educated village and small-town youth who knew what it felt like to be oppressed, and who wanted action, not ideological sophistication."[30]

The curriculum of the Mahsum Korkmaz Academy combined military and ideological training, the latter often conducted by Ocalan himself. His lectures normally lasted four to seven hours, extempore and with no breaks. The emphasis of the training course was to help young recruits mobilize their own idealism to become different people, "new men" and "free women" who would cast aside the feudal or bourgeois ways of thinking of their former lives, and be reborn as revolutionaries. Much of the work consisted of self-criticism, oral and written, with input from both classmates and teachers and frequent reminders that "90% of the combat is against your old personality, the enemy within, and only 10% against the external enemy."[31]

As social scientist Hamit Bozarslan noted, this "really is Franz Fanon speaking: The responsibility for slavery lies also with the slave himself and it is only his resistance that will allow him to become a free man. Violence is the main key to reach this goal. So it is not only about changing the system but about creating a man who frees himself from his chains."[32]

The many new recruits who were students brought with them habits of questioning authority and wanting to know the reasons for decisions. But PKK culture could not easily assimilate people who asked questions. Ocalan was suspicious that police agents might incite division and ordered the head of the Academy to scrutinize new recruits for traits that might mean they were actual or potential police agents or traitors.[33]

Two years after the founding of the Academy, Martin van Bruinessen wrote, "Paranoia seems quite rampant among the members of the PKK. They see enemies and traitors everywhere, which is one reason for their violent tendencies. Other factors are the social backgrounds of most members and their youth. About half of the approximately 250 'martyrs' the PKK claims were below the age of 22 when they were killed, and almost all were described as of very humble origins. These are precisely the groups most susceptible to rigorous indoctrination and most receptive to the party's romantic doctrine of revenge."[34]

French sociologist Olivier Grojean, who interviewed nearly forty members and ex-members of the PKK and its network in Europe about their training, painted a picture of an education process designed to break down individual personality structures, push recruits to cut ties with their families, and agree to sacrifice their personal lives so they could devote themselves totally to the needs of the revolution. Punishment was severe for those who did not measure up.

"The Academy has its own tribunal in charge of judging deviant personalities," wrote Grojean, "and those appearing before the tribunal are held apart in a special building prior to trial to reflect on their acts. If the assembly considers the 'culprit's' personality to be susceptible to improvement, then the judgment may be lenient, but it can also be very severe and even result in the death penalty if the person is found guilty of having had a relationship with a member of the opposite sex or of having betrayed the party's principles. Judgment is then either followed by an execution or else commuted to a less severe sentence by Öcalan himself. Selim Çürükkaya states that over 50 people were executed between 1985 and 1992."[35]

Ocalan later had second thoughts about many of these executions. He ordered an investigation into killings at the Academy and ended up accusing its head of deliberately trying to undermine his leadership. The head was executed by a firing squad. But looking for traitors was part of a paranoid organizational style that did not stop. Even after his imprisonment, Ocalan continued to denounce some defectors. Of course, they also denounced him—there has been a steady stream of such denunciations, particularly since the PKK split in 2004.[36]

In 1986, the PKK guerrillas carried out the decisions made at the Third Congress and began "military conscription." In other words, they started to kidnap young men and demand they become guerrillas. They attacked Kurds who worked for the enemy, especially the village guards, targeting their tribes, their villages, even their families. They firebombed the houses of village guards late at night, when everyone was asleep inside. They shot up minibuses going to areas controlled by village guards. In Pinarcik, they killed thirty civilians in a firefight, most of them women and children. They also targeted people who worked for the state, even if they just built roads or taught school, and burned down schools and health clinics.[37]

As anyone could have predicted, this approach backfired. Though people were afraid to join the village guards for a while, when Turkey upped the pay and gave the village guards more security and equipment, recruitment climbed again. The PKK's forced conscription also miscarried because boys who were kidnapped often tried to run away and, when they did, carried information about PKK plans back to their towns where police and village guards were waiting.

As the PKK attacks increased in number, Kurds were rounded up at a great rate. In 1988, Leyla Zana was arrested for protesting in front of the gates of the jail where her husband was imprisoned. "I had gone to visit Mehdi. There were a lot of people in front of the jail. It was July and quite hot. Many of the women there were with babies and young children, there were also old women. There was no water and everybody was very uncomfortable, especially the young and the elderly. They took us in a garden where it was announced that we would not be allowed to see the prisoners. Then, on the other side of the wall we heard them beating the men we had come to see. We just revolted, we began shouting and throwing stones. I was arrested with another eighty-three people. A soldier said that I had tried to take his gun and finally I was accused of inciting people to revolt."

She was tortured in prison. "The first seven days in custody were terrible. They subjected me to all kinds of torture. I was blindfolded and led to the interrogation room where I was stripped completely naked by a number of interrogators, all men. They hit me, I collapsed and they splashed me with cold water to bring me round. After that they gave me back my clothes and took me back to my cells. They also tortured me with electricity."

While she had nightmares about her imprisonment for years, she also learned about solidarity in jail. "I was sharing a cell with common prisoners, thieves, prostitutes, and drug addicts but eventually they became friends. We cooked together, we ate and slept together, all kinds of people in the same situation. It was about that time that I began to be a political activist, and when I learned there were Kurdish women fighting with guns I was moved to action. This changes everything, I told myself, a woman is also a human being."[38]

The struggle of Turkey's Kurds had yet to attract much international attention, particularly during the Anfal, when all eyes were focused on Iraq and Saddam's atrocities. But by this time there was a substantial Kurdish diaspora in Europe, and in Paris a physicist named Kendal Nezan had founded a Kurdish Institute. In October 1989, the Institute organized the first-ever international conference on Kurdistan, cosponsored by human rights groups and the wife of Francois Mitterand, President of the Republic. Also at the conference were Claiborne Pell, head of the Senate Foreign Relations Committee, and his staffer Peter Galbraith, who told *The New York Times* that the Senate had wanted to apply sanctions to Saddam Hussein after the chemical attacks, but these sanctions were blocked by the Reagan Administration. "Too many governments are too concerned about alienating the oil-rich or politically powerful nations where the Kurdish people reside," he said.[39]

While nobody considered asking the PKK to the 1989 Paris conference, thirty members of Turkey's largest opposition party, the Social Democrats, including seven Kurds, were invited. Their party chairman, however, barred them from going, fearing their presence at a conference about Kurds would prompt heavy criticism in the Turkish press. They went anyway. When they returned, they were called before the party's disciplinary committee and expelled for "taking part in political activities contrary to the party's fundamental principles."[40] In Turkey, it seemed that fundamental social democratic principles did not include opposing genocide.

## Iraq: Free at Last

With the advent of the no-fly zone in 1991, for the first time in their history, Iraqi Kurds had enough breathing space to think about how they would govern themselves. But they had no food. The UN had put the whole country under economic sanctions until Saddam paid Kuwait war reparations, and though refugee agencies were sending in food supplies for war victims, Saddam had imposed a blockade above the green line and little food reached the Kurds. He had also stopped paying salaries in the region, and fighting still took place sporadically between his forces and the various *peshmerga.*

Wanting some form of self-government, the political parties in Iraqi Kurdistan decided to hold elections for an Assembly in May 1992. These were the first democratic elections ever held in Iraq. There was a 7 percent threshold, which meant a party needed to get 7 percent of the total vote to make it into the Assembly. When the votes were counted, only the KDP and PUK had passed the threshold; each had roughly half the total vote.

The parties had different geographical bases—the KDP was based in the northern part of the no-fly zone, and the PUK in the more urbanized southern part. Their politics were different, too: The Barzani KDP was conservative and tribal, the Talabani PUK more left-wing. But, as historian David McDowall explains, there were many other factors affecting the way people voted: "The overwhelming majority voted according to their sense of personal loyalty. Many were the beneficiaries of patronage networks, either directly to a political leader, or via intermediaries through whom services or supplies were obtainable. Others had moved in order to be in the same party as the majority of their family, a new kind of communal solidarity pattern. Many, who could sell their services, had 'shopped around.' Some had been lured by money, for example, into one of the Islamic parties funded by Iran or by Saudi Arabia, or by a better deal in another party. Others had become disenchanted. Many of the *jash* chiefs who had submitted to the KDP, PUK and KSP, had now withdrawn to form their own 'Society of Kurdish Tribes.' They were anxious to defend tribalism, a form of identity to which perhaps 20 percent of Kurds still subscribed, against what they perceived as the political and social transformation of Kurdistan, a process in which the political parties were the leadings agents." After the election, most joined the KDP, the most powerful defender of tribalism.

One of the first acts of the new Assembly was to establish a Kurdistan Regional Government. But unity still did not come easily. In practice, the KRG functioned as an alliance of two parties rather than as one government. All posts were divided equally: If a minister was KDP, his deputy had to be PUK. This created what McDowall called "two parallel administrations reaching down to the police on the street or the teaching staff in a school," each with its own patronage network. Nepotism, corruption, and inefficiency became epidemic. People could not rise in any profession without belonging to one of these two parties.

At the same time, Saddam's economic boycott grew more and more severe, completely circumventing UN rules. The UN commissioned a report laying out what needed to be done to rebuild the Kurdish economy, but failed to carry out any of its own recommendations, and international agencies refused to work directly with the KRG for fear of implying recognition of a separatist government. Under these circumstances, supplies had to be smuggled in from Turkey, benefitting people closest to the border. In the southern part of the region, even though the grain harvest was not enough to feed the local population, farmers would sell grain to Saddam because he paid them more than they could get otherwise.[41]

In this situation, with a divided government still based on family and tribal affiliations, tension between the two parties was inevitable. The situation was further complicated by the PKK, which was securely dug into the Qandil Mountains in northern Iraq. The KDP, which was economically dependent on Turkey, was pressured by it into joining an assault on the PKK's Iraq bases in October 1992, in which many were killed. The PUK meanwhile, was briefly allied with the PKK.

There were other causes for antagonism as well, particularly quarrels over division of revenue from smuggling. Barzani's people in North Kurdistan had an extremely lucrative smuggling business in and out of Turkey, exchanging oil products for tobacco and alcohol. The Talabani network in southern Kurdistan also raised its main revenue from smuggling, but only in and out of Iraq, where there wasn't much to smuggle because of the sanctions. Thus, people in the area controlled by the PUK were very poor.[42]

Women particularly did not fare well in the new autonomous region. The incorporation of the *jash* into party politics had been a fateful one for women, for it gave impunity to men who had raped and killed their own people, and thus institutionalized a culture based on violence. But women were starting to voice their anger. In the spring of 1994, when a war between the KDP and PUK broke out over a land dispute, women organized a 200-kilometer peace march from Suleimaniya (the PUK capital) to Erbil (the KDP capital). They sang songs pleading for a return to sanity and made speeches about brother fighting brother. One told a reporter, "Men are making the fire; we are trying to extinguish it."[43] The march had as little effect on the war as a similar women's peace march from Zagreb to Belgrade in the summer of 1991 meant to "surround the generals with a wall of love." That march was stopped by Serbian troops, and war began soon after.[44]

The KDP-PUK war continued, with neither party able to control its own *peshmerga*. Soon there were new floods of refugees from the war zones. The situation was further complicated by the emergence of an Islamist militia based in Halabja, in territory otherwise controlled by the PUK. The Islamist group, supported by Iran, had received 4 percent of the votes in the Assembly election, not enough to be part of the government, but significant nevertheless. Now they came into the war on the side of the KDP and seized three towns, including Halabja, and a large area of land.

The civil war went on for four years, with first one side winning, then the other. It featured alliances between Baghdad and the KDP, Tehran and the PUK, intermissions, invasions by Turkey hunting the PKK, and failed attempts by the US to broker peace talks.[45] Not until 1998 was the US able to organize a solid peace agreement. And not until the US invasion of Iraq and the fall of Saddam Hussein in 2003 did the Kurdish economy become viable.

The prospect of a US invasion had been building for while. Neocons in Washington had been calling for a ground war in Iraq for years, some moved by the plight of Iraqi citizens, most by their vision of the US as a force to bring democracy to the Middle East and make that volatile region safe for business. The calls were very loud after the Gulf War, when many said the US should have marched on to Baghdad instead of pulling back. At the time, Dick Cheney, who oversaw "Operation Desert Storm" as Defense Secretary under the first President Bush, told CNN that invading Iraq would be a big mistake: "There wouldn't have been anybody else with us. There would have been a US occupation of Iraq. None of the Arab forces that were willing to fight with us in Kuwait were willing to invade Iraq. Once you got to Iraq and took it over, took down Saddam Hussein's government, then what are you going to put in its place? That's a very volatile part of the world, and if you take down the central government of Iraq, you could very easily end up seeing pieces of Iraq fly off. . . . In the north you've got the Kurds, and if the Kurds spin loose and join with the Kurds in Turkey, then you threaten the territorial integrity of Turkey. It's a quagmire if you go that far and try to take over Iraq."[46]

He changed his mind when he became Vice President under George W. Bush, and, with Donald Rumsfeld, pushed for a full invasion of Iraq in 2003 on the pretext that it had "weapons of mass destruction." The invasion and occupation were driven by illusion, arrogance, venality, cronyism, and the foolish assumption that the US could simply export its own political system anywhere it chose and be welcomed with open arms. While Saddam Hussein was a genocidal dictator who ruled by terror, what came out of the war was also terrible, as Houzan Mahmoud of the Organization for Women's Rights in Iraq (OWFI) described in 2006:

"Since the invasion, more than 100,000 people have lost their lives and more than 1 million Iraqis have fled the country in order to seek safety. The UN has recently announced that 6,600 people have been killed in Iraq in the past two months alone. . . . Internal refugees are increasing, with both Sunni and Shia Muslims migrating between cities to escape sectarian violence and religious persecution. Most of these people are living in camps, tents or in abandoned buildings without the most basic living standards. Security is still the paramount issue but, three years after the 'liberation' of Iraq, basic water and electricity supplies are still a dream for many people there. Schools, hospitals and other civil institutions have no proper functioning and armed militias rule over numerous neighbourhoods, enforcing religious law and terrorising people at will."[47]

In this dismal picture, the only winners were the Iraqi Kurds. Finally their long-shot bet on the US had paid off. The UN sanctions were over and the economy was taking off. True, Baghdad still contested Kirkuk and the oil money being generated there. But in a newly weak and fragmented Iraq, Baghdad was willing to give the Kurds almost anything else they wanted just to keep them from seceding.

The US was determined that Iraq not be partitioned; therefore the interim constitution, ratified in 2003, held that "the country's permanent constitution needed an absolute majority to succeed in a popular referendum and could be voted down by a two-thirds majority in a minimum of three governorates—code for the three Kurdish governorates.

In other words, no constitution could be passed without the Kurds' approval," as journalist Joost Hilterman said.[48]

This was autonomy, but autonomy from the top down, dependent on the US. Though Islamists were part of the picture and many tribal leaders were not friendly towards the aspirations of women, once the constant wars stopped, women had enough room to maneuver to create a feminist movement. Choman Hardi described how it happened: "In the post-dictatorship era . . . political space was opened up for suspended issues to be addressed and sidelined voices to be heard. Women rapidly mobilised in response to the widespread gender-based discrimination, marginalisation and violence. Even though initially they were preoccupied with more urgent issues, such as protecting women from violence, gradually their aims and objectives broadened. After a period of working in isolation the women's organisations founded umbrella organisations to consolidate their efforts and exert greater pressure for change. The patriarchal system responded to the on-going pressure by making cosmetic changes."[49]

The first big struggle took place in 2007 around the draft KRG Constitution, which had been heavily impacted by the rising tide of Islamism. Article Seven said, "This constitution stresses the identification of the majority of Kurdish people as Muslims; thus the Islamic sharia law will be considered as one of the major sources for legislation making."

Secular feminists like Houzan Mahmoud opposed Article Seven, saying, "It is clear to the world that in those countries where sharia law is practised—or simply where groups of Islamic militias operate—freedom of expression, speech, and association is under threat, if not totally absent. The rights of non-Islamic religious minorities are invariably violated and women suffer disproportionately. The implementation of sharia law in Kurdistan would be the start of a new bloody chapter in the Islamists' history of inhuman violence against the people, of oppression sanctioned by religious law."[50]

Kurdish feminists met with the committee writing the constitution, held a press conference in the Parliament building, and managed to defeat "the forced Islamization of women's lives." In this they were considerably more successful than feminists in Baghdad, who were unable to defeat a similar article in the Constitution of Iraq, which, according to activists, "canceled equal rights for all Iraqis in personal status matters and devolved judgments related to marriage, divorce, inheritance, and child custody to the authority of religious leaders."[51]

Still, while women may have been better off in Iraqi Kurdistan than in the rest of Iraq, Houzan Mahmoud pointed out that they still suffered from "honour killings, FGM, forced marriages, early marriages, stoning, rape, marital rape and many other forms of violence."[52]

In 2007, the KDP and PUK agreed to divide up power: Barzani got Iraqi Kurdistan and Talabani got to move to Baghdad and be President of Iraq. Foreign investors, especially from Turkey, flocked into Iraqi Kurdistan, throwing up fancy apartment buildings for the newly rich and building five-star hotels for foreign investors. Erbil, an ancient Assyrian trading center and UNESCO world heritage site, became a city surrounded by a 100-meter ring road that sported "a Nevada-like environment of gated hamlets for educated elites and expatriate foreigners," wrote journalist Derek Monroe. "It is widely understood that any major building project has to have some type of business connection with the Barzanis, who are pivotal to the permitting process. . . . Colonies like Royal City, English Village, American Village, and others, along with the wholesale import of fast food restaurants, have absolutely nothing to do with local culture or people." Most of the people who lived in these gated communities were in the upper echelon of the KDP and PUK, plus their friends and relations.[53]

Iraqi Kurdistan has huge oil and gas reserves, as many as 55 billion barrels of oil, a quarter of the reserves in the whole country.[54] Thirty-nine different oil companies from nineteen countries moved in; China even set up a consulate in Erbil. Since the region was still part of Iraq, however, oil revenues were disputed from the moment the autonomous region was created, with Baghdad claiming a percentage. The issue came to a head in October 2013, when the KRG defied Baghdad by building a pipeline through Turkey to the Mediterranean, bypassing the center of Iraq. In response, Baghdad stopped government salaries and other KRG expenses. This caused an economic crisis in the region, since an estimated 1.4 million people, out of a total population of five to eight million, were on the government payroll.[55]

Between 2006 and 2014, more than $38 billion in foreign investment flowed into the KRG, but most of it went into construction, where investors could get a quick return, rather than into manufacturing and agriculture, where real wealth could be produced. As a result, the economy remained dependent on oil, which meant the fall in oil prices after 2004 hit the KRG hard.

Corruption also took its toll on the economy. While some people had to work two jobs to survive, others didn't bother to show up for any job. In a 2008 BBC report, a Kurdish businessman admitted that a $2 or $3 million dollar contract to build a road would be given to a relative of some political leader, regardless of whether the relative had the capacity to actually do the work. The relative would then subcontract to someone who would subcontract to someone else until eventually the contract would reach a real construction company, by which time half the money would be gone. A 2015 report by the Carnegie Middle East Center called the system sultanistic: "Sultanism is a particular form of rule that is based on cronyism, clientelism, nepotism, personalism, and dynasticism."[56]

The corruption of the Barzani and Talabani clans was legendary; as a local journalist put it, they turned Kurdistan into a "two family region—Barzanistan and Talabanistan."[57] But journalists had to be careful what they said, particularly about the Barzanis. At least two journalists were gunned down, while another was sentenced to thirty years in jail for writing about the clan's hold on the economy.[58]

Despite such attacks, journalistic criticism continued. Seval Sarukhanyan, an Armenian researcher, wrote in December 2015, that, while "family states" are common in the Middle East, the degree of overlap between state and family in Iraqi Kurdistan was something special. President Masoud Barzani refused to resign after two terms in office, as required by the law adopted by the Kurds. His nephew, Nechirvan Barzani, was prime minister. Barzani's elder son, Masrour, was minister of intelligence and another son, Mansour, was a general in the Kurdish army, as was one of Barzani's brothers. His nephew, Sirvan Barzani, was said to be the richest man in the country. And, solidifying his ties with Baghdad, Barzani's uncle, Hoshyar Zaberi, was Iraq's minister of foreign affairs from 2003 to 2014, when he became finance minister.[59]

Based as it was upon tribalism, a strong security apparatus, and "traditional values," the KDP was not friendly to either democracy or women's rights and, while the PUK was more progressive in words, it was not very different in practice. In 2009, a new anticorruption party called Gorran (Movement for Change) was started by people who had split from the PUK. In 2016, it remains to be seen whether it would or could make any difference.

Thus it was not remarkable that, even when activists managed to get a 25 percent quota for women in decision-making bodies, business continued as usual. When government posts were allotted to fill the quota, they were given to women "based on their political affiliations or familial and tribal connections and not because of their suitability or interest in women's issues and gender equality," wrote Choman Hardi. "These women are specifically chosen because they are not a threat to the system."

In Parliament, there were few women on important committees—and no men at all on the Women's Committee because "women's issues are considered women's problem and they are left to deal with them. The burden of combating gender discrimination is put on women activists who are blamed every time a woman is killed. This mentality fails to recognise that the responsibility of securing better rights for the various social groups (women, the poor, people with disabilities, ethnic and sexual minorities, etc.) must ultimately lie with the government," wrote Hardi.[60]

In 2011, popular dissatisfaction with the Kurdistan Regional Government boiled over and, as in other places during the Arab Spring, thousands of young people took to the streets in Suleimaniya, demanding more transparency and democracy from the PUK. (There were no such demonstrations in Erbil because the KDP did not allow protests.) These demonstrators sent shock waves through the Kurdistan Regional Government.

As Kawa Hassan wrote in a report for the Carnegie Middle East Center, "They renamed the city's central square Saray Azady (Liberation Square, after Tahrir Square in Cairo), demanded an end to economic monopolies and human rights violations, and called for social and economic justice and the democratization of the political system. A remarkable characteristic of this protest movement was that different forces—Gorran, Islamist parties, and civil society—jointly organized the demonstrations."[61]

At their peak, the demonstrations attracted thousands and they continued for two months. Then security forces surrounded the demonstrators and opened fire, killing at least two and wounding forty-seven, according to one reporter. Another put the toll at ten killed and more than five hundred injured. In retaliation for the protests, government supporters and security guards attacked independent press offices, and burned down both the independent NRT television station in Sulay-maniyah and the Gorran radio station in Erbil.[62]

The PUK reaped the fruit of its repression in the next election for Parliament in 2013. Gorran got one third of the votes and became the second largest party, ahead of the PUK. And the KDP came under intense pressure again in the fall of 2015, with weeks of protests because teachers and government employees had not been paid for three months and Barzani refused to call new elections or step down even though his term extension was up. Shenah Abdullah, an anthro-pologist in Suleimaniya, wrote in mid-October of 2015: "Two years of financial and political uncertainty have led to widespread hopeless-ness. This week marks the third week of strikes in many government sectors in the Suleimani, Halabja and Garmyain districts. Teachers and government employees have refused to go back to work and demand to be paid three months of overdue salaries. . . . The KDP has refused to come to a consensus with the other four political parties due to [its] insistence on extending the president's reign, which ended on 20 August of this year. Their grip on power is reaching a frightening stage and they threaten to dismantle the parliament. . . . For the past two years, the majority of people have survived thanks to sustenance and loans from relatives and friends. That lifeline has thinned out and is nearing its limit. In the meantime, the ruling elite and a growing afflu-ent class feeding on capitalist investments and oil revenues lead lives of luxury inconceivable even to their counterparts elsewhere. The gap between the classes is alarming and it is making people furious. . . . while American and European officials boast of this shining demo-cratic example, which they have been nurturing for decades."[63]

Many Kurdish feminists joined Gorran because of their inability to get the Kurdistan Regional Government to deal with increasing levels of violence against women. Even when new laws were passed, they were not enforced. In 2013, a feminist NGO called One Voice presented a letter to the government demanding better enforcement. It quoted sta-tistics for 2011 and 2012: "74 women were killed and only 16 people were punished, 709 cases of [alleged] suicide were recorded and only 3 were investigated, 1,681 cases of domestic violence were recorded and no one was charged, 279 women were raped and only 2 men were punished. In other words, a total 2,743 cases of violence against women were recorded and only 21 people were brought to justice."[64]

Much of the work of the women's movement in Iraqi Kurdistan has centered on issues of violence against women, particularly "honor killings," forced marriage, domestic violence, and FGM. There has been entrenched opposition to change in any of these areas, particularly "honor killings," which both the KDP and PUK have claimed are part of Kurdish culture. In 2009, when a law was drafted on gender equality, Barzani refused to sign it. In 2011, he also refused to sign a law banning FGM, although it eventually passed without his signature.[65]

Local advocacy work on violence against women has suffered from the problems of women's rights advocacy everywhere—financial instability and donor driven programming. In places where the government has no interest in combating violence against women—or, more accurately, is hostile to women's equality—the work is often carried on by NGOS that are dependent on external funding. Since such funding is generally given on a project-to-project basis, with no provision for organizational sustainability, NGOs tend to follow whatever issue is fashionable, switching from one program to another every few years to please donors. Choman Hardi and Shahrzad Mojab addressed these problems in the Iraqi Kurdistan women's movement, but they are endemic to women's rights work everywhere, as documented by the Association for Women's Rights in Development (AWID).[66]

And while NGOs can help in individual cases—setting up shelters, helping young women escape forced marriages—and do political lobbying and advocacy, broader cultural questions like violence against women require consistent political education and social intervention. The rising strength of Islamism in Iraqi Kurdistan has only added to the difficulty of making that happen.

Hardi has shown how a history of violence has compounded many of the problems women face. On top of the Anfal, in Saddam's time, "the Iraqi government through the use of imprisonment, torture, widespread surveillance, and public executions in the main cities had made political violence part of everyday life. Throughout the Iran-Iraq war the Iraqi TV stations broadcast a programme called Swar min Al-Maaraka (Images from the battlefield) which proudly showed images of the broken and mutilated bodies of Iranian soldiers as a symbol of . . . success. In this sense cruelty in Iraq was normalised and the society was brutalised. Similarly in the 1991 popular uprising, the Kurds showed no mercy when killing members of the Iraqi security and intelligence offices. These people were not only killed but parts of their bodies, such as ears, fingers and penises, were cut and they were exhibited on the streets and in the main squares for days. This should have been a warning signal to tell us that the new community which was just beginning was going to be as brutal and merciless as the one it was replacing."[67]

A feminist, democratic, people-centered cultural revolution is needed. While such a revolution has not yet come to Iraqi Kurdistan, it has blossomed across the border, in the Rojava cantons of Syria. It began in Turkey in the 1990s, when the PKK began to change its strategy and Leyla Zana began to speak up for peace and democracy and women's rights.

*Funeral after a Daesh suicide bomb attack on YPG-YPJ in Sinjar, 2015.*

CHAPTER 4

# The People Take Up the Struggle

THE PKK's FIFTH CONGRESS in 1995 was a turning point in its development, at which it reversed policy decisions made at the Third Congress in 1986, notably the policy of drafting and taxing Kurdish peasants. In a major step forward, it made a commitment to uphold the Geneva Convention, meaning it would no longer attack civilians, only the military and police—a commitment that was not matched by the Turkish government.[1] The Congress also advanced a startling new position on women's liberation, essentially saying that women, not the working class, were the motive force of revolution: "In today's world, women represent the strongest revolutionary dynamic force in the society."[2]

What had happened between 1986 and 1995? A mass movement had been born.

In the eighties, the PKK was a small and fairly isolated group of militants focused on armed struggle and willing to use violence against civilians like teachers and the families of village guards. In the nineties, their message of Kurdish liberation was taken up by an increasing number of ordinary Kurds, and the struggle was gradually transformed by mass civil resistance as well as battles for political representation. In both these arenas, women were leading activists. And from the nineties on, these three forms of political struggle—guerrilla warfare, mass civil resistance, and parliamentary work—were linked and had a cumulative effect on the consciousness of people in southeastern Turkey. It was not so much that Kurdish activists all followed the PKK, as the Turkish government asserted, as that they were all part of the same movement, reaching for the same goals. The Turkish government itself bore much of the responsibility for this change.

In 1996, Martin van Bruinessen wrote that the PKK's apparent strategy of provoking Turkish repression in order to make Kurdish villagers take sides had been "dramatically successful, which was due largely to the brutality with which the Turkish security forces have operated in the region. Unable or unwilling to distinguish between PKK partisans and ordinary villagers, the military and special forces, hunting for guerrilla fighters, made life in many Kurdish mountain villages miserable. It was from such villages that the PKK recruited many of its new fighters."[3]

Turkish brutality towards the Kurds was nothing new, but it had begun to attract international attention and this affected the situation inside Turkey. The Kurdish diaspora in Europe had made people more aware of the ongoing repression. Also, in 1987 Turkey had applied for membership in the European Union, which requires that countries wishing to join meet generally accepted human rights standards. And, unlike the situation in the 1930s, when the British Ambassador refused to believe Ataturk was butchering the Kurds, there was now an international human rights movement keeping score. In May 1990, the European Parliament passed a resolution that, while condemning the PKK as terrorists, called on Turkey to recognize the political, cultural, and social rights of the Kurds.[4]

That same year, Helsinki Watch (later Human Rights Watch) published the second of what would be many reports on Turkey's violations of Kurdish human rights. "Kurds told us again and again that they want to be able to speak Kurdish officially, to read Kurdish books, to sing Kurdish songs, to dance Kurdish dances, to celebrate Kurdish holidays, and to give their children Kurdish names," wrote Lois Whitman, who authored the report. "'We want the government to accept us as Kurds,' one businessman told us, 'and to leave us alone.'"[5]

But Turkish officials insisted this was out of the question. According to Helsinki Watch, "in May 1990, Ms. Fugan Ok, head of the human rights department of the Foreign Ministry, told Eric Siesby of the Danish Helsinki Committee that the Kurds are not a minority, since according to the Lausanne Treaty of 1923 only religious minorities are recognized. She also asserted that there is no discrimination against Kurds, but that such discrimination would exist if the Kurds insisted upon a separate language and a separate culture. Adnan Kahveci, Minister of Finance, also told Mr. Siesby in May that Kurds were not discriminated against, and that special Kurdish schools would create segregation and give rise to ethnic conflicts."

Finally, the Helsinki Watch report noted that, "support among the Kurds for the PKK (the Kurdish Workers' Party, a separatist group waging guerrilla warfare against the Turkish government in the southeast) appeared to have grown a good deal. . . . Most people now sympathized with the PKK because of the killings, harassment and abuse of Kurds by the security forces. The tactics used by the Turkish government appear to have been counterproductive—to have driven more and more civilians into the arms of the PKK."[6]

The period between 1990 and 1995 was critical in the development of the PKK. In 1990, the focus was still on inner-party struggle. The party held its Fourth Congress in Iraqi Kurdistan that December. Though Iraq had invaded Kuwait and a US attack was imminent, the congress concentrated on the party's military failures and the search for police agents in the ranks. One fighter after another was disgraced and led away for questioning in what participants described as "an atmosphere of terror."[7]

For the first time, Ocalan was not present—he wanted the congress to be in Iraqi Kurdistan as a political statement, but could not leave Syria himself for fear of arrest. In his absence he put Mehmet Cahit Sener, a member of the party's executive committee, in charge. Sener had spent eight years in Turkey's Diyarbakir Prison for being in the PKK, then a year in Damascus working with Ocalan. By the time of the Fourth Congress, he had many criticisms of the way leading guerrillas were being targeted and, after talking with Sari Baran, another executive committee member, decided to express them.

"Friends," he told the congress, "the situation has been evaluated and every action has been judged to have been wrong. I think that those fighting can make mistakes, but to take a gun and go to the mountains is a courageous act . . . If what the fighters did is a crime, if the activities they carried out are crimes, then the party line itself must be looked at and judged." He demanded an investigation into policies like the killing of civilians and recruits; he also proposed a structure of more collective leadership. All this was a direct challenge to Ocalan.

Suddenly, in the middle of the congress, delegates heard that the US-led coalition was preparing to attack Saddam Hussein's forces, and they would have to leave immediately to avoid being caught in the war. Sener stayed behind; ten days later he was put under arrest by the PKK. Eventually he and Sari Baran, who was about to be arrested himself, escaped and fled to the mountains, where they decided to form a new group called PKK-Vejin (Revival). They sent out a call to PKK members to cut their ties to Ocalan and join the new party.[8]

Besides having been a member of the PKK executive committee, Sener had additional prestige from having led hunger strikes and rebellions in the harsh conditions of Diyarbakir prison. He had many contacts among former prisoners, while Baran knew a lot of the PKK cadres. "Our idea wasn't to break off from the PKK, but to persuade people of our ideas and turn the organization in the right direction," Baran later told Aliza Marcus. But their arguments got little traction and they could find few recruits for their new party in 1991.

Baran stayed in northern Iraq, under the protection of Masoud Barzani, but, for unknown reasons, Sener crossed the border into Syria and went to Qamishli, where the PKK was strong. On November 1, 1991, he and a woman companion were executed by the PKK in the apartment where they were staying. Baran eventually made his way to Europe and joined with other dissidents—including Ocalan's ex-wife Kesire Yildirim—to try to keep PKK-Vejin alive.[9]

But while the party was focused on its internal struggle and Ocalan was looking for traitors and dissidents, back home in Turkey the Kurdish people were starting to change. Women in particular were becoming radicalized and politically active, seizing on opportunities offered by civil resistance to break out of confining gender roles.

A 1990 uprising in Nusaybin, a small town in Turkey near the Syrian border, sparked several years of popular protests usually called the *Serhildan*, the Kurdish word for uprising. It began when thirteen PKK guerrillas were killed in a border skirmish. It was PKK policy to ask villagers to claim the bodies of guerrillas who had been killed in fighting and whom they considered martyrs, but normally people were reluctant to do so for fear of arrest. This time, however, one of the murdered fighters was twenty-year-old Komaran Dundar, who came from a prominent Nusaybin family with nationalist politics, and his father went to the police to claim his body. But the police would not give the body up, and Dundar remained in the police station for hours, arguing with them. During this time a crowd began to gather at his house, waiting for news and fearing the worst. When Dundar finally got home at four in the morning with his son's body, hundreds of people were waiting for him, tearing their hair and crying.

The police had ordered that the funeral be over by seven that morning, only a few hours away, but adding to the impossibility of holding such an early ceremony, the boy's mother was in Izmir and could not get back home until afternoon. The police had also stipulated that only family members could attend, but people who had been at the house all night spread the word, and thousands showed up for the funeral, marching in a vast cortege to a mosque at the other end of town, then to the cemetery. On the way back from the cemetery, some of the crowd began to throw stones at the police. When the police tried to cordon them off, a shot was fired, nobody knew by whom, and the funeral procession became a free for all, with many injured on both sides and hundreds arrested.[10]

The next day the protest spread to Cizre, a much larger town. This time 15,000 people—half the town—demonstrated. At least five were killed, eighty were injured, and 150 were arrested. Similar demonstrations spread to other towns and cities in southeastern Turkey throughout the spring of 1990, particularly during the forbidden Newroz holiday.[11]

As the Mayor of Nusaybin told reporters, the demonstrations were a spontaneous response to intolerable repression: "There didn't even have to be a leader of the protests. Everything has come to the point of explosion from the inside, because of bad policies, state terrorism, and torture."[12] Protestors were also inspired by the Palestinian *intifada*, which had been going on since 1987 and seemed to finally be resulting in negotiations. Many Kurdish demonstrators wrapped keffiyehs around their heads, Palestinian style.

Trying to cool things down, the Turkish government made a few cosmetic concessions—allowing people to speak Kurdish in private conversations, listen to Kurdish music at home, and even celebrate Newroz—but the struggle continued to heat up, particularly when police turned Newroz celebrations into bloodbaths by firing at the crowds. Clashes between police and protestors continued to take place throughout 1991, some involving the PKK and some not.

In fact, although the police and government papers blamed the uprising on the PKK, the party was as surprised as anyone. It had little organizational strength in the cities and towns where the demonstrations took place and had done nothing to organize them. Still focused only on armed struggle, the PKK saw the *Serhildan* mainly as a chance to recruit new fighters.[13]

In April 1991, the Turkish government announced rigid new censorship laws that allowed the governor general of a province to close any publishing house that revealed things he didn't want people to know. The state also reinstated the policy of emptying rebellious towns and razing them; between August and November over 80,000 people were left homeless.[14] The *Serhildan* was one reason for these measures; another was the growing number of Kurdish refugees coming into Turkey to escape the war in Iraq. The last thing the Turkish government wanted was more Kurds. In June, police were filmed by members of the international press using truncheons to beat back hundreds of refugees trying to cross the border.[15]

In a process that sociologist Ali Kemal Ozcan called "the massification of the PKK," people in southeastern Turkey were becoming increasingly restive, especially the young.[16] Some went to the mountains to join guerrilla encampments. Others searched for a legal way to do political work as Kurds. They found it when a group of Kurds who had been elected to the Turkish parliament as members of the Social Democratic Party decided to found a new left-wing party and make Kurdish civil rights part of its program.

The People's Labor Party (HEP) announced its existence on June 7, 1991 and immediately began to organize in the towns and cities of the southeast. It was not officially a Kurdish party—that would have been legally impossible—but soon was one in effect because most of the left-wing Turks who had been involved initially dropped out, not wanting to be associated with something that would be focused on Kurdish rights.[17]

Though the PKK itself was still anathema to most Turks, for the first time the Kurdish problem was actually being discussed in the press. The Social Democratic Party even published a report on conditions in the southeast, containing what David McDowall described as "startling recommendations to ease the situation: free expression of identity and linguistic freedom of expression; abolition of the village guards, the governor general and state of emergency; and a major programme of regional development." Kurds saw the report as electorally motivated—the Social Democrats did not want to lose their share of the Kurdish vote.[18] But there was a widespread sense that something needed to be done as repression grew and unrest mounted.

Increasing numbers of Kurdish activists were disappearing or were found dead after being arrested. Just one month after HEP's inception, its chairman, Vedat Aydin, was arrested and a few days later his body was found in a garbage dump, showing signs of torture. Twenty-five thousand mourners attended his funeral, where they shouted PKK slogans. The police attacked, leaving twelve dead and 122 wounded.[19]

International human rights organizations noted the growing number of violations of Kurdish life and liberty by "the deep state"—the government, the secret police, and the paramilitary groups that worked with them. A 1994 Helsinki Watch report summarized the toll: "Kurds in Turkey have been killed, tortured, and disappeared at an appalling rate since the coalition government of Prime Minister Suleyman Demirel took office in November 1991. In addition, many of their cities have been brutally attacked by security forces, hundreds of their villages have been forcibly evacuated, their ethnic identity continues to be attacked, their rights to free expression denied and their political freedom placed in jeopardy."[20]

Researchers were beginning to reveal the extent to which the deep state's development involved the CIA, which had set up secret counterguerrilla units in various NATO countries after World War II. These were supposed to swing into action in the event of a communist invasion. They were run by the CIA's Office of Project Coordination, the charter of which called for "propaganda, economic warfare; preventative direct action, including sabotage, anti-sabotage, demolition and evacuation measures; subversion against hostile states, including assistance to underground resistance movements, guerrillas and refugee liberation groups, and support of indigenous anticommunist elements in threatened countries of the free world."[21]

In Turkey, the secret police set up with CIA help were called the Special Warfare Department or the contra-guerrillas. Members of the Special Warfare Department received training from the CIA at the School of the Americas, a notorious US program for exporting subversion, as well as at various Turkish centers and US bases in Germany. They were taught "assassinations, bombings, armed robbery, torture, attacks, kidnap, threats, provocation, militia training, hostage-taking, arson, sabotage, propaganda, disinformation, violence, and extortion." They were also trained to counter peaceful movements for social change, which were seen as subversion. The Special Warfare Department had its own prisons, torture centers, and special "State Security Courts," separate from the normal judicial apparatus.[22]

In addition to help from the CIA, the Turkish secret police had another ally in their war against the Kurds—Kurdish Hezbollah (KH), an Islamist group financed by both Saudi Arabia and Iran, which in the early nineties began to penetrate the Kemalist state and work in league with its death squads against the Kurdish Left.[23] Although KH shares a name with the Lebanese Hezbollah, the two are not connected; Kurdish Hezbollah is Sunni and the Lebanese organization is Shia.[24]

Martin van Bruinessen described the relationship between Kurdish Hezbollah and the PKK as a blood feud: "The Hizbullah ('army of God'), most of whose members are also Kurdish, was originally firmly opposed to the existing political order, though for other reasons than the PKK. The section that came to clashes with the PKK, however, appears to have offered its co-operation to counter-insurgency operatives in the police and/or gendarmerie force. Turbaned, bearded and in baggy trousers (the conservative Muslim outfit), and armed with sticks and butcher's knives, they frequently attacked meetings of young Kurdish nationalists and raided cafes and other gathering places. Many persons in these towns were assassinated with the butcher's knives, which were [seen] almost as a signature; nevertheless Hizbullah members were rarely arrested, even those whom witnesses said they had recognised in broad daylight. Public opinion became convinced that these Hizbullah killers acted with connivance or even on instructions from the cloak-and-dagger departments of the counter-insurgency forces, popularly known in Turkey as 'Kontragerilla'."[25]

Despite the murder of its activists and officials, the newly-formed HEP ran candidates for Parliament in the general election of October 1991. They ran on the slate of the Social Democratic Party (SHP), since, under the 1980 Turkish constitution, a party could not be officially represented in Parliament until it received 10 percent of the national vote. But the Kurdish candidates did very well, particularly after the PKK told people to get out and vote for them. They won 22 seats; the election of so many Kurds gave the Social Democrats a stronger caucus and both parties hoped for a relationship which would be mutually beneficial.

But the honeymoon was brief. One of the new HEP members of Parliament was Leyla Zana, who had won 84 percent of the votes cast in her home district of Diyarbakir. She was the first Kurdish woman ever elected to the Turkish Parliament. On entering Parliament, each deputy had to take an oath of office which contained a phrase about upholding Ataturk's principles. The Kurds of course hated this since Ataturk's principles meant their own cultural extermination. So Zana said the words of the oath as usual, but added a sentence in Kurdish, saying she did so only as a formality and would "fight for the fraternal coexistence of the Kurdish and Turkish people within the context of democracy." Her fellow deputy Hatip Dicle did the same—this in a government space where the Kurdish language was illegal. Immediately, all hell broke loose.[26]

"It created a scandal," said Zana. "The ceremony was broadcast live by television. All the deputies yelled out comments like: 'We have a terrorist in the parliament,' 'Dirty Kurd,' and 'Get out, this is not your place.' The next day they forced me to resign from the SHP [Social Democratic Party]."[27]

It didn't help that Zana had worn a headband in the Kurdish colors: red, yellow, and green. The idea that there could be something like a separate Kurdish identity, or any identity beyond the homogeneous ethno-nationalism of Ataturk, was intolerable to most Turks at the time, including the Social Democrats. Soon the State Security Court announced it was investigating whether Zana and Dicle could be tried for treason.

As members of parliament, they were immune from prosecution as long as their term lasted. But they had to operate in a very hostile environment. The other deputies did not want to hear from them, some refused even to look at them, others pointed fingers and yelled insults. Whenever they brought up human rights issues, they were accused of protecting the PKK.[28]

But even though the Kurdish deputies were unable to have much impact on Parliament, the fact that they were there, in a period that coincided with two years of popular uprisings, made Ocalan feel that the situation was changing and opening up new possibilities for the Kurds. He began to rethink the idea that the only way forward was through armed struggle and to put out feelers for negotiations with the government.

As early as March 1991, at the height of the *Serhildan*, a PKK spokesman said the party might welcome a federalist solution—that is, they were willing to discuss democracy within Turkey rather than pushing for an independent Kurdistan—an idea that Ocalan had dismissed scornfully in the past. That November, when a journalist asked Ocalan about a federation, he replied, "Unquestionably, this is what we see." A month later, he offered Ankara a ceasefire and negotiations if the state would release PKK prisoners; end its secret war in Kurdistan, including disappearances and unexplained deaths; permit free political activity; and adhere to its own ceasefire.[29]

But the government did not respond and the war continued. In early 1992, Ocalan wrote a letter to the *Turkish Daily News* calling for mass uprisings throughout the country on March 21, the day Newroz was celebrated. The military took this as an invitation to attack anyone who celebrated Newroz. The civilian death toll that day came to at least 102, including many journalists. Despite the fact that the military said they fired only in self-defense, there were no reports of military casualties.[30]

Eric Lubbock, Lord Avebury, a member of an international delegation that investigated the Turkish human rights abuses during Newroz, reported, "In Cizre, the security forces opened fire on unarmed revellers singing and dancing in the streets, killing an estimated 12 people and injuring many more. In Sirnak also, the military fired on civilian crowds and individuals, killing 22 and again injuring dozens more. The governor of Sirnak, Mustafa Malay, told a visiting delegation on April 19, 1992, that it was said that between 500 and 1,500 armed guerrillas had entered the town on March 21, but he conceded that 'the security forces did not establish their targets properly and caused great damage to civilian houses'. . . . In Sirnak, the armed forces and police went on the rampage over a period of some 22 hours from March 21 to 22, bombarding houses, shops, and offices, and causing civilian casualties."[31]

In retaliation, the PKK staged more attacks on the military. The situation escalated and Turkey put heavy pressure on the Iraqi Kurds to rein in the PKK or kick them out of Qandil. Worried about Turkey, both Barzani and Talabani tried to persuade the PKK to move to a different part of Iraq. Not only did the PKK refuse to oblige, in September 1992 it organized a huge raid into Turkey, involving hundreds of guerrillas.

That was the last straw. Yielding to Turkish pressure, Barzani sent five thousand KDP *peshmerga* to attack Qandil. He coordinated with Turkey, which bombarded the PKK base from the air. PKK commanders in Qandil were unprepared for such a massive attack. Most of their experienced fighters were still in Turkey after the raid. Half the people in the camp were new recruits. The PKK felt they could not abandon Qandil because winter was coming and all their supplies were cached nearby. When Turkey moved ground troops into the mountains, while continuing bombing raids, PKK losses mounted and supplies began to run out. Unable to reach Ocalan in Damascus, his brother Osman, who functioned as a second-in-command, decided he had no choice but to make a deal with Barzani before everyone was killed. The PKK had already lost 161 fighters, with three hundred more wounded. So Osman Ocalan signed an agreement with the Kurdistan Regional Government, saying the PKK would withdraw from the border region and stop using Iraq as its entry point for raids on Turkey. In return, the Iraqi Kurds gave the PKK a new camp at Zeli, near the Iranian border.[32]

But the PKK did not remain in Camp Zeli for long. After a few months, cadre started to filter back to Qandil, from which they could again infiltrate guerrillas into Turkey. By this time, the futility of seeking a purely military solution to a political problem should have been evident to the Turkish government. As Aliza Marcus pointed out, "In this war and in subsequent large-scale Turkish crossborder raids in 1993 and 1997, the Turkish military always faced the same insurmountable problems. First, the mountains and ravines that made up the border formed natural defenses that were hard to breach. By the time they were breached, the rebels were long gone—after the 1992 war, the PKK never again tried to defend territory and instead relocated fighters as necessary. Air campaigns were only of limited success, thanks again to the rough terrain and the difficulty of pinpointing the caves where rebels took shelter. And even if the military raid did manage to disrupt PKK camps and operations, this ended the minute the troops withdrew. Then the rebels were free to relocate themselves back near the border."[33]

Kurdish deputies in the Turkish Parliament were deeply disturbed by the police violence at Newroz and the 1992 acceleration of Turkey's war with the PKK. When the coalition government voted to support the military and extend the state of emergency in the southeast, fourteen Kurdish deputies left the Social Democratic Party to join Hatip Dicle and Leyla Zana in a HEP caucus.

Such an enlarged caucus was impressive in theory but in real life the Kurdish MPs couldn't get anything accomplished. They had no allies in Parliament and, whenever they went home to meet with the people they represented, the police harassed them, and their constituents were arrested. On one such trip, a local chief of police told the MPs he would crush them like rats and drink their blood. And large numbers of HEP officials continued to be killed or disappeared: twenty-seven in 1992, seventeen in 1993, eighteen in 1994.[34]

Leyla Zana told a reporter in 1993, "I no longer believe in the Turkish parliament. Its role is to cover up the action of the State, to conceal the misdeeds of the army and the police. The people who take the decisions in Turkey are the members of the national security council. Members of parliament are like notaries, they merely register the decisions. In fact, it is against everything I believe in, I do not have a voice."[35]

The Kurdish movement needed new tactics. The armed struggle had been badly damaged, and the parliamentary struggle had reached an impasse. In March 1993, Ocalan once again proffered a limited unilateral ceasefire, to last a month.

This time there was some hope that the government would respond. The President of Turkey was Turgut Ozul, who had been Prime Minister of the first civilian government after military rule and was more liberal than most in his party; he thought it was time to negotiate with the Kurds. But conservatives—including Suleyman Demirel, the Prime Minister—and the military were totally opposed to any concessions. They thought Ocalan's offer of a ceasefire meant that the PKK was defeated and they had won the war.

Still trying to get some response, Ocalan renewed the ceasefire, listing basic human rights demands that were no more than what the EU and even some Turkish politicians had suggested: "We should be given our cultural freedoms and the right to broadcast in Kurdish. The village guard system should be abolished and the emergency legislation lifted. The Turkish authorities should take the necessary measures to prevent unsolved murders and should recognize the political rights of Kurdish organizations."[36]

It didn't seem like much to ask. But all demands became moot the next day when President Ozul suddenly died of a heart attack. The PKK thought he was murdered to forestall negotiations, a question which has remained unresolved.[37]

Ocalan tried to maintain the ceasefire, but the military now had free rein and Demirel, the new president, made it clear that his objective was complete annihilation of the PKK. The army and police renewed efforts to hunt down any guerrillas who remained in Turkey and, over the next six weeks, killed at least one hundred Kurds, both guerrillas and civilians, and arrested hundreds more. They also went back to demolishing villages.

Semdin Sakik, one of the PKK commanders in Turkey, warned Ocalan that the party was losing people's respect because they were not retaliating. When Ocalan told him to go ahead and do so, Sakik ordered units in Diyarbakir to set roadblocks up after dark on all the main roads in the area, something the PKK did frequently to reinforce the idea that they ruled the night. On May 24, 1993, an unmarked bus full of off-duty unarmed conscripts came along one of the roads. PKK guerrillas manning the roadblock ordered the thirty-three soldiers off the bus, along with four teachers, and shot all of them. According to McDowall, this was the work of a rogue commander who wanted to end the ceasefire, but the PKK did not disown the attack.[38]

The war got much worse after the killing of the soldiers. The PKK did everything possible to show its strength, which was considerable. It attacked tourist sites and took Western oil and archeological workers hostage. In November 1993, it banned all schools, which it saw as bases for Turkish indoctrination; it killed thirty-four teachers that year compared with ten the year before.[39]

But the state had far more resources at its disposal than the PKK, and was willing to punish not just the guerrillas but the entire Kurdish population, shelling civilians and wiping out villages. According to Turkish journalist Ismet G. Imset, "By the end of 1994, at least 2,664 Kurdish villages and hamlets in Turkey's troubled southeast region were recorded as completely evacuated or partially destroyed by government forces." The people who lived in such villages were rounded up at sunrise, and told they could either join the village guards and fight the PKK or get out. Between three hundred thousand and a million Kurds were driven from their homes into the slums of Diyarbakir, Adana and other Kurdish cities; some made their way farther west to Istanbul and Izmir. The army also beefed up its checkpoints and arrested anyone who might be bringing supplies to the guerrillas.[40]

This counterinsurgency strategy is known as "draining the swamp"— the object is to empty the villages and small towns on which guerrillas depend for supplies, thus starving them out. As noted by journalists Robert Jensen and Rahul Mahajan, the strategy inevitably involves major war crimes: "The phrase has roots in Mao's description of guerilla fighters as fish swimming in the sea of the people. US counterinsurgency experts after World War II took up the phrase in their strategies of 'draining the sea' to counter guerilla warfare. Drain the sea: Deprive a fighting force of cover. Drain the civilian population. For those unlucky civilians who make up the sea, to be 'drained' means one of two things. Either they are forcibly driven out of their villages and towns, often with their homes, property, and crops destroyed, or they simply are killed."[41]

Such a strategy requires complete ruthlessness towards civilians. But this was not a problem for the Turkish government. It wanted to stamp out every sign of resistance. Kurdish offices were bombed. Unsolved murders of activists rocketed. And the HEP was declared illegal. Anticipating that this would happen, the Kurdish MPs had already registered another party, the Democratic Labor Party (DEP) and transferred their memberships there. But the Constitutional Court moved to close that down as well. In March 1994—just before an election—a parliamentary commission lifted the immunity of six Kurdish deputies, the first step toward trying them for treason in a State Security Court. When the six were arrested, the rest of the DEP deputies fled the country and set up a Parliament in Exile in Europe. These events focused European attention on Turkey and made its entrance to the EU more problematic.[42]

Leyla Zana was one of the Kurdish deputies arrested and put on trial. The year before, she had made a speech at the Carnegie Endowment for International Peace in Washington in which she spoke of the destruction of Kurdish villages, and of the inability of the Turkish and Kurdish political leaders to address the Kurdish question with frankness and candor. She encouraged Congress to work with democratic forces in Turkey and to help bring about a peaceful resolution to the Kurdish conflict.[43]

That speech was to cause her a great deal of trouble when she appeared before the Security Court. Zana was tried for treason and sentenced to fifteen years in jail. To show its disapproval, the European Union gave her its major human rights award, the Sakharov Prize, in 1995. But the Turkish military didn't care how many EU resolutions were passed or prizes given out; they were running the show.

The "Special War" was a disaster not only for the Kurds but for everyone in Turkey, not least the conscripts who were sent to die by the thousands—sons of poor families, since rich ones got their sons out of the draft.[44] Turkish democracy became an ever-receding prospect, as Ismet G. Imset observed in 1995: "Any Turkish scholar, scientist, researcher or journalist seeking a peaceful solution to the problem through debate has been arrested. Scores of journalists working on Kurdish issues have been assassinated or imprisoned. The low intensity civil war . . . has not only robbed the troubled region of its own economic resources along with possible investments, but also drains approximately 7 billion dollars a year out of Turkey's budget."[45]

## Beginnings of Change in the PKK

By the time of the PKK's Fifth Congress in 1995, the group was under more pressure than it had ever been. It had grown substantially: By 1994, the party had a full-time active membership of 15,000 guerrillas, while Turkish military officials estimated that PKK supporters in the southeast numbered at least 400,000. The broader Kurdish liberation movement had also come a great distance in ten years: The armed struggle had changed popular consciousness and affected the political climate enough to make a legal above-ground party possible.[46]

The program and resolutions that came out of the Fifth Congress show both the strengths and weaknesses of the organization. The program begins with a sweeping narrative of world history, PKK history, and the history of revolution. It makes a strong critique of the Soviet approach to socialism, calling it "the lowest and most brutal level of socialism. . . . Ideologically, there was a decline to dogmatism, vulgar materialism, and pan-Russian chauvinism; politically, there was the creation of extreme centralism, a suspension of democratic class struggle, and the raising of the state's interests to the level of the determining factor; socially, there was a reduction in the free and democratic life of the society and its individuals; economically, the state sector was dominant and there was a failure to overcome a consumer society which emulated what was abroad; militarily, the raising of the army and acquiring weapons took precedence over other sectors. This deviation, which became increasingly clear to see during the 1960s, brought the Soviet system to a condition of absolute stagnation."[47]

The program acknowledged that the defeat of the Soviet system meant the US faced no opposing power and was "trying to bring all regions of the world under its control with its notion of a 'New World Order,'" but stated that the removal of Soviet-era stagnation had opened up "new possibilities for the development of socialism and revolutions." These possibilities were being realized in the PKK, "whose understanding of socialism is one of the most developed in the world." Explaining what this meant in unmistakably Ocalanian prose, the program put major emphasis on the transformation of individual consciousness: "In the reality of our party ... a type of person is created who goes from a situation of incurable confusion to a condition of development and the ability to solve problems. A leading militant personality is created, one which is marked by great self-control and the attempt to become like other great leading personalities, taking examples from the history of the Middle East. A personality which, with great care, understanding, effort, and determination, seeks to overcome all difficulties and change the negative into something positive; a personality which, under all conditions, exerts a strong force of will and a fascination for the developing struggle of humanity, without seeking personal gain, to the point of being willing to give up one's own life to that cause."[48]

The program did not explain how one was to attain this ideal personality, or how transformations in individual consciousness would lead to social revolution. Instead it went on to develop a strategic analysis of the state of the Kurdish revolution, noting the acceleration of Turkey's dirty war: "In addition to traditional army units, there are new creations such as the special corps, the special army, and the special teams, as well as the village guard system and the contraguerrilla forces which have been created. With the aid of these forces, and not obeying any rules, all forms of war and unimaginably brutal methods are being deployed in Kurdistan."

Despite this, the Fifth Congress took a rosy view of the situation: "In the struggle against the political and military control of the Turkish Republic in Kurdistan, our party has developed a political and military dominance. . . . There is now a form of dual power in Kurdistan. The feelings and thoughts of the Kurdish people have become revolutionized. The mass organizations . . . together with their various legal and illegal associations, form a broad leading force, and the Kurdish population are to a large degree led by this force. The People's Liberation Army of Kurdistan (ARGK), which our party developed during the course of the war, now has tens of thousands of fighters; this people's army is stationed in all the strategic regions of Kurdistan and it has placed the Turkish army in a position of immobility there."

The resolutions that came out of the Fifth Congress struck a far less optimistic note, referring to serious losses and organizational errors, for which cadres were blamed, avoiding any implication that there could be a problem with the party's approach to armed struggle.[49]

In the words of a female guerrilla, "Ocalan would say the tactic is not the problem, that the problem has to do with the individual. But we didn't have enough military supplies, what does that have to do with it? You get blown up by a landmine—that has nothing to do with the individual—that has to do with the lack of mine detectors. . . . Ocalan would say, everything is fine, the problem is you."[50]

The PKK would not have gotten as far as it had if it had not emphasized the ability of motivated, self-sacrificing people to overcome all obstacles. Without attention to changes in conditions on the ground, however, its approach risked taking its people over over a cliff into the complete denial of reality. The resolutions of the Fifth Congress reflected a struggle to come to terms with this problem. Realizing that Turkey was depopulating the Kurdish countryside in order to deprive the guerrillas of logistical support, the Congress resolved "to prohibit migration from the country's territory," unless "front line committees" had granted permission. The resolution did not say how cadre were supposed to stop people who were being forced by the government to flee. On the other hand, the Congress also resolved to set up committees to help people who were forced to migrate, and to organize them wherever they went.[51]

Part of the problem was a weakness in the PKK's collective leadership. While most successful revolutions have had a charismatic, far-seeing leader like Ocalan, they also have had strong group leadership and a number of striking personalities, as, for example, was the case in India, South Africa, China, Vietnam, and Russia (though any semblance of real collective leadership ended in Russia after Stalin took charge and killed off his rivals).

Because of Ocalan's dominance, and because inner-party relations could be described as ruled by fear, people who split from the organization described him as a "despot comparable to Stalin or Hitler" and said he ordered the murders of many cadre.[52] Chris Kutschera, a French journalist who covered the Kurdish struggle for many years, wrote that "Abdullah Ocalan frequently displayed a tendency to megalomania which amazed foreign journalists, who would watch with disbelief as the party's top leaders stood seemingly in awe while the 'chairman' spoke or clapped frenetically when he scored a goal during a football game organised for the benefit of a television crew."[53] The scholar Paul White saw him as a leader of the narcissistic or inspirational type; Aliza Marcus referred to his paranoia and inability to tolerate rivals.[54]

Many observed that the organizational culture of the PKK was skewed by a cult of personality. But while the party was probably as tightly controlled from the top as Ocalan could make it, the total control attributed to him was logistically impossible. Living in Damascus, he could not be reached by phone from most places in the mountains; commanders on the ground, including his brother Osman, had to make many decisions on their own. The idea that everything good in the PKK came from Ocalan is the corollary to the idea that everything bad that happened was caused by a traitor in the ranks. The flip side of idolatry is purges. Both overestimate the power of the individual.

Despite the optimistic tone of many of the resolutions issued by the Fifth Congress, it was clear by 1995 that Ocalan was rethinking the question of the state and the whole nationalist project.

Being a nation without a state was the problem Kurdish nationalists had been trying to overcome for decades. They had assumed the way forward was to have a nation-state of their own. By 1995, Ocalan had begun to think that this might be wrong. Such a state seemed to be forming next door in Iraq, under the protection of the US, but it was a conservative state dependent on oil and Turkey. What would this mean for the future of Kurdistan?

The PKK had never seen Kurdishness primarily in ethnic terms. Their whole problem with Turkish nationalism was that it permitted only one culture and one language, ignoring the rich diversity of its people. The PKK was certainly not going to duplicate that mistake. The Fifth Congress program stated that "our national liberation struggle is the basis for unity for all disadvantaged groups adversely affected by Turkish colonialism, and in it they are able to find their own identity. Our party does not wish to lapse into a narrow form of nationalism, and our party views all the many cultures in Kurdistan as a richness; that's why all cultures are to be guaranteed and supported in their cultural freedom."[55]

But was it possible to have a state that wasn't based on ethnic nationalism? Maybe something like Switzerland? Or was the whole idea of the nation-state outdated, an artifact of a previous period of development? Ocalan began to ponder on his people's ancient history, before the rise of empires in the Fertile Crescent, thinking back to a time when women and men were equal and managed to govern themselves in small local units, defending themselves without the need for a state apparatus. Women, as the first subjugated group, were central to this rethinking, in which the Kurds assumed world-historical importance as early inhabitants of the Fertile Crescent.[56]

Ancient Mesopotamia, located in the rich agricultural delta between the Tigris and Euphrates Rivers, is often called "the cradle of civilization" because it is the place where human beings first settled down and became farmers rather than hunters and gatherers.[57] Mesopotamia and Sumer, the southernmost region of Mesopotamia, are also where people first began to live in cities and develop a more complex and hierarchical mode of social organization than had previously existed. In the mythology of ancient Sumer, Ocalan traced the lineaments of patriarchy and the origins of the state. To him, Sumer was the site of original sin, the place of transition from a horizontal society based on kinship groups to a hierarchical state based on slavery. Under one of Mesopotamia's early rulers, Sargon the Great, wrote Ocalan, "the slaughtering of people through a well-planned use of force, the appropriation of all their belongings and resources, the deportation of captives as slaves, and the creation of tiers of colonial dependence, became principal features of historical development."[58]

In Ocalan's vision, Kurdistan, the place of original sin, would become the place where the sin is reversed, and the long historical trajectory of war, suffering, and domination would be replaced by local self-management, direct democracy, gender equality, and fellowship between all its peoples.[59]

Although Ocalan's thinking on democracy did not fully flower until the 2000s, when he began to read and to re-examine all his old ideas while in prison, his new vision was clearly taking shape by 1995. In a 1998 discussion with US diplomat David A. Korn, he said that the PKK was definitely not striving for the kind of socialism in which "the individual is shrunk to its bottom limit but the State is swollen to its top limit. . . . Rights for the individual as much as the needs of society, social benefits and social order as much as the needs of the individual, is what we are trying to be loyal to as a principle."[60]

But the Kurdish struggle needed a particular kind of individual, and Ocalan's vision of "rights for the individual" did not allow for much deviation from that ideal type. He was obsessed with the problem of how to build cadre who were more developed than the society that shaped them. In his last interview before he was captured, he alluded to what he saw as deficits in the Kurdish personality structure: "Our problems are partly the result of the situation within the party, the central committee, the leadership. Reform will allow us to improve. We don't want to cheat, there are shortcomings and we must correct them. Our activities during the last 15 years should have brought other results. The Turks should not be so free with us. We made tactical mistakes. Our political leadership did not play its role. These shortcomings were caused by faults in the Kurdish character: its individualism, its lack of foresight, its incapacity for collective action, its narrow-minded vision. So I want to transform this personality."[61]

As in so many of his other writings, he seemed to want to create a new kind of human being. This emphasis on individual development harks back to the romantic and prefigurative socialism of the period before Lenin. Ocalan's language, in fact, sometimes sounds like that of Ibsen, that great nineteenth-century modernizer and critic of bourgeois hypocrisy—phrases like "a splendid search for freedom in the framework of my personality" and "a noble, sacred, and very necessary peace" could have come out of the mouths of Ibsen's Master Builder or his Enemy of the People, characters who rebelled against stifling social pressures in their search for "something great, something splendid . . . to live for!"[62]

In fact, by the nineties, as Ali Kemal Ozcan's history of the PKK indicates, Ocalan had abandoned both the rhetoric of classical Marxism and the ideology of national liberation struggles for "an idiom peculiar to himself, engaged with more universal and philosophical concepts such as 'humanization,' 'socialization,' 'human emancipation,' 'analysing the Self,' 'freed personality,' 'pure human being,' and so on."[63]

The personal transformation of PKK cadre called for an intensive, continuing program of socialist education. This was a challenge because many of the peasant recruits were barely literate due to Turkish policies of limiting the number of schools in Kurdish areas and refusing to let Kurds be taught in their own language. Facing a similar challenge in Brazil, the activist educator Paolo Freire developed a "critical pedagogy" that emphasized active learning and dialogue, without a set curriculum, as discussed in his groundbreaking work, *The Pedagogy of the Oppressed* (1970). But this kind of participatory education did not mesh with Turkey's pedagogical traditions, which emphasize rote learning, memorization, and respect for authority.[64]

The PKK training program at the Mahsum Korkmaz Academy, set up at the Third Party Congress in 1986, was largely oral, consisting of lectures by Ocalan, followed by criticism/self-criticism sessions in which cadre would discuss their own shortcomings and be criticized by other participants and by Ocalan. By this means, he hoped to achieve the transformation in consciousness that Freire managed by developing his students' critical thinking skills.[65]

By the late nineties, the curriculum of a twenty-day training session consisted of the history and sociology of Kurdistan; PKK history, morality and culture; Turkey's bourgeoisie and army; the nature and tactics of Turkey's "Special War" against the Kurds; people's war; guerrilla war; military leadership; and party style and behavior. These subjects were taught by Ocalan in long lectures, which often lasted four to seven hours and were delivered without notes, with Ocalan drawing largely on his own experience.[66]

Between 1980 and 1999, all of Ocalan's lectures were recorded, transcribed, edited, printed, and distributed to party organizations all over the world in both written and cassette form under the title *Onderlik Çözümlemeler* (Analyses by the Leadership).[67] Such an exclusive emphasis on Ocalan's thought inevitably led cadre towards seeing his words as catechism and venerating him as a prophet. This was not good for democratic dialogue and independent thinking in the PKK.

Nevertheless, considering the history of other Marxist-Leninist groups, the wonder is not that the PKK had serious problems of authoritarianism and handled internal conflicts poorly, but that, unlike most similar organizations, they eventually focused on the importance of democracy. This change must be attributed to the growing strength of the mass democratic movement in southeastern Turkey, which virtually demanded that the PKK pay attention to it, although the PKK did not fully grapple with this need until years after Ocalan was jailed.

By the early nineties, however, Ocalan had recognized the importance of democracy, at least in theory, as is evident in statements such as "Democracy is a phenomenon that absolutely needs to be taught and kept alive to the utmost both by education and by experience," (1990) and "Party cadres must assimilate themselves into democratic culture, be absorbed into democracy and convert democracy into a lifestyle for themselves."(1993) He said he longed for people to challenge his views, and berated party members for their "naïvety and blind adulation," "obstinate-blind repetition," and "incredible slow-motion progress."[68] But slavishness on the part of cadre was the inevitable result of a low educational level combined with teaching methods that treated his words as the only source of wisdom.

One of the chief lessons taught to PKK cadre was the need for self-sacrifice and the subordination of private life to the cause. Joining the PKK was like entering into a marriage: One made a commitment for life, forsaking all others. Sociologist Olivier Grojean, who based his analysis of the PKK on interviews between 2001 and 2005 with "forty-odd PKK activists and sympathizers in Europe, some still actively involved, others not," described what was expected of cadre at the training academies: "The Çözümlemeler [Ocalan's Analyses] need to be applied, and this should result in the activists renouncing both their former life (they are obliged to cut ties with their family, spouse, children, friends, and so on) and certain attitudes and habits. They are for instance not allowed to cross their legs (only Öcalan is allowed to do that), to make hand gestures when speaking (Öcalan's privilege), or to sit before being instructed to do so (attitudes typical of the 'enemy's style'). . . . Drinking alcohol, smoking tobacco, and having sexual or even purely platonic relationships are also forbidden, as 'recommended' by Öcalan in his talks."[69]

Complete personal sacrifice, including separation from family and lifelong celibacy, was considered necessary in order to become new men and free women—fully-developed human beings who had left behind all traces of feudal and tribal personality and had thus become capable of transforming Kurdistan.

Central to this vision was a transformation of relations between the sexes. According to Grojean, Ocalan taught that "in the same way as the Turkish people, who stand out for their masculinity, have colonised and enslaved the Kurdish people, Kurdish men have colonised and enslaved Kurdish women. Since the 'traditional' masculine personality traits were associated with domination, violence, superiority, and arrogance, male PKK activists needed to free themselves from this sort of way of living and behaving and adopt the personality of the New Man, whose characteristics – inspired by those of the 'free' woman – are peace, communion with nature, culture, 'sociality', and a sense of patriotic duty." His goal, wrote Ocalan, was to kill the dominant male, which he saw as "the fundamental principle of socialism. This is what killing power means: to kill the one-sided domination, the inequality and intolerance. Moreover, it is to kill fascism, dictatorship, and despotism."[70]

Ocalan has written that one of the life events that radicalized him was seeing his older sister Havva, the main one in the family who cared for him, sold in marriage to a man from a village several days away for "a few sacks of wheat and a little money." He later recalled thinking that if he were a revolutionary, he would have been able to stop them from taking her away.[71]

As in other patriarchal societies, the "honor" of the traditional Kurdish family depended on the sexual purity of its women. To make sure she did not stray, a Kurdish girl was denied education, kept in the home, and secluded from social life. She was forced to marry whomever her father chose, often at a very young age, and, once she was married, her chastity was closely supervised. Girls were property, bought and sold as wives, with polygamy practiced by men who could afford it. "Honor killings" were common, as was male violence in general. And of course, since Kurdistan was economically underdeveloped, poverty was the norm.[72]

Revolutionary movements in other patriarchal societies have had to deal with similar feudal or tribal gender relations, overlaid and reinforced by colonialism and capitalism. The PKK's uniqueness lay in seeing the transformation of gender relations not as a sidebar to nationalist revolution but as the central task that would determine the success or failure of the whole endeavor. As the Fifth Congress resolution that founded the women's army in 1995 stated: "History has always been the history of male domination, because regardless of what class characteristics determined the society, it was always the men who determined social development and power relations. A careful analysis of all the revolutions which have taken place up until today will show that women were never really able to achieve their full political-military strength and were not effectively included in the movement. ... This reality is most clear when we look at real-existing socialism, where women took part in the revolution, but where an equal power balance between men and women was never achieved, therefore these women were not free, hence these were not free societies."[73]

The rising influence of women must be seen as central to the PKK's growing interest in democracy, mass organization, and a strategy of negotiation rather than an exclusive emphasis on armed struggle. The first PKK women's organization, the Union of the Patriotic Women of Kurdistan (YJWK) was formed in 1987 as a result of problems Kurdish women were experiencing in the movement and the diaspora. But the organization was based in Europe. The initial effort of this kind in Kurdistan itself came in 1992, shortly after the brief move to Camp Zeli when the PKK was fleeing attacks by Turkey and the KDP. Women guerrillas issued a call for an all-Kurdistan Women's Congress, which brought five hundred women from all the sections of the PKK to the camp, and had the explicit goal of forming an autonomous women's organization.

There is not much information on the Congress since its resolutions were not translated into English, nor is it mentioned in English-language histories of the movement on PKK websites. Some information can be gleaned from a poorly translated caption under an anonymous YouTube video of Kurdish women's militias, which says,

"The first Women's Congress of the PKK was conducted in late 1992. Among other things, the law was called for to get married. The Congress was eliminated by Abdullah Ocalan as a test, the PKK (tasfiyecilik) and considered canceled."[74]

According to Aliza Marcus, *tasfiyecilik* is PKK jargon that in context means "expelled, usually used in reference to those who somehow oppose the group or had 'anti-revolutionary' views."[75] Apparently, the first PKK women's congress passed a resolution that cadre should be allowed to marry, which was later annulled by Abdullah Ocalan on the grounds that these women had failed the test of confronting patriarchal ideas.

According to PKK historiography, this first Women's Congress was a failure. The blame fell on Abdullah Ocalan's younger brother Osman, the commander at Camp Zeli, who later left the PKK. As the story goes, Osman Ocalan and some of his friends contended that it would be better if PKK cadre could marry. The majority of women at the meeting were new recruits, not yet used to standing up to men and susceptible to pressure from leadership. Thus Osman and his friends derailed the larger discussion of forming a women's organization to focus specifically on marriage, creating a major setback for women's autonomy.[76]

A trainee at the Mahsum Korkmaz Academy reported that Mehmet Sener, the PKK leader who openly disagreed with Ocalan at times and who was executed in 1991, had also been pushing for freedom to marry: Sener "first garnered support," the trainee told historian Paul White, "by saying things like 'guerrillas should be allowed to marry each other.'" A PKK lecturer responded to Sener by telling trainees that marriage "would totally undermine the ARGK [the name of the PKK army in the nineties] as a fighting force, given the huge number of women fighters and mixed-sex guerrilla units. Then, at the party's Fourth Congress, Sener apparently argued that the guerrilla war period of the PKK's struggle was over; a new period was opening up, that of revolution through popular uprising. Once again, Ocalan and his supporters claimed that this was an indirect way of smashing the PKK."[77]

Turkish sociologist Nazan Ustundag, who studied the Kurdish women's movement, takes a more feminist view of the beginnings of women's organizing in the PKK: "According to Ocalan's writings and the women guerrillas I interviewed, the guerrilla organization PKK suffered from the danger of turning into gangster squads and para-militaries in the early 1990s, when the war in Kurdistan was most intense. Guerrilla leaders who monopolized authority, arms, trade routes, information, and relations with villagers threatened the Leftist path to liberation. Women and their struggles kept these risks under some control as they started challenging the patriarchal structures of PKK. Ocalan facilitated women's struggles by encouraging them to form an independent army and independent institutions in 1993. The women's army and institutions not only guaranteed women protection against men, both in the Turkish army and in guerrilla forces, but also disrupted channels of secrecy, transformed relations with locals, and effectively developed an opposition to the abuse of power."[78]

This was a long way from the First Congress in 1978, when only two women, Kesire Yildirim and Sakine Cansiz, attended, and Yildirim, who was married to Abdullah Ocalan, was the only woman chosen for the Central Committee.[79]

Kesire Yildirim was a strong-willed woman from a family con-nected with the military. Ocalan later said, "I didn't consider it very likely that the relationship would succeed, but I also was dragged along by the desire for love, emotion, and marriage." The marriage was over by the mid-eighties—the period of internal PKK terror—and Yildirim was arrested in an internal purge and held for a time, then "rehabilitated" enough to be sent off to organize in Europe. In 1988, according to Aliza Marcus, she tried to stage a coup against Ocalan. When that failed, she left the PKK and organized a splinter group. "It is widely rumored," wrote Marcus, "that Ocalan bought her silence in exchange for a financial stipend and a promise that she would not be killed. Still the PKK leader never forgot her betrayal. Her life—and their marriage—was turned into a rhetorical device, something Oca-lan used to underscore the constant dangers he and the PKK faced and the need to be ever-vigilant against traitors. He also used it to buttress his views on marriage and sexual relationships, both later banned for PKK militants."[80]

But if Kesire Yildirim was merely a blip in the graph of PKK gender dynamics, its other female founding member, Sakine Cansiz, became a revolutionary hero.

*Berivan, PKK commander in Makhmour.*

CHAPTER 5

# Kurdish Women Rising

S AKINE CANSIZ WAS the iconic PKK woman leader, always pictured with her thin intense face surrounded by a flaming cloud of bright henna hair. "We grew up hearing about Sakine Cansiz, how she withstood torture when she was in prison, spitting in the face of her torturers," Sebahat Tuncel, an MP for Turkey's pro-Kurdish Peace and Democracy Party [now the HDP], told Reuters. "She was a very important name for Kurdish women. She was a feminist, and her struggle was always double-edged: against male dominance and for Kurdish rights."[1]

Born in 1958 to an Alevi family in Dersim, Cansiz first encountered Kurdish activists as a teenager. After she hung out with them for a while, "a comrade visited our house one day and told us the history of Kurdistan. Me and my siblings all listened to him with great interest and till late hours after his leave [departure], we told each other about what he had told us. Everything he said was of importance for us because I learned from his telling that we were Kurd and came from Kurdistan. Impressed by the ideology of this movement, I started to live a contradiction with my family who were . . . preventing us from taking part in the revolutionary movement.

"As it became clearer . . . I left my family and secretly went to Ankara. Maybe it was just our weakness to fail to convince the family and to provide proper conditions so that I could stay and join the fight there. However, as a woman, I couldn't display a strong resistance against all those pressures and approaches. As I developed a strong will to absolutely take part in the movement and to dedicate my everything to it, I objected to the pressures and insisted on revolutionism."[2]

In Ankara, she went to the university neighborhood to look for people she knew and saw a group sitting under a tree around Ocalan. She listened to their discussion with great excitement, and soon became part

of the study group around him that engaged in debate and ideological struggle, held meetings, and went on marches. She was arrested in
Izmir, but after her release came back and, with the group, "conducted
training activities," then went to Elazig to engage in popular education,
speaking at high schools around the area. Gultan Kisanak, another
Alevi Kurd, who later became a mayor of Diyarbakir, remembered
hearing Cansiz speak "during my senior high school years at an all-girls
teachers training school. Sakine Cansiz . . . came to us and began telling
us about the Kurdish cause and how we needed to organize. The PKK
had not yet been officially formed but Abdullah Ocalan . . . had started
to plan a strategy for the Kurdish nationalist movement. The PKK's co-
founders included like-minded Turkish revolutionaries as well. . . . She
was incredibly practical and dynamic. She left a big impression."[3]

In 1978 the Ocalan study group moved toward forming a party and
Cansiz was appointed a delegate to the First Party Congress. The Congress assigned Cansiz to "propaganda-agitation works predominantly in
Antep and then in Elazığ in time. We were producing our notice papers,
leaflets and other means of propaganda and agitation and sending them
to other regions. I stayed in Elazığ and took an active part in works until
I was arrested."[4]

That was in 1979, when, in the leadup to the military coup, activists
were being picked up and sent to Diyarbakir prison, noted for its brutality. Gultan Kisanak was there also. She later described the treatment the
women suffered: insults, curses, and harassment; sexual abuse; torture
with bandoliers, police clubs, planks, sticks, bayonets, electric cables,
and hosepipes. Kisanak told an interviewer: "The whole world now
knows what went on there. The abuse was of barbaric proportions. People died, killed themselves. It was an inferno. There was torture around
the clock. But I don't see any merit in debating Diyarbakir prison in
these terms. The worst thing they did was to try to steal our honor. And
if one talks about the sexual abuse then they will have succeeded. This
is what they want. There is no need to go into details. It's obvious. All
the prison staff from the wardens up were male and part of the military.
They tried to beat us down, to rob us of our dignity, to stamp out our
Kurdishness, to crush our feminine identity. The torture was unrelent-
ing. But we resisted."[5]

Kisanek says morale building by Sakine Cansiz was the main reason the women held up so well under torture. "The key is that we stuck

together. There was a unique sense of solidarity among us. If a physically frail woman was singled out for punishment, say for speaking Kurdish, a stronger one would step forward and bear the punishment instead. We used to help each other bathe. There was no hot water. We would wash secretly in the toilet by using a small bowl that we would fill with water from the kettle. The winters were freezing cold. The summers could be unbearable because at times there were as many as 85 of us in a single cell. . . . The proof of our resilience is that unlike some of the male prisoners not a single woman broke down and became an informer. And Sakine's contribution was paramount in this regard."[6]

Cansiz spent ten years in prison. After her release, she went through the required cadre training course at the Mahsum Korkmaz Academy, then insisted on going to the mountains to fight. Using the code name Sara, she served under Osman Ocalan in northern Iraq and became the leading voice of women in the PKK. Mehmet Ali Ertas of the pro-Kurdish DIHA news agency called Cansiz "the most prominent and most important female Kurdish activist. She did not shy away from speaking her mind, especially when it came to women's issues."[7]

She spoke her mind in 1991 about the murder of Mehmet Sener, her comrade from prison. She did not think he was a traitor and said it was wrong to execute him.[8] After this, she was removed from active military duty but, unlike Sener, she was not sentenced to death and unlike Kesire Yildirim, she did not feel she had to leave the PKK. She was probably protected by her immense prestige and Ocalan's respect for her. In an interrogation after his capture, he said, "I started the women's movement to free [women] from the feudalism of men and to create a strong type of woman. I wanted lively discussions. In relation to that I do remember the name of Sakine Polat [Cansiz]." He added: "In mind and emotions she is loyal to the party."[9]

After leaving the army, she was sent to Europe in 1992. After a stint in Germany, she settled in France and continued to work for the PKK as an organizer and fund-raiser—according to Wikileaks, the US Embassy in Ankara identified her as one of the PKK's "most notorious financiers" and sought her capture.[10] She is also credited with recruiting a number of women who became suicide bombers in the nineties.[11]

"She was always plainspoken and was not afraid of an argument, even with her own organisation. Sakine Cansiz was a fighter," said Eren Keskin, a lawyer who first met Cansiz in 1991 while defending members of the PKK. "Sakine was a feminist before everything else. She possessed a woman's perspective, even on war."[12]

Because the PKK was first and foremost a guerrilla organization, the strength of women's voices was intimately related to their military strength. Aliza Marcus estimated that, by 1993, one-third of the new PKK recruits were women.[13] This influx prompted the formation of the first separate women's guerrilla units that year. A PKK essay on the subject quoted Ocalan as saying, "a woman's army is not only a requirement for the war against the patriarchal system, but is also a requirement in opposition to sexist mindsets within the freedom movement. Instead of traditional lifestyles and relationships, relationships based on freedom must be adopted; the synthetic dependence of women to men must be overcome by free choice."[14]

But despite the growing number of women in guerrilla units, patriarchal ideas lingered. A 1997 German analysis of the PKK, signed by Andreas (Marburg), pointed at some of the contradictions that arose from traditional gender relations, such as "Men who want to hinder an independent development of women and hold onto their positions of power and don't want to accept women as commanders," and "Women who hang onto men and can't get rid of their dependence and have no self-confidence, have avoided leadership positions, and don't want to accept other women in those positions." The author reported that PKK leadership recognized that "in order to destroy the roles that have been around for centuries, the strengthening of women became a necessity. Independent women's militias had to be established."[15]

These women-only units were key in giving women the confidence and leadership experience to make the leap to a fully separate women's army. At the Fifth Congress, the PKK resolved to form such an army, which was named the Free Women of Kurdistan Troops (YJAK), and later became YJA-Star. According to an article on the Kurdistan women's liberation movement in a PKK online journal, its purpose was to enable members "to develop their own social and political perspective instead of copying male-like characteristics or assuming themselves as a back-up force."[16] The Fifth Congress's resolution in January 1995 made it clear that the PKK saw this initiative as one of long-term strategic importance and a first step in forming autonomous women's organizations that would parallel all the other structures of the PKK:

"This army seeks to destroy all the characteristics and modes of conduct created by the status quo of class society. Therefore, it's not only of military significance that a women's army be created, but rather it is significant for all aspects of our movement. In all sectors of the economy, all social institutions, and even in the realm of culture, organizations will be created and modeled after this army. It will be largely the responsibility of women militants in leadership positions to realize the potential of women to organize, become educated, and join the struggle. . . . The goal of this is not simply to achieve independence for women, to make them reliant on their own strengths and not be dependent on men, and to achieve their full resistance and struggle potential, but this will also play an important role in the development of men. In this sense, work and living together will be characterized by freedom, equality, and comradery."[17]

An interview at the time with "a representative of the Free Women's Movement of Kurdistan (TAJK), who has herself taken part in the guerrilla struggle" further described the importance of a women's army: "In order to gain full recognition in Kurdish society and among the guerrillas, a military mode of organisation has to be introduced alongside the political one. In this way women have the possibility of developing independently, freely and to stand on their own feet, without feeling themselves to be mere shadows of the men. Each free practical step taken on her own accustoms the woman to build confidence in herself. The achievement of the 'revolution' can only come to fruition via a women's army."[18]

Prior to the development of the single-sex units, "Female commanders rarely found that the role they played was an acceptable one in the eyes of either men or women," according to the woman ex-guerrilla leader being interviewed. "Some men still found it difficult to take orders from women commanders. Equally, at first they did not receive respect from women either. The inferiority complex of women resulting from social conditioning was the decisive reason for this failure to accept women commanders. At the same time the fact that a woman could become a commander could be a source of self-confidence for women."

Mixed-sex units in other revolutionary groups have had similar problems. In the 1930s, three thousand women participated in the Long March of China's Red Army, fighting the Kuomintang and warlords as they went. Two thousand were in its Women's Independence Brigade, but rather than engage in actual combat, they mainly provided supply and logistical support, and built roads and bridges. After the Long March, all the special women's units were disbanded; women were integrated into the regular military and, during the anti-Japanese war, they were sent away from the front lines into support functions.[19]

After World War II, women guerrillas were more common in mixed units in liberation struggles. They were active in Asia in China, Vietnam, Sri Lanka, Nepal; in Africa in Angola, Eritrea, Mozambique, South Africa, Zimbabwe; and in Latin America in Cuba, El Salvador, Nicaragua, and the battles of the Zapatistas in Chiapas, Mexico—and this is far from an exhaustive list. In the sixties, their images were everywhere: a Vietnamese women shooting down an American fighter plane; an African woman with a baby on her back and a rifle in her arms; Palestinian hijacker Leila Khaled wearing a keffiyeh and holding a gun. But they rarely achieved leadership roles or led male troops. In the Kurdistan Regional Government in Iraq, female *peshmerga* members were no longer allowed on the front lines after 2013.[20]

Many national liberation struggles sought to enlist women in combat mainly because they needed more soldiers, not because the men running things saw a battle for women's rights and autonomy as essential to the struggle. In addition, male soldiers, or at least the commanders, sometimes assumed women fighters were sexually available, whether by choice or not.[21]

In her work on the Sandinistas of Nicaragua, Maxine Molyneux discussed the reasoning behind many woman friendly policies: "The policies from which women derived some benefit were pursued principally because they fulfilled some wider goal or goals, whether these were social welfare, development, social equality, or political mobilization in defense of the revolution. . . . This kind of qualified support for women's emancipation is found in most of the states that have pursued socialist development policies."[22]

After victory, such movements have often passed laws that improved women's lives economically, but their male leaders have seldom wanted to change their own behavior or share the sources of real power. They may have women loyal to them run parts of government they don't think are very important, like education or social services, while keeping a firm grip on finances, patronage, and the military.

Because the empowerment of women has so seldom been a priority for movements engaged in armed struggle, the PKK's emphasis on building an autonomous women's army was remarkable. Their explicit intention was not merely to increase the number of fighters but to actually strengthen women cadre and change the consciousness of both sexes.

By 1997, five thousand women were fighting in the separate women's militias and eleven thousand more were in mixed units. The women's militias had their own commanders and planned their own actions. At the time, some mixed units had women commanders as well. In 1999, the PKK formed a parallel women's party structure for the same reasons it had organized the women's militias and army. After several name changes, it became the Party of Free Women of Kurdistan (PAJK). With some pressure by women in the PAJK, PKK military camps at Qandil even began to share housework between the sexes.[23]

In a traditional rural culture where women were subordinated to men, not having to wash men's socks must have felt revolutionary; it certainly did to one young woman interviewed by *The Guardian* in August 2015: "Hejîn, a young woman who left home over four years ago, comes from a poor family in a neighbouring province where she was herding sheep instead of going to school. She jokes about her broken Turkish, but says she learned to read and write in the mountain camps of the PKK. 'I learned about many things there,' she recalls. 'For the first time I experienced an egalitarian lifestyle. Back at home I never dared to speak up with anyone, especially not with men. In our organisation, we share all the tasks equally. It is considered deeply shameful to wash another man's socks, for example, and we all cook together.'"[24]

Or, as Nesrin Abdullah, a commander in the Rojava women's army, the YPJ, put it, in implicit contrast with the women who joined the Iraqi *peshmerga*, which was a paid job, and where they were expected to go home at night to take care of homes and families, "We are not soldiers, we are militants; we are not paid to make war, we are partisans of revolution. We live with our people, follow a philosophy and have a political project. At the same time we are carrying out a gender struggle against the patriarchal system."[25]

Although not all militant Kurdish women took up arms, the women's militias and the idea of women's self-defense deeply affected consciousness. Newroz Seroxan, who worked in the Cizire canton's committee for work and social projects, said that at first many of the local women had a "patriarchal mindset" and were reluctant to get involved in work or political activity outside their homes. But they were inspired by interacting with women guerrillas. At the time she was interviewed in 2015, 60 percent of the local workforce was female. "If women can fight and carry a gun, that means they can do anything—this is the approach that has developed in society."[26]

The PKK's emphasis on building a women's army contrasts with the more common feminist approach of protesting militarism and imperialism and trying to develop a women's peace movement. As described by sociologist Cynthia Cockburn, this focused on gender relations in war, critiquing "the persistence of male dominance, accompanied (and indeed achieved) by the insistent shaping of masculinity, the ideal, preferred, form of manhood, as mentally competitive and combative; psychologically ready to use coercion; and physically equipped to prevail through force."[27]

The signal achievement of the women's peace movement was the adoption of Resolution 1325 by the UN Security Council in 2000, spearheaded by the work of WILPF, the Women's International League for Peace and Freedom, an organization which dates back to World War I. Resolution 1325 notes the particular kinds of impact war has on women and girls and calls for a gender perspective in peace negotiations and postwar programs, including the presence of women at the negotiating table.

While 1325 was a significant breakthrough, the daily life problems of making peace require additional measures. A major issue is the way people at the negotiating table are selected, since such negotiations are usually structured by the UN and regional powers rather than those on the ground. The Kurds, for example, have been repeatedly excluded from negotiations on Syria because of pressure by Turkey.[28] And more attention is needed to practical means and programs beyond the negotiating table, as outlined in the Nairobi Declaration of 2007, which addressed the need for special reparations and restorative practices for women.[29]

Many of the actions of the women's peace movement can be seen as a form of street theater, dramatizing a claim to power by people who do not have the capacity to actually get it. Because there never was a peace treaty at the end of the Korean War in 1953, for instance, prominent international feminists, including Gloria Steinem and Nobel peace prizewinners Leymah Gbowee and Maire McGuire, made a six-day trip to North Korea in 2015. Dressed in white with colored sashes, they then held a peace march in a nearby city of South Korea.

Steinem said there was an analogy between victims of domestic violence and the citizens of the divided Koreas. She called on women to use their experience of life as mothers and nurturers to give Koreans "proof of a humane alternative" to the status quo. Unburdened by male needs to show aggressive masculinity, she said that women had a "special ability to make connections between people."[30]

Iraqi Kurdish activist Houzan Mahmoud took issue with such claims: "To those who wish to see women return to their stereotypical roles as peace brokers and peace makers, I would ask exactly who are they supposed to be making peace with? With ISIS, who are one of the most brutal terrorist organisations on the face of the planet; who have as their main mission to drag society back into the dark ages; who force female children and women into Jihad Alnikah [sexual jihad], who rape and sell them in slave markets under their own control? . . . In the case of Kurdish women, taking up arms and fighting on the front line is perhaps their best option. To refuse to become slaves, to be raped, killed or ruled by Islamic Sharia Law under ISIS is only viable through armed resistance."[31]

Writer Dilar Dirik offered a similar criticism: "Over the last year, the world witnessed the historic resistance of the Kurdish city called Kobane. That women from a forgotten community became the fiercest enemies of the Islamic State group, whose ideology is based on destroying all cultures, communities, languages, and colors of the Middle East, upset conventional understandings of the use of force and warfare. It was not because men were protecting women or a state protected its 'subjects' that Kobane will be written in humanity's history of resistance, but because smiling women and men turned their ideas and bodies into the ideological front line on which the Islamic State group and its rapist worldview crumbled apart. Especially in the Middle East, it is no longer enough for women to 'condemn violence' when violence has become such a constant factor in our lives, when our perceived, or constructed status as 'victims' is used as a justification by imperialists to launch wars on our communities. The rise of the Islamic State group showed the disasters that full dependency on men and state-armies bring: nothing other than femicide."[32]

Militarization is central to the ideology of the Kurdish women's

movement. Because of the extreme inequality in traditional Kurdish society, says a spokeswoman for the PKK women's army YJA-Star,
women had to become soldiers; they could only deal with their subordination by "becoming a power themselves. In such context, the women's
militarization had organized itself rather as an instrument of equality
in social, political and cultural spheres instead of a simple military organization with only combat related purposes." The point is to break "the
false sense of power that develops in men."[33]

One of the central and unique tenets of the Kurdish women's army
is the rule of celibacy. Rural Kurdistan is an extremely conservative
society; many of the female cadre went to the mountains to escape
forced marriages and traditional family structures. Nevertheless,
they often felt they needed parental approval to leave. Most parents
allowed them to go only on the condition that the women would
remain virgins. If not for this guarantee from the PKK leadership,
which ensured that the family's "honor" would not be compromised,
the party would have been culturally separated from the community
they were fighting to liberate.

Gandhi, wanting women to be active in India's national liberation
struggle, in a society that was equally conservative, had a similar position in favor of celibacy. He developed this position, at least in part, as a
response to child marriage, forced marriage, the oppression of widows,
and the general subordination of women, though other ways of dealing with repressive traditions were certainly possible and many Indian
women activists rejected his approach.

To Ocalan, as to many feminists, marriage as an institution was
so oppressive to women it was to be avoided whenever possible. "It is
impossible to imagine another institution that enslaves like marriage.
The most profound slaveries are established by the institution of marriage, slaveries that become more entrenched within the family. This is
not a general reference to sharing life or partner relationships that can
be meaningful depending on one's perception of freedom and equality. What is under discussion is the ingrained, classical marriage and
family. Absolute ownership of woman means her withdrawal from all
political, intellectual, social and economic arenas; this cannot be easily
recovered. Thus, there is a need to radically review family and marriage
and develop common guidelines aimed at democracy, freedom and
gender equality. Marriages or relationships that arise from individual,

sexual needs and traditional family concepts can cause some of the most dangerous deviations on the way to a free life."[34]

Thus the PKK made celibacy a "red line." Sexual relationships between cadre were considered a grave violation of the party's commitment to women's independence and autonomy, an indication of misplaced priorities, and a dangerous distraction to anyone in combat conditions. People who broke the rule were thrown out, and in the early days of the armed struggle, some were executed. The rule applied only to guerrillas and people in PKK leadership, not to people who worked in PKK-linked mass organizations or to civilians.

Ocalan's theoretical position on the necessity of celibacy was that a new culture had to develop before sexual intimacy could be detached from power relations. Personal love relationships turned women into slaves, he insisted. "Woman's true freedom is only possible if the enslaving emotions, needs and desires of husband, father, lover, brother, friend and son can all be removed. The deepest love constitutes the most dangerous bonds of ownership."[35] In other words, women's liberation needed to be tackled right away, but sex would have to wait until after the revolution. This was partly because of priorities and partly because women had to attain more power in society at large before real love between equals could become possible.

There are of course other possible ways besides celibacy to address the contradictions in traditional gender relations, among them the anarchist or bohemian ethos of "free love;" the current redefinition of the family unit by feminist and gay activists; and the various alternative and communitarian solutions to be found in utopian communities over the ages. Feminists all over the world have put enormous emphasis on women being able to decide for themselves what they want, rather than having their love relations dictated by fathers, brothers, husbands or social convention. From this came the commitment to reproductive rights and the idea that women should be the ones choosing when and whether they bore children.

Handan Caglayan, author of the book, *Mothers, Comrades, Goddesses*, described the PKK taboo against love relationships as one more form of patriarchal restriction upon women, a new kind of honor code: "Women are asked to desexualize themselves when entering the public sphere much as they are in other anticolonial promodernization national movements. Respectable participation in the public sphere is strictly predicated upon an amorous attachment to the homeland, and to fighting for it. Substituting sexual love for the love for the homeland is enough reason to be excluded from the 'liberated' and 'trustworthy' female identity and being labeled as 'woman who pulls down.' Therefore, the same discourse that enables women to leave their homes by overcoming the *namus* [honor] barrier also establishes a new patriarchal control in the public sphere."[36]

And indeed, the PKK regularly subordinated individual freedom to the strategic necessities of what it would take to organize a revolution in Kurdistan—or, more accurately, the PKK saw individual fulfillment as coming not through personal relationships but by giving oneself to the cause. The large number of young PKK women who became suicide bombers and immolated themselves as a political protest in the nineties is another indication of the high value put on self-abnegation.[37]

During the nineties, when the PKK developed its position on marriage, the transnational women's movement was focusing on issues of child, forced, and arranged marriage, violence against women, and "honor crimes," particularly in the Middle East and South Asia. Rather than ban sexual relationships, the movement developed rights-based strategies to deal with abuse, as human rights activist Gita Sahgal noted in an article on the subject:

"Although there is a long feminist and radical tradition of critique of the institution of marriage as a fundamental cornerstone of patriarchy, not least in antinomian religious traditions, there are no attempts to outlaw marriage, which still remains globally the central apparatus to ensure sexual access and unpaid reproductive labour. Comparisons of marriage to the institution of slavery are not inapt. But the legislative battle has consisted of trying to criminalise coercive and violent elements within marriage, such as domestic violence, marital rape, and forced marriage, as well as to change the nature of marriage itself by extending rights of marriage to same-sex partners and by making the dissolution of marriage easier."[38]

To Western intellectuals, as anthropologist Michael Taussig noted, the question of celibacy evoked the intellectual battles between followers of Sigmund Freud, who thought it was a good thing that sexuality be sublimated so that people could turn their energy to other creative endeavors, and followers of Wilhelm Reich, who thought the free expression of sexuality was fundamental to all other freedoms. Taussig visited Rojava in 2015 and wrote:

"A justification of celibacy was proffered: that celibacy eases the anxieties of the women's families, the honor of their girls is intact; that romantic involvements get in the way of doing your job; and that your capacity for love gets transmuted into love for the group (which brings to mind the polemic concerning sex and repression between Wilhelm Reich and Freud.) Do the Kurdish guerrillas therefore provide their women and men with a new 'family,' merging something like a nation-state that is also an anti-state with something like a family that is not a family but an anti-family? Are the guerrilla forces castes of beings serenely distant from the flesh, like nuns and monks in the Christian Church, but with M-16s and rocket launchers? Does celibacy ensure a type of sacred purity and a mythical status of magical power?"[39]

Some answers to these questions can be found in an open "chat" held in July 2015 on Reddit, the online news and networking services with an anonymous male PKK fighter who had been at university in both Germany and Canada before he joined the PKK, and had fought in Kobane and Cizre in Syria, as well as in Turkey and Iraq. He freely admitted that he was pretty sexist when he joined the PKK; he didn't believe women could be good fighters and hadn't given a thought to feminism. But as a result of serving in battle with women commanders and comrades, he changed.

Asked about homosexuality, he said "the organization is equally sexually repressive—to both homosexuals and heterosexuals. No sex allowed—ever." He was then asked about his own sex life. He said:

"I personally quite like being able to interact with women without the actual practice [of] sex being an issue. We smile, laugh, speak together, but we're comrades. It ends there. ... I quite like that the many fighters I've known who are women, for example, don't need me (a man) in order to complete their life. They ... have left home and are doing something proactive, productive, and indeed revolutionary by going out and fighting and defending their ideas. Why would you need to ruin it by getting into a sexual relationship?

"I mean, seriously, what's with Westerners and their whole thing about sex, sex, sex, sex, sex? A lot of Kurds who come back from the West seem obsessed with this thing. Who ever put it in their mind that it was so important?"[40]

As far as Janet Biehl, the late Murray Bookchin's partner, could observe on her trips to Rojava, sex was not an issue. Interviewed by Biehl, the female Minister of Culture indicated that, while Rojava's feminists would fight adamantly for women's equality and against domestic violence, they would proceed very cautiously when it came to sex. And when Biehl asked about a new law on book publishing, which set up a committee to determine whether a book should be published on the basis of "its compatibility with the general legal system and its suitability to the morals of society," the minister replied that no book promoting teen sex before marriage would be permitted. "We should respect traditions in our society. Teenagers can't sleep with each other . . . before marriage," she told Biehl.[41]

## The PKK: Denouement and Transition

After three years of draining the swamp, in 1997 the Turkish government felt it had damaged the PKK to such an extent that it could lift the state of emergency. But it ignored Ocalan's call for a ceasefire. When he offered one again in 1998, the Turkish military concluded the PKK was really on the ropes and should be hit even harder.

This time they got help from the US, which, as usual, saw the Kurds as a destabilizing force in the region. Despite the end of the Cold War, the CIA retained a residual desire to fight communism, if it could find any communists to fight, and the PKK appeared to fit the bill. Israel, which acted as a US proxy in the region, helped Turkey devise a plan. In October 1998, Turkey suddenly massed ten thousand troops on its border with Syria and said they would invade unless Damascus handed over Ocalan. Syrian president Hafez Assad was not willing to risk war with Turkey and Ocalan was quietly asked to leave.[42]

He went on the run, first to Moscow, then to Rome, where he was arrested. Italy didn't know what to do with him but was unwilling to hand him over to the Turks, who had the death penalty. So there he stayed, wondering how things had gone so wrong. A change in strategy was clearly needed. Being in the West made him feel even more strongly that it was essential to negotiate a peace agreement. On November 18, 1998, he told an Italian paper: "We have abandoned terrorism and are ready for a peace accord. . . . My presence here [in Italy] testifies to a change in the strategy of the Kurdish national movement." The next week he released a press statement, saying that the Kurds wanted to demobilize and work for peace along the lines of the Basques and the Irish Republican Army. The statement contained a peace plan setting seven conditions that Turkey would have to meet: stop attacking Kurdish villages; let Kurdish refugees from these villages return home; end the village guard program; give political autonomy to the Kurdish region within Turkey's borders; give Kurds the same democratic freedoms allowed Turks; recognize Kurdish identity, language and culture; and allow freedom of religion. He also called for an international conference on the Kurdish question.[43]

All the demands fit into a human rights framework and deserved consideration. But power politics trumped human rights. Italy could not hold out under pressure from both Turkey and the US, and considered two options: putting Ocalan on trial in an international court or expelling him. So Ocalan fled again, first returning to Russia, then flying to Athens, where the PKK had friendly connections because of the longstanding enmity between Greece and Turkey. Now Greece came under pressure; Turkey said it would invade any country that sheltered Ocalan and, though led by a left-wing prime minister, Greece buckled. The government suggested Ocalan take refuge in the Greek embassy in Kenya and seek political asylum somewhere in Africa. So Ocalan flew to Kenya.

As CIA historian Tim Weiner reported, this was bad timing: "More than 100 American intelligence and law-enforcement officers, along with Kenyan security officials, are in Nairobi investigating the terrorist bombing of the American Embassy there in August, which took 213 lives. Members of that team quickly discovered that Mr. Ocalan had arrived in Nairobi, American officials said. They placed the Greek Embassy under surveillance and monitored his cell phone conversations while he placed calls to political contacts, seeking sanctuary."[44]

In February 1999, Ocalan was told he could go to the Netherlands. A car with a Kenyan police escort came to take him to the airport, but instead of being allowed to board a flight to Amsterdam, he was taken to an outlying part of the airport where he was put on a private plane for Turkey. As soon as he arrived, the government broadcast his picture, bound, handcuffed, and looking dazed, being guarded by two ski-masked Turkish commandos.

The Kurdish diaspora went ballistic. Demonstrations and occupations took place all over the world. In addition, between October 1998 and March 1999, seventy-five people set fire to themselves.[45] In London, the Greek embassy was occupied by fifty hunger strikers for three days while a large crowd demonstrated outside. Greek and Kenyan embassies or consulates were also occupied in most of Europe's major cities and many countries in Asia and the Middle East. Demonstrators forced their way into several UN buildings in Switzerland. In Berlin, two hundred Kurds stormed the Israeli Embassy. When security guards opened fire, four protestors were killed and twenty injured.[46]

Ocalan went on trial for treason that May. Though everyone expected his defense to feature stirring denunciations of Turkish oppression that would vindicate the PKK's struggle and tactics, his pretrial statements, released on video, sounded confused but hardly defiant. He said his mother was a Turk, he loved his country, and if he could be of service, he would. His comrades thought he had been drugged. Soon the Turkish media began to report that he had made all kinds of confessions. But they had reported similar confessions from other PKK prisoners who later said the reports were false, so people did not believe the stories about Ocalan. They waited to see what he would say at his actual trial.

The trial was held at a specially constructed prison on the small island of Imrali in the Sea of Marmara. Ocalan began his defense with a call for peace, stressing that, in order for him to be able to bring about peace and brotherhood, he had to remain alive. Far from blaming Turkey for Kurdish suffering, he apologized to the families of conscripts who had been killed, saying he understood their pain. He praised Ataturk and said the Kurds should have tried to solve their problems through human rights, not armed struggle.[47]

People in PKK circles were completely disoriented by this line of argument. They assumed Ocalan had a plan but they didn't know what it was. Many found his praise of the Turkish state and his failure to mention Kurdish grievances extremely hard to take. His critics outside the party sneered, calling him a coward who would say anything to save his life.

Leading cadre left the PKK. Selim Curukkaya, who had spent eleven years in prison and been a member of the Executive Committee, told journalist Chris Kutschera, "Abdullah Ocalan, the man who used to call people 'traitor' has himself betrayed us." Kutschera wondered how long the PKK could "stagger on."[48]

Ocalan was sentenced to death in May 1999. Two months later he publicly called on the PKK to withdraw from Turkey and unilaterally end the armed struggle. The party did as he asked, though the Turkish military killed as many as they could find in transit. Ocalan then asked certain cadre to turn themselves in as a token of good faith; they did so and were immediately arrested.[49]

When Ocalan fled Damascus, the PKK had formed a Presidential Council to manage things while he was on the run, and in January 2000, they called an emergency Seventh Congress. Ocalan was re-elected leader even though he was in jail, and the congress voted to support his new line of preferring negotiation to armed struggle. The autonomous women's units in particular backed Ocalan and an approach of finding a way towards peace negotiations.

The next few years were ones of ideological struggle and confusion within the PKK, as described by the scholars Ahmet Hamdi Akkaya and Joost Jongerden: "For the movement, the period between Ocalan's trial of 1999 and the reorganization of the party in 2003, was a period of retreat and consolidation. The PKK levelled down its demands, ceased military activities, withdrew the majority of its guerilla forces from Turkey into Northern Iraq and consequently gave an impression of introversion. The political activities of the PKK were confined to Ocalan's case, the sentencing in particular."[50]

Ocalan appealed his sentence to the European Court of Human Rights, and, because Turkey wanted to join the European Union, which bars the death penalty, his death sentence was commuted in 2002 to life imprisonment on Imrali. (Turkish leader Recep Tayyip Erdogan later said that if he had been prime minister at the time of the arrest, he would have made sure Ocalan was executed.)[51]

Ocalan continued to lead the PKK from his cell via messages transmitted by his lawyers and close family members, mainly his sister, who was allowed to visit him once a month. He read voraciously, everything from ancient history and mythology to contemporary political theory. In the eighties, his writing had referred mainly to such writers as Marx, Engels, Lenin, Stalin, Mao, Dimitrov, Giap, and Le Duan. In contrast, his bibliography in *Prison Writing I* cites sources on mythology and prehistory including Joseph Campbell, Samuel Noah Kramer, James Frazer, Gordon Childe, and feminist Merlin Stone, as well as political thinkers ranging from Bakunin to Seyla Benhabib, Karl Popper, Ernesto Laclau, and Judith Butler; he was particularly influenced by Benedict Anderson,

Michel Foucault, Murray Bookchin, and Immanuel Wallerstein.[52] Despite all these influences, his thinking remained his own, rooted in Kurdish experience and his own life history, and moving in new directions, particularly in regard to women.

He wrote his defense for the European Court of Human Rights in the form of political articles, which he gave his lawyer in their one-hour weekly visits. These articles centered on the idea of democracy based on local councils. Digging into the history of the Middle East, he reframed his ideas about the state much more systematically than before, developing a theory he called "democratic confederalism," which consisted of parallel democratic structures that would coexist with the state—provided it was a democratic state that respected human rights.

In all the countries where they lived—Iran, Iraq, Syria and Turkey—Kurds and others in the same area would establish local systems of self-organization and eventually link them into a regional "confederal system. Within Kurdistan democratic confederalism will establish village, town and city assemblies and their delegates will be entrusted with the real decision-making, which in effect means that the people and the community will decide." The confederal system would not reject the laws of the states involved, but these laws would have to be reconciled with those of the EU and "the democratic confederal law."

He envisioned democratic confederalism as promoting an ecological model of society, "opposed to all forms of sexual oppression," and called for the establishment of "democracy in all spheres of life of Kurdish society, which is based on ecology and equality of the sexes and struggles against all forms of reaction and backwardness. It conjoins individual rights and freedoms with the development of democracy."[53]

Ocalan's conception of local control and democratic autonomy owed a lot to Murray Bookchin, with whom he corresponded before Bookchin's death. But as Ercan Aybola, a Kurdish activist interviewed by Janet Biehl in 2011, pointed out, these ideas were further developed by the movement, which drew on its own years of experience and that of other movements to make something new: "The Kurdish freedom movement developed the idea of 'democratic confederalism' not only from the ideas of communalist intellectuals but also from movements like the Zapatistas; from Kurdish society's own village-influenced history; from the long, thirty-five-year experience of political and armed struggle; from the intense controversies within

Turkish democratic-socialist-revolutionary movements; and from the movement's continuous development of transparent structures for the broad population."[54]

The issue of the state was central. Here Ocalan's thinking was particularly influenced by Benedict Anderson's *Imagined Communities,* in which Anderson traced the origins of the notion of ethnic nationhood and described the state as a social construction, rather than an eternal organizing principle that existed in nature and was inevitable and unchangeable. Ocalan wrote: "In isolation I grasped the alternative modernity concept, that national structures can have many different models, that generally social structures are fictional ones created by human hands, and that nature is malleable. In particular, overcoming the model of the nation-state was very important for me. For a long time this concept was a Marxist-Leninist-Stalinist principle for me. It essentially had the quality of an unchanging dogma. . . . When you said nation there absolutely had to be a state! If Kurds were a nation they certainly needed a state! However as social conditions intensified, as I understood that nations themselves were the most meaningless reality, shaped under the influence of capitalism, and as I understood that the nation-state model was an iron cage for societies, I realized that freedom and community were more important concepts."[55]

In a world order where everything is based on states, including all international institutions, this was a big leap. Ocalan was definitively rejecting the claim for an independent Kurdish state that had been a foundational demand of the movement—and, what's more, he was doing it at the same time that Kurds right across the border in Iraq were getting closer and closer to having such a state.

If many cadre felt betrayed by the new approach, nobody wanted to oppose it openly. Hating the way Ocalan had seemed to capitulate in his speech to the court and disgusted that the party had maintained him as leader even when he was under duress, some quietly left fairly soon after his arrest, finding ways to get to Iraq and from there, to Europe, where they could ask for political asylum.[56]

Others waited, hoping the line would change again, while increasingly looking to the Iraqi Kurds for leadership. They argued that if the PKK was going to stop the armed struggle and make peace with Turkey anyway, why not partner with Iraq's Kurdistan Regional Government, which was already allied with Turkey? An opposing group maintained that they were not giving up the armed struggle; they had only halted it temporarily for tactical reasons. This difference led to a major split in 2004, when a faction supporting an alliance with the KRG left the PKK and moved to Iraq. To make their defection even more scandalous, the group included Executive Committee members Osman Ocalan and Nizamettin Tas, who immediately got married.[57]

As if to prove their guerrilla bona fides, the PKK leadership in Qandil, headed by founding member Cemal Bayik, declared an end to the cease-fire and the war started up again. There was another unilateral ceasefire that lasted from 2009 to 2011, then a resumption of battle.

The costs of this war over the years were staggering; The figures of thirty thousand to forty thousand dead are usually given, although there is no hard data on either side. As the numbers and costs of the war, estimated at $300 billion, mounted, pressure grew for some kind of political settlement. In September 2011, Prime Minister Erdogan announced that Hakan Fidan, head of military intelligence (MIT) had been meeting secretly with PKK representatives in Oslo. A year later, on December 31, 2012, he announced that the MIT had also been nego-tiating with Ocalan in Imrali prison.[58]

But the old Kemalist establishment and the deep state saw any nego-tiations with the PKK as conciliation with terrorists. At the beginning of the new year, they struck. In the early morning of January 10, 2013, Sakine Cansiz, Fidan Dogan, Paris representative of the Kurdistan National Congress, and Leyla Soylemez, a youth leader, were found dead in the locked offices of the Kurdish Information Center in Paris. According to French police, all had been shot execution-style. The office door had a combination lock so the assassin either knew the combination or was let in. The door to the room where the bodies were found was locked from the outside.[59]

Most of the press were convinced Cansiz was the target of the assas-sination, and the other two women just happened to be with her. Many, including Susan Fraser of the Associated Press, thought the purpose of the assassinations was to stop peace talks: "The killings come at a time when Turkey has resumed talks with jailed rebel leader Ocalan in a bid to persuade the group to disarm and end the nearly 29-year-old conflict that has killed tens of thousands of people. Some speculate that the slay-ings may have been an attempt to derail peace efforts."[60]

The French police quickly arrested Omer Guney, who had acted as an occasional driver and volunteer in the Kurdish office. He had made several trips to Turkey in the period before the killings. The investigation went nowhere for a year, then a recording was posted on the internet by an anonymous source "close to Omer Guney."[61] According to Rudaw, the Iraqi Kurdish press agency, the tape recorded a conversation between Guney and two agents of MIT, arranging the assassination. While the tape could not be verified, an internal document allegedly from MIT, published in the Turkish press, also seemed to indicate MIT's involvement in the killings. MIT responded by claiming that the tape was part of a plot to discredit them because of their role in pushing forward the peace process.[62]

Rudaw accused the French police of foot-dragging in the investigation to avoid offending Turkey. In July 2015, the case was cleared to go to trial. *Le Monde* said Guney's friends described him as a right-wing Turkish nationalist and the French police said he had a direct phone line to the Turkish secret service, which refused to let them interview one of the people he had called. "For the first time ever an official inquiry has implicated a foreign intelligence service in a political murder committed in France," said Radio France Internationale.[63]

The assassinations did not immediately destroy the peace talks; they dragged on for several more years, but brought no result because, while Turkish politicians frequently spoke of peace, they failed to address specific Kurdish demands for human rights. Meanwhile, a broad-based movement for Kurdish autonomy grew in strength.

*International Women's Day celebration, Qamishlo, Cizire Canton, Rojava, 2015.*

CHAPTER 6

# Democratic Autonomy in
# Turkey and Syria

THE MOVEMENT FOR democratic autonomy in southeastern Turkey began in 2005, when people in the Association of Communities in Kurdistan (KCK)—the umbrella organization of groups in the PKK network—started experimenting with local programs that could test their theories in practice. These programs brought cadre to work with recently urbanized, very poor peasants whose villages had been destroyed. Americans would call what they were doing community organizing, setting up organs of self-rule and decision-making from the bottom up. This work represented a huge change in approach for an organization that had been dedicated to revolution through people's war.

Though Turkey had expected the PKK to fall apart without its leader, it was actually strengthened by the struggle that developed after Ocalan's arrest. Now that he was in prison, Ocalan's tremendous intellectual strengths could be focused on long-range political strategy rather than tactical and organizational questions which others could handle as well as he. This meant that the collective leadership that every revolution needs had more room to emerge.

As Aliza Marcus put it, "Ocalan had created a system that was able to function as if he were present even when he is not. Day-to-day leadership passed to a small cadre of loyal senior commanders who had been with Ocalan since he began organizing the PKK in the mid-1970s. It did not matter that Ocalan could no longer weigh in on the daily details of military targets and political plans. In many ways, it was even better not to have him so closely involved."[1]

The Kurdish liberation movement's political transformation continued to evolve in counterpoint to the armed struggle, the civil resistance, and electoral politics. From the relationship among them, a new vision developed for bringing democracy and autonomy to the Kurds.

Shortly after the PKK split in 2004, when the party leadership in Qandil restarted the armed struggle, the Kurdish ex-parliamentarians Leyla Zana, Orhan Dogan, Hamit Dicle, and Selim Sadak were released from prison. The European Court of Human Rights had ruled against their prosecution. Since Turkey still wanted to join the EU, it staged a face-saving retrial in which the sentence was reaffirmed, and then the High Court ordered them all released on a technicality.

Zana's first act was to call for a "new page" in Kurdish-Turkish relations, beginning with another six-month ceasefire. The leadership in Qandil immediately rejected her call, and some predicted there would be a breach between the PKK and the parliamentarians. But this was not what the popular movement wanted. When Zana returned to her home base in Diyarbakir, she was greeted by an ecstatic crowd shouting PKK slogans and calling for Ocalan's release. The message was they loved the parliamentarians, they loved the PKK, and they wanted unity.

"Her return to the southeastern Turkish city of Diyarbakir was triumphant, yet illustrated the extremely fine line she and her close supporters must now tread," said *The Washington Report*. "Upon Zana's release, Turkish commentators of a more liberal stripe wondered if she might not be the one person who could turn around decades of fighting and produce a nonviolent Kurdish nationalist movement based within the Turkish state. This may well be Zana's intention—and [that] of a group of Kurdish intellectuals around her. If so, it is an extraordinarily difficult objective. To put it bluntly, she may end up shot by both sides."[2]

The next year Zana and the other Kurdish deputies founded the Democratic Society Party (DTP) as the successor to their old party, DEHAP, which had been banned. In the July 2007 parliamentary election, the Democratic Society Party won twenty-two seats, enough to allow its members to function as a caucus. The Kurdish liberation movement now had a legal above-ground party that would actually turn out to have some muscle.[3]

Meanwhile, the PKK had committed itself to a line that emphasized flexible tactics: keeping the possibility of armed resistance alive while stressing the need for peace negotiations, and working with the new electoral party. Together the PKK, the parliamentary group, and local activists worked out a bottom-up democratic strategy that combined education, cultural work, provision of services, and the development of alternative structures to bypass the official ones of the Turkish government.

In this they took direction from a new expansiveness in Ocalan's thinking. One of his first essays, written as part of his appeal to the European Court of Human Rights and released in 2005, was titled the "Declaration of Democratic Confederalism in Kurdistan." It focused on community organizing, with a clear statement of how such local work would relate to the Turkish state, laying out a profoundly radical reorientation of PKK politics.

"The Middle East is going through a period of conflicts and chaos in what has been deemed the Third World War and at the centre of these conflicts and contradictions is Kurdistan," he wrote. "Despite attempts to maintain the former political status quo and the endeavours of the forces of global capital to find solutions in line with their own interests, the peoples seek the development of their own democratic systems based on freedom and to overcome the current situation of chaos and conflict."

Ocalan further developed his thinking about the nation-state, arguing that the UN didn't work because the model of the nation-state was obsolete and had become an obstacle to progress, as demonstrated by the Gulf War and the US invasion of Iraq. "The only way out of this situation is to establish a democratic confederal system that will derive its strength directly from the people, and not from globalisation based on nation-states."

Ocalan's general ideas about organization and democracy became central to the practical program worked out by the movement itself. In October 2007, following its electoral breakthrough, the Democratic Society Party called a conference to form a new mass organization: the Democratic Society Congress. The conference brought Kurdish representatives from every part of Turkey to Diyarbakir to discuss what they called democratic autonomy, which, like Ocalan's "democratic confederalism," was a bottom-up, participatory, culturally diverse method of getting things done. Joost Jongerden and Ahmet Hamdi Akkaya, historians of the PKK, reported that the congress "called for radical reforms in Turkey's political and administrative structure in order to ensure democratisation and to develop problem-solving approaches for which the local level should be strengthened. Instead of autonomy based on 'ethnicity' or 'territory', it suggested regional and local structures which allow for the expression of cultural differences."[4]

Party activists immediately began to organize local councils and, by the next local elections, two years later, these were strong enough to successfully encourage people to boycott the electoral rallies of Turkey's ruling Justice and Development Party (AKP). In March 2009, the Democratic Society Party won control of nearly one hundred local governments, including Diyarbakir and seven other important cities. This was almost twice as many as they had won two years earlier.[5]

Such a rapid political rise made the AKP and other conservative parties that depended on the Kurdish vote extremely nervous, and a new wave of repression began, described by Aliza Marcus: "In December 2009, the constitutional court shut down the Democratic Society Party for allegedly helping the PKK. (It reopened as the Peace and Democracy Party or BDP.) Thirty-seven senior executives of the party, including two parliamentarians, were banned from politics for five years. On October 18, Turkish prosecutors in Diyarbakir opened the trial of 152 political party executives and members, including eight sitting mayors, charged with working for the PKK. It seems Turkey is having trouble differentiating between peaceful dissent and armed violence."[6]

Abdullah Demirbas, a former philosophy professor and teachers' union activist who was elected mayor of Sur, a municipal district of Diyarbakir, in 2007, was one of the most prominent local Kurdish politicians. He was also an exemplar of the movement's changed organizing approach. In his campaign for mayor, he promised to provide municipal services in the banned Kurdish language, which was often the only language of his constituents. Once in office, he also provided information to constituents in Assyrian and English. Ankara removed him from office within a year. When he was re-elected in 2009 by a much larger margin than in 2007, the government prosecuted him for "language crimes" and for being connected to the Association of Communities in Kurdistan. He was sentenced to two years in prison.[7]

Demirbas suffered from deep vein thrombosis and, after a campaign to free him, was released from prison on medical grounds in 2010, although he was not allowed to leave the country for treatment, as his doctors had recommended. Despite his legal problems, he was re-elected again in 2012, at which time seventy-four different prosecutions against him were underway. His lawyer told him that if he were convicted in every case, he could be sentenced to prison for 483 years.[8]

As mayor, one of his main projects—and one for which he was being prosecuted—was the repair of Surp Giragos, a nineteenth-century Armenian cathedral that fell into ruins when the Armenians fled Turkey after the genocide. Referring to the role played by some Kurds at that time, he said, "Our grandparents, incited by others, committed wrongs, but we, their grandchildren, will not repeat them."[9]

Another crime of which he was accused was misusing municipal funds by printing Diyarbakir tourist brochures in Armenian, Assyrian, Arabic, Russian, and Turkish. He asked a reporter, "Why is it . . . that tourists who visit Topkapi Palace in Istanbul can get an audio listening guide in English, French, Spanish, German, or Italian, but when I publish a small tourist brochure in Armenian, as a welcoming gesture to Armenian tourists who want to visit their ancestral home, I am accused of committing a crime?"[10]

## Democratic Autonomy at the Grassroots

In 2011, a group of German activists called TATORT Kurdistan, which means Crime Scene Kurdistan, went to Turkey to investigate the growing movement for local self-rule. They published their interviews in a book called *Democratic Autonomy in North Kurdistan: The Council Movement, Gender Liberation, and Ecology—in Practice*. According to their report, the newly-developed basic unit of democratic autonomy in southeastern Turkey was the neighborhood council. These councils were elected by smaller units called communes, which might consist of only a few blocks.

This structure was the product of a long process of home visits by organizers. One of the points of such laborious one-on-one organizing was to involve women, who were sometimes reluctant to leave the house to attend meetings. There was a minimum quota of 40 percent women on every council and committee and each was chaired jointly by a woman and man. The other purpose of such intensive outreach was to ensure that all the different ethnic and religious groups in a neighborhood were included in the citywide body to which the neighborhood councils would send representatives.

Democratic autonomy seeks to guarantee the protection and development of all the cultures present in Turkey, wrote the TATORT authors. "Its activists seek to organize all these diverse social groups and identities democratically, by creating councils in the urban neighborhoods and by civil society organizing."[11]

By 2011, the Kurdish movement for democratic autonomy was strong enough to call a conference that brought a thousand people together in Diyarbakir. It elected a coordinating group and set up committees to focus on municipal government, religion, language, women, and youth.

In cities where the elected officials were movement people, the government and the local democratic autonomy councils worked together to solve community problems. Much of the energy of these local councils went into restorative justice and conflict mediation. Since people had little faith in Turkish courts and were not permitted to speak Kurdish in state institutions, they preferred to bring their problems to the councils. A local activist described the process: "We work with conversation, dialogue, negotiation, and when necessary, criticism and self-criticism. When someone does something wrong, the party who perpetrated the harm has to make it up to the people he injured. We accomplish a lot that way. There's no death penalty, we don't put perpetrators in prison or penalize them financially. Instead, we use social isolation. Relationships with people freeze up, until the person acknowledges the mistake and corrects it. I was mayor for a year. . . . I've seen many cases of blood feuds and honor killings, for which the state has no solution. We stepped in and, because we better understood people's sensitivities, we were able to solve the problem."[12]

Such intensive local work was key to organizing women, particularly peasant women who had relocated from the countryside and were not accustomed to being seen in public, much less working outside the home or participating in politics. The problems such women faced were described by an organizer for the local women's council who set up sewing cooperatives modeled on those of the Zapatistas in Mexico. The women she was trying to recruit were mostly married, in their thirties and older, without education or previous work experience outside the home, and unable to speak Turkish so they couldn't get regular jobs. They were totally lacking in self-confidence and told the women's council they didn't know how to do anything. Their husbands were also a problem. Said the organizer: "The attitude of the husbands is not really positive. But we have a clear advantage in that the movement exists— even in relation to the women's question. The husbands who are tied to the movement try somehow to overcome their negative view of women. They have to work on themselves. That helps us—especially in the councils, where you'll notice men giving up their places to women. . . .

"At first many women came here secretly, without their husbands knowing, or they had to argue in order to be allowed to come here. But over time something's changed in the society. If a woman comes home with money and says, 'Look, I'm also contributing to the budget. I'm also bringing money in,' then maybe it doesn't change a man's complex opinion, but it weakens some of his reservations a little. Husbands become more open to their wives going outside and working. And another fact: the stronger a woman becomes and the more self-confident she gets, then the less likely she is to allow her husband or other men to oppress her."[13]

The movement set up thirteen educational institutions, called academies: nine were political, two were women's, and two were religious, one for Alevis and the other for Sunnis. Part of the purpose of the religious academies was to offer a progressive Islamic education to counter the aggressive propaganda of Islamist groups, some of which had enough money to give students stipends for attending classes. All the academies had three levels of program: a three-month course aimed at cadre, a one-month course for community activists, and popular education programs offered on demand. The head of the Amed [Diyarbakir] General Political Academy was explicit about what they didn't teach: "Stay away from nationalism. Stay away from scientific knowledge that has been warped by discrimination, the science that produces weapons, the cancerous science that's responsible for the destruction of nature. Stay away from religion that's been warped by domination and has become an instrument of the powerful. Stay away from sexism. We come into the world as women or men, and then certain roles are attributed to us. But if you want to be in this movement, if you want to build this society with us, you have to cut yourself loose from these traditional gender roles and relations."[14]

Although the PKK and its organizational partners were secular, in that they believed in the separation of religion and politics, they were not antireligious. Beginning in 2011, according to Aliza Marcus, they even organized Friday prayer services. "The PKK promotes environmentalism, women's rights (women make up around half of BDP [now HDP] candidates, more than in any other political party in Turkey), and a certain tolerance, at least in the media, of gays and lesbians," she wrote.

"The PKK has also taken on Prime Minister Erdogan in an area where he claims to be supreme: Islamic piety. PKK supporters and BDP politicians have encouraged attendance at the alternative Friday prayer services run by Kurdish imams and Kurdish Islamic scholars in Diyarbakir and other cities in the region. The prayer services . . . [are]

led by Kurdish religious figures who were frustrated by the state's long-standing requirement that salaried imams recite the prayers in Turkish and give their weekly speech in Turkish (reading from a prepared text sent by Ankara). Barred from the state mosques, these Kurdish imams and scholars started holding services in empty lots, construction sites, and in courtyards near mosques. In Diyarbakir, these weekly Friday prayers can attract thousands of people."[15]

Organizing on this scale could not have happened in the nineties, when most of the Kurdish population was still rural. But as social scientist Hamit Bozarslan wrote in 2014, "During the last decades, Kurdish society in Iraq and Turkey has become a predominantly urban society, where thousands of villages were systematically destroyed during the 1980s and 1990s, and in Iran and Syria, where developments gave way to the emergence of a middle class, distinct from the former urban notabilities or craftsmen. The emergence of this class metamorphosed the Kurdish urban landscape and gave birth to a new habitus, new ways of consuming, living, socialising, thinking, and struggling.

"An intellectual 'class', distinct from the politicised intelligentsia of the 1950s and 1960s, also appeared and became the agent of new forms of socialisation, political mobilisations, as well as cultural production. In the 1970s and 1980s, but also in the 1990s, being a 'Kurdish militant' primarily meant being a member or sympathiser of a political party; in contrast, the intellectuals of the 2010s develop non-partisan forms of being, behaving, and struggling. Both the middle classes and this intellectual stratum are widely integrated across Kurdistan and entertain close relations with the outside world."[16]

In the nineties, the only way to work with the PKK was to become a guerrilla and go to the mountains. The new, more flexible approach allowed for much broader recruitment. While joining the PKK itself still meant becoming a soldier, now people could help the movement in other ways. Instead of training as guerrillas, they could work in mass organizations, neighborhood committees, or a political party. These new activists were joined by more seasoned ones who were newly released from jail, where they had served time for PKK activities. They were "trusted, respected, and experienced," according to Aliza Marcus, and had a strong influence over decision making. "By offering people a route to get involved and show support for the PKK without having to risk their lives in armed struggle, the rebel group has gained new adherents and respect. It's not that the group has become democratic, but that it acknowledges the importance of (and in fact, need for) nonviolent activism, be it through the political party BDP or in a center teaching illiterate women to read."[17]

Ultimately the three earlier strands of Kurdish activism—the PKK, the electoral parties, and the popular civil resistance and movement for democratic autonomy—melted together in popular consciousness and the Kurdish population as a whole became much more radical. In 2012, Zubeyde Zumrut, co-chair of the BDP in Diyarbakir, told Marcus, "'The PKK has become part of the people. You can't separate them anymore."[18]

The new party line led to a profound change in organizational structure. As Marcus wrote, it was not so much that the inner core of the PKK had changed as that it was now surrounded by a proliferation of other organizations. The number and variety of groups in the PKK network was staggering.

At the top of the pyramid was Ocalan, referred to as "the Leadership," and the Executive Committee of the KCK, the Association of Communities in Kurdistan, the administrative group for the entire structure. The KCK was governed by a periodic general assembly or legislature, with an elected Executive Committee of thirty-one members. In 2013 the whole PKK network, with the exception of the armies, adopted the co-chair system, with one male and one female leader for every structure.[19]

The armed groups, the People's Defense Forces (HPG) and Free Women's Forces (YJA-Star) were also part of the structure, as were the series of electoral parties, each of which was made illegal by the government and replaced by a successor. In 2016, the party was a combination of the BDK, which was based in southeastern Turkey and largely Kurdish, and the HDP, an urban party of Leftists, progressives, feminists, and LGBTI activists. The two had merged in 2014 under the name of the HDP and won more than 13 percent of the national vote the following year.

While the HDP was not organizationally affiliated with the PKK, there were many overlapping members. Moreover, after thirty years of struggle, the PKK's prestige and ideological leadership were so great that opposing them—as the Turkish government and even the EU pressured the HDP to do—would have been politically impossible. Like all the other organizations within the orbit of the PKK, the HDP had an autonomous organization for women.[20]

Government repression made it impossible to fully implement democratic autonomy in Turkey, because Kurdish elected representatives were constantly being jailed, along with any journalists who wrote about the movement. The first place where these new ideas could be fully tested in practice was, ironically, in the middle of a war zone—Syria.

## The PYD and the Rojava Revolution

The history of the Kurds in Syria is not different in essence from that of Iraq and Turkey. They are a smaller percentage of the population but they suffered from similar policies of cultural genocide and land theft, particularly after 1963, when the Baath party took power in Syria and developed its plan to break the Kurds up geographically by creating an "Arab Belt" and settling Arab villages between Kurdish ones. Thus even the most underdeveloped agricultural regions of Rojava were, by 2016, a mixture of Arab and Kurdish peasants, plus refugees.

According to Dr. Amaad Yousef, the Minister of Economy in Afrin (also called Efrin) Canton, smallest of the three Rojava cantons, the Syrian government deliberately kept Rojava underdeveloped. "60% of Syria's poor were Kurds," he told a Kurdish newspaper. "Because they did not allow factories to be open, or development or any form of enrichment in the region of Rojava. For example in Efrîn there were close to 200 olive processing plants. Outside of this there was not even the smallest workshop. ... The regime passed a law in 2008 in order to force Kurds to migrate. With this law it was made very difficult for Kurds to own property. At the same time it made it much easier for Arabs to buy this property.

"There were elementary and middle schools in every village in Efrîn. These schools were built for assimilation. You would not find a single high school or professional school and they were forbidden. Kurdish language education was forbidden. ... The one thing that developed was loansharking. In Efrîn's Reco district you would know which house belonged to whom. You could look at a house and say that's the house of a usurer. ... They rendered the Kurds homeless and propertyless. ... They were taking their property and forcing them to migrate."[21]

Inevitably under such conditions, Kurdish nationalism developed in Syria, beginning with a sister party of the Iraqi KDP called the KDP-S; this kept splitting, and by the nineties there were numerous small nationalist parties, each grouped tribal fashion around one leader and seeking a share of whatever resources were available.[22] When Salih Muslim, a civil engineer, decided to become politically active, at first he joined the KDP-S, but was frustrated by their lack of impact and in

2003 became one of the founders of the PYD, the Democratic Union Party, an offshoot of the PKK. In response to a police attack on Kurds at a soccer game in 2004, the PYD helped organize the Qamishli uprising against Assad.[23] After that, Muslim spent a few months in jail every year—"the Middle East type of prison with the underground rooms for torture," he told the BBC.[24] When criticized for going their own way since 2011, Syrian Kurds often point to the lack of solidarity they received from Syrian left-wing groups in 2004.

In 2010, Muslim and his wife fled to Iraq to avoid another arrest, and that's where he was in April 2011 when the Syrian uprising began. He immediately decided to return to Syria. Five hundred to a thousand guerrillas came back with him, and established the party's military wing, the People's Defense Units and Women's Defense Units, the YPG-YPJ that fought in Kobane.[25]

The Syrian Kurdish parties kept their distance from the rest of the Syrian opposition, even though the opposition was at first led by progressives. As international relations specialist Kamran Matin said: "We should remember that for many months after the outbreak of anti-Assad protests, secular-progressive forces such as the Local Coordination Committees of Syria were in the forefront of the popular uprising. They lost their political clout only when Assad's forces' incessant violence against peaceful protests led to the militarisation of the opposition, which was in turn quickly sectarianized as a result of the indirect intervention of regional reactionary pro-Western, anti-Assad states of Jordan, Qatar, Saudi Arabia, and Turkey, all of which sought Assad's downfall at any price."[26]

While many of the Local Coordination Committees were indeed progressive, the Muslim Brotherhood was a presence in the Syrian National Council from the beginning and soon came to dominate it, pushing for an armed uprising.[27] The Syrian Kurds distrusted the Brotherhood and were wary of an uprising over which they would have no control. When the Syrian opposition refused to discuss Kurdish autonomy until after Assad was overthrown, all the Kurdish parties withdrew from the coalition. After that break, Kurds affiliated with the PYD concentrated on building their own base in Rojava. They called this strategy the "Third Path" or "Third Way," since they were not aligned with either the rebellion, increasingly dominated by Islamists, or the Assad government.[28]

The democratic Syrian opposition, vulnerable, overwhelmed, and furious about it, considered the Kurdish withdrawal a betrayal. Members of the opposition frequently accused the PYD of collaborating with Assad. In an interview early in 2016, Yassin al-Haj Saleh, a widely respected Syrian Marxist intellectual and dissident who spent sixteen years in Assad's prisons and then went into exile, voiced a vision of what Syria needed that was not that different from Abdullah Ocalan's:

"The new Syria could be built on a number of essential principles: decentralisation; thinking of different ethnic, religious, and confessional communities as equal constituent communities; full equality among individual citizens (Arabs, Kurds, and others; Muslims, Christians, and others; Sunnis, Alawites, and others; religious, secular, and others)." But when he spoke about the Syrian Kurds and the PYD, his bitterness was palpable. His feelings were likely shared by many in the Syrian Left: "There is a real war in the Kurdish regions in Turkey, with poor people being humiliated, displaced, and killed. To Syria, the Turkish government exported its bad experience in dealing with the Kurds. And to make things worse, the Syrian PYD imported from Turkey its experience there, [and] people to apply this experience ... What we are witnessing is, in my view, the building of an ultranationalist, one-party system, with hidden connections to the Assad regime and Iran, and less hidden ones with the US and Russia."[29]

Though it would not be accurate to call the PYD nationalist in any ethnic sense, this accusation was often made by the Syrian opposition, whose rancor against the Kurds was a strong indication that the elements needed to build a new Syria would take a long time to come together. Yet the original Local Coordinating Committees, which still existed in some places in 2016, resembled Rojava communes in many ways, although they were more disparate ideologically, and some were dominated by Islamists. Syrian-British journalist Robin Yassin-Kassab described them as "practical, not ideological organisations. Their members are civil activists, family and tribal leaders, and people selected for technical or professional skills. They do their best in the very worst conditions to provide humanitarian aid and fulfill basic needs where the state has either collapsed or deliberately withheld them, including water, electricity, waste disposal and healthcare. ... Council members are appointed by some form of democratic process, though the form differs from place to place, and is most severely restricted in regime- or ISIS-controlled areas where the councils must operate in secret ..."

Although Yassin-Kassab too had many criticisms of the PYD, he shared with the Kurds a decentralized vision of Syria's future: "The myth that a strong central state ensures the strength and dignity of its people runs deep in oppositional consciousness—nationalist, Leftist, and Islamist—despite all the evidence to the contrary. But decentralisation is the best way to deal with Syria's currently explosive ethnic and sectarian polarisations. It would mean a recognition of autonomy for the Kurds, who have set up their own council system. It would also mean that different areas could govern themselves according to their social and sectarian composition."[30]

Unfortunately, he was one of the few Syrian intellectuals to take this ecumenical view of the Kurds. It was far more common for members of the Syrian opposition to reiterate the charge that the Rojava Kurds were allied with the Assad government—otherwise they would not have been able to establish an autonomous area so fast. The PYD denied this from the beginning. In 2011, Salih Muslim argued that the Kurds were merely taking advantage of the upheavals in the region to achieve a degree of independence. Speaking of the 2004 Kurdish uprising, he said, "We fought then, too. Many of our members were imprisoned. But now we have established that since the beginning of the unrest, the regime has had no possibility to attack us. If it does attack us, it will see what happens. We are profiting from the unrest. It is a historical chance for us. We have a right and are making use of it. We do not kill anyone and we also do not fight against anyone. We are preparing our people and ourselves for the period after the fall of the regime. . . . The state knows that if PYD leaders are arrested, there will be serious protests everywhere. This is not in the state's interest."

When pressed to say whether the PYD supported the opposition in calling for the downfall of the regime, Salih Muslim replied, "We demand a fundamental change to the oppressive system. There are some who hold up the slogan: the fall of the regime. In contrast we demand the fall of the oppressive authoritarian system. Our problems are not problems of powers. The ruling powers in Damascus come and go. For us Kurds, this isn't so important. What is important is that we Kurds assert our existence. The current regime does not accept us, nor do those who will potentially come into power. Our politics differ from a politics that seeks power. That needs to be clear."[31]

The PYD's own narrative was that, in the chaos of the Syrian civil war, their party was able to organize openly for the first time since its founding. In July 2012, the Syrian government had pulled most of its troops out of Rojava to fight in Damascus, Aleppo, Homs, and Idlib, and the PYD's local council took over Kobane without firing a shot.

"This action was planned for almost one and a half years," explained Ehmed Sexo, one of the two elected heads of Kobane's council after the takeover. "Because of this long preparation, we managed to take over the city without any bloodshed. Not one Syrian Army soldier was killed, and all surrendered." The soldiers were stripped of their uniforms and weapons, then allowed to return to their home cities. If they could not return because of the civil war, they were placed under house arrest in the old army buildings.[32]

Benjamin Hiller, a German freelancer, was in Kobane during this period, and spent time with the troops protecting the city from incursions. "In Kobani, the outer city perimeter was quickly fortified with checkpoints on all major roads (flying the Kurdish flag) and heavily armed fighters controlling each incoming car. 'We want to prevent any members of the Free Syrian Army, but also regime spies, from entering the city,' said one masked fighter, proudly displaying his newly acquired shotgun. Some of the weapons used by the Kurdish fighters were smuggled into the country via northern Iraq. Other weapons were acquired on the black market or confiscated from [the] Syrian Army and police forces."[33]

The Syrian government managed to maintain small garrisons in a few cities in Rojava, and also continued to pay the salaries of local employees like teachers. Critics of the PYD pointed to this to prove the Kurds were collaborating with Assad. But as Afrin Canton's Minister of Economy pointed out, the Syrian government had continued to pay the salaries of civil servants and teachers all over the country, including in areas controlled by the opposition: "Right now in the whole of Syria there are former state employees who are going and applying to the regime saying 'I am on duty and doing my job' and take their salary. It makes no difference whether or not they are doing their job, they say this. It is like this in areas under the control of the Free Syrian Army, and it is also like this in areas under the control of other powers." According to the Carnegie Middle East Center, the point of the policy was that it allowed Assad "to claim that the regime is the irreplaceable provider of essential services."[34]

## Democratic Autonomy in Rojava

Even before 2011, while the PYD was still underground, it had begun to develop local councils along the lines of those in Turkey, concentrating mainly on conflict mediation and restorative justice. As soon as the uprising began, as Salih Muslim told an EU conference in Brussels in December 2012, "local councils popped up everywhere. Developed under the umbrella of democratic confederalism, these councils had been active already as a parallel structure of government to that of the state since 2007, organizing justice and mediating in conflict; with the collapse of the state, they came out into the open. Since the summer of 2011, the de facto elections for those councils have been held in different cities and towns of the West Kurdistan and Syrian areas in which the Kurds live. For example, in Aleppo, the largest city in Syria, Kurds voted for their de facto representatives in 35 electoral boxes in different districts."[35]

Salih Muslim viewed local councils as part of a structure that could eventually replace a repressive state with local self-governing administrations in all of Syria, not just in the three liberated cantons of Rojava: "We call it the Western Kurdistan People's Council. It is organized everywhere and it includes the Self-Defense Committees, also in the villages, and they are guarding the people. I mean the people themselves have organized the People's Defense Units. They are armed groups and protecting the society. For daily demands and daily work, in the municipalities and towns, we have committees, so we don't need the central authorities or the main government. Everywhere and in every place we have a kind of self-rule, self-government, and till now it is very successful. I think if we could have done it for whole Syria, the situation in Syria would have been different."[36]

In 2016, the elected councils were the overall administrative wing of Rojava's self-administration—they refused to use the word "government"—while the multi-party coalition, TEV-DEM, put democratic autonomy and economic self-organization into practice at the grassroots level. All of a city's ethnic and religious groups were represented in TEV-DEM by quotas, along with civil society organizations and political parties. Many parties were represented, though the coalition's ideological leadership clearly came from the PYD. TEV-DEM working groups and assemblies focused on project areas like the economy, education, the environment, women's issues, defense, and more.

In the opinion of journalist Joris Leverink, the Rojava revolution was "one of the most important political projects being pursued in the world today.... The TEV-DEM can be singled out as one of the main reasons why the revolution in Rojava didn't succumb to the destructive internal conflicts that haunted so many other opposition groups that have sprung up in the context of the Arab Spring. . . . The four principles of the TEV-DEM go a long way in explaining its appeal to the oppressed and marginalized people of Rojava. These are: the revolution must be bottom up; it has to be a social, cultural, educational as well as a political revolution; it should be directed against the state, power, and authority; and finally it must be the people who have the final say in all decision-making processes."[37]

Following the liberation of Kobane, local councils took over other Syrian Kurdish cities with only a few glitches, except in Derik, where there was oil. There fighting broke out. "Around 30 Syrian soldiers holed up in the main military headquarters. The gun battle lasted for several hours, with bursts from AK-47s echoing through the narrow streets. Neighbors watched the escalating firefight with awe, applauding each Kurdish fighter, until the first bullets hit civilian houses. The YPG started clearing the streets and setting up traffic controls. . . . Eventually, Kurdish fighters brought in heavy weapons, including RPGs [rocket-propelled grenades] and a heavy machinegun, and the government soldiers surrendered. Kurdish forces now control several oil fields around the city."[38]

By the end of 2012, the PYD had organized all three Rojava cantons. Feeling that the councils were too remote from the neighborhoods, they set up communes as the basic unit of administration and decision-making. An academic delegation visited Cizire canton in December 2014,[39] and met with Cizire Co-chair Cinar Salih, who told them how the self-administration system worked: "Our system rests on the communes, made up of neighborhoods of 300 people. The communes have co-presidents [one male, one female], and there are co-presidents at all levels, from commune to canton administration. In each commune there are five or six different committees. Communes work in two ways. First, they resolve problems quickly and early—for example, a technical problem or a social one. Some jobs can be done in five minutes, but if you send it to the state, it gets caught in a bureaucracy. So we can solve issues quickly. The second way is political. If we speak about true democracy, decisions can't be made from the top and go to the bottom, they have to be made at the bottom and then go up in degrees. There are also district councils and city councils, up to the canton. The principle is 'few problems, many resolutions.' So that the government doesn't remain up in the air, we try to fill the bottom of it."[40]

Eighteen communes made up a district, and the co-presidents of all of them were on the district people's council, which also had directly-elected members. The councils decided on matters like garbage collection, heating oil distribution, land ownership, and cooperative enterprises. While all the communes and councils were at least 40 percent women, the PYD—in its determination to revolutionize traditional gender relations—also set up parallel autonomous women's bodies at each level, including the highest level, the TEV-DEM. These determined policy on matters of particular concern to women, like forced marriages, honor killings, polygamy, sexual violence, and discrimination. Since domestic violence remained a problem, they also set up a system of shelters. If there was a conflict on an issue concerning women, the women's councils were able to overrule the mixed councils.[41]

For people to be able to carry out this kind of self-administration, they had to learn how to think politically. "Democratic autonomy is about the long term," Salih Muslim said. "It is about people understanding and exercising their rights. To get society to become politicized: that is the core of building democratic autonomy . . . You have to educate, twenty-four hours a day, to learn how to discuss, to learn how to decide collectively. You have to reject the idea that you have to wait for some leader to come and tell the people what to do, and instead learn to exercise self-rule as a collective practice."[42]

On January 29, 2014, when the Rojava cantons declared autonomy, they adopted a remarkable constitution they call their Social Contract or Charter, which explicitly incorporates the Universal Declaration of Human Rights, the International Covenant on Civil and Political Rights, the International Covenant on Economic, Social and Cultural Rights, and other internationally recognized human rights conventions. Its Preamble reads:

"We, the people of the Democratic Autonomous Regions of Afrin, Jazira and Kobane, a confederation of Kurds, Arabs, Assyrians, Chaldeans, Arameans, Turkmen, Armenians and Chechens, freely and solemnly declare and establish this Charter, which has been drafted according to the principles of Democratic Autonomy. In pursuit of freedom, justice, dignity and democracy and led by principles of equality and environmental sustainability, the Charter proclaims a new social contract, based upon mutual and peaceful coexistence and understanding between all strands of society. It protects fundamental human rights and liberties and reaffirms the peoples' right to self-determination. Under the Charter, we, the people of the Autonomous Regions, unite in the spirit of reconciliation, pluralism and democratic participation so that all may express themselves freely in public life. In building a society free from authoritarianism, militarism, centralism and the intervention of religious authority in public affairs, the Charter recognizes Syria's territorial integrity and aspires to maintain domestic and international peace. In establishing this Charter, we declare a political system and civil administration founded upon a social contract that reconciles the rich mosaic of Syria through a transitional phase from dictatorship, civil war and destruction, to a new democratic society where civic life and social justice are preserved."[43]

Sociologist Nazan Ustundag observed that, while Rojava aspired to a total lack of traditional government, it was at war and in transition, and could not reach that condition quickly: "As a result of war and embargo and the need to present themselves diplomatically at the global stage, as well as represent their cantons internally to people as emerging systems, canton governments often end up performing stateness. They collect information, speak in the name of the people, assume a Rojavan economy, and desire to create education and healthcare systems."

She called Rojava "a movement that is situated in the dialectic between state-ness and society," and argued that TEV-DEM and the people's local militias and asayish (local police) would be key in preventing a state from emerging in future. Since state-like activities needed to be performed, and there was no functioning state in Syria, she worried that what had happened in the past could also be the future if care was not taken:

"Armed warriors, polygamous chiefs who had unequal access to resources, and prophets promising a good life always carried the potential of becoming ruling figures, overtaking functions of production, reproduction, and defense from collectivities. Fighters against ISIS, canton officers who conduct diplomacy and make rules, and political cadres embodying revolutionary ethics bear a surprising resemblance to warriors, chiefs, and prophets."

Her interviews with TEV-DEM members persuaded her that they consciously saw themselves as the first line of defense against the spontaneous development of government-like relationships: "The relationship between the canton government and assemblies is conceived not in terms of representation but in terms of self-defense. In other words, the primary aim is not to achieve the representation of assemblies in the government, although that could be the case. Rather assemblies, academies, and communes will be the means by which localities maintain their autonomy against the canton governments, unmake the latter's claims to state-ness, and eventually appropriate their functions, proving them redundant."[44]

The whole society was only a few years old when she wrote this, and still at the test-drive stage; only time can tell how this tension will play out.

## Democratic Economy

Because the Rojava cantons were under siege on all sides, their people had to become economically self-sufficient in a hurry, even though 70 percent of their resources were going to fund the war. They knew how to grow food, but gasoline and electricity were enormous problems, as were weapons. They had shortages in many areas but by the time the academic delegation visited in December 2013, Rojava had moved towards setting up what one of their economic advisors called a "community economy." Janet Biehl, who was part of the delegation, was immensely impressed by what she saw: "'If there is only bread, then we all have a share,' the adviser told us. We visited an economics academy and economic cooperatives: a sewing cooperative in Derik, making uniforms for the defense forces; a cooperative greenhouse, growing cucumbers and tomatoes; a dairy cooperative in Rimelan, where a new shed was under construction. The Kurdish areas are the most fertile parts of Syria, home of its abundant wheat supply, but the Baath regime had deliberately kept the area pre-industrial, a source of raw materials. Hence wheat was cultivated but could not be milled into flour. We visited a mill, newly constructed since the revolution, improvised from local materials. It now provides flour for the bread consumed in Cizire, whose residents get three loaves a day."[45]

The same month the academic delegation visited Cizire, a Turkish journalist interviewed Dr. Amaad Yousef, the Minister of Economy for Afrin, the smallest canton, cut off from the other two and almost completely farmland. Yousef proudly listed all they had built in a year and a half, with virtually no outside help. "Right now in Efrîn there are fifty soap factories, twenty olive oil factories, 250 olive processing plants, seventy factories making construction material, four hundred textile workshops, eight shoe factories, five factories producing nylon, fifteen factories processing marble. Two mills and two hotels have been built. We are the first and only place producing soap in Syria. We are working on developing commerce around dairy products, fruit, and other foodstuffs. We are doing all of this in the villages so that the people return to their villages. . . . A dam was built to provide drinking water.

We created a 'made in Efrîn' brand. We forbid the founding of any more olive factories from an environmental perspective. We also forbid workshops melting lead, to protect human health."[46]

All this progress was in spite of the fact that Afrin had been blockaded for three years, cut off by Turkey on one side and surrounded by Jabhat al-Nusra and other jihadi groups on the others. As the war in nearby Aleppo intensified, Afrin came under sharper attack by al-Nusra, beginning in July 2015. On February 3, 2016 its democratic self-administration committee sent an urgent appeal to the UN, the US, and the EU, saying:

> For three years, the Afrin Canton has been under a dual siege. On the one hand, there are armed groups in the east and south that launch assaults, block roads, ban the entry of food and medical aid to the canton, obstruct movement of civilians from and to the canton and kidnap them. On the other hand, the Turkish government imposes a firm closure on the border from north and west, and toughens the siege, despite the fact that the Democratic Self-Administration areas make up the largest part of the Syrian-Turkish border and are the safest on both sides. . . .
>
> The siege laid on Afrin and the loss of food, medicines, and babies' milk, etc. puts the lives of hundreds of thousands in danger and worsens their suffering. The canton hosts tens of thousands of displaced families from different areas of Syria and cities, opens its doors to all Syrians from different ethnic and sectarian backgrounds fleeing war, and provides them a shelter. This has caused extra burden for the canton due to lack of capability, life difficulties, the shortage of basic and urgent life necessities of food and medicine, and the difficulty getting them due to the siege. All these foretell a humanitarian catastrophe intensified due to complete absence of international organizations and the non-reaching of aids offered by international sides. . . . In light of the substantial US influence and role in the Syrian crisis, and considering the American administration's positive and effective role in finding a peaceful and democratic solution to the Syrian crisis, we appeal to your immediate and urgent support intervention to lift the siege on Afrin Canton . . .[47]

The canton's self-administration or management committee had done its best to handle these scarcities. In the beginning of the siege, during the winter of 2013, the price of flour in Afrin went from 3,000 to 65,000 Syrian pounds per sack, putting it out of reach for many people. The canton management made a rule that any flour sold for more than 4,100 would be confiscated. Then they decided the canton should set up two more mills and stop exporting flour. The price went down to 3,500.[48]

This exemplified the PYD view of how to build a cooperative economy that was nothing like the centralized command economies of Cold War Eastern Europe, where everything was owned by the state. Dr. Dara Kurdaxi, an economist and a member of the committee for economic revival and development in Afrin, explained how the cooperative economy operated: "The oil industry is under the control of the councils and managed by the workers' committee. The refineries produce cheap benzine for the cooperatives and the staff of the autonomous government. A great deal of land which was previously nationalised under Assad as part of the anti-Kurdish policies is now managed by free Rojava through agricultural cooperatives. Doctors' committees are working to form a free health system." She contrasted this with the economy of the Kurdistan Regional Government in Iraq, "where the social contradictions between the system of the client state . . . and the socially disadvantaged are becoming ever sharper."

In Kurdaxi's view, such a system was no longer viable: "The artificial creation of needs which ventures forth to find new markets, and the boundless desire for ever more gigantic profits makes the gap between rich and poor ever wider, and expands the camp of those who are living on [the] poverty line, those who die of hunger. Such an economic policy is no longer acceptable to humanity. The greatest task of a socialist politics lies therefore with the implementation of an alternative economic policy, one based not on profit but on the fairer redistribution of wealth."[49]

Because so much of the Rojava economy has had to be devoted to war, the cantons have not been able to move very quickly towards a democratic, cooperative and ecologically sound form of economic development. For this reason, one cannot say for sure what form such development will take. But a conference on Democratic Economy held in Van, Turkey, in November 2014, provided a fascinating glimpse of the combination of visionary and practical thinking that has been going on to integrate women's needs into every section of the economic program—"Women" actually was the first section in the document that contained the decisions of the Conference. The first three proposals under that heading were extraordinary for their forthright depiction of women's lives and the need for change. The first stated that the male-dominated capitalist economy made women invisible and called for a new conceptual framework and a change in language to allow women to see themselves as part of the economic structure. The next two decisions declared that:

- A campaign needs to be organized to counter the governmental social policies that put women into the position of having to take care of the disabled, the elderly, and children under conditions of underpaid and undocumented work without any social security. This struggle must be undertaken on the grounds of international agreements.
- Women must be able to participate in all decision-making processes regarding local resources. Urban spaces must be planned with an aim to ease the lives of women, the disabled, and children. Not just parks but all common life spaces must be transformed in accordance with women's perspectives, and women-focused cities need to be swiftly brought into existence.[50]

The Rojava Women's Council began implementing these goals by founding shelters for women who were being abused, where they could be physically safe and learn how to become economically self-sufficient. Workplaces that employed women were required to operate nurseries for babies and small children; women received three months' paid maternity leave plus two hours off per day for nursing or childcare. Sewing workshops were set up for women in the refugee camps in Rojava so they could earn money.[51]

As women's economic needs were given a central place in economic planning, so were their needs for justice and defense against violence. The asayish—the local police force largely made up of women—was seen as the main way to manage the need for peace and justice on the community level. One of its main tasks—framed in terms of self-defense—was dealing with cases of violence against women, including such issues as child marriage and polygamy, both illegal. The asayish proceeded on the basis of complaints, most of which came from housewives. An asayish member in Cizire explained that "as soon as a complaint is received, the force begins an investigation into the man in question and a process of one-on-one communication and support with the woman survivor."[52]

In Turkey, women in the Kurdish youth movement—the Union of Patriotic Revolutionary Young Women (YDG-K)—had their own, somewhat more confrontational method of dealing with violence against women, as the Kurdish women's news agency JINHA reported in September 2015: "For four years, C. A.'s husband I. A. has physically and psychologically abused her. C. A. then applied to the YDG-K. The women warned her husband several times to stop his behavior. The women of YDG-K then beat him until he promised that he would never abuse his wife. The women of YDG-K called on all women suffering from violence to apply to them, and noted that they struggle to protect their fellow women."[53]

Asayish members in Rojava went through a training process that was primarily ideological. As described by Nazan Ustundag, it involved topics such as "women's history and liberation, Middle Eastern history, the history of Kurdistan, the state, truth, and diplomacy. Far from being only conceptual, the lessons are also practical, involving enactments of life in nature and scarcity whereby students are brought to the outdoors and taught to live without electricity and food. Self-reflexivity and criticism constitute another important part of the lessons: people are invited to collectively contemplate their desires for power, revenge, and conformity. Once asayiş members take their posts, they are expected to perform an ethics of equality with people and not make themselves too present in their lives. There are a number of cases where complaints by the public led certain asayiş members to be punished. Punishment involves more education . . ."[54] Here as in other areas of policy, the goal is not to set up a punishing quasi-state but to enable the community to reach for both justice and unity.

*People's Protection Unit (YPG) campfire outside grain silos after capture of Tel Hamis, Cizire Canton, Rojava.*

## Chapter 7

# The Battle of Kobane and Its Backlash

Rojava's radical, transformational vision of social change in the Middle East was bound to be seen as a threat by conservatives, including Kurdish and Syrian Islamists and nationalists, Barzani's KDP in Iraq, and, of course, Turkey. As long as no one in the international community noticed the existence of the Rojava Kurds, the war on them was primarily military and could be left to Daesh and Jabhat al-Nusra, abetted by Turkey. All this changed with the battle of Kobane.

The battle of Kobane lasted from the spring of 2014 until January 2015, completely destroying the town, and drawing international attention for the first time to the liberated Rojava cantons and their women's militias. It also brought US bombers into the Syrian war, though not until after much of Kobane had been destroyed and the Kurdish militias had lost hundreds of fighters. The YPG-YPJ's defeat of Daesh was made more exquisite by the fact that so many of the victorious Kurdish fighters were women—apparently Daesh members believe that if they are killed by a female, they will not be able to immediately proceed to paradise and their allotted 72 virgins.[1]

Until the Syrian uprising and the war that followed, Kobane had a population of perhaps 200,000, but it grew much larger after 2012 due to an influx of refugees. Before the war, 90 percent of the population was Kurdish, but the city of Kobane has about a hundred outlying villages and the population in some is made up of Sunni Arabs who were settled there by the Assad regime to fragment Kurdish territory.[2]

As the central of the three Rojava cantons—Afrin is quite far to the west, and Cizire to the east—Kobane was of key importance to the future of Rojava. If Daesh succeeded in capturing it, Kobane would be cut off from contact with the other two cantons and the dream of an autonomous Kurdish region in Syria would be dead.

Daesh wanted Kobane for logistical reasons. It had already captured two other towns on the Turkish border, Jarabulus and Tal Abyad, but because Kobane lay between them, Daesh vehicles had to go 160 miles out of their way in order to travel between them.[3] But once it started the battle, Daesh had to win or suffer an immense blow to its prestige. A Daesh victory over the Kurds in Kobane would show the strength of Islamism—both its ferociously violent version and the "moderate" nationalistic version of Turkish president Erdogan, who clearly hoped for a Kurdish defeat.

Turkey's objective was to prevent a strong contiguous Kurdish presence on its border that could give aid and comfort to Turkish Kurds. As the strategic consultants of the Soufan Group, a consulting firm specializing in security and intelligence, put it, "Given a choice between having the Islamic State or Kurdish groups along its border with Syria, Turkey would almost certainly choose the former."[4] Though Turkey was a member of NATO, many observers noted its accommodating attitude toward both Daesh and Jabhat al-Nusra. Jihadis traveled freely through Turkey, where they were known to meet in certain coffeehouses; these coffeehouses were never raided by police. Foreign fighters were allowed to cross the border into Syria in large numbers. Daesh moved large quantities of military supplies through Turkey as well. Besides allowing Daesh fighters and supplies to regularly cross the border into Syria, Turkey set up a program to offer wounded Daesh and al-Nusra fighters treatment in private hospitals.[5]

Daesh first attacked Kobane in March 2014, after driving Jabhat al-Nusra and the Free Syrian Army out of the area. This left Kobane surrounded by Daesh on three sides with the fourth side being Turkey. The combined People's Protection Units and Women's Protection Units (YPG-YPJ) turned back the first attacks, but on July 2, Daesh began a concerted assault, using thermal missiles and heavy artillery they had captured from the Iraqi Army in Mosul. They also had Humvees, night vision goggles, M-16 rifles, and at least one $4 million tank, not to mention a seemingly unlimited supply of jihadis. In fact, Daesh had so many weapons they were able to fire three thousand mortar rounds at Kobane over a period of four days in July.[6]

Because none of the Western powers were willing to supply the Syrian Kurds with weapons, the YPG-YPJ had only vintage Russian Kalashnikovs bought on the black market, handmade grenades, and tanks they put together out of construction vehicles and pick-up trucks. They had only 500 soldiers, many young and inexperienced.[7]

On July 6, the Association of Communities in Kurdistan (KCK) called for a general mobilization of Kurds to come to Kobane. Daesh had cut the power lines and water supply and Turkey was not letting food through. It was essential to break the Turkish embargo. As Daesh mounted heavy coordinated assaults on villages near Kobane, Turkey dug trenches ten feet wide on its side of the border to stop refugees from getting in and supplies and volunteers from getting out.[8]

The citizens of Rojava were trying to help themselves. In Cizire canton, the Qamishli people's council had organized a water supply by digging wells, and neighborhood communes, each covering several streets, had begun to acquire commercial generators capable of producing ten hours of electricity a day. Kobane tried similar methods of popular mobilization to cope with the siege. Their most serious problem was health care. They had converted an old building into a 210-bed hospital but, as Enver Muslim, president of the Kobane canton, explained, "we have no tomography, endoscopy, X-ray, or MR machines. We have no incubators for new-born babies who need them. We do not have the medical equipment to treat the injured. We are facing serious medicine shortages."[9]

They also had no construction materials or equipment to repair roads and buildings. Nevertheless, they dug eighteen wells in the West Kobane village of Qeynter Oxan, laid 320 meters of pipe to bring water into the city, and bought generators for every street. They grew some fruits and vegetables, peanuts, and cotton, but they badly needed more food as well as supplies.[10]

Turkish Kurds were determined to help. The HDP, the pro-Kurdish party in Turkey's parliament, immediately began to hold solidarity events to raise money for food and supplies, and to try to find ways to get them into Kobane. In the second week of July, they managed to send seven trucks of sugar, milk, rice, dates, olive oil, bulgur wheat, pasta, and other food.[11] On July 19, the second anniversary of the liberation of Kobane, thousands of Turkish Kurds massed at the border and stormed the fence. Despite the army's use of tear gas and water cannons, at least one thousand broke through.[12] By one means or another, they moved about three tons of food and medical supplies into Kobane during the rest of the month, and two new brigades formed with volunteers from all over Kurdistan.

The Daesh assault became a brutal siege. At the end of July, Meryam Kobane, commander of the local Women's Defense Forces, described the situation to *Özgür Gündem,* a sympathetic Turkish paper: "There is no trade. Nothing comes from outside and nothing goes outside. This is a war in its own right. Forcing people to migrate by depriving them of work and bread is a special kind of war. It is the most merciless road to surrender."[13]

Until August 2014, the siege of Kobane had gone almost unnoticed by world media, but after Daesh attacked the Yazidis on Sinjar Mountain and the YPG-YPJ rescued thousands of refugees, reporters began to pay attention. Once Western journalists arrived, Turkey was embarrassed into opening the border, at least long enough to let 45,000 refugee Kurds in. Three hundred crossed in the other direction to help defend Kobane.[14]

Information about Turkey's relationship with Daesh was also starting to trickle out. On September 17, an Alawite nurse who worked at a private hospital near the border wrote a letter to Parliament and the police saying she was sick and tired of having to care for wounded jihadis. "The ISIL commander named Muhammet Ali R. who was admitted to our hospital on Aug. 7 was treated at room number 323. Many of his bodyguards kept watch around the hospital. Many other ISIL commanders like him and soldiers have been treated at our hospital, and returned to war after the completion of their treatment. I don't want to help these people. I want you to inspect these hospitals. And I am referring the owners of the hospital and its management to God." It later came out that the person who had been placing Daesh fighters for care in Turkish hospitals was none other than Erdogan's daughter Sumeyye.[15]

After the battle of Sinjar, the Obama administration debated whether to give air support to the Syrian Kurds. As the attack on Kobane continued, pressure to do something mounted. What was holding the President back? He had already authorized airstrikes in Iraq and air drops of supplies in the Sinjar Mountains. "We're not going to let them create some caliphate through Syria and Iraq," he told Thomas L. Friedman of *The New York Times* in August, but the US could not get more involved without "partners on the ground who are capable of filling the void."[16]

He meant partners who wouldn't offend Turkey; even if the Kurds were the only ones willing to fight Daesh, they had to be kept at arm's length. The Obama administration's position made no sense to anybody who knew what was actually going on. David Romano, a Middle East specialist at the University of Missouri with a weekly column in *Rudaw*, an Iraqi Kurdish publication, wrote on July 26: "Let us look at the PYD's [Democratic Union Party] concrete record of action since it took control of large parts of northern Syria and declared autonomy in the cantons of Kobane, Cizre and Afrin. They held municipal elections. They provided refuge to Arab, Turkmen, Christian, and other refugees from all over Syria. They incorporated not just Kurds, but also Arabs, Turkmen and Christians into the autonomous administrations of all three cantons. They protected all of them from both Daesh and the Assad regime. They empowered women, arming them, and placing females into leadership positions of every single municipality the PYD controls. They have committed no massacres, and they continue to insist that they want only good relations with Turkey and the Iraqi Kurds. They did all of this while being isolated, starved economically, and pressured militarily from all sides."[17]

Daesh attacks on Kobane kept getting worse. Kurds in Turkey and other parts of Rojava were desperate to join the fight, but the Erdogan government was determined to keep the border closed in both directions. Asya Tekin, a Turkish reporter for *Jinha*, the Kurdish women's online news service, described the scene at the border, with thousands of refugees on the Syrian side trying to flee Kobane. "They were mostly women, children, elderly people. People were crossing with giant bags of stuff, with their cars and sheep. There was no water and food. The [Turkish] police opened fire with teargas. People on this side of the border know about teargas, but people from Rojava had never experienced it before and they thought it was a chemical weapon attack against them. That was what they were most familiar with, so they hid under blankets. A reporter ... ran to help them and told them that they needed to run away from the teargas. A lot of women were screaming because they couldn't find their children. There were hundreds of journalists there and they were also attacked. A lot of journalists stopped their journalism role, abandoned our jobs, because we needed to help the people urgently. That was the first day. After that there was an attack every day. Turkish police and soldiers were there in their thousands and launched attacks with teargas, batons, and with live ammunition. There were tanks, soldiers on foot, and bullets being fired."[18]

On October 2, the Syrian Observatory for Human Rights, a small London nonprofit that was the most trusted group tracking the Syrian war and its victims, reported that Daesh had surrounded Kobane with thirty to fifty tanks, which were shelling the city, sections of which were going up in flames. Daesh and the YPG-YPJ were clashing only hundreds of meters away from Kobane to the east and southeast of the city, and two or three kilometers to the west. It was clear that Kobane was about to fall and that Daesh would massacre anyone still there. Three hundred thousand people had already fled; now the PYD moved the rest into makeshift refugee camps at the Turkish border, to clear Kobane for street fighting. On October 3, Daesh captured the eastern part of the city and raised the black flag on Mistenur Hill above the town.[19]

That same day, Turkish Prime Minister Ahmet Davutoglu promised that Turkey would do whatever was necessary to prevent the fall of Kobane but refused to make any definite commitment. The next day, Erdogan held a press conference. He said, "For us, the PKK is the same as ISIL. It is wrong to consider them as different from each other." He refused to send any help, saying Turkey was helping enough already by taking in refugees and was not going to bow to people "involved in PKK terrorism."[20]

The Turkish Army massed tanks at the border, but their only purpose seemed to be to prevent Kurds who wanted to get to Kobane from crossing. In protest, the HDP and the Kurdish youth group YDG-H organized massive demonstrations all over Turkey. As protestors crowded the streets, they were attacked by fascists and the police; there were fifty-five deaths between October 7 and October 10.[21]

The siege of Kobane convinced most Kurds that the Turkish government was secretly supporting Daesh. Abu Khaled, the *nomme de guerre* of an ex-jihadi interviewed by journalist Michael Weiss, told him, "During the Kobani war, shipments of weapons arrived to ISIS from Turkey. Until now, the gravely wounded go to Turkey, shave their beards, cut their hair, and go to the hospital. Somebody showed me pictures in Kobani. You see ISIS guys eating McDonald's french fries and hamburgers. Where did they get it? In Turkey."

He also told Weiss that Daesh openly proselytized in Turkey. The border town of Kilis, he said, had two important mosques. "This one [is] for the Islamic State. You go there, everybody says, 'You want to go to Syria?' They arrange your travel back and forth. And the other mosque is for Jabhat al-Nusra."[22]

Knowing that an air war alone could not defeat Daesh, the Pentagon had been searching in vain for Syrian Arab "partners on the ground" who would be willing to fight the jihadis without insisting on fighting Assad as well. There weren't any. Still the State Department resisted the idea of an alliance with PKK-connected groups and did not confront Turkey strongly on the ways it was enabling Daesh. On October 9, Secretary of State John Kerry told the press that preventing the fall of Kobane was not a US strategic objective.[23]

This was two days after Erdogan had once more predicted the end of resistance in Kobane, pooh-poohing the idea that US airstrikes could help. He said only a ground campaign could do the job, implying that the Turkish army was the one force capable of such a campaign. "Months have passed but no results have been achieved. Kobane is about to fall," he said, in a televised speech at, of all places, a Turkish camp for Syrian refugees.[24]

Against all odds, the Rojava Kurds continued to resist. They absolutely refused to admit defeat. And as the days passed, the Pentagon began to push the administration, convinced that the YPG-YPJ forces were the "partner on the ground" needed to defeat Daesh. On October 11 and 12, the State Department met secretly with representatives of the PYD in Paris. Shortly thereafter Vice President Joe Biden, never known for his diplomatic tongue, mentioned that Turkey was letting an awful lot of foreign fighters pass through its territory to join Daesh. Erdogan had a fit and insisted that Biden apologize, which he did, but the wind was changing.[25]

On October 19, the press again asked Erdogan if he would agree to the US arming the PYD militias in Syria. "The PYD is for us, equal to the PKK. It is a terror organisation," he answered. "It would be wrong for the United States with whom we are friends and allies in NATO to talk openly and to expect us to say 'yes' to such a support to a terrorist organisation."[26]

But finally, on October 21, the Obama administration took a clear position. A State Department spokesperson announced that, as far as the US was concerned, the PYD was a different organization from the

PKK; the PYD was not on the terrorist list and the US was not barred by law from giving it aid.[27]

In fact, the US had already begun air strikes though these were not very effective until the Air Force developed a system of coordinating with Kurdish fighters on the ground. And, though YPG-YPJ commanders were happy about the air support, they still needed better weapons. They told *The Guardian*, "Air strikes alone are really not enough to defeat Isis in Kobani. . . . They are besieging the city on three sides, and fighter jets simply cannot hit each and every Isis fighter on the ground."[28]

By this time thousands of Syrian Kurds from Cizire and Afrin had gathered on the Turkish border, trying to get into Kobane from the one side that wasn't controlled by Daesh. But Turkey still would not let them in. On October 28, Meysa Abdo, a woman commander in Kobane, wrote an op-ed for *The New York Times*: "We will never give up. But we need more than merely rifles and grenades to carry out our own responsibilities and aid the coalition in its war against the jihadist forces. . . . Last week, following domestic and international criticism, Turkish leaders at last said they would open a corridor for a small group of Iraqi peshmerga fighters, and some Free Syrian Army brigades, to cross into Kobani. But they still will not allow other Syrian Kurds to cross Turkish territory to reach us. This has been decided without consulting us. As a result, the Islamic State can bring in endless amounts of new supplies and ammunition, but we are still effectively blockaded on all sides—on three by the Islamic State's forces, and on the fourth by Turkish tanks."[29]

At the beginning of November, Turkey finally allowed 150 *peshmerga* from Iraq into Kobane. A new Arab brigade, the Euphrates Volcano, also formed, made up of volunteers who had previously fled Raqqa. On November 8, the YPG-YPJ announced that they and the Euphrates Volcano had killed three thousand Daesh fighters since September 15.[30]

US forces were now collaborating more closely with the YPG-YPJ forces, who would call in coordinates to the bombers, and the airstrikes were beginning to hurt Daesh. On November 11, the Syrian Observatory for Human Rights said they had heard from reliable sources that "a very important military leader in IS said that IS militants [had been] shocked by the fierce resistance of the YPG fighters" after Daesh had detonated more than 20 booby-trapped vehicles. "He also said that the battle of Kobani has drained hundreds of IS fighters."[31]

On November 29, Daesh sent four cars of suicide bombers into

Kobane from the Turkish side of the border, where they had been using government-owned grain silos as their base. Turkey assisted them with an unannounced power cut that plunged the border area into darkness so the attack took the Kobane forces by surprise. Clashes went on through the night, and many were killed on both sides.

At a protest rally, Selahattin Demirtas of the HDP said the government could no longer deny supporting Daesh: "ISIS terrorists opened fire on Kobanê from wheat silos belonging to the (Turkish) Agricultural Products Department all day." He said that it was obvious that some officials at the border were collaborating with Daesh: How else could vehicles packed with bombs have gotten through the Turkish border to carry out suicide attacks at an official crossing?[32]

By this time, the battle of Kobane had lasted seventy-seven days. Between IEDs (improvised explosive devices), suicide bombers, and US aerial bombardment, the city had been reduced to rubble. Now fighting began to take place street to street as the Kurds tried to clear out areas occupied by the jihadis. A YPG fighter interviewed on the online networking service Reddit described the day-to-day battle.

"Look, the Daesh don't really give up (especially en masse). So you have to clear the place house by house, street by street. Clearing an area (I think Americans call this "mopping up") is a lot harder than it sounds. It leads to a lot of loss of life on our side. As the city fell into ruins, Daesh's tanks and heavy weapons ceased to be so advantageous. Because so much of the city was ruined we had plenty of cover. They couldn't use the tanks in the blocked streets. They also were incapable of defending specific buildings from our assaults. . . . which were launched at night and when they couldn't take advantage of their heavy-weapons at once (they couldn't see what they were shooting at)."

The battles were very intense, he said; at least seven hundred fighters died during this period. "There was dozens of Alamos in that city no one will read about. . . . hundreds of small little battles in small ugly broken houses no one will ever care about. It was like Stalingrad. At night, it was haunting to see how much of it looked like the moon."[33]

By December 1, the Kurds had retaken three-fourths of the city. On January 27, 2015, the YPG-YPJ captured Mistenur Hill, where Daesh had planted its black flag in October, and replaced it with the Kurdish flag. As the PYD announced victory, celebrations broke out everywhere Kurds lived.

Daesh was badly hurt by the battle of Kobane. As Michael Weiss wrote, it no longer had "its aura of invincibility." When he interviewed Abu Khaled, the former jihadi told him that Daesh had lost five to six thousand fighters in Kobane, most of them foreigners who had been sent "to their slaughter, without any tactical, much less strategic, forethought." Twice that many had been wounded and could no longer fight. The defeat had been devastating for recruitment, he said. Before Kobane, "We had like 3,000 foreign fighters who arrived every day to join ISIS. I mean, every day. And now we don't have even like 50 or 60."[34]

As soon as the town of Kobane was declared safe—though many surrounding villages had yet to be cleared of Daesh—the international press corps, which had been camping on a hill in Suruc just across the border, watching the bombs but unable to enter the city, poured into Rojava. An English freelancer, Yvo Fitzherbert, reported that "more than 80 percent of the city has been destroyed entirely, reduced to little but a heap of rubble. . . . Unexploded bombs are scattered everywhere, often going unnoticed. Some are buried into the road, while others lie unobtrusively beneath the rubble. Children play alongside these bombs, not giving them a moment's thought. Every now and then, a loud explosion pierces through the city, and civilians exchange fearful looks, hoping that nobody was harmed. Half a dozen people have died as a result of such accidents in the last week alone."[35]

The area was still far from peaceful. When Canadian photographer Joey Lawrence went to Rojava in March 2015, the YPG-YPJ took him to battles in progress, including one unanticipated suicide attack. The fighters he was with immediately grabbed their Kalashnikovs and headed for the front lines to support the fighters and drive wounded back to the base. He kept wondering why they didn't wear some of the helmets and bulletproof vests they had captured, but they didn't want to. "Their tactics rely on speed and stealth, and remaining fluid on a constantly changing battlefield. It's these same guerrilla tactics that led to major successes against their adversaries. Sure ISIS has tanks, heat seeking missiles, and night vision technology, but even with these technological advantages, the jihadist group can still struggle against a force like YPG/J."[36]

Daesh attacked again on June 26, 2015, when dozens of jihadis dressed in Free Syrian Army uniforms snuck into town in the middle of the night and went on a rampage, setting off car bombs, shooting whomever they saw in the street, and raiding houses. They slaughtered over 150 people before they were killed. A YPG spokesman told Reuters, "The Daesh attack was a suicide mission. . . . Its aim wasn't to take the city but to create terror."[37]

Still, in the year following the liberation of Kobane, despite very difficult living conditions, losing a flood of refugees who hoped for a better life in Europe, and having to guard against attacks at any time, the Rojava Kurds went from strength to strength. In June, they captured Tal Abyad, a key border town that was essential to the Daesh supply route from Turkey to its capital at Raqqa. The liberation of Tal Abyad freed the area between the Kobane and Cizire cantons and gave the Syrian Kurds control of a much larger contiguous space. These successes brought new recruits. In August 2015, a Reuters analysis put YPG-YPJ numbers at forty thousand fighters, and said they controlled twice the amount of territory they had the year before.[38]

In 2016, Kobane remained a wreck, still full of Daesh bombs and mines that needed to be cleared by experts. An international campaign to rebuild it had begun, but the effort needed more support than it was getting, particularly from international agencies. Kobane was now home to two hundred thousand refugees whom the Kurdish community was supporting without much help from anyone. There were not enough standing buildings to house the refugees and none could be built without materials, construction equipment, and financial aid. And Turkey continued to refuse to open the border, so the few supplies that were available could not get through.[39]

The border between Syria and Iraq was also closed most of the time. Not only did Barzani's Kurdish Democratic Party have a long and contentious rivalry with the PKK and, by extension, the Syrian PYD, but its commercial interests tied it to Turkey, as Heval Dostar, the head of the Kobane Reconstruction Board, told reporters from the English left-wing journal *Red Pepper* in January 2016. "For two months now there has been an absolute embargo and for one month there has even been no cement allowed through. This is a big problem as winter is coming. We urgently need a humanitarian corridor opened. . . . Sometimes they allow things to come through but it requires a lot of politics on our side. They will not allow building materials to pass. They allow basic things after a lot of political pressure from us, but nothing that will make a positive long-term impact to our reconstruction work.

Ther journalists saw no sign of international foreign aid anywhere. Dostar explained, "On 1 July 2015, there was a large conference in Brussels about the reconstruction of Kobanê. A lot of NGOs and parliamentarians attended and their reaction was supportive and positive in providing aid to us. But this has not been so in practice. Many NGOs have been here and have made many promises to remove mines and work on water and sewage, for example, but not much has been delivered. Also, when major NGOs try to bring over medicines and equipment, it's often not allowed to come through. An individual with a small package can come through, but this has a very small impact. It's the same on both borders." After the November 2015 election, Turkey prevented any international NGO from entering Kobane; they even turned away Doctors Without Borders.[40]

The military front was progressing more rapidly than reconstruction. In October 2015, the PYD announced the formation of the Syrian Democratic Forces, a new unified military grouping comprised of the YPG-YPJ, new Yazidi militias formed under the leadership of the PKK, and Arab brigades, including the Euphrates Volcano. The US Congress had already appropriated $721 million to supply Syrian rebels; the formation of the SDF permitted some of these supplies to get to the Kurds. On October 12, US planes dropped the first 50,000 tons of ammunition. There was speculation that one of the new force's first tasks might be to capture Raqqa.[41]

Sinjar had already been recaptured on November 12, 2015, after fifteen months in the hands of Daesh. It was taken by a combined force of the Iraqi KDP *peshmerga*, Syrian YPG-YPJ, and the new Yazidi militias. The victory was not without its problems, as reported by *The New York Times*: "The head of the Iraqi Kurdish government, President Masoud Barzani, held a news conference on Mount Sinjar to hail the retaking of the town and made clear that it would formally be incorporated into Kurdistan. 'Aside from the Kurdistan flag, no other flag will rise in Sinjar.' As he uttered those words, however, a different flag was also prominently displayed in Sinjar—that of the rival PKK separatist movement, along with the banners of its Syrian Kurdish offshoot. After weeks of efforts by the Kurdistan government to sideline the PKK during the Sinjar campaign, the rival fighters bitterly insisted that they had in fact led the fighting . . . for months."[42]

Retaking Sinjar had been in the works for some time, but was held up by the rivalry between the PKK and the KDP. Nor were the Iraqi Kurds happy that the Yazidi had formed their own militias and were talking about setting up a canton. To Barzani's people this clearly meant that they were under PKK influence. According to Siddik Hasan Sukru, a political analyst in Erbil, Turkey was stirring the pot to keep the disagreement going, partly for logistical reasons: "If Sinjar stays in the hands of the PKK or its partisans, it will . . . provide Rojava with an outlet to the outside world. But if the KDP dominates Sinjar . . . the YPG and the PYD will be encircled."[43]

## The Backlash Begins

After the battle of Kobane, an ideological and political war heated up, led by Turkey, with support from its allies in the KDP and the Syrian opposition.

In 2012, after all the Kurdish groups walked out of the Syrian opposition's coalition, Masoud Barzani, in an attempt to become the major Kurdish power broker in Syria, put together a Kurdish National Council. It consisted of sixteen very small parties, most of them close to Barzani's KDP in Iraq. Despite major political differences, the PYD also joined this coalition and signed what was known as the Erbil Agreement that June, committing to form a united Kurdish front against the Syrian government.

Joining a coalition was one thing; agreeing on its structure was another. Integration of militias became a major issue; the tribal leaders of the small parties wanted to keep their own militias, which were classically a source of revenue. Remembering the fratricidal war between the Iraqi Kurdish parties in the nineties, as well as past KDP attacks on the PKK, the PYD insisted that any Kurdish militia that wanted to operate in Rojava had to come under a unified YPG-YPJ command. (Barzani has had his own problems with similar issues in Iraq; despite considerable US pressure to form a single professionalized army, the KDP and PUK *peshmerga* have both remained under the control of their separate political parties, and a newly-formed Yazidi militia in Sinjar has struggled to remain independent from the KDP command.)[44]

In May 2012, a delegation from the Kurdish National Council visited Washington and met with former US Ambassador to Syria Robert Ford, Assistant Secretary for Near East Affairs Jeffrey Feltman, and Frederic Hof, the US envoy to the Syrian opposition. According to Ford, the KNC asked the US for military aid that would "allow them to challenge the PYD as the preeminent force in Syria's Kurdish areas, as well as megaphones, equipment for home hospitals, generators, satellite phones, and help setting up satellite TV channels." When asked by *Foreign Policy* if the KNC also wanted American weapons, Ford said, "Of course they did," but added that Washington did not offer to provide any. The KNC also asked for money to counter Muslim Brotherhood influence within the Syrian opposition, saying that the Brotherhood was buying people's votes and they needed to be able to do the same. This wish was not fulfilled either. At some point in 2012, the US realized the KNC had no base and opened up a back channel to negotiate directly with the PYD.[45]

Some of the sixteen parties in the Kurdish National Council eventually decided to work with the PYD and joined TEV-DEM, while others remained outside. None were very large, nor did they have the reputation of being able to get a lot done, while the PYD was seen as efficient, especially on security matters. Siamend Hajo, one of the editors of *Kurd-Watch*, an online human rights monitor, described the PYD as clearly having more experience "than the other Syrian Kurdish parties; they make the youth feel involved by giving them responsibilities, such as taking care of security in neighbourhoods. They have sold gasoline at a discounted price; they have paid house visits to poor families and provided similar services. By contrast, several youths complained that the KNC had squandered money it had received from the KRG [Kurdistan Regional Government in Iraq]. They sent a representative to the KRG to complain about its decision to give money to KNC individuals instead of to the KNC as an institution, and then this representative was given money ... and he also took it for himself."[46]

Meanwhile, Turkey was using its NATO position and the threat of loosing more refugees into Europe to create diplomatic and ideological opposition to Rojava. It made unfulfilled promises of participation in the war against Daesh to win Western support for its anti-Rojava position, and maintained a fleet of lobbyists to the tune of $5 million a year. In the summer of 2015 it hired former director of the CIA Porter Goss, among others, to make its war on the Kurds more palatable to the US.

According to Harut Sassounian, an Armenian-American journalist, Ankara's roster of lobbyists in 2016 included the law firm Squire Patton Boggs, which it paid $32,000 a month. Former Senators Trent Lott and John Breaux, and former White House official Robert Kapla were all on the payroll. But Squire Patton Boggs was merely a sub-contractor to the powerful lobbying firm The Gephardt Group, whose team for Turkey also consisted of other subcontractors, such as Greenberg Traurig, Brian Forni, Lydia Borland, and Dickstein Shapiro LLP (where Porter Goss worked). Other firms hired by Turkey, according to Sassounian, were: "Goldin Solutions, Alpaytac, Finn Partners, Ferah Ozbek, and Golin/Harris International. . . . Furthermore, several US nonprofit organizations serve as fronts for the Turkish government to promote its interests in the United States and take members of Congress and journalists on all-expense paid junkets to Turkey."[47]

While Turkey has spent millions on lobbyists, the Rojava self-administration has not even had the resources to set up a Washington office. It is thus no surprise that Salih Muslim has been unable to get a US visa since 2012, despite numerous speaking invitations.[48] Nor has Washington been alone in its deference to Turkey. The EU gave Erdogan strong, if unstated, support in his November 1 electoral campaign for absolute power, despite his countless violations of democratic norms, as Robert Ellis pointed out in *The Independent*:

"The AKP interim government's conduct prior to the elections has, by any democratic standards, been outrageous. Under the leadership of Erdogan's stooge, former foreign minister and now prime minister, Ahmet Davutoglu, it has instigated attacks on what is left of the free press, culminating in the takeover of the Koza Ipek media group, including two dailies and two TV stations, five days before the elections, converting it into a propaganda outlet for the government. . . . The EU's role in the whole business is entirely shameful. In an attempt to appease Erdogan, the publication of a critical progress report on Turkey has been delayed by the EU Commission until after the elections, and a fortnight before the elections Germany's chancellor, Angela Merkel, paid a visit to Turkey, which was seen as tacit support for Erdogan's regime. In an attempt to stem the flood of refugees heading for Europe, the EU has offered a number of incentives to Turkey: €3 billion in aid, the restart of membership talks, visa-free travel to the Schengen area from 2016, and an invitation to Turkish leaders to EU summits."[49]

After the battle of Kobane, an anti-Rojava narrative of war crimes and ethnic cleansing began to make the rounds among Western governments and NGOs. In 2015, the German Foreign Office funded a strategic report on dealing with Rojava by Khaled Yacoub Oweis, who had previously reported for Reuters and had good contacts in the Syrian opposition.[50] Entitled "The West's Darling in Syria," the report was subheaded "Seeking Support, the Kurdish Democratic Union Party Brandishes an Anti-Jihadist Image," and presented the PYD as a sinister force. The report warned that the US, despite the risks of "deepening an Arab Sunni backlash that has fanned radicalization," was set on the PYD retaking "mostly Arab Territory captured by the Islamic State." It dismisses the PYD's project of democratic autonomy as a mixture of Marxist jargon and "a vague form of social democracy," with emphasis on women's and minority rights.[51]

Oweis's main line of attack was clearly drawn from the Syrian opposition and, ignoring the fact that most Kurds are Sunnis, albeit secular ones, mobilized the same Sunni grievance narrative that is gospel to Daesh and other Islamists. He accused the PYD of building a "militia which could be allied to Assad from the country's minorities," and said people in the Syrian opposition preferred the Islamists as a "bulwark against perceived Kurdish expansionism at the expense of Arab Sunnis." He accused the PYD of having killed at least thirty Kurds who opposed them, and, recycling an old accusation that had been long since proven false, said the PYD murdered Mashaal Tammo, an activist who wanted the Kurds to stay in the Syrian National Council and was assassinated by Assad's intelligence service in October 2011.[52]

Although Tammo's murder had been publicly laid at the door of the Assad government, Oweis used this and other accusations of human rights abuses to discredit Rojava and try to persuade Europeans not to support the Syrian Kurds. He wrote that "it would be a mistake for Berlin to toe the US line and support the PYD/YPG in the fight against the Islamic State beyond the Kurdish areas. The PYD has not only silenced other Kurdish voices, it has also been accused of ethnic cleansing in villages and towns inhabited mainly by Arabs, and it maintains cooperation with the Assad regime. Too strong a support will also further antagonize Turkey as well as rebel formations."[53]

This tone of alarm at US aid to the Kurds was also, surprisingly, echoed in attacks on the PYD by Amnesty International. The press release for a report posted on October 13, 2015, by Lama Fakih, a Senior Crisis Advisor, was headlined, "Syria: US ally's razing of villages amounts to war crimes." The story alleged "a wave of forced displacement and home demolitions amounting to war crimes" committed by YPG-YPJ troops in villages recaptured from Daesh.

The second sentence says, "The Autonomous Administration is a key ally, on the ground, of the US-led coalition fighting against the armed group calling itself the Islamic State (IS) in Syria." But rather than directing its demands for redress of violations at the accused offender, as is normally done, the press release goes on:

"'It is critical that the US-led coalition fighting IS in Syria and all other states supporting the Autonomous Administration, or co-ordinating with it militarily, do not turn a blind eye to such abuses. They must take a public stand condemning forced displacement and unlawful demolitions and ensure their military assistance is not contributing to violations of international humanitarian law,' said Lama Fakih. 'In its fight against IS, the Autonomous Administration appears to be trampling all over the rights of civilians who are caught in the middle. We saw extensive displacement and destruction that did not occur as a result of fighting. This report uncovers clear evidence of a deliberate, co-ordinated campaign of collective punishment of civilians in villages previously captured by IS, or where a small minority were suspected of supporting the group.'"[54]

The report spread like wildfire through the media but, though it was taken as credible, a close examination of its approach raised many red flags. It is highly unusual for recommendations in a human rights report to be addressed to a third party, in this case the US, rather than the people who committed the alleged offenses. This alone would suggest a political agenda. Such was the conclusion of YPG commander Sipan Hemo, who forcefully rebutted the suggestions of ethnic cleansing in an interview two days after the Amnesty report was released:

"I can tell you that the timing and wording of this report is a bit suspicious. . . . [It] comes right after the coalition forces are giving us significant aid. . . . Thirty percent of YPG [is] made up of Arabs. . . . If such things were true, would they fight alongside us in Jazira and Kobane? We believe such reports want to harm our image. In our opinion, [the] Syrian National Coalition and forces behind it have a lot to do with this."[55]

The allegations in the Amnesty report were also challenged by the head of Dutch Catholic Charities who had been on the spot; by Macer Gifford, a British volunteer with the YPG; and by the YPG High Command, which offered a line-by-line rebuttal, calling the report "arbitrary, biased, unprofessional and politicized." The YPG noted that the report relied on aerial photos featured on Syrian coalition websites hostile to the Kurds, and that the destruction shown could easily have been the result of shelling or buildings being blown up by Daesh. "Under IS . . . village houses were looted, demolished, filled with oil tanks and burned to create smokescreens to mislead the coalition forces' jets and our fighters, before retreating from an area in which they were dispelled, leaving behind complete destruction."[56] The YPG also alleged that information for the report was provided by one Anwar Al Katav, the commander of an Islamic battalion, who was involved in deporting Kurds and looting their properties in Tal Abyad and its surrounding villages, and who now worked for the Syrian National Council in Turkey. Amnesty has not responded to the allegation that its report relied on tainted sources.

Around the same time, Amnesty also published a report accusing the YPG of arbitrary detention and blatantly unfair trials.[57] Feminist human rights activist Gita Sahgal, former head of Amnesty's gender desk who left the organization in 2010 after a public dispute about their relationship to a UK pro-jihadi organization, responded to the report, noting that the "PYD has engaged extensively with human rights organisations in the middle of an existential human rights struggle for its existence. They have, as Amnesty acknowledged, provided free access and opportunities to talk to prisoners. Governments do sometimes do this—but how many Middle East governments do so? How many can be found free from torture? How many attempt to, in the main, treat prisoners who may be fighters and constitute a wartime threat, humanely? They are not meeting the very highest international standards, but unlike most prisons in the Middle East they are not found to be torturing or ill-treating prisoners and Amnesty is not alleging that they are keeping black sites. In fact, for an armed group which has never had time to properly establish a state they are quite remarkable. The headline for this could very well be 'Western ally allows human rights access. No torture found though some concerns remain.'"[58]

In July 2015, Badirkan Ali, drawing on an investigation made by the UN Council for Human Rights, wrote in *Jadaliyya* that the only ethnic cleansing going on in northern Syria had been done first by Islamist and Arab nationalist groups in the Free Syrian Army and then by Daesh, and it had been directed not at Arabs or Turkmen but at Armenians and Kurds. Elements of the Free Syrian Army had destroyed the

Armenian church and driven Kurds from Tel Ahyad and surrounding villages. The false accusations against the Rojava Kurds, he wrote, further cemented "the idea that there is a zero-sum conflict between Kurds and Arabs in Syria. . . and were disseminated as propaganda to cover up what happened earlier, in which Kurds were uprooted from the area even before ISIS emerged in the region."[59]

The Oweis and Amnesty reports were part of a process of building an anti-Rojava narrative of war crimes and ethnic cleansing that began during the successful YPG-YPJ campaign to drive Daesh out of Tal Abyad. Rami Abdulrahman, founder of the Syrian Observatory for Human Rights, generally considered the most authoritative source on events in Syria, was asked in June 2015 about such allegations. He replied, "There's no 'ethnic cleansing' in Til Abyad against the Turkmen and Arabic population. If the YPG would have wanted to expel Arabs and Turkmens, it would have done so already during the liberation of the villages. Nevertheless . . . in some villages, like in Dogan or Al Bajela, the inhabitants were prevented from returning to the villages for a longer period of time because IS fighters were still expected to be in the villages. . . . Within the Syrian chaos, people need a perspective. . . . People in Syria have to see examples for a peaceful togetherness in their own country. And North Syria could become an example for [the] whole [of] Syria."[60]

Preventing such an example from taking hold may be the point of false human rights accusations, which represent a point of view that finds it inconceivable that different ethnic groups and religions could live together and treat one another decently, at least in the Middle East. This view is held not only by Arab nationalists, Islamists, and Daesh, but also by US conservatives like John Bolton, who said the only solution for Syria and Iraq was partition along ethnic and religious lines, as in the former Yugoslavia.[61] As the YPG Command stressed in its response to Amnesty, seeing Rojava through this prism could only "contribute to [the] deepening of ethnic tensions as it portrays the ongoing conflict as sectarian war between the Kurds and Arabs. . . . The reality on the ground is completely different and the area enjoys a peaceful coexistence among different ethnic and religious components."[62]

While war crimes by YPG-YPJ members are not impossible, from all accounts of how the Rojava cantons operate, if they occurred, they would have been taken very seriously. As Sahgal noted, the Rojava administration has been unusually open to human rights investigators and, far from waiting for pressure from international agencies, the YPG-YPJ investigates and prosecutes possible human rights violations themselves.

For example, the fighter interviewed on Reddit during the siege of Kobane blew up a house that had been booby trapped by ISIS and the fire spread and burned down half the village. He was arrested and jailed until an investigation showed the property destruction had been accidental.[63]

It was no surprise that members of the Syrian opposition who believed, with the Muslim Brotherhood, that "Islam is the solution," would become uneasy when facing the very different solution being developed by radical Kurds. Rojava represents a secular, democratic, and feminist way forward in a region stereotyped by many as hopelessly backward.

Salih Muslim proudly summed up the first two years of the autonomous cantons: "We have created, in the middle of the civil war in Syria, three independent cantons in the Rojava region that function by democratic, autonomous rule. Together with the ethnic and religious minorities of the region—Arabs, Turkmen, Assyrians, Armenians, Christians, Kurds—we have written a collective political structure for these autonomous cantons: our *social contract*. We have established a people's council including 101 representatives from all cooperatives, committees, and assemblies running each of our cantons. And we established a model of co-presidency . . . and a quota of 40 percent gender representation in order to enforce gender equality throughout all forms of public life and political representation. We have, in essence, developed a democracy without the state. That is a unique alternative in a region plagued by the internally conflicted Free Syrian Army, the Assad regime, and the self-proclaimed Islamic State."[64]

Rojava has also taken in hundreds of thousands of refugees in a flood that seems neverending, while the aid to refugees that was supposed to reach them has been siphoned off by the Syrian opposition or blocked at the border by Turkey. To date, there has been no significant economic investment in Rojava by anyone, and certainly no open political support, least of all from the US. Instead, NATO has fretted over how to make Turkey behave without finding an answer, and the attention of world leaders has been fixed on either war or great power negotiations.

Through it all, Rojava has continued to struggle to support and protect its people. Hawzhin Azeez, an Australian Kurdish academic and member of the Kobane Reconstruction Board, posted a cry from the heart in January 2016 that echoed the appeal from Afrin Canton:

"There is a big difference between bags of cement and iron and glass not being allowed to come to Kobane across the borders versus life-saving medicine and equipment. I was just informed by the health board that they are desperately running out of medicine. They have equipment to conduct surgery but no medicine for the surgery. They have ambulances but there is no point in sending sick people from villages to hospitals empty of medication where their lives can't be saved. . . . We have boxes and containers of medicine and equipment that are sitting on the Basur [Iraqi Kurdistan] and Bakur [Turkey] borders but deliberately not allowed through, and the medicine expires and babies die and we are left feeling unbearable anguish—a state of permanent emotional existence for the choiceless, the colonized, those whose lives and that of their communities are designated as worthless by invisible hands, voices, and faces but who determine our fates every day."[65]

These conditions helped create the massive refugee crisis in Europe. Rather than trying to bribe Turkey to keep the refugees from fleeing, a far better solution would have been for the EU to pressure the KRG and Turkey to open their borders, so the Rojava cantons could rebuild and some of those who thought they could only find a better life in Europe could try to make one where they were.

*Captured Daesh flag, Tel Hamis, Cizire Canton, Rojava.*

CHAPTER 8

# The Birth of Daesh

No ONE WOULD CALL the members of Daesh "moderate Islamists."
But while Daesh is a grotesquely violent version of Islamism,
its beliefs on the subject of women differ only in degree, not in kind,
from those of the Muslim Brotherhood, Turkey's AKP, and Iran's Shia
militias. This is why distinctions between violent and non-violent
Islamists do not hold up for feminists; both kinds are purposefully
violent against women.

Like other fundamentalists—Christian, Hindu, or Jewish—Islamists
do not believe there should be any separation between religious and
civil law. They want to impose their own codes on everyone else. Their
goal is a caliphate—a state founded upon the strictest possible interpretations of seventh century laws that systematically discriminate against
women along with sexual and religious minorities.

Some Islamists, like those of al Qaeda, think only a world war with
the US could bring the caliphate into being. Others, like the Muslim
Brotherhood, believe in a strategy of charity work and organizing
as a means to win power through elections; once in power, they can
impose their version of sharia law on others. The deposed government
of Mohamed Morsi in Egypt followed that plan. Its politicization of
religion became so unpopular that a million people turned out in a
demonstration calling for its removal, which ended up bringing the
military back into power a year after it had been overthrown. Turkey's
AKP, a similar party, has exhibited the same combination of grandi-
osity, paranoia, and authoritarianism. But whether their strategy is
to seize power by force or to win it through elections, Islamist groups
share a certain set of beliefs. In *The Looming Tower*, his book about al
Qaeda, journalist Lawrence Wright explains:

They believe that the five hundred Quranic verses that constitute the basis of Sharia are the immutable commandments of God, offering a road back to the perfected era of the Prophet and his immediate successors—although the legal code actually evolved several centuries after the Prophet's death. These verses comment upon behavior as precise and various as how to respond to someone who sneezes and the permissibility of wearing gold jewelry. They also prescribe specific punishments for some crimes, such as adultery and drinking, but not for others, including homicide.

Islamists say the Sharia cannot be improved upon, despite fifteen centuries of social change, because it arises directly from the mind of God. They want to bypass the long tradition of judicial opinion from Muslim scholars and forge a more authentically Islamic legal system that is untainted by Western influence or any improvisations caused by the engagement with modernity. Non-Muslims and Islamic modernists, on the other hand, argue that the tenets of Sharia reflect the stringent Bedouin codes of the culture that gave birth to the religion and are certainly not adequate to govern a modern society.[1]

Sunni fundamentalists are often called salafis, because they want to return to the time of the "salaf" (past) and discard the entire body of interpretation since. Those who want to get there by making war—jihad—are called salafi-jihadis. Salafis are extremely intolerant of other versions of Islam and have a deeply conservative and patriarchal view of the family, gender, sexuality, and women.[2] They stand against the politics and culture of the modern world (though they are happy to adopt its weapons and social media), which is to them a corrupt world of unbelief called *jahiliyya,* tainted by materialism, secularism, and women's liberation.

In addition to other salafi beliefs, jihadis embrace the notion of the "defense of Muslim lands," meaning not only the lands of the historical caliphate but any country where a lot of Muslims live, including places where people practice other forms of Islam and therefore must be brought to the correct path. Some Muslim groups, such as the Shia, Sufis, and Ahmadis, are considered *kuffar* (unbelievers) who must convert or be killed. Christians and Jews, the "people of the book," must also convert or else be made to pay a special tax on non-Muslims called *jizya*; Hindus, atheists, and polytheists—like the Yazidis—are so low they must be killed or enslaved.

The salafi-jihadis of al Qaeda and, later, Daesh, view jihad in military terms, as a physical fight, not a spiritual one, and make no distinction between killing civilians and noncivilians. In their view, every believer is obligated to take up military jihad, and not just for defense. They are expected to use the sword to make converts to the faith. In the words of Anwar al-Awlaki, the American-born jihadi killed by US drones in Yemen, the intention of jihad is to establish the Muslim community or *umma* as a global caliphate in which unbelievers would either be "wiped out" or live under Sharia law as religious minorities, second-class citizens with few rights.[3]

Conservatives and anti-immigrant bigots in the West attribute salafi beliefs to all Muslims. They say jihad is intrinsic to Islam because the Koran is full of references to it. By the same logic, one could say that polygamy is intrinsic to Judaism because the first five books of the Bible are full of patriarchs with multiple wives, or that all Catholics believe heretics should be burnt at the stake because that's what they did in the early Church.

But if most Sunni Muslims are not fundamentalists, how did Islamists get so strong?

While there are many answers to this question, including dictator-ships, stagnant economies, and US-led wars, one is certainly Saudi Arabia. The Saudis and their oil money have played a seminal role in spreading Islamism around the world. According to Vali Nasr of Georgetown University, "Saudi Arabia has been the single biggest source of funding for fanatical interpretations of Islam, and the embodiment of that inter-pretation in organizations and schools has created a self-perpetuating institutional basis for promoting fanaticism across the Muslim world."[4] In cables released by Wikileaks in 2010, then-US Secretary of State Hill-ary Clinton acknowledged that Saudi donors were the most significant source of support for jihadi groups worldwide, and that, despite the US-Saudi alliance, the US had not been able to put a dent in this support.[5]

Saudis were essential to the development of al Qaeda, the parent group of Daesh—as were the US and Pakistan. In 1979, when the Soviet Union invaded Afghanistan, a radical Islamist scholar named Abdullah Azzam—a key figure in the Muslim Brotherhood, who was originally from Palestine but had taught in Saudi Arabia and was then teaching in Pakistan—issued a fatwa, or Islamic legal ruling, "Defense of the Muslim Lands: The First Obligation after Ima[n]."[6] Azzam said that defending Muslim lands against invaders was an absolute duty and called upon young men to make jihad by coming to Afghanistan to fight the Soviets. With money and help from Osama bin Laden, a rich Saudi, he set up the Afghan Services Bureau, which recruited thousands of foreign fighters and bought air tickets for them to come to Peshawar in Pakistan, where he established military training camps and guest houses for them. The US and Saudi Arabia helped finance and equip these jihadis, channeling most of their aid through Pakistan's Inter-Services Intelligence (ISI).[7]

In 1989, the USSR, exhausted and at the point of dissolution, pulled its troops out of Afghanistan. By that time, Osama bin Laden was already looking farther afield. In February 1988, he and Abdullah Azzam had organized a secret meeting with leaders of the Egyptian group, Islamic Jihad, and others at which they agreed to internationalize the struggle once the Soviets left. This was the founding meeting of al Qaeda, whose long-term goal was to build a caliphate, but whose immediate strategy was to provoke a US invasion of Muslim countries that would radicalize believers and make them want to fight.[8]

While al Qaeda had a strong desire to injure the West and start a world war between the US and Muslims everywhere, it had no clear strategy for doing so. Its leaders assumed that if they could design actions that would terrify the West and make it seem vulnerable, Muslims would rise up and the caliphate would follow.

Meanwhile, in southern Afghanistan, the Taliban took power and imposed an extreme form of Islamist rule in which women were forbidden to work outside the home, go to school, or leave the house without being accompanied by a male relative, even if they had no living male relatives or were being rushed to the hospital. Kite flying, music, and mixed gatherings were forbidden, and men were forced to grow beards. In 1996, with military support from Pakistan and money from Saudi Arabia, the Taliban moved north and proclaimed the Emirate of Afghanistan. A new civil war ensued, during which the Taliban committed a number of massacres, notably against Shia Muslims, many of whom belonged to the Hazara ethnic minority. Some eight thousand Shia were murdered in 1998 when the Taliban captured Mazar-e-Sharif.[9]

During this civil war, more foreign fighters found their way to Afghanistan. The Taliban re-opened training camps that had been set up by the CIA and the Pakistani intelligence service and began to train young men from places as far away as China, Bosnia, Algeria, and Chechnya, among others. These young men came to Afghanistan for many reasons: religious fervor, anger at Serbian atrocities against Muslims during the Bosnian war, unemployment, lack of a future in their own countries, idealism, disenfranchisement, racism, a desire for adventure—reasons similar to those that brought foreign fighters to Syria more than a decade later. Some had already fought in Islamist militias in Algeria or Bosnia. They saw Afghanistan as a utopia in the process of being created and wanted to fight alongside the Taliban to make this vision real. Once there, they made contacts that would enable them to eventually bring the war home to their own countries.

When Kabul fell to the Taliban in 1996, Afghanistan became a secure base from which al Qaeda could plan attacks on the West, including the 1998 truck bombings of US embassies in Tanzania and Kenya; the 2000 suicide attack on the USS Cole in Yemen; and the September 11, 2001 suicide attacks on the World Trade Center and Pentagon. After the US invaded Afghaistan in response, al Qaeda was forced to regroup in Pakistan but continued to stage operations: the 2002 bombing of a historic synagogue in Tunisia and an Israeli-owned hotel and plane in Kenya; four 2003 bomb attacks in Istanbul targeting two synagogues, the British consulate, and the HBSC Bank; the 2004 bombing of the Madrid train station; and the 2005 London suicide bomb attacks on trains and a bus.

These attacks were meant to ignite a world war—and they succeeded after 9/11, when President George W. Bush declared a "war on terror," and the US invaded Afghanistan in search of Osama bin Laden. The US-led coalition then followed with the disastrously ill-conceived and mismanaged invasion of Iraq in 2003, based on cooked evidence of "weapons of mass destruction" and fantasies of a connection between al Qaeda and Saddam Hussein. Seizing the opportunity, al Qaeda's foreign fighters brought their skills and weapons to the Middle East.

The year before the American invasion, a Jordanian named Abu Musab al Zarqawi had left Afghanistan to set up an al Qaeda branch in Iraq. By this time bin Laden, hunted by the Americans, was less visible than he had been, and operational leadership had been assumed by an Egyptian, Ayman al-Zawahiri.

Bin Laden and Zawahiri had no problem with killing Muslims they considered *kuffar* but they didn't make it their main emphasis. They assumed that al Qaeda in Iraq (AQI) would focus, as they did, on driving out the American imperialists.[10] But Zarqawi had other ideas. He belonged to a school of salafi-jihadism called Takfir, which believes that Islam itself must be purified before it can take on external enemies. After 2003, Takfirism gained support among al Qaeda's middle leadership and rank and file, and under Zarqawi's leadership, the major emphasis of al Qaeda in Iraq became to kill as many Shia as possible.[11]

The writer David Ignatius described what happened next. When the Americans invaded Iraq, "[Zarqawi] proved willing to ally with remnants of Saddam's intelligence network. Four months after the US invasion, Zarqawi's organization attacked three well-chosen targets—UN headquarters in Baghdad, the Jordanian embassy in Baghdad, and the Imam Ali Mosque, a Shia shrine, in Najaf—that signaled the dirty war ahead. These bombs shattered the ground for reconciliation: Iraq would be a no-go zone for the international organizations that might have lightened the burden of US occupation; Iraq's links would be severed with its mainstream Sunni patron, Jordan; and Iraq would be cleaved apart by a vicious sectarian war between Sunni and Shia Muslims, whose coexistence had been a feature of modern Iraqi life."[12]

Al Qaeda in Iraq might not have made so much headway had the American authorities behaved more intelligently. The Iraqi Army soon crumbled and Saddam went on the run, but nobody in Washington seemed to have made any real transition plan. George W. Bush put Paul Bremer, a not particularly distinguished diplomat with no Middle East expertise, in charge. His first two acts in power were to disband the Iraqi Army and to bar all members of the Baath party from professional positions—which meant, essentially, that he dissolved the government. As journalist Dexter Filkins reported, "Overnight, at least two hundred and fifty thousand Iraqi men—armed, angry, and with military training—were suddenly humiliated and out of work. This was probably the single most catastrophic decision of the American venture in Iraq. In a stroke, the Administration helped enable the creation of the Iraqi insurgency. . . . We'll never know for sure how many

Iraqis would have stayed in the Iraqi Army—and stayed peaceful—had it remained intact. But the evidence is overwhelming that former Iraqi soldiers formed the foundation of the insurgency."[13]

The new dispensation put in place by the US was based on a thoroughly sectarian view of politics: Sunnis had been in charge under Saddam so now Shia should run the government. Paul Bremer handpicked members of the new Iraqi Governing Council, including a number of members of Shia Islamist parties. Among other things, these men declared they planned to change the family law or "personal status" code, which had been written in 1959 by a fairly left-wing government and was one of the most progressive family law codes in the region—it limited divorce proceedings to civil courts, gave women child custody and inheritance rights equal to men's, restricted child marriage, and required that a man get the permission of his first wife before he could take a second one.[14]

Until the nineties, Iraq had had one of the most egalitarian climates for women in the Arab world. Women in the cities dressed as they pleased and went around freely by themselves. But after the Iran-Iraq war and the 1991 Shia and Kurdish uprisings, Saddam courted the support of conservative tribal leaders. He set up colleges for Islamic studies and inscribed "God is Great" upon the Iraqi flag. As Islamists began to gain influence, Baath party officers stopped drinking and started going to mosques and studying salafi texts, and the state began to impose ancient punishments like amputation for theft and beheading for prostitution.[15]

Like other fundamentalists, the rising Iraqi Islamists were obsessed with questions of women's mobility and dress. They assaulted women who wore short skirts, painting their legs as punishment. The government, instead of preventing the attacks, banned short skirts and said women could not go out at night without a male relative. One of the first actions of the new Iraqi Governing Council appointed by Bremer was to pass Resolution 137, overturning parts of the progressive family code. The Iraqi women's movement mounted such a strong protest that Bremer decided not to ratify the IGC's decision, but he would not meet the women's movement's other demands about representation in government and on the committee that was drafting a new constitution. Nor did he take any steps to prevent violence against women. As the violence increased, women soon realized that it was not just a consequence of war, but part of an Islamist strategy to create a state ruled by their version of sharia law.

Changes in the personal status code that Bremer allowed to go through also harmed women. A man was allowed to take a second wife without asking his first wife's permission, and he could be sentenced to as little as six months in jail if he killed a female relative he suspected of immorality.[16]

With the US occupation in full force, Islamization went nuclear, with a predictably devastating effect upon women. As a 2007 report by the American feminist organization MADRE described it, "In spring 2003, as the smoke began to clear from the US invasion of Iraq, a wave of kidnappings, abductions, public beatings, death threats, sexual assaults, and killings gripped the country. The targets were women. US authorities took no action and soon the violence spread. Killings of Iraqi men and foreigners became commonplace as Islamist militias launched a campaign of terror that mushroomed into the civil war now raging across Iraq. While the militias were taking to the streets, their political leaders were taking their seats in a new Iraqi government. With money, weapons, training, and political backing from the United States, Iraqi Islamists have put an end to 85 years of secular rule in Iraq and established an Islamist theocracy. As Yanar Mohammed, director of the Organization of Women's Freedom in Iraq . . . said, 'We used to have a government that was almost secular. It had one dictator. Now we have almost 60 dictators—Islamists who think of women as forces of evil. This is what is called the democratization of Iraq.'"[17]

According to the MADRE report, by the summer of 2003, Islamist "misery gangs" were patrolling the city, attacking women who were not "properly" dressed or who behaved in a manner the men disapproved of. "According to a woman musician, 'If the Islamists see me walking on the street with my flute, they could kill me.'" Female doctors were warned not to treat men and the reverse held for male doctors. Throughout Iraq, cities were "soon plastered with leaflets and graffiti warning women against going out unveiled, driving, wearing makeup, or shaking hands and socializing with men. Islamist "punishment committees" sprang up, manned by the Badr Brigade of the US-backed SCIRI Party and its rival, the Mahdi Army. . . . In Basra, the Mahdi Army ensured that women were virtually confined to their homes.

Wearing pants or appearing in public without a headscarf became punishable by death."[18]

As Shia fundamentalists took over the government and the streets of Baghdad, the Sunni fundamentalists of al Qaeda in Iraq organized resistance in Anbar Province in the Sunni heartland. Zarqawi's methods included rape, murder, theft, kidnapping, and public beheadings; in fact, al Qaeda in Iraq's rule in Anbar Province was so violent that other Islamists complained to the main al Qaeda leadership. In July 2005, Zawahiri sent Zarqawi a letter of reprimand, saying, "Many of your Muslim admirers amongst the common folk are wondering about your attacks on the Shia. The sharpness of this questioning increases when the attacks are on one of their mosques. . . . My opinion is this matter won't be acceptable to the Muslim populace, however much you try to explain it, and aversion to this will continue. . . . Among the things which the feelings of the Muslim populace . . . will never find palatable are the scenes of slaughtering the hostages."[19]

Zarqawi did not listen. In 2006, al Qaeda in Iraq blew up the al-Askari mosque in Samarra, one of Shia Islam's holiest sites. By doing this, he hoped to provoke a sectarian war between Sunnis and the Shia majority, who were now firmly in control of the Baghdad government. He thought that once his fellow Sunnis realized they could fight back, they would wake from their apathy and seize power from the Shia.[20] Zarqawi did succeed in awaking Sunni anger, but they turned against him, not the Shia. Al Qaeda in Iraq had ruled Anbar Province so harshly that the Sunni tribes who originally supported them changed sides in 2006 and joined the Sunni Awakening movement being promoted by the US.[21]

But this did nothing to improve things for Iraqi women, sexual minorities, religious minorities, and secularists. Houzan Mahmoud, the Iraqi Kurdish women's rights activist, wrote that "political Islamists who are friends of the US and who dominate its puppet regime are no less criminal than Zarqawi and his thugs. The Badr corps of the Supreme Council for the Islamic Revolution in Iraq (SCIR) has been a key force in imposing religious totalitarianism on the Iraqi people, wielding its sectarian violence against women, above all. And the Mahdi army of Moqtada al-Sadr was rewarded for its terrorist activities in southern Iraq with seats in the so-called Parliament. Both forces regularly kill women, gay men and lesbians, and trade unionists. In some places Islamists are even ordering farmers to put shorts on their female goats and sheep. And in certain street markets the display of tomatoes and cucumbers is banned due to their association with genital organs."[22]

Under the sectarian government in Baghdad, everyday life grew more and more difficult. While women continued to organize, they had to be extremely cautious to avoid becoming an assassination target for the government or Islamists. A reporter for *The Independent* wrote in 2006, "Across Iraq, a bloody and relentless oppression of women has taken hold. Many women had their heads shaved for refusing to wear a scarf or have been stoned in the street for wearing make-up. Others have been kidnapped and murdered for crimes that are being labelled simply as 'inappropriate behaviour.' The insurrection against the fragile and barely functioning state has left the country prey to extremists whose notion of freedom does not extend to women."[23]

According to scholar and activist Nadje al-Ali, writing in 2013, "Acute violence in the form of car bombs and targeted assassinations, as well as kidnapping, forced prostitution, trafficking, and honour-based crimes are only the tip of the iceberg of much deeper and widespread forms of gender-based violence. Furthermore, there is a constant policing of women's involvement in public activities, employment, general behaviour within the home and family, and dress code both by state and non-state actors."[24]

The situation became so bad that by 2016 much of the work of OWFI, the Organization for Women's Freedom in Iraq, was focused on setting up safe houses for battered and trafficked women trying to escape the militias.[25] Despite its talk of human rights, in Iraq as in Afghanistan, the US had merely supported one group of Islamists against another.

## Daesh is Born

In June 2006, Zarqawi was killed and the new leaders of al Qaeda in Iraq, Abu Ayyub al-Masri and Abu Omar al-Baghdadi, announced a name change to the Islamic State in Iraq. A lot of their people had been put in prison by the Americans, but that turned out to work in their favor, because the large American prisons—especially Camp Bucca, where al Qaeda/Islamic State in Iraq had its own wing—permitted inmates to meet freely. As a jihadi called Abu Ahmed told *The Guardian*, "We could never have all got together like this in Baghdad, or anywhere else. . . . It would have been impossibly dangerous. Here, we were not only safe, but we were only a few hundred metres away from the entire al-Qaida leadership."[26]

In Camp Bucca, al Qaeda members also met former Baathist security operatives and military men, including Samir Abd Muhammad al-Khlifawi, known as Haji Bakr, who had been a weapons expert and colonel in Saddam Hussein's intelligence service.[27] A number of former Baathists became Islamists in prison, at least nominally, and in 2010, when the two leaders of al Qaeda/Islamic State in Iraq were killed, these newly converted ex-Baathists became the power behind the throne. They chose a well-connected Iraqi cleric, Abu Bakr al-Baghdadi, to be their official leader.[28]

The Syrian civil war gave them their big opportunity. Syria was a dictatorship controlled by the Assad family and the Baathist party which, like Saddam Hussein's Baath party in Iraq, was nominally secular but was, in fact, founded on power politics and manipulating ethnic and religious differences. The Assads are Alawi, a minority Muslim sect that is considered Shia by salafis. In March 2011, the Arab Spring protests spread to Syria, and civil society groups and students began to demonstrate against the government. These demonstrations were initially peaceful and anti-sectarian, but Assad's military and police attacked the demonstrators so viciously that by the summer, soldiers began to defect and join the rebellion. At the same time, some demonstrators decided they had to take up arms to defend their villages from the government. Thus the Free Syrian Army was born, with the mission of overthrowing Assad; it was soon joined by various Islamist militias.

Since 2003 Bashar Assad, eager to embarrass the US, had been letting jihadis en route to fight in Iraq pass through his airports. Syrian Army officers would even escort them from their planes to the Iraq border. Some ninety percent of suicide bombers in Iraq entered through Syria.[29] Thus the Syrian security police had longstanding ties with members of the branch of al Qaeda now calling itself the Islamic State in Iraq. Some of its fighters were Syrians and, in 2004 and 2005, as their organization lost traction in Iraq, they began to come home. Anticipating that they would want to take on Assad's security forces, the Syrian government arrested them and put them in storage on a special floor of the Sednaya Prison, dubbing the floor the al Qaeda wing.

Like Camp Bucca in Iraq, Sednaya was a great place for Islamic

State members to get acquainted. One ex-prisoner told reporter Rania Abouzeid, "When I was detained, I knew four or five or six, but when I was released I knew 100, or 200 or 300. I now had brothers in Hama and Homs and Daraa and many other places, and they knew me."[30]

In 2011, as antigovernment demonstrations became bigger and more heated, Assad declared a selective amnesty. He let members of the Muslim Brotherhood and residents of the al Qaeda wing in Sednaya Prison out of jail, while continuing to imprison democratic opponents of the regime. Assad knew the jihadis he released from prison would take up arms, and thus allow him to say that the Syrian revolution was led by terrorists who wanted to kill Syrian minorities. It is fair to say that Daesh was fathered not only by al Qaeda and by ex-Baathists in Iraq but by the Assad government in Syria.[31]

In August 2011, during Ramadan, the Islamic State in Iraq sent eight men across the border into Syria, led by Abu Mohammad al-Julani, a Syrian who had gone to Iraq to fight the US and ended up in Camp Bucca. His mission was to start a branch of al Qaeda in Syria. Julani scooped up the prisoners released from Sednaya and recruited others eager to fight. On January 23, 2012, he released an audiotape announcing the formation of a new Islamist army to fight Assad, called the Jabhat al-Nusra, or the al-Nusra Front. He didn't say anything about his connection with al Qaeda. Zarqawi had given the organization in Iraq such a bad name that Julani decided that al-Nusra would have to prove itself before mentioning its origins. He told his troops that first they would "show our values, deal with people well, and then after a while we'd tell them, 'The al Qaeda that was smeared in the media? This is it. We are it. What do you think of us—Jabhat al-Nusra?'"[32]

Better armed, equipped, and trained than most of Assad's other opponents, Jabhat al-Nusra quickly made its mark. For one thing, they used suicide bombers, which other groups in Syria did not. And unlike al Qaeda in Iraq, killing Shia or minorities was not their first priority. Instead, they presented themselves as patriotic Syrian nationalists. To ingratiate themselves, they distributed flour to bakeries as well as fighting Assad, and villagers told reporters that al-Nusra did not impose its fundamentalism on the communities it controlled—not at first.

By the summer of 2012, Jabhat al-Nusra was the dominant fighting group in four provinces of Syria: Raqqa, Idlib, Dier ez-Zor, and Aleppo. By December 2012, they had become so popular that when the US put them on the terrorist list as an affiliate of al Qaeda in Iraq, demonstrators marched with signs saying the only terrorists were in the Assad government. Even Syrian opposition leaders in exile condemned the US listing.[33] They all thought Jabhat al-Nusra was a homegrown Syrian group that might be a little too religious but just wanted to fight Assad.

Back in Iraq, Baghdadi was not pleased. As the profile of Jabhat al-Nusra and Julani grew ever more shining in jihadi chat rooms, he no doubt started to wonder what the Islamic State of Iraq was getting out of all this publicity. Nobody even knew that Baghdadi was the emir who had sent Julani into Syria in 2011 and had funded Jabhat al-Nusra for more than two years. Surely the world had a right to know who was really responsible for all this success?

On April 8, 2013, Baghdadi released an audio message saying, "it is time to declare to the Levant and to the world that the al-Nusra Front is simply a branch of the Islamic State of Iraq." From now on, he said, the two organizations were officially merged; the new group would be called ISIL, the Islamic State in Iraq and the Levant—or, as its opponents call it in Arabic, Daesh. He did not bother to tell Julani before dropping this bombshell.

Within a few days, Julani announced that there would be no such merger. Clearly worried that other Syrians might think he was going to behave as Zarqawi had when he was in control of al Qaeda in Iraq, he said, "We reassure our brothers in Syria that al-Nusra Front's behavior will remain faithful to the image you have come to know, and that our allegiance (to al Qaeda) will not affect our politics in any way." Despite this effort, his announcement didn't reassure other Syrian jihadis. A spokesman of the Free Syrian Army rushed to put distance between them, saying, "There has never been and there will never be a decision at the command level to coordinate with al-Nusra."[34]

The quarrel between the two branches of al Qaeda buzzed around jihadi media to such an extent that Zawahiri became alarmed. In June 2013, *Al Jazeera* published a letter containing Zawahiri's official judgment on the feud. Strongly siding with Jabhat al-Nusra, the letter said Baghdadi should stay in Iraq and leave Syria alone. In his capacity as emir of al Qaeda, Zawahiri dissolved the Islamic State in Iraq and the Levant, saying Baghdadi had not been given the authority to set up any such merger. The two men were instructed to work separately for a year, after which they should report back so their work could be judged. In the meantime, they should stop quarreling and keep their men apart.[35]

Because Daesh was part of al Qaeda, Baghdadi was supposed to submit to Zawahiri's authority. But instead of agreeing to disband his operation in Syria and stop using the name Islamic State in Iraq and the Levant, Baghdadi posted on jihadi forums: "The Islamic State of Iraq and the Levant will remain, as long as we have a vein pumping or an eye blinking. It remains and we will not compromise nor give it up."[36]

An online media duel erupted, with each organization calling on the other's fighters to switch camps. On June 20, Islamic State spokesman Abu Mohammed al-Adnani went on the attack, accusing Zawahiri of causing "sedition" by trying to get Jabhat al-Nusra, which had, after all, been started by the Iraqi organization, to secede from it. He also said that in effect, by telling the two jihadi groups each to stay in its own country, Zawahiri was endorsing the national borders created by the hated Sykes-Picot treaty. Real jihadis knew that Islam had no national borders and no country.[37]

But the battle for leadership between Daesh and al Qaeda could not be resolved by polemics. It had to be resolved on the battlefield, by seeing who could take territory and hold it. Al Qaeda had never even tried to set up a governing organization. Would Daesh be able to do so?

Though Julani didn't know it, he was not the only member of the Iraqi organization who had infiltrated Syria. At the end of 2012, Haji Bakr, Saddam's former intelligence colonel, quietly moved to Tal Rifaat in Syria to develop sleeper cells there. The idea was to build a strong base in Syria and use it as a jumping-off place from which to retake Iraq from the Shia government.[38] Haji Bakr's objective was to seize enough territory in both Iraq and Syria to build his kind of caliphate— a pure Islamist state with an all-pervasive intelligence structure that would reach into every area of life, and from which no one would be protected. If this totalitarian vision was reminiscent of the Stasi, it's no accident, for Saddam Hussein's security people were trained by the East German secret police.[39]

Haji Bakr kept a little notebook full of his plans for founding the "Islamic intelligence state." In January 2014, he was killed by a rival militia, who found the notebook and eventually sold it to the German media giant *Der Spiegel*, where it was painstakingly examined by their

Middle East expert, Christoph Reuter. His analysis of Haji Bakr's note-book makes it easy to understand what happened in Raqqa.[40]

## Daesh Comes to Raqqa

In Bakr's game plan, the first step in infiltrating a Syrian town was to open a Dawah office—a missionary center from which to proselytize. Using it as a base, Daesh operatives were to carefully assess the local people who came in and pick one or two to train as spies, telling them to gather information on the most powerful families in the town, their leaders, and the sources of their money. The spies were also instructed to find out everything about other militias in town and their political and religious orientation. Most important, they were told to look for anything the town elite or rebel leaders were doing that violated sharia law and could be used to blackmail or accuse them. Finally, the spies were told to find out which of the powerful families had marriageable daughters, whom some of the "brothers" could be assigned to marry, "to ensure penetration of these families without their knowledge."[41]

And so it went in Raqqa, a relatively isolated city in central Syria, with a largely Sunni population variously estimated as 220,000 to 500,000.[42] Raqqa fell not to Daesh, but to a coalition formed by the Syrian Islamic Front, an umbrella group of Islamist opposition militias. According to Matthew Barber, co-editor of the online journal, *Syria Comment*, the best organized and equipped militia in the Islamic Front was Ahrar al Sham, which took the lead in capturing Raqqa. Its emir, Abu Kha-lid al Suri, was an experienced fighter from Afghanistan and a highly respected commander linked to the Madrid and London bombings.[43] Because he did not want Syrians to think that outsiders were attacking Raqqa, he set up a front group called Liwa Umana al-Raqqa (Brigade of the Trustees of Raqqa), whose fighters were all locals.[44]

On March 2, 2013, Ahrar al Sham led the Islamist coalition in driv-ing Assad's troops out of the city, capturing the governor and the head of the local Baath party. It seemed to have been an easy victory, possibly by prior arrangement, since regime forces manning the eastern check-point pulled out on the morning of the attack and at the same time, all the local members of Assad's security service left the army base.[45] They essentially handed the city's entire eastern district over to Ahrar al Sham and its ally in the battle, Jabhat al-Nusra. Also in the coali-tion that took the city were militias who identified themselves as the

Free Syrian Army, compounding, as Barber said, "the difficulty of distinguishing between Islamist and nationalist energies on the ground." Although a small regime presence remained in the city, on March 5, Liwa Umana al-Raqqa, Ahrar al Sham's front group, announced that it was in charge. Thus Islamism came to Raqqa wearing a familiar face.[46]

Raqqa had a brief flowering of democracy that spring: Doctors, lawyers, and journalists formed professional groups; women and youth organized. By the end of May, forty-two new civil society organizations had registered with the local government. A committee organized a propaganda campaign, "the revolutionary flag represents me," in which artists painted flags all over city walls to challenge the black Islamist flags that were starting to crop up.[47]

Some of those Islamist flags had been planted by Ahrar Al Sham, others by Jabhat al-Nusra, which was strong and had a number of local members. The rebel forces also included a number of other militias, most affiliated with the Free Syrian Army (FSA) and supported by Saudis or Qataris, such as Ahfad al-Rasoul, which means "Descendants of the Prophet."[48]

But under the radar, Haji Bakr's Daesh operatives had quietly infiltrated the city, where they set up a Dawah center according to plan, selected their spies, and went to work. They had competition from al-Nusra at first, but the public dispute between Daesh and al Qaeda broke out just a month after the fall of Raqqa, and when Zawahiri told the two groups to keep away from each other, al-Nusra withdrew and set up a new base 53 kilometers west of the city. Ahrar al Sham also pulled most of its people out of Raqqa and sent its main force north, where it seized the city of Tal Abyad and the border crossing with Turkey, expelling the local Kurds and Armenians.[49]

Once it had uncontested control of Ragga, Daesh began to eliminate anyone who might oppose its rule, starting with secularists and civil society activists. In May 2013, the head of the city council was kidnapped by men in ski masks. Next, the brother of a prominent writer disappeared, then the leader of the artists' group that had painted the revolutionary flags on city walls. People became afraid. On May 14, Daesh executed three Alawites in a public square, saying they were spies for the regime. After that, according to the Lebanese daily *al-Akhbar*, "the secular peaceful protest movement began to gradually wither, at least in the public sphere. Though activists called for peaceful protests to reject violence, their efforts did not pan out, especially as many activists were arrested."[50]

Increasingly threatened, civil society organizations appealed to other militias for protection. They distributed leaflets against Daesh and called on the Free Syrian Army brigades that remained in the city to do something.[51] In response, the FSA's more moderate militias announced they were forming an alliance to protect the people, the September 11th Division. They claimed their members comprised eighty percent of the combat-ready forces in the city.[52]

That year Ramadan began on July 8, and Father Paolo Dall'Oglio came to Raqqa to celebrate with his Muslim friends. An Italian Jesuit priest and lifetime proponent of Muslim-Christian understanding who fasted every Ramadan, Father Paolo had lived in Syria since the 1970s. After siding with the revolution against Assad, he was kicked out of the country, but he snuck back in. He told his friends in Raqqa that while he was there, he would be negotiating with Daesh on behalf of people who had been kidnapped.[53]

On July 29, he took part in a civil society demonstration organized by youth groups. He visited the Daesh headquarters in Raqqa that same afternoon and emerged in high spirits, telling his friends he was leaving for a few days to meet Baghdadi.

He never returned.

His old friend Souad Nawfal, a middle-aged schoolteacher and civil society activist, decided she had to do something. "I started demonstrating because they took Father Paolo," she told a reporter. "He used to come to break the fast at Ramadan in my house. He was coming to speak out against ISIS. He wanted to stop the killings and secrecy, all the stuff the regime does. He went in to speak to ISIS but he never came out."[54]

Defying the pleas of her family, and wearing a hijab (headscarf) and slacks despite the Daesh dress code, which mandated several layers of black niqab, a black head-to-toe garment that covers the face as well, Nawfal stood outside the Daesh headquarters every day. She held hand-made protest signs with slogans such as, "Muslims spilling the blood of Muslims are sinners," or "Our enemy is the criminal regime, not the people."[55] She told a reporter, "Apostate, laywoman, infidel: This is how ISIS members described me while poking me with their guns as I took part in protests. I did not fear them, I used to tell them they are the regime's men with a beard and mask."[56]

It was strictly forbidden for Raqqa civilians to take photos in the streets or record "provocative" behavior in any way. Offenders were beaten with leather straps or taken into custody. Nevertheless, a four-minute video of Souad Nawfal criticizing both Assad and Daesh began to circulate on the internet, titled "The Woman in Pants."[57] Wearing a striped blouse and pink hijab Nawfal spoke directly to the camera:

"What bothers people from the 'Islamic State' most are the pants. They can't imagine that I'm wearing pants. *'If you want to come out and demonstrate, sister, at least put on some decent clothes.'* To them . . . my clothes don't fit with the religion. But that's how I dress at home. And I've been dressing like this for 30 years. . . . *'I don't ask you about being dressed in the Afghan way! I don't ask you why you're sporting a beard! I don't ask why you're wearing a mask!'* How can pants be sinful and not the mask? . . . Masked people, they're up to no good in this area. They kidnap, they steal, they arrest. And no one can complain or anything because we don't know who they are."[58]

Ramadan ended on August 7. Almost immediately, Daesh attacked the largest and least doctrinaire brigade in the Free Syrian Army that remained in Raqqa.[59] The battle lasted days and many civilians died. On August 13, 2013, Daesh sent suicide bombers driving three cars loaded with explosives to the headquarters of the brigade, known as the Descendants of the Prophet. The whole building came down. Dozens of fighters were killed and the rest fled. Civilians were not allowed to tend the wounded or even remove the bodies. The other brigades in the FSA looked on and did nothing because Daesh had made deals and played one off against the other. Survivors from the brigade were either arrested or left Raqqa, while its commander for the whole of Syria said he wouldn't retaliate because of the need to preserve unity against Assad.[60]

A month later, on September 12, Jabhat al-Nusra, the al Qaeda affiliate, returned to Raqqa. Immediately upon the return of al-Nusra, the FSA militias in Raqqa self-destructed and everybody became an Islamist. Some fighters rushed to join al-Nusra; others went over to Daesh or Ahrar al-Sham. "There is no such thing as the FSA [here]. We are all al Qaeda now," said a top rebel commander in Raqqa Province. "Half of the FSA has been devoured by ISIS, and the other half joined

Jabhat al-Nusra." He pointed out that at least al-Nusra was fighting Assad, unlike Daesh. Many locals considered al-Nusra the lesser of two evils, saying they were mostly Syrian, not foreigners.[61]

But Jabhat al-Nusra did not last more than a few days in Raqqa. Its emir was kidnapped by Daesh and his car was found in Aleppo, with the explosive belt he always wore inside. On September 15, al-Nusra pulled out of Raqqa for the second time, vacating the governate, a large fancy building in the center of town. Daesh took it over and put up large signs on all the entrances saying, "The Islamic State of Iraq and Syria—Raqqa Province."[62]

Now in full control, Daesh tightened its stranglehold on the civilian population. It made new rules which segregated boys and girls at school; established sharia courts; set up a Daesh police force; banned smoking; promulgated an even stricter dress code for women; drove minorities out of the city; prevented everyone else from leaving; and arrested foreign aid workers, journalists, and anyone whom they could accuse of un-Islamic activities, including commanders of other militias.[63] The new rules included strict punishments, such as the loss of a hand for stealing. Punishments for rebellion or dissidence included beheading and crucifixion in the public square.

But the same harshness that had driven Iraqi tribesmen away from Zarqawi was now alienating Syrians. As Daesh solidified its hold in Syria, its kidnappings, murders, floggings, and bans on smoking and music became increasingly unpopular in the areas it controlled. In January 2014, revolts broke out in various provinces, aided by Jabhat al-Nusra and other militias. These led to Daesh's final split with al Qaeda. Zawahiri cut all ties, criticizing Baghdadi's lack of consultation and intransigence. "Clearly, Zawahiri believes that ISIS is a liability to the al-Qaeda brand," said Aaron Zelin of the Washington Institute, a US think tank.[64]

Raheb Alwany, a doctor who managed to get to the UK from Raqqa, told a reporter, "In Raqqa, when we were growing up, you could wear what you liked. People there always wanted to enjoy themselves—they loved going out with friends, people would fish or swim in the river." But all that changed when Daesh took control. "Women couldn't go out without being covered in black abayas and niqabs—even their hands. . . . I was the only woman working full time in the hospital, but they made it impossible for me."[65]

Daesh also began to attack churches, removing their crosses and replacing them with the black Islamist flag. When it burned the Sayidat al-Bishara Catholic Church on September 25, several dozen people came out to protest, among them Souad Nawfal. She told other demonstrators it was pointless to protest at the church. They had to go to Daesh headquarters, she said, and proceeded to lead them there. But by the time she arrived at headquarters, she was alone. Everyone else had dropped off along the way.

When Daesh attacked another church the next day, Nawfal went directly to headquarters with her sister Rimal. As usual she had a homemade sign. This time it said, "Forgive me." The message was meant for her family because she was sure she had reached the end of the road and would either be killed or kidnapped.[66]

"They ran after us and stopped us," she said. "My sister Rimal was crying and screaming, grabbing onto the barrel of the militiaman's gun as he screamed, 'You're as good as dead, you infidel, you collaborator,' . . . Rimal cried and begged them to leave me alone as the bullets rained down. I had no idea whether they were shooting at me or into the air."[67]

On October 23, 2013, Daesh invited local notables and religious leaders to a public meeting to discuss their policies. Two men dared to complain about all the killings. One of them, Muhannad Habayebna, a media activist, was found a few days later at the edge of the city, with his hands tied and a bullet through his head. Other civil society advocates received a picture of his corpse on their mobile phones with a text that said, "Are you sad now about your friend?" That night, twenty of the people who had led the democratic revolution in Raqqa fled to Urfa, across the border in Turkey.[68]

By this time, Souad Nawfal was so scared she moved houses every night. She told a reporter, "I love Syria, and my soul is here. We didn't start the revolution so that we can up and leave, but when it gets to the point where they're going to kill my whole family and I am the reason why, I would leave my mother but I will never forget her. And my mother stays inside my soul until she is free. And my mother is Syria."[69]

Nawfal managed to escape to Turkey that December, and later to Europe.[70]

In March 2014, a year after the takeover of Raqqa, Daesh captured Mosul, adding a big piece of Iraq to the area they already controlled in Syria. On June 29, they announced that these conquests meant that the caliphate had been restored, with Baghdadi as its caliph and "the leader of Muslims everywhere." In an audio recording, spokesman Abu Mohamed al-Adnani said, "The legality of all emirates, groups, states, and organisations becomes null by the expansion of the caliph's authority and the arrival of its troops to their areas. . . . Listen to your caliph and obey him. Support your state, which grows every day."[71]

This was a direct challenge not only to the West but to al Qaeda. The dream of all jihadis was a caliphate, an empire of their own. Now Daesh was saying it could not only conquer territory but hold and administer a state. Because the caliph is the leader of all Islamists, all other jihadis, including the members of al Qaeda, were thus being told they had to swear allegiance to Abu Baker al-Baghdadi—the first caliph since the end of the Ottoman Empire.[72]

The effects on al Qaeda were devastating. Jabhat al-Nusra lost so many fighters that two of its spiritual leaders told *The Guardian* al Qaeda was washed up in Iraq and Syria.[73] By founding a caliphate, Daesh had made itself the only game in town. In well-made videos and incessant posts on social media, they carefully defined their international image as a ferocious, seemingly invincible inspiration to Islamists from Nigeria to Pakistan. No alternate versions of their reality were to be tolerated.

Abdel Aziz al-Hamz, a former biology student from Raqqa, now a citizen journalist, told David Remnick of *The New Yorker*, "If you Googled 'Raqqa' in those early days you got their material first and only. . . . So that was one reason why a lot of foreign fighters emigrated. And this is why we began."[74]

In April 2014, after the first crucifixions in Raqqa, he and other young media activists who had fled to Urfa decided to start a website called "Raqqa is Being Slaughtered Silently." Working anonymously with reports and films from friends who had remained in the city, RBSS got the news out to the international media, which came to rely on it as the only solid source of information about what was going on in Raqqa under Daesh rule.

The Committee to Protect Journalists gave RBSS an award in 2015, saying, "Since its inception, RBSS has publicized public lashings, crucifixions, beheadings, and draconian social rules, thus providing the world with a counter-narrative to Islamic State's slickly produced version of events. . . . While RBSS was formed to document the atrocities of Islamic State, its members have also reported critically on the Assad government's bombings, other rebel forces, and civilian casualties caused by US-led airstrikes. The group has established itself as a credible source among Syria monitors and journalists globally."[75]

As soon as it surfaced, Daesh declared Raqqa Is Being Slaughtered Silently an enemy of God. Members of the group were risking their lives to get information out, as the Committee to Protect Journalists said in its award: "Al-Moutaz Bellah Ibrahim [a member of RBSS] was kidnapped by Islamic State and murdered in May 2014. In July 2015, Islamic State released a highly produced video, showing two men saying they worked for RBSS. The men are then strung up on trees and shot."[76]

Being in Turkey was no guarantee of safety, since Turkish intelligence gave Daesh freedom to operate there. On October 30, 2015, Ibrahim Abd al Qader, twenty years old and a founder of the RBSS collective, was found dead in his Urfa apartment together with his friend Fares Hamadi, 19, a journalist with another Syrian media collective. Both had been shot and then beheaded.[77] Filmmaker and journalist Naji Jerf was shot in broad daylight on December 27, 2015 in the Turkish city of Gazientep, the day before he was to leave for France with his wife and two children.[78] He had made a documentary about Raqqa is Being Slaughtered Silently and had recently aired another film, widely watched on YouTube, about Daesh killings of Syrian activists in Aleppo.[79]

Ruqia Hassan, a graduate in philosophy from the University of Aleppo, became a citizen journalist also. She was from a Kurdish family who left Raqqa when fighting broke out between al-Nusra and the Free Syrian Army militias, but she and other members of her family returned after a few months to protect their businesses in Raqqa. Hassan had no media outlets, but stuck inside the house month after month, growing more desperate and furious, she began to write a Facebook blog and post pictures of herself, along with sarcastic remarks about Raqqa daily life, using the name Nissan Ibrahim. Her blog focused on Daesh oppression and bombing raids by the Assad regime and its Russian ally: "People in the market crash into each other like waves," she noted, "not because of the numbers . . . but because their eyes are glued to the skies . . . their feet are moving unconsciously."[80]

On another day she wrote, "Today, a Tunisian fighter stopped me because of my Islamic dress code. I ignored her and walked away but I wished that I had a pistol to kill her. I wanted to stop this humiliation, these guys built their power on us. I'm sick of them and their power. I'm sick of being a second-class citizen. God, please help us."

Members of RBSS, to whom she sometimes sent articles, warned her to be more careful. A cousin told her not to post her picture on Facebook or she would be targeted, but that made her angry and she deleted him from her page. "She was stubborn and wanted to show the truth of what is happening, no matter what the cost," he said. She was arrested in the summer of 2015. Her family went to the prison every day, but were never given any news or allowed to see her. Finally, on New Year's Day, 2016, Daesh told her brother that she and five other women had been executed. They refused to give the family her body.

Her last Facebook post said "I'm in Raqqa and I received death threats. When Isil arrest me and kill me it's OK, because [while] they will cut [off] my head I will have dignity, which is better than living in humiliation."

*People's Protection Unit (YPG) patrol truck, Tel Hamis,*
*Cizire Canton, Rojava.*

CHAPTER 9

# Daesh vs. Kobane

I N THE SPRING OF 2015, Zainab Bangura, the UN Special Rapporteur on Sexual Violence in Conflict, made a tour of camps housing Syrian refugees from Daesh. She was no stranger to the horrors of war, having worked in the conflict zones of Bosnia, Congo, South Sudan, Somalia, and the Central African Republic, but she was sickened as never before by what she heard from women who had been captured by Daesh. "It was painful for me," she said. "I never saw anything like this. I cannot understand such inhumanity."[1]

Vian Dakhil, a Yazidi Member of the Iraqi Parliament, and her younger sister Deelan became spokeswomen for these enslaved women and girls. Deelan worked in the refugee camps in northern Iraq that housed many former captives. In December 2015, she was interviewed by a reporter for the *Daily Mail*, who wrote, "The stories she recounts sound like something from a horror film. One in particular stands out: that of a mother and her nine-year-old daughter. But one morning a man, thought to be in his 50s, decided he would take the little girl instead of one of the women. The mother was distraught, and fought to protect her, but it was in vain. The fighters shot her in the head, leaving her body lying on the floor. The fighter took the little girl: the woman who recounted the story to Deelan still hears her screams every night as she goes to sleep. 'They raped her, but her small body could not tolerate it, and from the first sexual experience she bled to death and she died,' Deelan told the audience in London. The first girl Deelan helped after escaping had thrown herself from a second-floor window and walked for three days to find safety. She had been sold six times, from fighter to fighter. Each time, she was raped every day. The last time her 'price' had dropped to just a cigarette."[2]

In 2014, Daesh had published a guide to the proper treatment of female slaves, which contained answers to such questions as "Is it permissible to have intercourse with a female captive immediately after taking possession of her?" The answer was yes, as long as she was a virgin. If she was not, her uterus had to be "purified" first, although it did not explain how to do that. Another question: "Is it permissible to have intercourse with a female slave who has not reached puberty?" Yes, as long as she is "fit for intercourse; if not, then it is enough to enjoy her without intercourse." Many salafis consider it acceptable to have sex with young girls, following the example of the Prophet, whom religious texts say married his last wife, Aisha, when she was six and consummated the marriage when she was nine. Apparently some fighters had been overstepping even the minimal restrictions placed on them, since Daesh subsequently published a series of fatwas laying down refinements, including the rule that it was not permissible to sleep with both a mother and her daughter.[3]

Because of the Daesh code separating the sexes, the policing of women had to be done by other women. In Raqqa and Mosul, the rules were enforced by the al-Khanssa Brigade, an all-female police force established a few months after Daesh took over the city. As a Daesh official said, "We have established the brigade to raise awareness of our religion among women, and to punish women who do not abide by the law. . . . Jihad is not a man-only duty. Women must do their part as well."[4]

For Sunni women, there was an elaborate, onerous dress code that reached extremes undreamed of by the Taliban. Not only were women required to wear a full burqa or niqab—a long black head-to-toe garment, with another black waist-length garment covering their head—and hide their faces behind so many veils they could hardly see; in addition, unmarried women were supposed to wear a white scarf over their faces underneath, to denote their availability for marriage. Color-coded veils were also required for other marital conditions: black for married women, green for widows, and blue for divorced.[5]

These rules were laid out in a manual written by the media committee of the al-Khanssa Brigades, published in January 2015. The manual targeted women in Arab countries, particularly Saudi Arabia.[6] In it, the dress code was discussed not only in terms of religion but of anticolonialism, and was framed as the right to be veiled: "In the years of mental and military colonialism, this right was banned by force or persuasion. Faces were forcibly revealed for identity checks to denote national identity. Women would not be allowed to travel out of the country unless they had a passport with a photo of their face in it."[7]

Dress code violation was a serious crime. In July 2015, a resident of Raqqa named Dalia told *Syria Deeply*, an independent online news source, "One of my neighbors was walking with her husband and she had forgotten to wear the 'shield,' a rectangular piece of thick material that stretches from eyes to knees. It was recently imposed in addition to the niqab. The Daesh police arrested him and his wife; they punished him with 100 lashes and forced him to pay a 25,000-pound ($137) fine. He divorced his wife out of anger at the same place where ISIS punished him."[8]

That same month, a seventeen-year-old married woman was in the market in Mosul with a group of friends. They lifted their veils to examine some clothes on display because it was impossible to see clearly through all the layers of fabric covering their faces. Members of an all-Russian (probably Chechen) Al-Khanssa Brigade rushed over and beat the offenders so severely that the seventeen-year-old died.[9]

The white veil for unmarried women was of particular interest to the Al-Khanssa Brigades: "When the female police spot the white scarf," a woman in Raqqa told a reporter from *Syria Deeply*, "they approach these women and their families, and often harass them, to ask for their hands for the Arab and foreign fighters who are looking for wives. Not many Raqqa families have married their daughters to ISIS fighters, but the ones who did have many privileges. Families that did not accept were picked on and punished for the slightest mistake."[10]

Three Raqqa girls who married fighters, and whose families benefitted as a result, escaped from Raqqa and told their stories to a reporter from *The New York Times* in November 2015. They complained that, as Syrians, they were held in much lower status by Daesh than the foreign girls who came to Raqqa. Though one young woman, named Dua, fell in love with her husband and wanted to have children, she was forced to take birth control pills because Daesh did not want its fighters held back from suicide by becoming fathers. When Dua's husband blew himself up, she found she was expected to marry another fighter almost immediately, even though that was contrary to Islam. As the *Times* reported, "Under nearly universal interpretations of Islam, a woman must wait three months before remarrying, mainly to establish the paternity of any child that might have been conceived. The waiting period, called idaa, is not only required but is a woman's right, to allow her to grieve. But even in the realm of divine law, the Islamic State was reformulating everything.

"'I told him that I still couldn't stop crying,' Dua said. 'I said: "I'm heartbroken. I want to wait the whole three months."' But the commander told her she was different from a normal widow. 'You shouldn't be mourning and sad,' he said. 'He asked for martyrdom himself, and you are the wife of a martyr. You should be happy.'"[11]

*Syria Deeply* reported the story of another woman, Lina, who was arrested for an infraction against the dress code. "Her husband was not around. The ISIS police freed her after three days. Her husband got suspicious. He asked her if ISIS fighters or police did anything to her. She said no. A few days later, he was not convinced, so he demanded she swear on the Koran that she was telling the truth. She could not lie. The truth was a horrifying story. She said that she was raped repeatedly every hour by a different ISIS fighter. Her husband divorced her on the spot."[12]

Veteran reporter Rania Abouzeid reported on the website Politico that she heard a similar story in a village in Idlib Province, where she was interviewing the wife of a Jabhat al-Nusra emir. A woman "relayed a tale about a crying woman who marched into the Nusra outpost one day, took off her hijab and told the emir she no longer wanted to be a Muslim. She said seven ISIL members had 'married' her, one after the other, in the same night. It was gang rape. "This is not our religion," the emir's mother said."[13]

These stories were very different from the romantic fictions being pushed by online recruiters for Daesh, which featured an idyllic religious commonwealth which women could share with men as long as they kept to their prescribed roles. *Women of the Islamic State: A Manifesto by the Al-Khanssa Brigade* presented an image of this ideal society: seventh century Arabia. "If we look back to the Prophet's community in Medina, it was the best of communities. With the best leaders, absolutely and indisputably. While it was a very simple society in terms of the material world and worldly sciences, it was strong in terms of its faith and the science of the next. People in it were hungry more than they were satisfied. They had houses of palm and mud, rode camels and horses and did not know physics, engineering or astronomy. Because of all this, God was kept at the forefront, and the Righteous were His slaves."[14]

The problem, according to the al-Khanssa manifesto, was that Muslims had forgotten that the purpose of their existence was to worship God. They had befriended the wrong people, including infidels and UN agencies, and looked to them for leadership. Relations between women and men had gone awry because women had forgotten that their one duty was to be a good wife and mother and had started to work outside the home, thus emasculating men.

Anyone familiar with the history of the struggle for women's emancipation will recognize these arguments, which have been made all over the world by conservatives of every religion. The starting premise is that men and women are different in essence. There is a wall between them and if you make a chink in it, society will fall apart: "Women have this Heavenly secret in sedentariness, stillness, and stability, and men its opposite, movement and flux, that which is the nature of man, created in him," according to the manifesto. "If roles are mixed and positions overlap, humanity is thrown into a state of flux and instability. The base of society is shaken, its foundations crumble and its walls collapse."[15]

When women go outside the home, they thus take the fatal step that leads to the destruction of society. There are a few exceptions: Women may leave their houses to study sharia; women doctors and teachers may work as long as they keep to sharia guidelines; and, on certain rare occasions, during a jihad, for instance, when there are not enough men around to protect the country, women may take up arms "if the imams give a fatwa for it, as the blessed women of Iraq and Chechnya did, with great sadness." Poor women are also permitted to work for a limited number of hours a day in places like market stalls, as long as their male relatives permit it and they are able to perform their household duties as well.

It follows from these limited expectations that women do not need an excessive amount of education. They merely need be literate and able to do simple arithmetic, in addition to knowing how to knit, sew, and cook. Of course, they also have to know the stories of the Prophet and the rules of sharia, especially those governing women's lives. The manifesto proposed a simple curriculum for girls between seven and fifteen. "No need for her to flit here and there to get degrees and so on, just so she can try to prove that her intelligence is greater than a man's." Bear in mind that "it is considered legitimate for a girl to be married at the age of nine. Most pure girls will be married by sixteen or seventeen, while they are still young and active. Young men will not be more than twenty years old in those glorious generations."[16]

What does this mean in practice? That even women who were Sunni and supported Daesh were unable to move freely; they could not go outside without a male relative; their education was strictly limited; they had to wear three veils over their faces and would be lashed if their eyes could be seen; and they would be stoned to death if they were accused of adultery.[17]

And what is one to make of these girls and young women in the al-Khanssa brigade who policed other women and supervised the sex slaves, girls like Mujahidah Bint Usama, formerly a British medical student, who posted a picture of herself in Raqqa holding a severed head, with the message, "Dream job, a terrorist doc," followed by smiley faces and hearts?[18] Or Aqsa Mahmood, formerly a twenty-year-old pre-med student from Glasgow, who wrote in a blog post on September 11, 2014, "Know this Cameron/Obama, you and your countries will be beneath our feet and your Kufr [unbelief] will be destroyed, this is a promise from Allah swt [abbreviation for 'glorified and exalted be He'] that we have no doubt over. If not you then your grandchildren or their grandchildren. But worry not, somewhere along the line your blood will be spilled by our cubs in Dawlah [your country]. We have conquered these lands once Beithnillah [God willing] we will do it again. Read up on your History, and know that it will repeat itself, you will pay Jizyah [tax on non-Muslims] to us just like you did in the past. This Islamic Empire shall be known and feared world wide and we will follow none other than the Law of the one and the only ilah [God]!"[19]

These young Sunni women bought into a sectarian caste system that gave them admission to a society run by an elite group of warriors with life and death power over other women—Yazidis, Shia, Ahmadis, Christians. Their bargain was the same as that made by other women who joined poisonous right-wing groups based on racial identity or religious sect—Nazi women, women of the Hindu Right, or the Ladies Auxiliary of the Ku Klux Klan.

## What Does Daesh Believe?

There has been considerable discussion of how Daesh's version of Islam compares to other, more mainstream practices, and whether religion is actually central to Daesh at all. A controversial piece in *The Atlantic* by

Graeme Wood focused on the way Daesh justified its practices by citing ancient Islamic texts. After interviewing all of three people—a Princeton professor, an Australian recruiter for Daesh, and a London preacher of jihad—Wood decided that Daesh was well within the Muslim tradition. His critics mostly responded by saying Islam-isn't-like-that.[20]

In fact, like other fundamentalist organizations, Daesh has cherry-picked ancient texts to justify whatever it wanted to do, then said its own selection was the only correct one. Centuries of interpretation of the texts are considered nothing but corruption and error, unless the interpretations agree with theirs.[21] Thus Daesh spokesmen cite scripture and say they are restoring the "true" traditions of the times of the Prophet in order to justify the most appalling acts of cruelty.

While Daesh constantly points to the Koranic foundations of its laws, the last time a lot of those laws were in effect was the seventh century. There have been plenty of Muslim-ruled states since then; some have even said they were based on sharia law, although they were actually following the dictates of *realpolitik,* like other states. Mouin Rabbani, formerly of the International Crisis Group and now a co-editor of the ezine, *Jadaliyya,* concluded that "few of the ideas promulgated by the IS are without theological foundation, nor are its practices entirely without precedent. Nevertheless, it can hardly claim to be rooted in well-established Muslim tradition or jurisprudence and should therefore be primarily understood as a thoroughly modern interpretation and application of a faith whose imagined past is a projection backwards of contemporary agendas rather than a revival of early Islamic rule. The IS's reclamation of Islam's essence is thus on a par with the Khmer Rouge's insistence that it represented the pure soul of communism."[22]

Aymenn Jawad Al-Tamimi, an online researcher of jihadi thought, found the whole "how-Muslim-is-it" debate misguided: "Firstly, the debate is largely between an 'academic' view of Islam and the divisions within it, peaceful or otherwise, and a normative view of Islam, which seeks to distance the rigid, conservative, and violent forms of the religion from the one practiced by the vast majority of Muslims around the world. To argue that ISIS isn't 'Islamic' in a normative sense is to argue, to some degree, that Salafism isn't a branch of Islam and that jihad isn't a noble concept in the religion, arguments that are false and misleading, and severely hinder attempts to understand these movements properly."[23]

Amal Ghazal, an historian, and Larbi Sadiki, a political scientist, are among those who believe it is ridiculous to think that Daesh is either religious or political when clearly it is both. They have argued that its goals are political, it arose out of special social and historical conditions, and religion is central to its self-definition. "Surely, theology is not the main or only drive behind ISIS, but denying its existence denies reality. Regardless of the regional and foreign politics shaping the emergence of ISIS, ISIS defines itself in religious terms, it vies for and fiercely rivals other groups over religiously sanctioned authority, and dutifully and conscientiously anchors itself and its vision in religious texts. ISIS's worldview, even if cultic, is a religiously-informed one par excellence while at the same time ISIS remains, first and foremost, a political organization with political goals."[24]

It has been important to many Daesh members that their practice be based on scriptural sources, however selectively these may be chosen. "The problem is that with such a huge corpus of Islamic literature and no central infallible authority like the Pope to regulate teachings, many of ISIS' actions, seen as heinous in this day and age, can find a place within the vastness of Islamic tradition," Al-Tamimi and fellow researcher Amarnath Amarasingam have noted. "We may dismiss such evidence by claiming that ISIS is only citing them in order to gain legitimacy and credibility among its followers, but that's precisely the point: they feel reassured that they have a coherent theological basis in their actions."[25]

In December 2015, under the heading "The ISIS Papers," *The Guardian* published a Daesh internal document entitled "Principles in the Administration of the Islamic State." The document, which was unearthed by Al-Tamimi, was written shortly after Abu Bakr al-Baghdadi declared the new caliphate and was directed largely towards answering administrative and economic questions about governance. In doing so, it laid out a historical and philosophical argument indicating that Daesh is principally focused on power and land acquisition.

The document states that the purpose of founding a caliphate was to regain what were seen as Sunni rights. These rights had been stolen by heretics, whom it was necessary to disperse and grind underfoot "to protect the power of the Sunnis," and enable the rightful owners of the land and its wealth to get back their proper position in the world. While some theological justification is mixed into this argument, it is basically a statement of revolutionary power politics.

The analysis begins with the Sykes-Picot agreement—the secret treaty between England and France that divided what remained of the Ottoman Empire after World War I into separate states. This led to a situation, the author writes, where everybody got land except the Sunnis. The Sykes-Picot treaty is seen as a deliberate plot whose purpose was "depriving the Sunnis from those assets, as the mountains were granted to the Kurds, Druze and Alawites [Shia], while the sea was granted to the Rafidites and Nusayris [more Shia], while the river and what surrounds it is investment for the Jews and the agricultural lands under their administration."[26]

This was all a plan, according to "The ISIS Papers," to prevent the Sunnis from establishing a state ruled by the correct interpretation of holy law. "All that has not merely been a coincidence, but it was a dirty political decision in order to implement a tightening stranglehold on the Sunnis and make them the most remote people and strip them of all assets for advancement or thinking of a rightly-guided Islamic State." The task, therefore, is to restructure the region and draw new boundaries that protect "the assets of the ummah . . . its wealth, the nature of its land, its inhabitants and its water."

As for the usurpers, and anyone else who stands in the way of the Sunnis, "special teams can be deployed for fundamental change in the structuring of the regions that are subject to the rule of the Islamic State. And that was what the companions [of the Prophet Muhammad] and after them the caliphs pursued against every heretic community: that is, dispersing their groupings so there no longer remained any impeding opinion, strength or ability, and the Muslim alone remains the master of the state and decision-making and no one is in conflict with him."[27] In other words, kill them all or drive them away.

This is a political agenda that uses religious pleading as an argument that a particular group deserves more wealth and political power, based on an essentially paranoid and tribal perspective that says: "The world is against us so we will be against the world. We will take as much as we can and kill anybody who's in the way and enslave their women."

So, while Daesh draws on Islamic texts operationally, its philosophy is a kind of fascistic nihilism. If you substitute "religion" for "race" and substitute "Shia and infidels" for "Jews," you come up with a view of the world very similar to that attributed to Hitler by European historian Timothy Snyder: "If you eradicate the Jews, then the world snaps back into what Hitler sees as its primeval, correct state: Races struggle against each other, kill each other, starve each other to death, and try and take land. . . . I was struck that Hitler explicitly said that states are temporary, state borders will be washed away in the struggle for nature."[28]

Daesh does not want to live peacefully alongside other kinds of Muslims any more than Hitler wanted to co-exist with the Jews. In fact, "The ISIS Papers" indict Saddam Hussein for fostering ideas of co-existence that led to stripping Sunnis of their identity. A tolerant, non-sectarian society is framed as a threat to Sunnis: "Discarding the difference with the disbelieving sects, and considering co-existence with them as the true societal bond that the ummah must operate in accordance with in order to preserve its goals, while in reality protection is implemented for the rights of all the communities of disbelief while oppressing the Sunnis and their principles."[29]

If the analogy with Hitler's view of the world is correct, the idea of dividing Syria and Iraq into new states—Shiastan, Sunnistan, Kurdistan—is based on a fundamental misunderstanding. Daesh may have called itself a state but that doesn't mean it would settle for boundaries. Snyder says of Hitler, "He's quite consciously manipulating German national sentiment to get to power and then to start the war, which he thinks will transform the Germans, as it were, from a nation into a race. So he's aware that German nationalism is a force in the world, but he's just using it in order to create the world that he wants, which is this world of racial struggle." As Hitler believed in the race, not the state, so Daesh has believed in its Takfiri version of Islam. It has used the idea of a state to transform the Sunnis into a warrior tribe, as Zarqawi hoped would happen when he bombed the al-Askari mosque in Iraq in 2006.

In "The ISIS papers" special attention is paid to oil, "gold and antiquities," and weapons. The trade in and ownership of these is to be reserved for the state. The state will also extract substantial revenue from taxes, fines, and the confiscation of the property of anyone who flees its rule. Like many other states in the Middle East, rather than trying to develop industry or agriculture, Daesh is dependent on oil, which makes it economically weaker and more vulnerable than states with a diverse economy.

The political scientist Charles Tripp described Daesh's sources of wealth as "oil extracted in Syria and in Iraq and sold to areas controlled by the Assad government, across the Turkish border or through middlemen in the Kurdish region of Iraq. The wells that IS has seized produce only a fifth of their pre-war levels, but in September 2014 they were bringing in a reported $2m a day. These assets have been supplemented by the vast sums poured into the Syrian conflict by various donors from the Gulf since 2011. Especially in Kuwait, Qatar and Saudi Arabia substantial 'private' donations seem to have had official blessing until recently. . . . An economy based on tribute and distribution prevails in the territories controlled by IS. Banks, military installations and other assets, both state and private, were looted and 'protection levies' imposed on businesses and on transport firms. The same applies to the smuggling of antiquities: direct sales and the sale of 'licences' to dig for antiquities provide a steady source of externally generated revenue."[30]

These sources of income are vulnerable to attack. Protection money, fines, and taxes depend on the number of people controlled. If Daesh lost territory, this revenue would decrease. A number of oil depots and tankers were bombed after Daesh took them over, but, more importantly, the price of oil dropped drastically for several years. The US had turned to producing most of its own oil, which meant the Arab states had to find other markets. At the same time, Chinese markets started to contract because of economic problems, while more oil continued to be pumped, creating an oversupply. On top of that, OPEC—the oil producers' cartel controlled by the Saudis and Gulf States—refused to fix the price, possibly to hurt the economy of its rival Iran, or to undercut US attempts to become a major oil exporter.[31]

In 2016, Daesh's annual income was an estimated $1.5 to $2 billion, which would be a lot for a jihadi group, but was not much for running a large state in the middle of a multifront war. In addition, Daesh did most of its business in cash; when US bombers started to target cash depots in Daesh-controlled areas, they destroyed tens of millions of dollars in currency. Rumors began circulating in 2016 that Daesh fighters were having to take a pay cut, which some believed might prompt those jihadis who were principally motivated by money to drift away.[32]

## The Logic of Terror

While some of the Daesh soldiers may be filled with genuine religious zeal, however warped, is this also true of Daesh strategists and leaders? Abu Hamza, a Syrian commander who became disillusioned and escaped to Turkey, isn't sure the leaders of Daesh are actually religious at all. "They pray and they fast and you can't be an emir without praying, but inside I don't think they believe it much. . . . The Baathists are using Daesh. They don't care about Baathism or even Saddam. They just want power. They are used to being in power, and they want it back. They want to run Iraq."[33]

Christoph Reuter of *Der Spiegel* takes a similar view: "If you see the statements and actions of Al-Qaeda, they were like the early left-wing terrorists in the 1970s in Europe. They always believed in the masses. 'We do something and then the masses will rise,' but the masses never rose. Not for Al-Qaeda, not for the Leftists. Daesh does not believe in the masses rising; Daesh believes in control: 'oppress the masses and they will obey.'"[34]

Daesh's rule by terror has been forced on a subject population by harsh laws, assassinations, and public beheadings. It has been projected at the world through videos and photos that present Daesh as a swarm of ski-masked, black-clad warriors jumping out of vehicles and shooting madly in all directions. Reuter notes that, we never see blurry images of Daesh, or pictures of fighters who are confused, tired, wounded or squinting at the camera. They are always in clear focus and perfect light. To Reuter, Daesh videos should be seen as theater:

"Strength is something relative, like when you had the early phase in 2013, and they would always be masked. And whenever something happens, immediately around 200 guys would appear. Bam! All masked. So the local people would not know how many they are, or who they are. During this period, for example, they were exaggerating their strength, but in general they tried to foment the image of the invincible warrior, with the mask you came like a ninja, you jump from the pick-up, you threaten everybody, you shout. . . . They create an image as a weapon where, for example, in Iraq they just needed to call ahead and say 'we will arrive in half an hour,' and the village would be empty. If it was an opposition village against Daesh, people would just run away."[35]

This image of brutal invincibility was designed to attract recruits as well as terrify opponents. Those photos of hundreds of Iraqi or Syrian bodies, those carefully staged 2014 beheadings of Westerners in orange jumpsuits—James Foley, Alan Henning, Stephen Sotloff, David Haines, Peter Kassig—were advertising, meant to terrify the West and attract young men from all over the world who wanted to feel more powerful than they did at home. Recruitment was the reason for the heads mounted on spikes around the public square in Raqqa, for the publication of a price list for female slaves, for the smile on the face of the executioner and, of course, for the attacks on European cities.

Foreign fighters have been central to Daesh strategy. Locals might have conflicting loyalties to family or old friends, but foreigners would have no such ties, and since they had no roots in Syria or Iraq and no local networks, they would be less likely to be able to desert and run away. They came in, were met at the border, brought to a training camp, and reshaped into members of an army whose loyalties were only to Daesh.[36]

Daesh media carefully targeted such recruits. Important messages were released not only in Arabic, but also in English, French, and German, and rapidly translated into Indonesian, Russian, and Urdu.[37] Special outreach via social media was targeted at young girls in the West who could be persuaded to leave their families and go to Syria. Some of the recruits were pious. Many were recent converts who know little about Islamic traditions.

In a brilliant analysis of of jihadi recruits, Olivier Roy, a scholar of Islam, wrote that one quarter of the jihadis arrested in France were converts, while a full 40 percent of those arrested in the US in 2011 were, showing the errors of "the (culturalist) idea that individual radicalisation reflects a radicalisation of a frustrated Muslim community." Some actually arrived in Syria carrying copies of *Islam for Dummies*.[38]

Some of these foreign fighters were probably psychopaths or sadists turned on by violence. Many were just bored young men looking for adventure, money, sex, a meaningful life, martyrdom, or all of the above. Roy described them as 21st century "rebels without a cause," the equivalent of US lone shooters: "Jihad is the only cause on the global market. If you kill in silence, it will be reported in the local newspaper; if you kill yelling 'Allahuakhbar,' you are sure to make the national headlines." He emphasized the importance of videogames and pop superhero narratives to the self-image of these young men, and the fact that they were usually recruited through peer networks. Internet recruitment was apparently mainly successful only with girls, at least in Europe.

In 2005, journalist Hind Fraihi interviewed disaffected young men in the Belgian city of Molenbeek, a hotbed of Islamism, later famous for its role in providing suicide bombers for the Paris and Brussels attacks of 2015 and 2016.[39] After the Paris attacks, *The Washington Post* reported that the young men told Fraihi they had quit school and "passed much of their time sleeping. Or they would hang around at the metro exits and snatch people's bags. They called it jihad because they would pick out Westerners. Fraihi told them that sounded like racism. They called it gangster Islam. They were ripe for picking by international recruiters. 'These young people don't have a job or a future, so they are very easy to indoctrinate if you give them a big story,' she said, 'a big collective story, a story of our society, a dream, an aspiration, an idealism.'"[40]

Religion is not the motivation behind the attraction of such young men to jihad. Many, like the Paris bombers, became interested in religion shortly before they acted. Researcher Lydia Wilson, who interviewed Iraqi jihadis imprisoned in Kirkuk, said, "They are woefully ignorant about Islam and have difficulty answering questions about Sharia law, militant jihad and the caliphate . . ." They were motivated by alienation and anger, not religion, she said. "They are children of the [US] occupation, many with missing fathers at crucial periods (through jail, death from execution, or fighting in the insurgency), filled with rage against America and their own government. They are not fueled by the idea of an Islamic caliphate without borders; rather, ISIS is the first group since the crushed Al Qaeda to offer these humiliated and enraged young men a way to defend their dignity, family and tribe."[41]

Young women also turned to Daesh, although not nearly in the same numbers as their male counterparts. Recruiting foreign women to bear "young lions" for the cause took on increasing emphasis in Daesh over the years. Though teenage girls who ran away to join Daesh probably had the same mix of motives as boys—the hope of adventure, an idealistic wish for a meaningful life, the desire to be part of a holy utopia, or a craving for power, plus the age-old teenage dream of getting away from one's parents—the version of the dream sold to girls emphasized romance with a dashing warrior. Once these girls made their way to Turkey, they were met by a fixer and taken over the border to Raqqa, where they were paraded before fighters looking for a wife. Men were allowed to see the women's faces just that one time. Then the girls were immediately married off.[42]

After Daesh made Raqqa its capital, foreign fighters came in droves and a dual economy developed in which many locals became impoverished while foreigners had money to burn and freedom to do whatever they liked, including forcibly marry local women and take over people's houses. They received subsidized gas and could cut to the front of the bread queues. They swaggered around the streets wearing suicide belts and scaring people.[43]

A resident who fled to Turkey said "locals were constantly subjected to harassment and interrogation by groups of foreign fighters, who, mistrustful of the more 'moderate' Syrians, operate pervasive brigades and religious police to enforce religious law and report violations under the threat of violence. 'They come into internet cafes and demand to see who you are talking to. They will confiscate your phone in the street and inspect your contacts.'"[44]

People must be made afraid to resist. They must be prevented from defecting by checkpoints that make it impossible to get out. The locals must be afraid of the foreign fighters; the foreign fighters must be afraid of their commanders; and the commanders must be afraid of the secret police.

In Haji Bakr's blueprint, one of the first things Daesh had to do once it was established in a town was to set up a council with an emir in charge of "murders, abductions, snipers, communication, and encryption." A separate council would be appointed to check up on the other emirs to make sure they were sufficiently pious and doing their jobs. The result would be a parallel state structure, like that of the East German Stasi or Iraq under Saddam Hussein: Public officials would rule the town by fear and a separate security state would spy on them.[45]

This rule by terror was the model of an ideal society being held out to Sunni Muslims all over the world. The weak states of Iraq and Syria were unable to defeat it. Only when Daesh got to Kobane did it encounter a society with a political vision as strong as its own, based on diametrically opposed ideas.

The seeming invincibility of Daesh went into decline after the battle of Kobane. According to the military intelligence research group IHS Conflict Monitor, it lost 14 percent of its territory in 2015, including the vital border crossing of Tal Abyad, Tikrit, the Bajji oil refinery in Iraq, and a stretch of road connecting Raqqa and Mosul.[46] Due to these losses and the falling price of oil, Daesh apparently failed to meet its $2 billion 2015 budget.[47]

These losses were a blow to morale and prestige, and in the fall of 2015 Daesh moved swiftly to balance them by attacking civilians in countries including Bangladesh, Egypt, Tunisia, Turkey, and Yemen. It downed a Russian plane in the Sinai on October 21, killing all 224 on board; staged a triple suicide bomb attack on a Shia neighborhood in Beirut on November 12, leaving forty-three dead and between two hundred and two hundred forty wounded; killed twenty-six with a road bomb and suicide attack in a Shia neighborhood of Baghdad on November 13; and, also on November 13, organized a coordinated attack by at least six jihadis in Paris at multiple sites, including a soccer stadium, a cafe, a public square, and a theatre. The death toll the next day was 129, with 352 wounded.[48] Nigerian terrorist group Boko Haram, which pledged allegiance to Daesh in June 2015, was also responsible for attacks in November of that year, when female suicide bombers, one only eleven years old, blew up a mobile phone market in Kano, Nigeria, killing fifty or sixty people, just hours after another bomb killed thirty-four and wounded eighty at a marketplace in Yola.[49] The carnage continued in 2016 with suicide bombers targeting civilians in Istanbul, Jakarta, and Homs; an attack on a Shia mosque in Syria; a second bombing in Istanbul; attacks on the Brussels airport and metro; and a suicide bombing during an Iraqi soccer game.

These widespread attacks indicated that Daesh's earlier concentration on capturing and holding territory might be changing. Confronted with so many powerful enemies, its would-be state in Iraq and Syria seemed less viable. It is worth noting that, despite Obama's stated intention to "degrade and ultimately destroy" Daesh militarily, his actual strategy has been one of containment—rather than bombing Daesh into smithereens along with all the civilians under its control or putting in those constantly referenced "boots on the ground," he has preferred to send in some advisors to train local forces and wait until Daesh fell apart of its own accord because it couldn't handle fighting such a big war and running a quasi-state at the same time.[50]

But defeating Daesh militarily is not the same as defeating its ideas, which continue to find other hosts. It is an amoeba-like organization, sending out arms to various places and taking in affiliates wherever it can. By late 2015, it had established a base at Sirte, Colonel Gaddafi's old hometown in Libya, where it had three thousand fighters. Some observers thought its leadership might settle there if Daesh were chased out of Raqqa.[51]

As Daesh territory has begun to shrink, that of Rojava has grown. According to the military strategists of the IHS Conflict Monitor, "Territory under their control expanded by 186 percent to 15,800 km in 2015. They have established control over nearly all of Syria's traditionally Kurdish areas, and are the largest component of the Syrian Democratic Forces (SDF), which are being nurtured to form a key part of the US ground campaign against the Islamic State in 2016."[52]

Polat Can, a founding member of the YPG who was head of the Kobane media center during the siege, expressed hope for the region for the first time in many years: "The whole region is on the verge of a deep and radical change. The region will not return to what it was before 2011, that era is gone forever—a new world and new system is forming and nothing will remain the same. . . . I am optimistic that the Kurdish people will defeat ISIS and terrorism and the Kurds will obtain their rights and no one will be able to keep the Kurdish people from determining their own future."[53]

*PKK guerrillas pose at Makhmour trench, Iraq.*

# CHAPTER 10

# War and Peace in Turkey

Recip Tayyip Erdogan came to power in Turkey as an Islamist allied with the powerful Gulen movement (also called the Hizmet movement, and described as perhaps "the world's biggest Muslim network"),[1] and an opponent of the Kemalist elite's narrow and restrictive form of secularism. For many years before his election, the military had ruled with an iron hand, exercising strict censorship, preventing any cultural expressions other than their own, staging coups whenever they got nervous, and focusing on what they saw as the two enemies of the Turkish nation: Islamists, who wanted to replace secular nationalism with Sunni nationalism, and Kurds, who refused to assimilate to the dominant culture. Even after the changeover to civilian rule, repression continued. In 2012 and 2013 Turkey won the distinction of having more journalists in prison than any other country; only in 2014 was it surpassed in this regard by China, which has a much larger population.[2]

Before becoming prime minister, Erdogan had been Mayor of Istanbul, representing the Islamist Welfare Party, a party with anti-Western politics and connections to the Muslim Brotherhood. He was a capable mayor who did a lot to curb pollution and improve the city's water supply, though residents were unhappy when he banned drinking in cafes. But his open Islamism made the military nervous and they looked for an excuse to go after him. They got one in 1997, when he recited the following lines from a poem at a rally in Sirt: "The mosques are our barracks, the domes our helmets, the minarets our bayonets and the faithful our soldiers." He was sentenced to ten months in jail for "inciting religious hatred," of which he served four, and the Welfare Party was banned in 1998.[3] But in 2001, he switched allegiances, founding the Justice and Development Party, the AKP,

which he framed as a Muslim version of Europe's Christian Democratic parties, combining religiosity with friendliness to capital and
the West.[4] It was a foregone conclusion that the AKP would win the
votes of religious Muslims but, since many urban secularists were
more worried about the military than Islamism, the AKP got their
votes, too. The party even got the votes of lots of Kurds, some because
they were religious, some because they thought a man who had been
in prison might be sympathetic to their cause.

The AKP won 363 seats out of 550 in in the 2002 parliamentary elections, becoming the first party in fifteen years able to govern without
a coalition. Though Erdogan's jail sentence had made him ineligible
for public office, Parliament amended the constitution and he became
Prime Minister in 2003.[5]

At that point he seemed to want to be a peacemaker. One was certainly needed. When the PKK split in 2004, a group called the Freedom
Falcons (TAK) suddenly emerged, and established themselves as more
violent than the PKK and much more willing to bomb civilian targets,
especially tourists. Soon attacks took place at a train station, a resort
town, a supermarket, a bus station. While the Turkish media called TAK
a PKK front, the PKK denied any connection with these attacks. Some
believe TAK is contolled by the Turkish deep state, the secret intelligence program set up by the CIA during the Cold War.[6]

In August 2005, Erdogan made a dramatic peacemaking gesture by
traveling to Diyarbakir, where he gave a speech saying that a great nation
like Turkey needed to accept the fact that it had made mistakes. He said
the Kurds needed more democracy, not more repression, and that the
Kurdish problem could not be solved through purely military means.
He was immediately denounced by politicians to his Right, including
some people in his own party.[7]

The Kurds waited for a year to see what the follow up would be. There
was none. Even so, in August 2006, the PKK announced yet another
unilateral ceasefire. TAK responded with a wave of bomb attacks on
tourist buses and resorts that killed three people and injured many
more. When the PKK condemned these attacks, TAK warned tourists
to stay out of Turkey and issued a statement saying, "From now on, every
attack against our people will be met immediately by even more violent
acts. We will start to harm not just property, but lives too. With our
actions, we will turn Turkey into hell."[8]

Although the PKK continued to disavow any connection to TAK, the Turkish government used the attacks as an excuse to attack the PKK camps in Iraq once again. It declared martial law in the southeast for three months, and embarked on another war with the PKK that lasted until 2008.[9] Erdogan's resumption of the war led to his party's loss of the southeast to the Kurdish Democratic Society Party in the election of March 2009. A wave of arrests of Kurdish politicians followed. Seizing the initiative, the PKK announced another ceasefire. This time Erdogan seemed to get the message and made an impassioned plea for peace negotiations, issuing a call for a "Democratic Initiative" to reform the constitution and address Kurdish demands. Meanwhile, in secret discussions, the PKK and the government had decided on a piece of political theatre to illustrate the PKK's desire to put down their arms and the government's willingness to let the guerrillas come home. They planned a dramatic "peace caravan" of eight guerrillas and their families who would cross into Turkey from Iraq in October 2009 and be granted immunity from prosecution.[10]

Unfortunately, the two sides did not have the same image of what the peace caravan would look like. Erdogan, who saw himself as the father of his people, may have imagined a handful of prodigal sons slinking over the border to ask his forgiveness. In reality, as soon as the guerrillas crossed into Turkey, they were met by a rapturous Democratic Society Party rally of thousands of Kurds, all waving PKK flags and pictures of Ocalan and shouting "Long live the PKK!"

A storm of criticism erupted on the Right, blaming Erdogan for allowing what they called a PKK victory demonstration. Erdogan couldn't stand the pressure. He abandoned all talk of peace in order to hold on to the support of the military. Despite Turkey's promise that they would have immunity, the peace caravan guerrillas were all arrested and tried as terrorists. In December 2009, the Democratic Society Party was banned and its officials were arrested. That was the end of the "Kurdish opening." It was also the end of any attempt by the AKP to lead Turkey in a more democratic direction.

The death of the "Kurdish opening" in 2009 led to another round of what author Paul White called the "deadly pattern" in which "wholesale bloodletting is followed by fruitless attempts at peacemaking—which are followed by even worse bloodletting."[11]

The pattern will sound all too familiar to anyone who has followed the other Oslo "peace process" between Israelis and Palestinians, in which negotiations that began in 1993 led to one betrayal and disappointment after another. But, unlike the Palestinian movement, members of the Kurdish movement in Turkey and Syria had a unified vision of what they were fighting for. They also had taken concrete steps to build an institutional base for what they wanted. Whatever one may feel about the Ocalan cult of personality, there can be no question that his ideological leadership enabled this transition.

## The AKP and "Moderate Islamism"

Turkey had been a NATO member since the organization's beginning and had been a candidate for membership in the European Union for many years. For these reasons, the US and the EU failed to take Erdogan's Islamism seriously. In fact, members of the US State Department used Erdogan as the poster boy for what they termed "moderate Islamism," meaning a kind of fundamentalism that was not only friendly to development, but allegedly moderate in its views.[12]

By 2013, Erdogan's moderation was not much in evidence, but his friendliness to development remained and was the source of many of the accusations of corruption against him and his associates. The planned destruction of Gezi Park in 2013 was a landmark in the convergence between "moderate Islamism" and real estate development: He would rebuild the center city for the rich and tourists, exile the poor to the outskirts, and console them with religion. This agenda also entailed cutting back public spending in favor of "faith-based" charity.[13]

In a scathing essay written six months after the Gezi protests, Nazan Ustundag called out Erdogan's manipulation of Turkish popular opinion, writing that "the AKP's rhetorical skill has been in its ability to rewrite the history of Turkey's multiple oppressions by putting itself at the center and by narrating the suffering of the prime minister and his friends as the suffering of the whole nation. In such an equation, defending public space, secular education, or a guaranteed job—that is, objecting in any way to the AKP's policies—is seen as an act of coup d'état against the nation's will."[14]

The AKP's Islamism was not just a foible. Like the Islamism of Egypt's Muslim Brotherhood, it was inseparable from authoritarianism, repression, censorship, and a willingness to impose its own beliefs by force.

The AKP was certainly not "moderate" when it came to women. Erdogan tried to outlaw abortion and the morning-after pill. He decreed that every Turkish woman should have three children. His Forestry Minister told women who were looking for jobs, "Isn't your housework enough?" And in the 2015 election, Prime Minister Davutoglu actually promised to find mates for people who voted for the AKP: "You have a job, a salary and a home. Now it's time for a spouse. We want people of this land to be bountiful. We want you to procreate. First, seek the help of your parents to find a spouse. God willing, this will work out. If it does not, apply to us. We will find you a blessed spouse."[15]

With this approach, it was no wonder that the AKP presided over a decline in the economic position of women relative to other countries. In November 2015, the World Economic Forum announced that "Turkey has moved down five places, ranking 130th among 145 countries in the "Global Gender Gap Index," placing Turkey among the three lowest performing countries in the Europe and Central Asia region alongside Malta (104) and Armenia (105). It did particularly poorly in areas of economic and political equality.[16] Women suffered in other ways after the AKP took office. Between 2002 and 2009, the murder rate for women increased by an astonishing 1400 percent. In 2002, sixty-two women were murdered; in the first seven months of 2009, 953 were.[17]

If AKP rule was problematic for Turkish women, it was a disaster for the Kurds, who, let us not forget, made up 20 percent of the Turkish population. Their increasingly united stand in favor of democratic autonomy was a threat to any hegemonic Turkish party committed to centralization. Erdogan tried to disrupt this unity with token concessions—a Kurdish language TV station run by the government, a university elective in the Kurdish language. But, as Aliza Marcus said, "They see what Ankara gives them: schools where students cannot speak or learn Kurdish; security forces who harass the local population. And they know what they do not have: democratic freedoms."[18]

They did not have democratic freedoms because whenever they started a new political party, it was banned, and whenever they elected local leaders, those leaders were likely to end up in jail. The Turkish constitution, written after the military coup of 1980, severely restricted freedom of speech and assembly, and minority rights, and entrenched the power of the military. Not just the Kurds but the entire country suffered under this dispensation.

Multiple promises to reform the constitution were never carried out, and after Erdogan reached his term limit as prime minister and had to accept the ceremonial office of president, rather than move the country towards greater democracy, he began to push for a revised constitution that would give the president almost unlimited power.[19] He was clearly willing to sacrifice Turkey's image in the world to maintain the old unitary state—only his version substituted Sunni identity politics for Ataturk's secularism, and his Islamism brought him closer to Daesh and other jihadi groups than the US was willing to admit. The battle of Kobane brought that lesson home.

In the fall of 2014, when Daesh mounted its assault, Kobane was surrounded on three sides, its fourth side being the Turkish border. Instead of trying to help, or at least letting supplies and volunteers through, Turkey closed the border, massed tanks, and refused to let anyone pass, while Erdogan confidently predicted that Kobane would fall any minute. But Kobane did not fall. Instead, the remarkable battle of the Syrian Kurds eventually brought long overdue US air support, a turning point for the Kurds and the cause of considerable diplomatic stress between Turkey and the US.

In December 2014, Erdogan further scandalized Turkey's Western allies by arresting twenty-four journalists, media workers, and police officers as part of his feud with the media empire of his onetime friend, Fethullah Gulen, the founder of the conservative Hizmet movement, whose newspapers had accused the Erdogan family of corruption. *The New York Times* published an editorial in response, headed "Turkey's Descent Into Paranoia." The editorial said that "Mr. Erdogan's efforts to stifle criticism and dissent show an authoritarian leader living in a parallel universe, one where being a democracy, a NATO ally and a candidate for membership in the European Union are somehow compatible with upending the rule of law and stifling freedom of expression."[20]

The political climate grew tense as the May 2015 election approached. Erdogan was banking on getting a large enough majority to protect his party and family members from being prosecuted for under-the-table deals. Although the Turkish presidency was supposed to be an office above politics, he campaigned ferociously for the AKP to win a majority large enough to permit them to change the constitution and make him an imperial president.[21]

Under the 1980 constitution, a party needed 10 percent of the national vote to become a recognized parliamentary entity. Previous Kurdish parties had been unable to reach that percentage because their base was limited to the southeast. But the game changed with the 2014 merger of the Kurdish BDP and the progressive Left and feminist HDP. Despite AKP attacks on their offices and arrests of party activists, in the June election, the merged HDP won 13.1 percent of the vote and eighty-one seats in Parliament. Even conservative and religious Kurds who had previously voted for Erdogan's AKP switched their votes because of his refusal to allow aid into Kobane.[22]

Without a parliamentary majority, the AKP was supposed to try to form a coalition. But rather than let that happen, Erdogan scheduled a new "snap election" to be held on November 1, 2015, hinting that, unless people gave him the majority he wanted, things were going to get rough.

On July 20, a suicide bomber attacked a Kurdish rally in Suruc, killing thirty-three Kurds from socialist youth groups who were crossing the border to help rebuild Kobane. Turkey accused Daesh, but the HDP and the press raised questions about how Turkey's omnipresent security apparatus could have let a suicide bomber through when everyone else at the event had been searched.[23]

On July 22, a local PKK group killed two Turkish security police in retaliation for the Suruc attack. That was all the excuse Erdogan needed to begin arresting HDP leaders and start bombing PKK camps in Iraq for the first time in four years. On July 23, HDP co-chairman Selahattin Demirtas called for an immediate ceasefire, saying, "No one has anything to win from a civil war in Turkey. Just look at Syria and Iraq." Appealing to the PKK as well as the government, he insisted that killing individual soldiers and policemen was not the way to fight, saying, "They are also the children of this country, our children."[24]

A few days later he told Der Speigel that killing the two policemen was "a dark, dirty chapter. It was revenge for the attack in Suruc, committed by a local PKK unit. The broader organization did not claim responsibility. It seems to me that individual elements were looking to provoke the Turkish state. . . . We urgently call on the PKK and the Turkish government to put down their weapons."[25]

Instead of listening, Prime Minister Davutoglu bragged that government planes had hit 400 targets in their raids n PKK bases in Iraq. In a furious response, the PKK rejected the call for a ceasefire just as they had when Leyla Zana made a similar appeal in 2004. PKK Executive Committee member Duran Kalkan explained that the PKK was not looking for a fight and had not started this one but it was "not right to talk about the actions by PKK without mentioning the most recent Amed (Diyarbakir) and Suruç massacres, and increasingly ongoing repression and arrests. On the other hand, guerrillas haven't pulled the trigger yet. Their current actions are limited retaliation."[26]

The situation continued to escalate. On July 29, someone blew up the oil pipeline between Turkey and Kirkuk, and the PKK attacked a Turkish police station in Hakkari. By the third week in August, at least fifty Turkish police had been killed. Despite HDP calls for a ceasefire, the Turkish state followed its usual procedure of treating the PKK and HDP as if they were the same organization. As political scientist Nicole Watts has observed, Turkish electoral politics can be almost as dangerous as armed struggle, at least for Kurds.[27] By August 2015, 1,464 HDP elected officials had been arrested, and 224 were in jail, including the co-mayors of Hakkari, Sur, Silvan, and Edremit. (Turkey considered the co-mayor system, one man and one woman, illegitimate, and Turkish repression often made it hard to carry out the vision behind the HDP's democratic autonomy program. During one period in 2015, for example, 60 percent of the women leaders in Diyarbakir were in jail.)[28]

The Erdogan government then began to put Kurdish cities in the southeast under martial law, treating regions that had voted HDP as conquered provinces whose people needed to be taught a lesson. In Cizre, for instance, the military put the whole town under 24-hour-curfew for nine days, refusing to let HDP deputies in to observe, and stationing snipers on mosque roofs to kill any civilian who dared to go outside.[29]

The Kurdish civil resistance movement responded by declaring autonomy in town after town, saying that, since the Turkish state would not protect them, they would protect themselves. Members of the Patriotic Revolutionary Youth Movement (YDG-H), made up of young urban guerrillas who sought to defend their communities against attacks by right-wing Turkish groups, such as the fascist Gray Wolves, the Islamist Huda-Par, as well as the Turkish police,[30] began digging ditches and throwing up barricades, preparing to defend the cities which they correctly estimated would soon be attacked in force. Early in September 2015, the government issued an executive order putting thirteen predominantly Kurdish provinces under martial law and authorizing their civilian governors to use military operations against terrorists. The PKK called on all citizens to form armed self-defense forces.[31]

The first towns attacked were Silopi and Cizre. In defiance of every human rights convention, the Turkish military continued to put snipers on the roofs of high buildings, from which they shot civilians at random; imposed 24-hour curfews, leaving people without food and water; burst into houses and shot whoever was there; prevented ambulances from picking up the wounded, so people bled to death; shot into crowded buildings; shot people who tried to help the wounded or retrieve the bodies of relatives from the streets; and prevented burials.[32]

All this was in the lead-up to the critical snap election of November 1. On October 10, two Daesh suicide bombers blew themselves up at a Kurdish peace march in Ankara, killing 102 people and wounding hundreds more. The HDP accused the state of being involved, and the accusations gathered force as evidence came out that the Turkish security service had been watching the bombers and monitoring their communications.[33]

After this attack, the HDP decided it could no longer hold rallies for fear its supporters would again be killed, while Erdogan cited the Ankara bombing as proof that voters would be safe only under a strong leader. His government also went on the offensive against the press, taking over newspapers hostile to the AKP and arresting their editors, journalists, and anyone who criticized Erdogan.

On October 20, Prime Minister Davutoglu made a speech in the Kurdish city of Van, saying that if the AKP failed to regain its parliamentary majority in the snap election, they could expect "the return of the 'white Toros,'" the Turkish name for the Renault 12, the car used by the secret police who had murdered so many Kurds in the nineties. "This was a remarkably overt threat for a head of government to make to his own people," wrote the journalist Christopher de Bellaigue in *The New York Review of Books*, "and a sign of the perversion of democratic norms that has become common in Turkey."[34]

Under these circumstances, it would have been a miracle if the HDP had received the same level of support it had in May, and it did not. At the cost of bringing Turkey closer to a dictatorship and seriously damaging its economy and its political credibility abroad, the AKP won a parliamentary majority, freeing it from the need to form a coalition government. But it did not succeed in eliminating the HDP as a threat: The party received 10 percent of the vote, enough to keep it in Parliament—at least, until it is declared illegal again, which may happen at any time.

HDP co-chair Figen Yuksekdag tallied up the carnage after the election: "258 civilians, including 33 children, lost their lives during the period of 5 months since [the] June 7 election. Over 100 people were killed in [the] Ankara massacre. 500 executives and members of our party were arrested. 190 HDP buildings were attacked." Yuksekdag's co-chair, Selahattin Demirtas, added: "It was not a fair election under equal circumstances. We couldn't run an election campaign during this process. We just tried to save our people from the massacres targeting us."[35]

Despite its electoral victory, the government stepped up its attacks on Kurdish cities after the election. Using the misleading term "curfews," Erdogan's government instituted an urban scorched-earth campaign meant to depopulate targeted areas. The Turkish Human Rights Foundation reported that from August to the end of December 2015, seventeen different Kurdish towns were subjected to a total of fifty-two round-the-clock curfews in which whole neighborhoods were leveled and many civilians killed. Some of these towns were bombed from the air or shelled by tanks. Prime Minister Davutoglu told the press on December 15, "All those towns will be cleansed of terror elements. If necessary, neighborhood by neighborhood, house by house, street by street."[36]

Rather than cowing the Kurdish population, the undoing of the HDP electoral victory and the attacks on civilians pushed people further towards civil resistance. On August 11, 2015, after three civilians were murdered by special forces, the province of Sirnak joined other Kurdish regions in declaring autonomy, stating, "No appointed governor shall rule us in this way. . . . We will govern ourselves from now on and won't allow anyone rule over us."[37] Despite heavy bombardment and many civilian casualties, one Kurdish city after another declared autonomy. Self-defense groups spread throughout the region, many of them organized by youth and women, including older women.

One of these women, identified as Serife, told the Kurdish media, "Whenever the police enter our neighborhood we go into action. They used to torture our children right in front of our eyes. They would break down our doors and come into our homes. They would go up to our roofs to position their snipers. We decided together to take up arms against all of this. The President and Prime Minister of Turkey are saying that the PKK is here, however there is no PKK in Sûr, there [are] the people. We are defending ourselves and our children in our own neighborhood. We are the people, and it is us who are building these positions. We are not afraid of death, we have nothing to lose."[38]

On December 28, one thousand Kurdish activists, including Selahattin Demirtas, attended a special self-rule conference called by the Democratic Society Congress (DTK). The conference's final resolution stated, "We as the DTK embrace the declarations of self-rule by local people's assemblies and the just and legitimate popular resistance in all areas. We consider it essential that the Kurdish people and all peoples of Turkey join and support this resistance as part of the struggle for democracy and freedom. This is a matter of democracy rather than a trench and barricade problem like the AKP government asserts. The aggressive policy of the AKP is intended to break the popular will for local democracy and a free life." Participants resolved to further develop the concept of self-rule and support individual and collective self-defense against policies of war and violence.[39]

The situation continued to deteriorate. In January 2016, a coalition of Turkish human rights groups issued an urgent call for help to the international community, saying, "Since August 2015, long-term and consecutive curfews have been declared in the provinces of, and the towns attached to Sirnak, Mardin, Diyarbakir, Hakkari, and Mus, and are still underway in certain cities and towns. During these prohibitions, national and international media, human rights or professional organizations as well as representatives of the parliament who wanted to identify violations of rights have been denied access to these cities and towns. According to the findings in reports drawn up by the very small number of civil society organizations which could make their way into the region in the face of huge obstacles, it has been determined that the civilian population has become the target of both snipers and heavy weaponry, which has been used in an arbitrary fashion.

"According to reports prepared by rights based organizations, 1.3 million people have been impacted by the curfews; more than 150 civilians—including children and the elderly—have lost their lives. Many people have been injured, and hundreds of thousands of people have been displaced. Arbitrary detentions and arrests have occurred; and civilians are being subjected to torture and maltreatment in detention centres and in the open. Intrusion in telecommunication networks restricts the right to information and freedom of communication. By an official decision to send away teachers from the region, education has been disrupted without a deadline, and health services have also been suspended. Due diligence in protecting civilians is not being demonstrated in any sense and they are not even provided the opportunity to meet minimum daily needs such as the right to food and water. After the curfews, no immediate and explicitly effective investigations have been conducted. Trial and punishment of those security forces that violate rights are being rendered impossible. The policy of impunity expands and continues, getting more severe."[40]

As southeastern Turkey descended into chaos, the entire country moved closer to dictatorship. Journalists, artists, and academics were particularly targeted. On January 11, 2016, over one thousand Turkish academics, plus various foreign luminaries including Etienne Balibar, Judith Butler, Noam Chomsky, and David Harvey, released a petition entitled "We will not be a party to this crime." The petition condemned Turkish attacks on civilians in the southeast and called for a resumption of peace talks between the government and the PKK.[41]

Immediately labeled traitors by President Erdogan, the signatories were attacked in the press and the Turkish ones were publicly threatened by a nationalist gangster who said he would bathe in their blood. Prosecutors launched an investigation into everyone who had signed, on charges of "making propaganda for a terrorist organization" and "insulting the Turkish nation." Thirty-three were hauled in for questioning. A number lost their jobs, while many more received menacing phone calls and death threats from right-wing student organizations. Erdogan said the academics were "committing the same crime as those who commit massacres" and invited university authorities and judicial organs to "do their duty."[42]

At the end of January 2016, Abdullah Demirbas, the beloved former mayor of Sur—which was being pounded into dust by the military—wrote in *The New York Times*, "In 2007, Sur became the first municipality in Turkey to offer services in local languages . . . a move that infuriated the authorities in Ankara, the capital, and led to my removal as mayor. In 2009, months after being re-elected with two-thirds of the vote, I was arrested on charges of separatism. . . . As I was rounded up along with hundreds of Kurdish activists and elected politicians, my teenage son left our house to join the PKK. 'You are wasting time with your politics and dialogue,' he told me. I dedicated my life to trying to prove him wrong and bring him home in peace. I have been discouraged before, but never lost hope. Today, I struggle to keep that hope alive."[43]

And how did the US government respond to Turkey's lurch towards dictatorship and war on civilians? It criticized Turkish violations of free speech. Selahattin Demirtas, cochair of the HDP, expressed his frustration with this approach in *The New York Times*:

"Many American policy makers are horrified by Mr. Erdogan's efforts to kill off what is left of free speech in Turkey. Even President Obama admitted that he was 'troubled' by the direction of the country, a NATO ally. While the American public is right to be concerned about Mr. Erdogan's efforts to stifle free speech and imprison journalists, as a Kurd I am saddened that the criticism ends there. There has been hardly any real mention of the government's abuses in the fight against the Kurdistan Workers' Party, or P.K.K., the deportations of civilians, the destruction of Kurdish towns and the imprisonment of Kurdish politicians in Turkey."[44]

The US failure to factor human rights into its Kurdish policy goes back to the Cold War.

In 1948—at a time when it was cultivating a relationship with Turkish military intelligence and planning Operation Gladio, which would arm and train clandestine groups in NATO member countries and elsewhere in Europe—the CIA made a study of the "Kurdish problem." This report, declassified, under the Freedom of Information Act, begins:

"The almost three million Kurdish tribesmen of Turkey, Iran, Iraq, and Syria constitute a factor of some importance in any strategic estimate of Near East affairs by virtue of their tradition of armed resistance to the governments over them and the efforts the USSR is making to stimulate and capitalize upon their grievances. Because of the narrow tribal loyalties of the Kurds and the rudimentary nature of the Kurdish nationalist movement, a unified attempt to set up an independent state over all of the traditional mountain homeland of 'Kurdistan' is unlikely. Nevertheless, the Kurdish tribes can be expected to continue to break out in sporadic local uprisings . . . capable of furnishing propaganda for the USSR before world opinion and of disrupting operations of Iraq's Mosul oilfields, which are in the Kurdish area. Moreover, the delicate balance of the present Near East state system creates the possibility that a Kurdish revolt, by drawing on security forces and by stimulating other dissident groups, might lead to further disruption of the political and economic stability of that region."[45]

With minor changes, this paragraph could have been written in 2016. Washington continues to see the Kurds mainly in terms of their proximity to oil fields and their capacity for disrupting existing states. Nor have the various branches of the US government yet found a way to reconcile their longstanding relationship with Turkey with the need to ally with the Kurds against Daesh.

In July 2015, Secretary of Defense Ash Carter publicly acknowledged that the US had found the YPG-YPJ a reliable partner to act as a ground force against Daesh. That October, Ilham Ehmed of the TEV-DEM Executive Committee was optimistic that the relationship was moving in the right direction, saying US representatives had "said that they would support the Kurds and work together with them in a diplomatic relationship built on friendship. In this respect we can say that the United States has opened a new diplomatic door."[46].

Of course, Mullah Mustafa Barzani thought the same thing until Kissinger threw him under the bus. While one can hope that this story will end differently, the US and EU have not insisted that the Rojava Kurds be part of Syrian peace talks despite their leading role in the war. In January 2016, after Ehmed and Salim Muslim were excluded from the talks in Geneva, the Kurdish delegation criticized the attitude of the US, which they said was obscuring the PYD's role and treating them as a military, but not a political ally.[47]

This was an accurate description of the situation. For decades the US and EU have gotten away with relating to the Kurds in a purely instrumental way, seeing them as a military resource, rather than as a people with an agenda of their own. The Cameron government in the UK baldly stated as much in a March 2015 report on the Iraqi Kurds: "We are also concerned that the PYD is attempting to pre-empt discussions on a final settlement for the Syria conflict. We do not support the PYD's unilateral announcement in November 2013 of forming a temporary administration in the Kurdish areas of Syria. This move was not conducted in consultation with the wider Syrian population or the international community. It will be for all Syrians to decide the exact nature of the political settlement in Syria as part of a transition process, including whether an autonomous region will be created for the Kurds in Syria."[48] In other words, the Syrian opposition will decide what happens to Rojava, not the Kurds.

To futher complicate matters for US and EU diplomacy, Russia is also courting the Rojava Kurds, who set up their first diplomatic office in Moscow in February 2016. By failing to give Rojava more diplomatic and economic support, and by continuing to tolerate Turkey's attacks on the Syrian Kurds and its own Kurdish citizens, the US could drive Rojava into the arms of Russia, which is surely not the object of its Middle East strategy.

Rather than continuing to pursue a foreign policy with so many internal contradictions, the US needs a fundamental reorientation of its attitude towards the Kurds, as well as a re-examination of its relationship with Turkey. Aliza Marcus and another longtime student of Kurdish politics, Andrew Apostolou, believe that the US has not caught up with facts on the ground: "The arguments against Kurdish independence are obsolete. It's not a question of whether the world should allow Kurds to have independent states. It's a matter of the international community catching up with what the Kurds have already done. In Iraq and Syria, Kurdish groups have established their own states—albeit *de facto*—without waiting for anyone's permission. These are not fully fledged independent countries with diplomatic missions at the United Nations and international recognition. They don't need to be. Kurds have shown they can manage without that. . . . Given how Kurds have been treated in the countries in which they live, it's no surprise that they have demanded the right to govern themselves and are willing to fight. So it's time that the international community caught up with Kurdish desires and helped Kurds build stable, democratic institutions, instead of taking the side of those who want to rule over the Kurds."[49]

*Tekoshin, PKK Sniper, Makhmour.*

# Some Questions Remain

I WROTE THIS BOOK TO ANSWER my own questions about what kind of revolution was possible in the 21st century, how it could happen and what it would look like. Was it imaginable that the Left would ever put women at the center of its politics, and what would happen if it did? And how would a decision to focus so much on women, a decision which would probably have to be made from the top at the beginning, mesh with democracy?

These questions preoccupied me long before the battle of Kobane. As I learned about the struggle of the Kurds, I reframed them, as I have said in the preface to this book. I hope some answers have emerged from the history I have recounted.

After the battle of Kobane, as Western journalists and activists began to hear about Rojava and even go there, progressives in many parts of the world started to get interested in Ocalan's thought and in Kurdish feminism. The YPG had begun to recruit foreign fighters online, and a number of young men from Europe and North America had already made their way to Syria to join the "Lions of Rojava," while solidarity groups emerged in a number of Western cities.

The Ocalan cult of personality could be a stumbling block in such solidarity work. Janet Biehl observed that "Western visitors who admire the remarkable accomplishments they witness in Rojava quickly also notice something that many find disquieting: seemingly every interior space (a notable exception being the self-government buildings) features an image of Abdullah Öcalan, the imprisoned PKK leader, affixed to the wall. The disquiet arises from memories of assorted twentieth-century dictators—Stalin, Hitler, Mao Zedong—whose images, in the many nations they long tormented, were similarly ubiquitous."[1]

Another stumbling block was the counter-narrative, sometimes influenced by Turkey or the Syrian opposition, sometimes coming out of left-wing purism, that said the PKK could not have changed from a totalitarian terrorist organization to a democratic one, pointing to the fact that some of the men who led it during its most Stalinist period, including Cemal Bayik and Murat Karayilan, were still in charge. These voices said that Rojava was one big Potemkin Village. They reminded the world that naive visitors had gone overboard on revolutions in the past, revolutionary tourism being a tradition at least as old as John Reed— dumb, over-privileged Americans blissing out on the idea that the work- ers' paradise had finally arrived in Russia or Albania, China or Vietnam, Cuba, Nicaragua or Peru, India, Nepal, Tanzania, or Zimbabwe.

I take such criticisms seriously, having had my own experience of revolutionary tourism in China in 1973 at the height of the Cultural Revolution, too credulous to question what I was looking at half the time. I remember how I wanted everything people told me to be true and tried to disregard my own misgivings. But I also agree with David Graeber when he says that this is a real revolution and that's the rea- son it scares people:

"I don't think there's any guarantee this one will work out in the end, that it won't be crushed, but it certainly won't if everyone decides in advance that no revolution is possible and refuse[s] to give active sup- port, or even devote their efforts to attacking it or increasing its iso- lation, which many do. If there's something I'm aware of, that others aren't, perhaps it's the fact that history isn't over. Capitalists have made a mighty effort these past thirty or forty years to convince people that current economic arrangements—not even capitalism, but the peculiar, financialized, semi-feudal form of capitalism we happen to have today— is the only possible economic system. They've put far more effort into that than they have into actually creating a viable global capitalist sys- tem. As a result the system is breaking down all around us at just the moment everyone has lost the ability to imagine anything else."[2]

I am excited by Rojava because the people there are trying some- thing new, and women are in the center of it all. This is not to say that complete equality has already been achieved; nobody with any sense would make such a claim after so short a time. So when debunk- ers note that women don't talk very much in mixed meetings; that the women co-chairs are less well known than the men; and that you don't see many women driving cars or starting businesses, I am not so concerned. It takes time and mutual support for women to get the confidence to speak up, learn how to drive, and claim equal space after generations of oppression. Those things will come.

Other questions remain. How strong is the position of women, really? How much are women in leadership really listened to? Is there more rotation among them than among the men, especially the veterans at the top? Are women stronger in Rojava, where they actually have the power to create a new society—though under very difficult conditions—than in the Kurdish regions of Turkey? There are no answers to these questions yet.

To me, there are inherent contradictions in trying to mesh a top down party-type organization like the PKK with the bottom-up grassroots democratic politics of communes and councils. What happens when differences of opinion arise? Under peacetime conditions, these differences can be worked through. The process will not be painless but time is on the side of the young, who are more likely to understand new models than are hard-bitten old warriors. But under conditions of war, a disciplined party and military command structure will probably prevail in most cases.

In other words, as long as the war goes on, the voices of the PKK military leaders in Qandil are likely to overrule the voices of civilian politicians like Leyla Zana and Selahattin Demirtas—especially if Ocalan, who tends to push for ceasefires, continues to be held incommunicado in a Turkish island prison.

I don't mean to say that democracy is impossible under conditions of war. But it is more likely to thrive under conditions of peace, when all the differences of opinion, affiliation, and material interest can come out into the open, unconstrained by the need for unity against an external enemy. On the other hand, any revolutionary society is likely to be threatened from the outside, so there will still be pressure to conform even if no shooting war is going on. Add to that a strong sense of group identity and a view that individualism is tied to capitalist modernity, and you have a model where freedom of thought and expression could become problematic. In the Rojava-to-come, how much room will there be for open discussion of basic points in "the Philosophy?"

This all remains to be seen. There are reasons, based on past revolutions, to fear the worst and there are reasons to believe that, like the rest of us, the Kurds have learned from these past revolutions and are looking for a different way. It is already clear that, even under wartime conditions, Rojava may well be the best place in the Middle East to be a woman. One can only imagine what such a place could mean for the region—a liberated area with a secular, egalitarian approach to gender, governance, economics, land usage, and ecological sustainability. Dissidents all over the region would have a place to get a secular education, escape the draft, and run away from forced marriages.

And, with all the new educational institutes being set up, and so much contact with people from other countries, young activists in Rojava are likely to be more sophisticated politically than earlier generations of militants in other revolutions—for one thing, they will have access to a much wider range of educational materials, not just Marxist classics or speeches by Ocalan, though they will certainly have those too. Widespread education is likely to temper uniformity of party thought and language—what the Chinese call "stereotyped party writing"—and allow for more individual variations of tone.

Will the commitment to democracy remain as strong as it is today? One of the problems with past struggles led by men with guns has been that, after the revolution, the men turned into an elite with police powers. What happens in a revolution where women also have guns? Will the guns wielded by the asayish and community self-defense brigades be enough to prevent the emergence of elites and a quasi-state? Maybe, but even thinking such a thought in a country plagued by the National Rifle Association and "lone shooters" is enough to make me nervous.

And what about Ocalan's idea that the state is becoming an obsolete form of organization?

By the end of the 20th century, global financial institutions like the World Bank and transnational treaties like the North Atlantic Free Trade Agreement (NAFTA)—including some, like the Trans-Pacific Partnership (TPP),[3] that are so destructive of state control that the politicians favoring them have tried to keep them secret from their own people—have already eroded the authority of the nation-state. The European Union is an attempt, though hardly a completely successful one, to make a political unit that overrides national control and dispenses with borders. And though Daesh calls itself a state, the classic salafi vision of a caliphate is more like a vast cultural union without borders where everyone (at least everyone who counts) is the right sort of Muslim, living under sharia law. In contrast, we have the radical local democracy of the Syrian and Turkish Kurds who hope to form some kind of federation that leaves state relations up to various national governments but keeps everything else—administration, law, education, economics—close in hand.

In the end, what will happen to the state is still a road unforeseen. Perhaps the question is not whether the ethnic-nationalist state will eventually be superseded, but what it will be superseded by—a globalized form of capitalism that leaves current social and political relations largely in place, but sucks out all the money for a tiny elite? An Islamist theocracy combining some aspects of capitalism (like oil extraction) with violent and repressive seventh-century social customs? Or the radical local control envisioned in Rojava, based on democracy, equal citizenship for all, feminism, and ecology?

If these are the choices, I know where I would put my energy.

—New York, April 2016

*Photographer Joey Lawrence with YPG-YPJ, Tel Hamis,*
*Cizire Canton, Rojava.*

# Notes

AUTHOR'S NOTE: In March 2016, the Turkish newspaper *Today's Zaman* was seized by the Erdogan government and its archive was taken offline. Due to this and other reasons, some of the following URLs may no longer be viable. Archived pages may still be accessed using a search engine or web applications such as the Way Back Machine.

## Introduction: A Road Unforeseen

1 Samantha Rollins, "France says the name 'ISIS' is offensive, will call it 'Daesh'" instead," *The Week*, September 17, 2014, http://theweek. com/speedreads/446139/france-says-name-isis-offensive-call-daesh-instead; Zeba Khan, "Words matter in 'ISIS' war, so use 'Daesh'," *The Boston Globe*, October 9, 2014, https://www.bostonglobe. com/opinion/2014/10/09/words-matter-isis-war-use-daesh/ V85GYEuasEEJgrUunodMUP/story.html; Amanda Bennett, "Daesh? ISIS? Islamic State? Why what we call the Paris attackers matters," *The Washington Post*, November 25, 2015, https://www.washingtonpost.com/ news/in-theory/wp/2015/11/25/daesh-isis-islamic-state-why-what-we-call-the-paris-attackers-matters/.

2 Justin Sink, "Obama makes ISIS enemy No. 1," *The Hill*, August 22, 2014, http://thehill.com/policy/international/215797-obama-makes-isis-enemy-no-1.

3 David Graeber, "Why is the world ignoring the revolutionary Kurds in Syria?" *The Guardian*, October 8, 2014, http://www.theguardian.com/ commentisfree/2014/oct/08/why-world-ignoring-revolutionary-kurds-syria-isis.

4 Danny Postel, "Should We Oppose the Intervention Against ISIS?" *In These Times*, December 18, 2014, http://inthesetimes.com/article/17423/ should_we_oppose_the_intervention_against_isis.

5 J.R.R. Tolkien, *The Fellowship of the Ring* (London: George Allen & Unwin Ltd, 1965), 280.

6 Meredith Tax, "The Revolution in Rojava," *Dissent*, April 22, 2015, http:// www.dissentmagazine.org/online_articles/the-revolution-in-rojava.

7 Meredith Tax, *The Rising of the Women: Feminist Solidarity and Class Conflict, 1880–1917* (New York: Monthly Review Press, 1980; 2nd edition,

Champaign-Urbana: University of Illinois Press, 2001, with a new introduction), 256.

8   Memed Aksoy, "A(y)lan Kurdi and the Kurdish Question," *Kurdish Question,* Sept. 4, 2015, http://kurdishquestion.com/index.php/insight-research/aylan-kurdi-and-the-kurdish-question.html.

9   Karl Marx, *Critique of the Gotha Programme,* I, 1875, https://www.marxists.org/archive/marx/works/1875/gotha/ch01.htm.

10  See, for instance, Meredith Tax, "An Expedient Alliance: The Muslim Right and the Anglo-American Left," *Dissent,* February 26, 2013, https://www.dissentmagazine.org/online_articles/an-expedient-alliance-the-muslim-right-and-the-anglo-american-left; "The Antis: anti-imperialist or anti-feminist," *openDemocracy 5050,* November 19, 2014, https://www.opendemocracy.net/5050/meredith-tax/antis-antiimperialist-or-antifeminist-0.

11  A basic discussion of globalization myths can be found in John Gray, *False Dawn: The Delusions of Global Capitalism* (New York: New Press, 1998).

12  Ahdaf Soueif, "Image of unknown woman beaten by Egypt's military echoes around the world," *The Guardian,* December 18, 2011, http://www.theguardian.com/commentisfree/2011/dec/18/egypt-military-beating-female-protester-tahrir-square.

13  Handan Caglayan, "From Kawa the Blacksmith to Ishtar the Goddess: Gender Constructions in Ideological-Political Discourses of the Kurdish Movement in post-1980 Turkey," *European Journal of Turkish Studies,* 14, 2012, http://ejts.revues.org/4657.

14  Deniz Kandiyoti, "Fear and Fury: women and post-revolutionary violence," *openDemocracy 5050,* January 14, 2013, http://www.opendemocracy.net/5050/deniz-kandiyoti/fear-and-fury-women-and-post-revolutionary-violence.

15  Gita Sahgal, "Purity or Danger? Human Rights and Their Engagement with Fundamentalisms," *Proceedings of the Annual Meeting (American Society of International Law),* 100, March 29–April 1, 2006, 417, http://www.jstor.org/stable/25660137.

16  FGM stands for the mutilation or complete removal of the female clitoris, an operation with many attendant psychological and medical complications performed on young children or adolescents, particularly in parts of the Middle East and Africa.

17  Susan Waltz, "Who Wrote the Universal Declaration of Human Rights?" *IIP Digital,* November 19, 2008, U.S. Department of State Publications, http://iipdigital.usembassy.gov/st/english/publication/2008/11/20081119135247xjyrrep6.023806e-02.html

18   Gita Sahgal, "Who wrote the Universal Declaration of Human Rights/," *openDemocracy 5050*, December 10, 2011, https://www.opendemocracy.net/5050/gita-sahgal/who-wrote-universal-declaration-of-human-rights.

19   Sonia Alvarez with Nalu Far and Miriam Nobre, "Another (Also Feminist) World Is Possible: Constructing Transnational Spaces and Global Alternatives from the Movements," trans. Arturo Escobar, *World Social Forum: Challenging Empires,* eds. Jai Sen, Anita Anand, Arturo Escobar, and Peter Waterman (New Delhi: Viveka Foundation, 2004), http://www.choike.org/documentos/wsf_s313_alvarez.pdf; Jenny Burchall and Jessica Horne, "World Social Forum: Integrating feminism and women activists into visions and practices of 'another world,'" *Bridge,* April 2013, http://socialmovements.bridge.ids.ac.uk/case-studies; Ara Wilson, "Feminism in the Space of the World Social Forum," *Journal of International Women's Studies,* 8.3, April 2007, http://vc.bridgew.edu/jiws/vol8/iss3/2.

20   "WLUML Statement to the World Social Forum—Appeal Against Fundamentalisms," *WLMUL,* January 21, 2005, http://www.wluml.org/node/1850.

21   Nadje Al-Ali, "A Feminist Perspective on the Iraq War," *Works and Days,* 29, 2011, http://eprints.soas.ac.uk/12116/.

22   Meredith Tax with Marjorie Agosin, Ama Ata Aidoo, Ritu Menon, Ninotchka Rosca, and Mariella Sala, *The Power of the Word: Culture, Censorship and Voice* (Women's WORLD: New York, August 1995), http://www.meredithtax.org/gender-and-censorship/power-word-culture-censorship-and-voice. For an article on the organization's work, see Meredith Tax, "Women's WORLD: A Transnational Organization of Women Writers: The Targeting of Feminist Writers," *Meridians: feminism, race, transnationalism,* 2, 1, 2001, pp. 177–185.

23   Caglayan, "Kawa the Blacksmith," 2012.

24   Friedrich Engels, *The Origin of the Family, Private Property and the State,* 1884, https://www.marxists.org/archive/marx/works/1884/origin-family/ch02c.htm.

25   Sveinung Legard, interview with David Graeber, "We Have a Lot to Learn," *New Compass,* September 17, 2015, http://new-compass.net/articles/we-have-lot-learn.

26   Christa Wolf, *Cassandra,* trans. Jan van Heurck (New York: Farrar Strauss and Giroux, 1984).

27   Gonul Kaya, "Why Jineology? Re-Constructing the Sciences Towards a Communal and Free Life," *Kurdish Question,* n.d., http://www.kurdishquestion.com/index.php/kurdistan/north-kurdistan/why-jineology/533-why-jineology.html.

28   Tax, *Rising of the Women*, 2001; Meredith Tax, "The Sound of One Hand
     Clapping: Women's Liberation and the Left," *Dissent*, Fall, 1988, http://
     www.meredithtax.org/us-movement-history-strategy/sound-one-hand-
     clapping-women's-liberation-and-left.

29   Ali Kemal Ozcan, *Turkey's Kurds: A Theoretical Analysis of the PKK and
     Abdullah Ocalan* (London: Routledge, 2006), 148.

## Chapter 1: The Kurds

1    Martin van Bruinessen, *Agha, Shaikh and State: on the social and
     political organization of Kurdistan* (PhD Diss., University of Utrecht,
     1978). This was made into a book: Martin van Bruinessen, *Agha,
     Shaikh and State: The Social and Political Structures of Kurdistan*
     (Zed Books: London, 1992), https://universiteitutrecht.academia.edu/
     MartinvanBruinessen/Books. My page numbers refer to the thesis.

2    Erika Solomon, "Isis aims to erase regional borders," *The Financial
     Times*, June 23, 2014, http://www.ft.com/intl/cms/s/0/aa5dafc2-fae6-11e3-
     8959-00144feab7de.html; Martin Chulov, Fazel Hawramy, and Spencer
     Ackerman, "Iraq army capitulates to Isis militants in four cities," *The
     Guardian*, June 11, 2014, http://www.theguardian.com/world/2014/jun/11/
     mosul-isis-gunmen-middle-east-states.

3    Dexter Filkins, "The Fight of Their Lives," *The New Yorker*, September 29,
     2014, http://www.newyorker.com/magazine/2014/09/29/fight-lives.

4    Filkins, "Fight," 2014; Anna Fifield, "Corruption fatigue fuels critics of
     Kurdistan's twin dynasties," *The Financial Times*, July 25, 2009, http://
     www.ft.com/intl/cms/s/0/d6dfe914-78b1-11de-bb06-00144feabdco.html;
     Derek Monroe, "Kurdistan: The Next Autocracy?" *Foreign Policy in
     Focus*, June 13, 2011, http://fpif.org/kurdistan_the_next_autocracy/.

5    Luay Al Khatteeb, "Kurdistan's Slow Rolling Coup d'état," *Huffington
     Post*, October 15, 2015, http://www.huffingtonpost.com/luay-al-khatteeb/
     kurdistans-slow-rolling-c_b_8306984.html.

6    "Seven Days In Iraq, Syria, Rojava And Turkey," *Harvest*, June 12,
     2014, http://turkeyharvest.blogspot.co.uk/2014/06/seven-days-in-iraq-
     syria-rojava-and.html; Asya Abdullah, "A joint defense force is a must
     for the Kurds," *Harvest*, June 28, 2014, http://turkeyharvest.blogspot.
     co.uk/2014/06/asya-abdullah-joint-defense-force-is.html; "'ISIS Crisis
     Urges Kurdish Unity' says Salih Müslim," *Harvest*, June 12, 2014, http://
     turkeyharvest.blogspot.co.uk/2014/06/isis-crisis-urges-kurdish-unity-
     says.html.

7    Sebastian Maisel, "Sectarian-Based Violence: The Case of the Yezidis
     in Iraq and Syria," *Middle East Institute*, July 23, 2014, http://www.mei.
     edu/content/map/sectarian-based-violence-case-yezidis-iraq-and-syria;
     Raya Jalabi, "Who are the Yazidis and why is ISIS hunting them?" *The

*Guardian,* August 11, 2014, http://www.theguardian.com/world/2014/
aug/07/who-yazidi-isis-iraq-religion-ethnicity-mountains.

8     "ISIS Commits Atrocities, Syrian Government Attacks Aleppo And
      Kurdish Forces Are In Solidarity With Communities In Iraq," *Harvest,*
      June 13, 2014, http://turkeyharvest.blogspot.co.uk/2014/06/isis-commits-
      atrocities-syrian.html.

9     Necla Acik, "Kobane: the struggle of Kurdish women against Islamic
      State," *openDemocracy Arab Awakening,* October 22, 2014, https://
      www.opendemocracy.net/arab-awakening/necla-acik/kobane-struggle-
      of-kurdish-women-against-islamic-state; Reuters, "Kurds, Islamic
      State Clash Near Kurdish Regional Capital," *The New York Times,*
      August 6, 2014, http://www.nytimes.com/reuters/2014/08/06/world/
      middleeast/06reuters-iraq-security-kurds.html?_r=1.

10    "A Day of Tremendous Resistance Across Northern, Western And
      Southern Kurdistan," *Harvest,* August 3, 2014, http://turkeyharvest.
      blogspot.co.uk/2014/08/a-day-of-tremendous-resistance-across.html.

11    "Salih Muslim Calls For Unified Military Council Following New
      ISIS Attacks," *Harvest,* August 4, 2014, http://turkeyharvest.blogspot.
      co.uk/2014/08/salih-muslim-calls-for-unified-military.html; Acik,
      "Kobane," 2014; Yvo Fitzherbert, "A new kind of freedom born in
      terror," *openDemocracy Arab Awakening,* August 26, 2014, https://www.
      opendemocracy.net/arab-awakening/yvo-buxton/new-kind-of-freedom-
      born-in-terror.

12    Tugba Akyilmaz, "Ezidi women refuse to give up in the face of Daesh,"
      *Jinha,* July 22, 2015, http://jinha.com.tr/en/ALL-NEWS/content/
      view/27022?page=1.

13    Jane Arraf, "Islamic State persecution of Yezidi amounts to genocide,
      UN says," *The Christian Science Monitor,* August 7, 2014, http://
      www.csmonitor.com/World/Middle-East/2014/0807/Islamic-State-
      persecution-of-Yazidi-minority-amounts-to-genocide-UN-says-video.

14    Zeinab Karam and Bram Janssen, "In an IS Training camp, children told:
      Behead the doll," *Associated Press,* July 19, 2015, http://bigstory.ap.org/
      article/f852b2d021254f06b9a002dfe25c7538/training-camp-children-told-
      behead-doll.

15    Rukmini Callimachi, "ISIS Enshrines a Theology of Rape," *The New
      York Times,* August 13, 2015, http://www.nytimes.com/2015/08/14/world/
      middleeast/isis-enshrines-a-theology-of-rape.html?_r=0.

16    Ishaan Tharoor, "Islamic State burned a woman for not engaging in
      an 'extreme' sex act, U.N. official says," *The Washington Post,* May 22,
      2015, http://www.washingtonpost.com/blogs/worldviews/wp/2015/05/22/
      islamic-state-burned-a-woman-alive-for-not-engaging-in-an-extreme-
      sex-act-u-n-official-says/?postshare=4031432347480556.

17    Olivia Goldhill, "This man risks his life every day to rescue kidnapped women from ISIS," *The Telegraph*, July 8, 2015, http://www.telegraph. co.uk/women/womens-life/11723360/Islamic-State-Meet-the-man-who-helps-kidnapped-women-escape-horrors.html; Mohammed A. Salih, "Father of the brave: the man who rescues enslaved women from Isis," *The Guardian*, July 13, 2015, http://www.theguardian.com/world/2015/jul/13/father-of-the-brave-the-yazidi-christian-who-rescues-hostages-from-isis; "Escaping ISIS," *Frontline,* July 14, 2015, http://www.pbs.org/wgbh/pages/frontline/escaping-isis/.

18    Goldhill, "This man risks everything," 2015.

19    Callimachi, "Theology of Rape," 2015.

20    Adam Withnall, "Isis releases 'abhorrent' sex slaves pamphlet with 27 tips for militants on taking, punishing and raping female captives," *The Independent*, December 10, 2014, http://www.independent.co.uk/news/world/middle-east/isis-releases-abhorrent-sex-slaves-pamphlet-with-27-tips-for-militants-on-taking-punishing-and-raping-female-captives-9915913.html; Rukmini Callimachi, "To Maintain Supply of Sex Slaves, ISIS Pushes Birth Control," *The New York Times,* March 13, 2016, http://www.nytimes.com/2016/03/13/world/middleeast/to-maintain-supply-of-sex-slaves-isis-pushes-birth-control.html.

21    "Liberating Şengal/Sinjar, Rabiaa And Maxmur/Mexmûr—Defending Rojava—Protecting HPG Guerillas—In Solidarity With Ezidis," *Harvest,* August 8, 2014, http://turkeyharvest.blogspot.co.uk/2014/08/liberating-sengalsinjar-rabiaa-and.html.

22    Reuters, "Kurds, Islamic State Clash," 2014.

23    Reuters, "Obama Authorizes Air Strikes in Iraq," *The New York Times,* August 7, 2014, http://www.nytimes.com/reuters/2014/08/07/world/middleeast/07reuters-iraq-crisis-usa.html.

24    Reuters, "US Weighs Options to Rescue Desperate Yazidis From Iraqi Mountain," *Newsweek,* August 11, 2014, http://www.newsweek.com/us-weighs-options-rescue-desperate-yazidis-iraqi-mountain-263759.

25    Hassan Hassan, "Isis, the jihadists who turned the tables," *The Observer,* August 9, 2014, http://www.theguardian.com/world/2014/aug/10/isis-syria-iraq-barack-obama-airstrikes.

26    Acik, "Kobane," 2014; "Late-breaking news—victories in Sinjar and Maxmur/Makhmour," *Harvest,* August 10, 2014, http://turkeyharvest. blogspot.co.uk/2014/08/late-breaking-news-victories-in-sinjar.html; "Our news today from Rojava and northern Iraq," *Harvest,* August 14, 2015, http://turkeyharvest.blogspot.co.uk/2014/08/our-news-today-from-rojava-and-northern.html.

27   Isabel Coles, "Iraqi Kurds liberate besieged Sinjar mountain, freeing hundreds," *Reuters,* December 18, 2014, http://www.reuters.com/article/us-mideast-crisis-sinjar-idUSKBN0JW22G20141218; Michael R. Gordon and Rukmini Callimachi, "Kurdish Fighters Retake Iraqi City of Sinjar from ISIS," *The New York Times,* November 13, 2015, http://www.nytimes.com/2015/11/14/world/middleeast/sinjar-iraq-islamic-state.html.

28   Filkins, "Fight," 2014; Barzani made a similar statement in January 2016, quoted in *The Guardian,* http://www.theguardian.com/world/2016/jan/22/kurdish-independence-closer-than-ever-says-massoud-barzani.

29   Filkins, "Fight," 2014.

30   Mouin Rabbani, "The Un-Islamic State," *Jadaliyya,* September 9, 2014, http://www.jadaliyya.com/pages/index/19181/the-un-islamic-state.

31   "ISIS Proposes Truce to Kurdish Peshmerga South of Kirkuk," *Rudaw,* June 16, 2014, http://rudaw.net/english/kurdistan/150620143.

32   Hanin Ghaddar, "ISIS's strategy of terror: interview with Christoph Reuter," *NOW Media,* July 15, 2015, https://now.mmedia.me/lb/en/10questions/565586-isiss-strategy-of-terror.

33   Hayri Demir, "The Betrayal of Shingal," *Ezidi Press,* August 9, 2015, http://ezidipress.com/en/the-betrayal-of-shingal/.

34   "Asya Abdullah: a joint defense force is a must for the Kurds," *Harvest,* June 28, 2014, http://turkeyharvest.blogspot.co.uk/2014/06/asya-abdullah-joint-defense-force-is.html.

35   Justin Huggler, "The world's largest nation without a state seeks a new home in the West," *The Independent,* February 19, 2001, http://www.independent.co.uk/news/world/europe/the-worlds-largest-nation-without-a-state-seeks-a-new-home-in-the-west-692440.html.

36   This overview is drawn from van Bruinessen, *Agha, Shaikh and State,* 1978, and David McDowall, *A Modern History of the Kurds* (London: I.B.Tauris & Co., 2004).

37   Robert Reich, "Tribalism is tearing America apart," *Salon,* March 25, 2014, http://www.salon.com/2014/03/25/robert_reich_tribalism_is_tearing_america_apart_partner/.

38   "Anglo-French Declaration," November 7, 1918, http://www.balfourproject.org/anglo-french-declaration/; "President Woodrow Wilson's Fourteen Points," *The Avalon Project,* January 8, 1918, http://avalon.law.yale.edu/20th_century/wilson14.asp.

39   Ali Kemal Ozcan, *Turkey's Kurds: A Theoretical Analysis of the PKK and Abdullah Ocalan* (London: Routledge, 2006), 2.

40   Shahrzad Mojab, ed., "Introduction," *Women of a Non-State Nation: The Kurds* (Costa Mesa: Mazda Publishers, 2001), 11–12.

41    Martin van Bruinessen, "From Adela Khanum to Leyla Zana: Women as Political Leaders in Kurdish History," in Mojab, ed., *Women of a Non-State Nation*, 100–103.

42    "Female Genital Mutilation in Iraqi Kurdistan: an empirical study by WADI," 2010, 5, http://www.stopfgmkurdistan.org/study_fgm_iraqi_kurdistan_en.pdf; Christina Asquith, "Under the Knife: Grading Iraqi Kurdish Progress Against Female Genital Mutilation," *Foreign Affairs*, July 27, 2015, https://www.foreignaffairs.com/articles/turkey/2015-07-27/under-knife.

43    Before the 1979 revolution that brought the Ayatollah Khomeini to power, Iranian Kurds had small separatist movements, as well as a strong Communist Party; today they have a nationalist party, the KDPI, whose leader was assassinated by the Iranian government in Vienna in 1989, and a Marxist-Leninist party, Komala. Both these parties are split into two factions. A PKK affiliate, the Free Life Party of Kurdistan (PJAK), is the most rapidly growing Kurdish party in Iran; its militias are camped in the Qandil mountains near those of the PKK.

44    Roger Morris, "A Tyrant 40 Years in the Making," *The New York Times*, March 14, 2003, http://www.nytimes.com/2003/03/14/opinion/a-tyrant-40-years-in-the-making.html.

45    McDowall, *Modern History*, 348.

46    McDowall, *Modern History*, 382–3.

47    "Iraqi Kurds' protests over economic crisis turn violent," *Al-Jazeera*, October 8, 2015, http://www.aljazeera.com/news/2015/10/iraqi-kurds-protests-economic-crisis-turn-violent-151008155126148.html.

48    Hamit Bozarslan, "The Kurds and Middle Eastern 'State of Violence': the 1980s and 2010s," *Kurdish Studies*, May 2014, 7, http://tplondon.com/journal/index.php/ks/article/view/349.

49    McDowall, *Modern History*, 472.

50    McDowall, *Modern History*, 474; "The Time of the Kurds," *Council on Foreign Relations*, June 3, 2015, http://www.cfr.org/middle-east-and-north-africa/time-kurds/p36547?cid=nlc-news_release-news_release--link2 20150604&sp_mid=48807925&sp_rid=Z2FlcmZAYWpjLm9yZwS2 - !/;

51    McDowall, *Modern History*, 475.

52    James Brandon, "The PKK and Syria's Kurds," *Terrorism Monitor*, 5,3, February 21, 2007, *Jamestown Foundation*, http://www.jamestown.org/single/?tx_ttnews%5Btt_news%5D=1014; Soner Cagaptay, "Syria and Turkey: The PKK Dimension," *The Washington Institute*, April 5, 2012, http://www.washingtoninstitute.org/policy-analysis/view/syria-and-turkey-the-pkk-dimension.

53    David L. Phillips, *The Kurdish Spring: A New Map of the Middle East* (New Brunswick: Transaction Publishers, 2015), 79–80.

54    J. Michael Kennedy, "Kurds Remain on the Sidelines in Syria's Uprising," *The New York Times*, April 17, 2012, http://www.nytimes.com/2012/04/18/world/middleeast/kurds-remain-on-sideline-in-syrias-uprising.html?_r=0; Aliza Marcus, "Kurds in the New Middle East," *The National Interest*, August 22, 2012, http://nationalinterest.org/commentary/kurds-the-new-middle-east-7377; Phillips, *Kurdish Spring*, 159.

55    "The Kurdish Democratic Union Party," *Carnegie Middle East Center*, March 1, 2012, http://carnegie-mec.org/publications/?fa=48526&reloadFlag=1; Marcus, "Kurds in the New Middle East," 2012.

56    H. Akin Unver, "Turkey's 'Deep-State' and the Ergenekon Conundrum," *Middle East Institute*, April 1, 2009, http://www.mei.edu/content/turkeys-deep-state-and-ergenekon-conundrum; Kerem Oktem, "Return of the Turkish 'State of Exception,'" *MERIP*, June 3, 2006, http://www.merip.org/mero/mero060306.

57    Greg Bruno, "Inside the Kurdistan Workers' Party," *Council on Foreign Relations*, October 19, 2007, http://www.cfr.org/turkey/inside-kurdistan-workers-party-pkk/p14576; McDowall, *Modern History*, 189.

58    McDowall, *Modern History*, 442.

59    Kamran Matin, "Why is Turkey bombing the Kurds?" *openDemocracy Arab Awakening*, August 4, 2015, https://www.opendemocracy.net/arab-awakening/kamran-matin/why-is-turkey-bombing-kurds.

60    Adam Barnett, "The Rojava Spirit Spreads," *Dissent*, February 25, 2015, https://www.dissentmagazine.org/online_articles/turkey-erdogan-putin-rojava-kurdish-democracy.

61    Joost Jongeren and Ahmet Hamdi Akkaya, "Democratic Confederalism as a Kurdish Spring: The PKK and the Quest for Radical Democracy," in Mohammed A. A. Ahmed and Michael M. Gunter, eds., *The Kurdish Spring: Geopolitical Changes and the Kurds* (Mazda Press: Costa Mesa, 2013), 166, https://www.academia.edu/3983109/Democratic_Confederalism_as_a_Kurdish_Spring_the_PKK_and_the_quest_for_radical_democracy.

62    Acik, "Kobane," 2014.

63    These include Abdullah Ocalan, *Democratic Confederalism* (Cologne: International Initiative Edition, 2011), and *Liberating Life: Woman's Revolution* (Cologne: International Initiative Edition, 2014), http://www.freeOcalan.org/?page_id=267.

64    Abdullah Ocalan, *War and Peace in Kurdistan* (Cologne: International Initiative Edition, 2009), http://www.freeOcalan.org/?page_id=267.

65    Abdullah Ocalan, *Prison Writings III: The Road Map to Negotiations*, trans. Havin Guneser, (Institute Initiative Edition: Cologne, 2012), 21–2.

66    Ocalan, *Prison Writings III: Road Map*, 30.

## Chapter 2: Separated at Birth

1    Martin van Bruinessen, *Agha, Shaikh and State: on the social and political organization of Kurdistan* (PhD Diss., University of Utrecht, 1978), 16, 35–37, https://universiteitutrecht.academia.edu/MartinvanBruinessen/Books.

2    van Bruinessen, *Aghas*, 23.

3    David McDowall, *A Modern History of the Kurds*, (New York: I.B.Tauris, New York: 2004), 157.

4    van Bruinessen, *Aghas*, 91.

5    Blood feuds are not a thing of the past nor are they peculiar to Kurdistan. An August 2015 Google search of *The Guardian*, using the term "blood feud," turned up news stories about Afghanistan, Albania, Calabria, Corsica, Georgia, Ingushetia, Pakistan, Syria, Turkey, and Yemen.

6    van Bruinessen, *Aghas*, 90.

7    McDowall, *Modern History*, 246.

8    It was at first called the Kurdish Democratic Party but changed its name to Kurdistan Democratic Party in 1956 to avoid any implications of ethnic exclusivity.

9    McDowall, *Modern History*, 294, 296–7, 303–4.

10    McDowall, *Modern History*, 307–312.

11    Martin van Bruinessen, "Kurds, states and tribes," in *Tribes and power: nationalism and ethnicity in the Middle East*, ed. Faleh A. Jabar and Hosham Dawod (London: Saqi, 2002), 165–183, https://www.academia.edu/2521393/Kurds_states_and_tribes; McDowall, *Modern History*, 354.

12    McDowall, *Modern History*, 314–16.

13    McDowall, *Modern History*, 323–331.

14    Interview with Said Aburish, "The Survival of Saddam: Secrets of his Life and Leadership," *Frontline*, PBS, January 2000, http://www.pbs.org/wgbh/pages/frontline/shows/saddam/interviews/aburish.html.

15    McDowall, *Modern History*, 335, 331–2.

16    Douglas Little "The United States and the Kurds: A Cold War Story," *Journal of Cold War Studies*, 12, 4, Fall, 2010, https://www.academia.edu/9687244/The_United_States_and_the_Kurds.

17    McDowall, *Modern History*, 333.

18    McDowall, *Modern History*, 337–8.

19   Little, "Cold War Story," 2010.

20   McDowall, *Modern History*, 339–40.

21   "Minority groups face increasing discrimination in Turkey," *Today's Zaman*, March 20, 2014, http://www.todayszaman.com/national_minority-groups-face-increasing-discrimination-in-turkey_342607.html.

22   McDowall, *Modern History*, 192.

23   McDowall, *Modern History*, 192–200.

24   McDowall, *Modern History*, 207.

25   McDowall, *Modern History*, 208–9.

26   Erdem Yoruk, "Turkey: Kurds, the working class, and the new left," *Links International Journal of Socialist Renewal*, June 6, 2015, http://links.org.au/node/4457.

27   Aliza Marcus, *Blood and Belief: The PKK and the Kurdish Fight for Independence* (New York: New York University Press, 2007), 24.

28   Marcus, *Blood and Belief*, 28–35.

29   Alex de Jong, "Kurdish Autonomy Between Dream and Reality [Interview with Joost Jongerden]," *Roar Magazine*, June 4, 2015, http://roarmag.org/2015/06/kurdish-autonomy-jongerden-interview/.

30   Marcus, *Blood and Belief*, 38–41.

31   McDowall, *Modern History*, 421.

32   Joost Jongerden and Ahmet Hamdi Akkaya, "Born from the Left: The making of the PKK," in *Nationalism and Politics in Turkey: Political Islam, Kemalism and the Kurdish Issue,* ed. Marlies Casier and Joost Jongerden (London: Routledge, 2011), 10, footnote 6, https://www.academia.edu/376932/Born_from_the_Left_the_making_of_the_PKK.

33   Marcus, *Blood and Belief*, 56–8.

34   Chris Kutschera, "Turkey: Leyla Zana, the only Kurdish woman MP," *The Middle East*, October 1993, http://chris-kutschera.com/A/leyla_zana.htm.

35   "About Leyla Zana," *Writings from prison* (Watertown MA: Bluecrane Books, 1999), http://www.hist.net/kieser/ma11/About_Leyla_Zana.html; Kutschera, "Leyla Zana."

36   Kutschera, "Leyla Zana," 1993.

37   Kutschera, "Leyla Zana," 1993.

38   Aysegul Sert, "A Woman, a Kurd, and an Optimist," *The New York Times*, February 19, 2013, http://www.nytimes.com/2013/02/20/world/europe/20iht-letter20.html?_r=0.

39   "About Leyla Zana," 1999.

40  Kutschera, "Leyla Zana," 1993.

## Chapter 3: Insurrection and Genocide

1   David McDowall, *A Modern History of the Kurds*, (New York: I.B.Tauris, New York: 2004), 261–274.

2   David L. Phillips, *The Kurdish Spring: A New Map of the Middle East* (New Brunswick: Transaction, 2015), 36.

3   Interview with Said Aburish, "The Survival of Saddam: Secrets of his Life and Leadership," *Frontline*, PBS, January 2000, http://www.pbs.org/wgbh/pages/frontline/shows/saddam/interviews/aburish.html.

4   McDowall, *Modern History*, 343–356.

5   Middle East Watch, *Genocide in Iraq: The Anfal Campaign Against the Kurds* (New York: 1993), http://www.hrw.org/reports/1993/iraqanfal/ANFALINT.htm.

6   Middle East Watch, *Genocide in Iraq*, 1993.

7   Dave Johns, "The Crimes of Saddam Hussein: 1988, the Anfal Campaign," *PBS Frontline*, January 24, 2006, http://www.pbs.org/frontlineworld/stories/iraq501/events_anfal.html.

8   Middle East Watch, *Genocide in Iraq*, 1993.

9   McDowall, *Modern History*, 362–3.

10  Aburish, *Frontline*, 2000.

11  Phillips, *Kurdish Spring*, 41.

12  McDowall, *Modern History*, 371–2.

13  "Endless Torment: The 1991 Uprising in Iraq and Its Aftermath," *Human Rights Watch*, June 1991, http://www.hrw.org/reports/1992/Iraq926.htm.

14  McDowall, *Modern History*, 373.

15  Phillips, *Kurdish Spring*, 42.

16  Ismet G. Imset, "The PKK: Freedom Fighters or Terrorists," *American Kurdish Information Network*, December 7, 1995, 22–3, http://kurdistan.org/the-pkk-freedom-fighters-or-terrorists/.

17  Aliza Marcus, *Blood and Belief: The PKK and the Kurdish Fight for Independence* (New York: New York University Press, 2007), 83–5.

18  Joost Jongerden and Ahmet Hamdi Akkaya, "Born from the Left: The making of the PKK," in *Nationalism and Politics in Turkey: Political Islam, Kemalism and the Kurdish Issue*, ed. Marlies Casier and Joost Jongerden (London: Routledge, 2011), 130.

19  Che Guevara, "Message to the Tricontinental," *Che Guevara Internet Archive*, https://www.marxists.org/archive/guevara/1967/04/16.htm.

20  Walter Isaacson, *Kissinger: A Biography* (New York: Simon and Schuster, 2005), 160.

21  Marcus, *Blood and Belief*, 70.

22  Marcus, *Blood and Belief*, 79–82.

23  Jongerden and Akkaya, "Born from the Left," 132; Martin van Bruinessen, "Between Guerilla Warfare and Political Murder: The Workers' Party of Kurdistan," *MERIP*, 153, July-August 1988, http://www.merip.org/mer/mer153/between-guerrilla-warfare-political-murder.

24  Marcus, *Blood and Belief*, 97.

25  Martin van Bruinessen, *Kurdish Ethno-Nationalism versus Nation-Building States: Collected Articles*, (Istanbul: ISIS, 2000), 5, http://www.let.uu.nl/~Martin.vanBruinessen/personal/publications/index.html.

26  Marcus, *Blood and Belief*, 109–10.

27  Jongerden and Akkaya, "Born from the Left," 137.

28  Marcus, *Blood and Belief*, 89–96.

29  Marcus, *Blood and Belief*, 118–9.

30  Van Bruinessen, "Between Guerrilla Warfare and Political Murder," 1988.

31  Olivier Grojean, "The Production of the New Man Within the PKK," *European Journal of Turkish Studies*, July 2014, http://ejts.revues.org/4925. The article was originally published in French in 2008 by the same journal: http://ejts.revues.org/2753.

32  Hamit Bozarslan, "Between integration, autonomization and radicalization. Hamit Bozarslan on the Kurdish Movement and the Turkish Left," *European Journal of Turkish Studies*, 14, 2012, http://ejts.revues.org/4663.

33  Marcus, *Blood and Belief*, 135.

34  van Bruinessen, "Between Guerrilla Warfare and Political Murder," 1988.

35  Grojean, "New Man," 7. Selim Curukkaya was a founding member of the PKK who joined its core group in 1974; he left the PKK in 1992 after a disagreement with Ocalan and now lives in Germany. He is the author of a memoir about the PKK that has not been translated into English, and a prison memoir translated as *Sing That Song*, an excerpt of which can be found online at http://www.epubli.de/shop/buch/39397/excerpt.

36  For Ocalan's reflections, see Chapters 7 and 9 of *Prison Writings: The PKK and the Kurdish Question in the 21st Century* (London: Transmedia Publications, 2011); there is actually a section called "Conspiracies and the Course of History." For criticisms by ex-PKK members see van Bruinessen, "Guerrilla Warfare and Political Murder," 1998; and Marcus, *Blood and Belief.*

37  Marcus, *Blood and Belief*, 115–17.

38  Chris Kutschera, "Turkey: Leyla Zana, the only Kurdish Woman MP," *The Middle East*, October 1993, http://chris-kutschera.com/A/leyla_zana.htm.

39  Steven Greenhouse, "Paris Talks Seek Attention for Plight of Kurds," *The New York Times*, October 15, 1989, http://www.nytimes.com/1989/10/15/world/paris-talks-seek-attention-for-plight-of-kurds.html.

40  Marcus, *Blood and Belief*, 127.

41  McDowall, *Modern History*, 378–85.

42  This description comes from 2001 but the situation was the same before and after, until 2003. Isam al-Khafaji, "Almost Unnoticed: Interventions and Rivalries in Iraqi Kurdistan," MERIP Press Information Note 44, *Iraq Watch*, January 24, 2001, http://www.iraqwatch.org/perspectives/merip-pin44-012401.htm.

43  Choman Hardi, "Killing in the name of honour," 2007; Susan McDonald, "Kurdish Women and Self-Determination: A Feminist Approach to International Law," in Shahrzad Mojab, ed., *Women of a Non-State Nation: The Kurds* (Mazda Publishers: Costa Mesa, 2001), 150; Mirella Galletti, "Western Images of Women's Role in Kurdish Society," in Mojab, ed., 219.

44  Meredith Tax, "World Culture War," *The Nation*, May 17, 1999, http://www.thenation.com/doc/19990517/tax.

45  McDowall, *Modern History*, 388–92.

46  Eric Garris, "Cheney vs. Cheney: Invasion of Iraq Would Lead to 'Quagmire'," *Antiwar Blog*, August 12, 2007, http://antiwar.com/blog/2007/08/12/cheney-vs-cheney-invasion-of-iraq-would-lead-to-quagmire/.

47  Houzan Mahmoud, "A Dark Anniversary," *The Guardian*, September 27, 2006, http://www.theguardian.com/commentisfree/2006/sep/27/ontheoccasionof24thseptember.

48  Joost Hilterman, "To Protect or to Project: Iraqi Kurds and Their Future," *MERIP 247*, June 2008. file://localhost/, http/::www.merip.org:mer:mer247:protect-or-project.

49  Choman Hardi, "Women's activism in Iraqi Kurdistan: Achievements and obstacles," *Kurdish Studies*, October 2013, http://tplondon.com/journal/index.php/ks/article/view/30.

50  Houzan Mahmoud, "We say no to a medieval Kurdistan," *The Guardian*, April 13, 2007, http://www.theguardian.com/commentisfree/2007/apr/13/thefightforsecularisminku1.

51  Nadje Al-Ali and Nicola Pratt, "Between Nationalism and Women's Rights: The Kurdish Women's Movement in Iraq," *Middle East Journal of Culture and Communication*, July 28, 2011, http://booksandjournals.

brillonline.com/content/journals/10.1163/187398611x590192; pdf at http://www2.warwick.ac.uk/fac/soc/pais/people/pratt/publications/.

52   Houzan Mahmoud, "Day 16/16 of Activism Against Gender Violence: Women Rights and War," *Women Living Under Muslim Laws,* December 10, 2012, http://houzanmahmoud.blogspot.com/2013/06/this-is-my-interview-for-wluml-website.html.

53   Derek Monroe, "Kurdistan: The Next Autocracy?", *Foreign Policy in Focus*, June 13, 2013, fpif.orghttp://fpif.org/kurdistan_the_next_autocracy/; Kawa Hassan, "Kurdistan's Politicized Society Confronts a Sultanistic System," *Carnegie Middle East Center*, August 18, 2015, http://carnegie-mec.org/2015/08/17/kurdistan-s-politicized-society-confronts-sultanistic-system/ieta.

54   Dexter Filkins, "The Fight of Their Lives," *The New Yorker,* September 29, 2014, http://www.newyorker.com/magazine/2014/09/29/fight-lives.

55   Jenna Krajeski, "How the War With ISIS Has Exposed Kurdistan's Internal Divisions," *The Nation,* April 6, 2015, http://www.thenation.com/article/celebrated-its-stability-iraqi-kurdistan-actually-plagued-corruption-nepotism-and-int/.

56   Hassan, "Sultanistic System," 2015.

57   Anna Fifield, "Corruption fatigue fuels critics of Kurdistan's twin dynasties," *Financial Times,* July 25, 2009, http://www.ft.com/intl/cms/s/0/d6dfe914-78b1-11de-bb06-00144feabdc0.html.

58   Monroe, "Next Autocracy," 2013.

59   Seval Sarukhanyan, "Independent Kurdistan 'family' state, unlikely," *Ekurd*, December 18, 2015, http://ekurd.net/kurdistan-family-state-unlikely-2015-12-18 - .VnQDBg0-WvU.facebook.

60   Hardi, "Women's Activism," 2013.

61   Hassan, "Sultanistic System," 2015.

62   Filkins, "Fight of Their Lives," 2014; Hassan, "Sultanistic System," 2015.

63   Shenah Abdullah, "Being Fed Up in the Kurdistan Region of Iraq: The Story You Are Not Told," *Pasewan*, October 17, 2015, http://pasewan.com/blog/2015/being-fed-up-in-the-kurdistan-region-of-iraq-the-story-you-are-not-told/.

64   Hardi, "Women's Activism," 2013.

65   Nazand Begikhani, "Kurds Develop Gender Studies to Face Fundamentalism," *Huffington Post,* May 21, 2015, http://www.huffingtonpost.com/dr-nazand-begikhani/kurds-develop-gender-studies-_b_7344338.html; Christina Asquith, "Under the Knife: Grading Iraqi Kurdistan's Progress Against Female Genital Mutilation,"

*Foreign Affairs*, July 27, 2015, https://www.foreignaffairs.com/articles/
turkey/2015-07-27/under-knife.

66  Hardi, "Women's Activism," 2013; Shahrzad Mojab, "On women's NGOs
in Iraqi Kurdistan: military occupation, 'imperialist democracy' and
'colonial feminism,'" *Revolution*, July 1, 2007, http://revcom.us/a/094/
awtw-ngo-en.html; Lydia Alpízar Duran, "20 Years of Shamefully Scarce
Funding for Feminists and Women's Rights Movements," *AWID*, May
14, 2015, http://www.awid.org/news-and-analysis/20-years-shamefully-
scarce-funding-feminists-and-womens-rights-movements.

67  Hardi, "Killing in the name of honour," 2007.

**Chapter 4: The People Take Up the Struggle**

1   "PKK Statement to the United Nations," January 24, 1995, http://www.
hartford-hwp.com/archives/51/009.html.

2   "5ème Congrés, *Programme du PKK*, 1995 (en Anglais)," http://apa.online.
free.fr/imprimersans.php3?id_article=746&nom_site=Agence Presse
Associative %28APA%29&url_site=http://apa.online.free.fr.

3   Martin van Bruinessen, "Turkey and the Kurds in the early 1990s:
Guerrilla, Counter-insurgency, and Emerging Civil Society," originally
published as "Historical background" and "Developments since Newroz
1993," *Violations of Human Rights in Turkish Kurdistan. Report of a Fact-
finding Mission of Pax Christi and the Netherlands Kurdistan Society to
Newroz 1993*, (Amsterdam: Netherlands Kurdistan Society, 1996), https://
kurdishissue.wordpress.com/2014/05/29/1-15/.

4   Eric [Lubbock, Baron] Avebury, Chair of the Parliamentary Human
Rights Commission, "Turkey's Kurdish Policy in the Nineties," (paper
presented at the Middle East Studies Association in Washington, DC,
December 1995), http://kurdistan.org/turkeys-kurdish-policy-in-the-
nineties/.

5   Lois Whitman, "Destroying Ethnic Identity: The Kurds of Turkey,"
*Helsinki Watch*, July 1990, 2–3, http://www.hrw.org/reports/pdfs/t/
turkey/turkey907.pdf.

6   Whitman, "Destroying Ethnic Identity," 1, 11.

7   Paul White, *Primitive Rebels or Revolutionary Modernizers? The Kurdish
National Movement in Turkey* (London: Zed Books, 2000), 144–46.

8   Aliza Marcus, *Blood and Belief: The PKK and the Kurdish Fight for
Independence* (New York: New York University Press, 2007), 147–49.

9   Marcus, *Blood and Belief*, 150–51.

10  "The Kurdistan Women's Liberation Movement for a Universal Women's
Struggle," *Komalen Jinen Kurdistan*, March 2011, http://www.kjk-online.
org/hakkimizda/?lang=en; Marcus, *Blood and Belief*, 141–2.

11    Minorities at Risk Project, *Chronology for Kurds in Turkey*, 2004. http://www.refworld.org/docid/469f38e91e.html.

12    White, *Primitive Rebels*, 164.

13    Marcus, *Blood and Belief*, 142–3.

14    David McDowall, *A Modern History of the Kurds* (London: I.B.Tauris & Co., 2004), 430.

15    Minorities at Risk Project, *Chronology*. This was when the US-led Coalition finally set up a no-fly zone in Iraqi Kurdistan.

16    Ali Kemal Ozcan, *Turkey's Kurds: A Theoretical Analysis of the PKK and Abdullah Ocalan* (London: Routledge, 2006), 15.

17    Marcus, *Blood and Belief*, 128.

18    McDowall, *Modern History*, 430.

19    McDowall, *Modern History*, 430–2; Minorities at Risk Project, *Chronology*.

20    Lois Whitman, "The Kurds of Turkey: Killings, Disappearances and Torture," *Helsinki Watch*, March 1994, https://www.hrw.org/report/1993/03/01/kurds-turkey/killings-disappearances-and-torture.

21    "Counter-Guerilla," *Operation Gladio,* December 3, 2012, http://operation-gladio.net/counter-guerilla.

22    Serdar Celik, "Turkey's Killing Machine: The Contra-Guerrilla Force," *Kurdistan Report No. 17*, February-March 1994, http://www.hartford-hwp.com/archives/51/017.html.

23    McDowall, *Modern History*, 434.

24    It was repressed by the government in the late nineties, when it got out of control, and went quiet for a while but in 2012 founded a legal party called Huda-Par. Kadri Gursel, "New 'Party of God' Will Divide Kurdish, Turkish Islamists," *Al-Monitor,* December 23, 2012, http://www.al-monitor.com/pulse/originals/2012/al-monitor/hizbullah-turkey-islamist.html.

25    van Bruinessen, "Turkey and the Kurds in the early 1990s," 1996.

26    Marcus, *Blood and Belief*, 165. Leyla Zana took the oath in Kurdish again in 2015 and once more it was ruled invalid by the speaker of the house. Gulsen Solaker and Ayla Jean Yackley, "Once-jailed lawmaker again uses Kurdish in Turkey's parliament," *Reuters*, November 17, 2015, http://www.reuters.com/article/2015/11/17/us-turkey-politics-kurds-idUSKCN0T627T20151117.

27    Chris Kutschera, "Turkey: Leyla Zana, the only Kurdish Woman MP," *The Middle East*, October 1993, http://chris-kutschera.com/A/leyla_zana.htm.

28    Marcus, *Blood and Belief*, 207.

29    McDowall, *Modern History*, 432.

30    Minorities at Risk Project, *Chronology*; White, *Primitive Rebels*, 166.

31    Avebury, "Turkey's Kurdish Policy," 1995.

32    Marcus, *Blood and Belief,* 203–5.

33    Marcus, *Blood and Belief,* 206.

34    Marcus, *Blood and Belief,* 207–8.

35    Kutschera, "Leyla Zana," 1993.

36    McDowall, *Modern History*, 438.

37    Andrew Finkel, "Turkey's Nagging Whodunit," *The New York Times*, December 19, 2012, http://latitude.blogs.nytimes.com/2012/12/19/turkeys-nagging-whodunit/?_r=0.

38    McDowall, *Modern History*, 438.

39    Marcus, *Blood and Belief,* 214–20.

40    Ismet G. Imset, "The PKK: Freedom Fighters or Terrorists," *American Kurdish Information Network*, December 7, 1995, 3, http://kurdistan.org/the-pkk-freedom-fighters-or-terrorists/; Marcus, *Blood and Belief,* 221-3.

41    Robert Jensen and Raul Mahajan, "Drain the swamp?" *Znet*, September 24, 2001, http://uts.cc.utexas.edu/~rjensen/freelance/attack6.htm.

42    Marcus, *Blood and Belief,* 325–8.

43    "About Leyla Zana," *Writings from prison* (Watertown MA: Bluecrane Books, 1999), http://www.hist.net/kieser/ma11/About_Leyla_Zana.html.

44    The stories of some of the conscripts were published in 1998 as oral histories by Nadire Mater, in *Mehmed's Book: Soldiers Who Have Fought in the Southeast Speak Out*. The book was censored and she and her publisher, Metis Press, were accused of insulting the military; their trial got international attention and they were acquitted in 2000. The book has been published in English under the title *Voices from the Front: Turkish Soldiers on the War with the Kurdish Guerrillas* (New York: Palgrave Macmillan, 2005).

45    Imset, "Freedom Fighters or Terrorists," 1995.

46    Imset, " Freedom Fighters or Terrorists," 1995.

47    5ème Congrés, *Programme du PKK*, 1995.

48    5ème Congrés, *Programme du PKK*, 1995.

49    "PKK Fifth Conference Resolutions," *Weşanên Serxwebûn*, May 1995, http://theirwords.org/media/transfer/doc/ut_tr_pkk_hpg_1995_07-aebf7 c10072070be75858618879b7c88.pdf

50    Marcus, *Blood and Belief,* 241.

51    "PKK Fifth Conference Resolutions," 1995.

52  Chris Kutschera, "Kurdistan Turkey: PKK Dissidents Accuse Abdullah Ocalan," *The Middle East Magazine*, July 2005, http://www.chris-kutschera.com/A/pkk_dissidents.htm.

53  Chris Kutschera, "Kurdistan Turkey: Abdullah Ocalan's Last Interview," *The Middle East Magazine*, April 1999, http://www.chris.com/A/Ocalan Last Interview.htm.

54  Marcus, *Blood and Belief,* 211, 217–18, 245, 254–5, 260; White, *Primitive Rebels or Revolutionary Modernizers:*, 109–11. In his lectures, Ocalan offered himself as a positive example of what can be achieved: "Why then can I be so effective? I am currently considered to be a miracle; this is because I revealed the state of ideologylessness and absence of morale in the Kurdish existence within the framework of my personality, and the extent of my own self-realization through this very unveiling corresponded quite easily with the concrete circumstances of this phenomenal social and political existence. In fact, the miraculous quality of every historical leap emanates from such a conjunction." Ozcan, *Turkey's Kurds,* 104.

55  5ème Congrés, *Programme du PKK*, 1995.

56  Ferdinand Hennerbichler, "The Origin of Kurds," *Advances in Anthropology*, 2.2, May 2012, http://www.scirp.org/journal/PaperInformation.aspx?paperID=19564; Andrew Curry, "Kurdistan Offers an Open Window on the Ancient Fertile Crescent," *Science* 4, April 2014, http://www.sciencemag.org/content/344/6179/18.

57  V. Gordon Childe, *Man Makes Himself* (London: Watts, 1936).

58  Abdullah Ocalan, *Prison Writings: The Root of Civilisation,* trans. Klaus Happel (London: Pluto Press, 2007), p. 12.

59  Ahmet Hamdi Akkaya and Joost Jongerden, "The PKK in the 2000s: Continuity through breaks," in Marlies Casier and Joost Jongerden, eds., *Nationalism and Politics in Turkey: Political Islam, Kemalism and the Kurdish Issue* (Routledge: London, 2011), 152, https://www.academia.edu/376934/The_PKK_in_the_2000s_Continuity_through_breaks; Abdullah Ocalan, *Serxwebun*, March 1993, as quoted in Ozcan, *Turkey's Kurds*, 103.

60  Ozcan, *Turkey's Kurds,* 107.

61  Kutschera, "Abdullah Ocalan's Last Interview," 1999.

62  Henrik Ibsen, *Rosmersholm,* Act III.

63  Ozcan, *Turkey's Kurds,* 95.

64  Ipek Uzum, "What is really missing from Turkish education?" *Today's Zaman*, May 12, 2014, http://www.todayszaman.com/blog/i-pek-uzum/what-is-really-missing-from-turkish-education_347572.html; David Lepeska, "New Turkey turns to old Ottoman," *Al-Jazeera America,*

December 23, 2014, http://america.aljazeera.com/opinions/2014/12/erdogan-turkey-ottomanlanguage.html.

65  Olivier Grojean, "The Production of the New Man Within the PKK," *European Journal of Turkish Studies*, July 9, 2014, http://ejts.revues.org/4925.

66  Ozcan, *Turkey's Kurds*, 149; Grojean, "The New Man," 2014.

67  Ozcan, *Turkey's Kurds*, 146.

68  Ozcan, *Turkey's Kurds*, 141, 143, 180–1.

69  Grojean, "The New Man," 2014.

70  Abdullah Ocalan, *Liberating Life: Woman's Revolution* (Cologne: International Initiative Edition, 2014, 51, http://www.freeOcalan.org/?page_id=267.

71  Vamik Volkan, *Blood Lines: From Ethnic Pride to Ethnic Terrorism* (New York: Farrar, Strauss & Giroux, 1997), 174–5.

72  Andreas (Marburg), "Zur Geschichte und Politik der Arbeiterpartei Kurdistans (PKK)," ["The History and Politics of the PKK"] 1997, passages translated for the author by Miriam Frank, https://www.nadir.org/nadir/initiativ/isku/hintergrund/geschichte/hausarbeitpkk.htm.

73  Kurdistan Committee of Canada, "Women's Army: PKK 5th Congress Resolution," August 1995, http://mailman.greennet.org.uk/pipermail/old-apc-conference.mideast.kurds/1995-August/000972.html.

74  "March 8, International Day of Kurdish Womens Amazons," March 7, 2012, https://www.youtube.com/watch?v=lbgfg_87sx4.

75  Email communication from Aliza Marcus, October 2, 2015.

76  This information is from a PKK internal educational resource translated from the German by Miriam Frank.

77  White, *Primitive Rebels*, 146. In addition to annulling the decisions of the Women's Congress in 1992, Abdullah Ocalan accused his brother of having mishandled the war with Turkey and relations with the KDP, and organized a conference to explore his "collaborationist" mistakes. Osman Ocalan fled to Iran, but the PKK brought him back and he was imprisoned for five months, eventually returning to leadership after a protracted process of self-criticism. He told journalist Chris Kutschera in 2004, after he left the party: "In June 1993, they removed all my powers . . . I was isolated in a cell for three months and interrogated for 52 days before being tried in February 1995. The trial lasted only one day. I was warned that if I continued to defend my ideas, I would be executed. If not, I would be pardoned. A lawyer? Out of the question. The trial was conducted under the law of the mountain." Chris Kutschera, "Kurdistan Turkey: PKK dissidents accuse

Abdullah Ocalan," *The Middle East Magazine*, July 2005, http://www.chriskutschera.com/A/pkk_dissidents.htm.

78  Nazan Ustundag, "Self-Defense as a Revolutionary Practice in Rojava, or, How to Unmake the State," *South Atlantic Quarterly*, January 2016, http://saq.dukejournals.org/content/115/1/197.full.pdf+html.

79  Ozcan, *Turkey's Kurds*, 84. The members of the PKK's first Central Committee were General Secretary Abdullah Ocalan, M. Hayri Durmuş, Cemil Bayik, Mazlum Dogan, Mehmet Karasungur, Kesire Yildirim, and Sahin Donmez.

80  Marcus, *Blood and Belief*, 42–44. At Ocalan's trial, he suggested that Yildirim's splinter group may have been involved in the unsolved assassination of Swedish Prime Minister Olaf Palme. "Ocalan denies role in key rebel actions, Palme assassination," CNN, June 1, 1999, http://www.cnn.com/WORLD/meast/9906/01/Ocalan.02/.

## Chapter 5: Kurdish Women Rising

1  Darren Butler, "Slain Kurdish activist Cansiz leaves stamp on militant PKK," *Reuters*, January 12, 2013, http://in.reuters.com/article/2013/01/11/france-kurds-cansiz-idINDEE90A0GU20130111.

2  "The Foundation of the PKK in the Words of Sakine Cansiz," *Kurdish Question*, November 2014, http://kurdishquestion.com/index.php/kurdistan/north-kurdistan/the-foundation-of-the-pkk-in-the-words-of-sakine-cansiz/493-the-foundation-of-the-pkk-in-the-words-of-sakine-cansiz.html.

3  Amberin Zaman, "One woman's journey from prisoner to mayor," *Al-Monitor*, March 23, 2015, http://www.al-monitor.com/pulse/originals/2015/03/turkey-woman-in-middle-east-gultan-kisanak.html.

4  "Foundation of the PKK," 2014.

5  Zaman, "One woman's journey," 2015.

6  Zaman, "One woman's journey," 2015.

7  Constanze Letsch, "Sakine Cansiz, 'a legend among PKK members,'" *The Guardian*, January 10, 2013, http://www.theguardian.com/world/2013/jan/10/sakine-cansiz-pkk-kurdish-activist.

8  Michael Gunter, "Murder in Paris: Parsing the Murder of Female PKK Leaders Sakine Cansiz," *Militant Leadership Monitor*, 4.1, 2013, http://www.mesop.de/murder-in-paris-parsing-the-murder-of-female-pkk-leader-sakine-cansiz/; "Three PKK members killed in Paris attack," *Daily Hurriyet*, January 10, 2013,http://www.hurriyetdailynews.com/three-pkk-members-killed-in-paris-attack.aspx?pageID=238&nID=38748&NewsCatID=338.

9  Letsch, "Sakine Cansiz," 2013.

10   Susan Fraser, "Sakine Cansiz Murdered: PKK Founder's Execution Highlights Women's Role in Kurdish Insurgency," *AP*, January 11, 2013, http://www.huffingtonpost.com/2013/01/11/sakine-cansiz-pkk-execution-kurdish-women_n_2457081.html.

11   "Sakine Cansiz," [obituary], *The Telegraph*, April 11, 2013, http://www.telegraph.co.uk/news/obituaries/9988186/Sakine-Cansiz.html.

12   Butler, "Slain Kurdish activist Cansiz leaves stamp," 2013.

13   Aliza Marcus, *Blood and Belief: The PKK and the Kurdish Fight for Independence* (New York: New York University Press, 2007), 173.

14   Delal Afsin Nurhak, "The Kurdistan Women's Liberation Movement," n.d., http://www.pkkonline.com/en/index.php?sys=article&artID=180.

15   Andreas (Marburg), "Zur Geschichte und Politik der Arbeiterpartei Kurdistans (PKK)," ["The History and Politics of the PKK"] 1997, passages translated for the author by Miriam Frank, https://www.nadir.org/nadir/initiativ/isku/hintergrund/geschichte/hausarbeitpkk.htm.

16   "The Kurdistan Women's Liberation Movement for a Universal Women's Struggle," *Komalen Jinen Kurdistan*, March 2011, http://www.kjk-online.org/hakkimizda/?lang=en.

17   "Women's Army: PKK 5th Congress Reso," *Kurdistan Committee of Canada*, August 6, 1995, http://mailman.greennet.org.uk/pipermail/old-apc-conference.mideast.kurds/1995-August/000972.html.

18   Deryagul Beran, "Women's Army In Kurdistan," *Kurdistan Report*, 20, January–Feburary, 1995, http://www.hartford-hwp.com/archives/51/011.html.

19   Xiaolin Li, "Chinese Women Soldiers: A Legacy of 5,000 Years," *Social Education* 58 (2), 1994, National Council for Social Studies, 180; http://www.socialstudies.org/system/files/publications/se/5802/580201.html.

20   Benedetta Argentiers, "Iraq's Largest Kurdish Faction Excludes Women From the Front Line," *War Is Boring*, November 10, 2015, http://warisboring.com/articles/iraqs-largest-kurdish-faction-excludes-women-from-the-front-line/.

21   Aaronette M. White, "All the Men are Fighting for Freedom, All the Women are Mourning Their Men, But Some of Us Carried Guns: Fanon's Psychological Perspectives on War and African Women Combatants," *Boston Consortium for Gender, Security and Human Rights, Working Paper No. 302*, 2006, http://genderandsecurity.org/projects-resources/working-papers/all-men-are-fighting-freedom-all-women-are-mourning-their-men-some.

22   Maxine Molyneux, "Mobilization without Emancipation? Women's Interests, the State, and Revolution in Nicaragua," *Feminist Studies*, 11:2, Summer 1985, 245.

23  Maya Arakon, "Kurdish Women's Unknown History of Struggle," *Revolutionary Strategic Studies,* March 31, 2015, https://revolutionarystrategicstudies.wordpress.com/2015/03/31/kurdish-womens-unknown-history-of-struggle/.

24  Constanze Letsch, "Kurdish women pray for peace as fears of civil war in Turkey mount," *The Guardian,* August 15, 2015, http://www.theguardian.com/world/2015/aug/16/women-join-kurdish-rebel-ranks

25  Giuliana Sgrena, "Commander Nesrin Abdullah: The Other Half of Rojava," *The Bullet,* July 7, 2015, http://www.socialistproject.ca/bullet/1137.php.

26  "Rojava: the women who wove a revolution," *Jinha,* July 17, 2015, http://jinha.com.tr/en/ALL-NEWS/content/view/26719.

27  Cynthia Cockburn, "World disarmament? Start by disarming masculinity," *openDemocracy 5050,* April 30, 2015, https://www.opendemocracy.net/cynthia-cockburn/world-disarmament-start-by-disarming-masculinity.

28  Madeleine Rees, "Syrian women demand to take part in the peace talks in Geneva," *openDemocracy 5050,* January 12, 2014, https://www.opendemocracy.net/5050/madeleine-rees/syrian-women-demand-to-take-part-in-peace-talks-in-geneva; "PYD Co-chair Moslem: We won't recognize a Geneva-3 excluding Kurds," *ANF,* January 31, 2016, http://anfenglish.com/features/pyd-co-chair-moslem-we-won-t-recognise-a-geneva-3-excluding-kurds.

29  "Nairobi Declaration on Women and Girls' Right to a Remedy and Reparations," 2007, https://www.fidh.org/en/issues/women-s-rights/NAIROBI-DECLARATION-ON-WOMEN-S-AND.

30  John Power, "Can Women End Korean War? After DMZ Crossing, Gloria Steinem says, 'Yes,'" *Christian Science Monitor,* May 25, 2015, http://www.csmonitor.com/World/Asia-Pacific/2015/0525/Can-women-end-Korean-War-After-DMZ-crossing-Gloria-Steinem-says-Yes.

31  Houzan Mahmoud, "Kurdish Female Fighters and Kobane Style Revolution," *Huffington Post,* October 7, 2014, http://www.huffingtonpost.co.uk/houzan-mahmoud/kurdish-female-fighters-_b_5944382.html.

32  Dilar Dirik, "Kurdish Women's Radical Self-Defense: Armed and Political," *Telesur,* July 7, 2015, http://www.telesurtv.net/english/opinion/Kurdish-Womens-Radical-Self-Defense-Armed-and-Political-20150707-0002.html.

33  Evren Kocabicak, "Interview with the World's First Army of Women: YJA-Star," *Maoist Road,* March 23, 2015, http://maoistroad.blogspot.com/2015/08/interview-with-worlds-first-army-of.html.

34  Abdullah Ocalan, *Liberating Life: Woman's Revolution* (Cologne: International Initiative Edition, 2014, 36, http://www.freeOcalan. org/?page_id=267.

35  Ocalan, *Liberating Life,* 52.

36  Handan Caglayan, "From Kawa the Blacksmith to Ishtar the Goddess: Gender Constructions in Ideological-Political Discourses of the Kurdish Movement in post-1980 Turkey," *European Journal of Turkish Studies,* 2012, 19, https://ejts.revues.org/4657.

37  "Sakine Cansiz," (obituary), *The Telegraph,* April 11, 2013, http://www. telegraph.co.uk/news/obituaries/9988186/Sakine-Cansiz.html; Fraser, "Sakine Cansiz Murdered," 2013; Olivier Grojean, "Self-Immolations by Kurdish Activists in Turkey and Europe," *Revue d'Etudes Tibétaines,* 25, December 2012, 159–168.

38  Gita Sahgal, "Legislating Utopia: Violence Against Women: Identities and Interventions," *The Situated Politics of Belonging,* ed. Nira Yuval-Davis, Kalpana Kannabiran, and Ulrike M. Vieten, SAGE Studies in International Sociology 55 (London: SAGE Publications Ltd, 2006), 217.

39  Michael Taussig, "The Mastery of Non-Mastery," *Public Seminar,* Aug. 7, 2015, http://www.publicseminar.org/2015/08/the-mastery-of-non-mastery/.

40  "We reproduce below a very informative Ask May Anything (AMA) from Reddit with a verified PKK fighter active in Kobane, Cizre, Bakur (Turkey) and Bashur (Iraq)," *Workers Solidarity Movement (Ireland), Facebook,* July 20, 2015, https:// www.facebook.com/WorkersSolidarityMovement/photos /a.974071899285290.1073741894.132000150159140/ 1175786155780529/.

41  Janet Biehl, "Paradoxes of a Liberatory Ideology," *Biehl on Bookchin,* November 22, 2015, http://www.biehlonbookchin.com/paradoxes-liberatory-ideology/.

42  McDowall, *Modern History,* 442.

43  Paul White, *Primitive Rebels or Revolutionary Modernizers? The Kurdish National Movement in Turkey* (London: Zed Books, 2000), 122, 184.

44  Tim Weiner, "U.S. Helped Turkey Find and Capture Kurd Rebel," *The New York Times,* February 20, 1999, http://www.nytimes.com/1999/02/20/ world/us-helped-turkey-find-and-capture-kurd-rebel.html; Tony Karon, "Behind Ocalan's Capture: Deceit, Abduction—and the Mossad," *TIME,* February 17, 1999, http://content.time.com/time/arts/ article/0,8599,20031,00.html; Marcus, *Blood and Belief,* 270–79.

45  Olivier Grojean, "Self-immolations," 2012; "Syrian Kurds Find Refuge in Camp Named after Suicide Bomber," *Agence France Press,* October 20,

2014, http://www.ndtv.com/world-news/syrian-kurds-find-refuge-in-camp-named-after-suicide-bomber-682131; Ahmet Hamdi Akkaya and Joost Jongerden, "The PKK in the 2000s: Continuity through breaks?" in Marlies Casier and Joost Jongerden, *Nationalism and Politics in Turkey: Political Islam, Kemalism and the Kurdish Issue* (London: Routledge, 2011), 143, https://www.academia.edu/376934/The_PKK_in_the_2000s_Continuity_through_breaks.

46    "Capture of PKK Leader Causes Worldwide Kurdish Protest," *Transnational Communities Program, Economic and Social Research Council,* Oxford, n.d., http://www.transcomm.ox.ac.uk/traces/iss5pg1. htm; "Kurds storm UNHCR headquarters; new protests erupt," *CNN,* February 17, 1999, http://www.cnn.com/WORLD/europe/9902/17/Ocalan. protest.02/.

47    Marcus, *Blood and Belief,* 282–4.

48    Chris Kutschera, "Kurdistan Turkey: Revelations on the Ocalan System," *The Middle East Magazine,* May 20, 2000, http://www.chris-kutschera. com/A/Revelations PKK.htm.

49    Marcus, *Blood and Belief,* 286–7.

50    Akkaya and Jongerden, "PKK in the 2000s," 2011.

51    "Erdogan: Kurdish leader should have hung," *Al Jazeera,* June 10, 2011, http://www.aljazeera.com/news/europe/2011/06/201161010254112644.html.

52    Ali Kemal Ozcan, *Turkey's Kurds: A Theoretical Analysis of the PKK and Abdullah Ocalan* (London: Routledge, 2006), 91; Abdullah Ocalan, *Prison Writings: The Roots of Civilisation* (London: Pluto Press, 2007) 312–13; Nick Danforth, "An Imprisoned Nationalist Reads Benedict Anderson," *Dissent,* March 7, 2013, https://www.dissentmagazine.org/blog/an-imprisoned-nationalist-reads-benedict-anderson; Janet Biehl, "Bookchin, Ocalan and the Dialectics of Democracy," *New Compass,* February 16, 2012, http://new-compass.net/articles/bookchin-öcalan-and-dialectics-democracy.

53    Abdullah Ocalan, "Declaration of Democratic Confederalism in Kurdistan," March 20, 2005, http://www.freeOcalan.org/wp-content/uploads/2012/09/Ocalan-Democratic-Confederalism.pdf.

54    Janet Biehl, "Kurdish Communalism," *New Compass,* September 10, 2011, http://new-compass.net/article/kurdish-communalism.

55    Danforth, "An Imprisoned Nationalist."

56    Aliza Marcus interviewed many of those who had left for *Blood and Belief.* See also Peter Nowak, "KURDISTAN: 'The PKK is threatened with decay,'" [interview with Selahattin Celik], *Green Left,* April 12, 2000, https://www.greenleft.org.au/node/22584.

57    "Osman Ocalan's Marriage Ties PKK Into Knots," *Today's Zaman*,
      March 3, 2004, http://www.todayszaman.com/national_osman-Ocalans-
      marriage-ties-pkk-into-knots_5937.html; Chris Kutschera, "Kurdistan
      Turkey: PKK dissidents accuse Abdullah Ocalan," *The Middle East
      Magazine*, July 2005, http://www.chriskutschera.com/A/pkk_dissidents.
      htm.

58    International Crisis Group, "Turkey: Ending the PKK Insurgency,"
      September 20, 2011, 1, http://www.crisisgroup.org/~/media/Files/europe/
      turkey-cyprus/turkey/213; Paul White, *The PKK: Coming Down From the
      Mountains* (London: Zed Books, 2015), 73, 100–101.

59    Dan Bilefsky and Alan Cowell, "3 Kurds Are Killed in Paris, in Locked-
      Door Mystery," *The New York Times*, January 10, 2013, http://www.
      nytimes.com/2013/01/11/world/europe/three-kurdish-activists-killed-in-
      central-paris.html?_r=0.

60    Fraser, "Sakine Cansiz Murdered," 2013.

61    Gianluca Mezzofiore, "Is Turkey Responsible for 2013 Paris Murder of
      PKK Founder Sakine Cansiz?" *International Business Times,* January 17,
      2014, http://www.ibtimes.co.uk/turkey-responsible-2013-paris-murder-
      pkk-co-founder-sakine-cansiz-1432756.

62    Harvey Morris, "Who Ordered the Killing of Sakine Cansiz?" *Rudaw*,
      January 29, 2014, http://rudaw.net/english/middleeast/turkey/29012014.

63    "French inquiry implicates Turkish secret services in Paris Kurds'
      murder," *Radio France Internationale*, July 23, 2015, http://www.english.
      rfi.fr/europe/20150723-french-inquiry-implicates-turkish-secret-services-
      pariskurds-murder.

## Chapter 6: Democratic Autonomy in Turkey and Syria

1    Aliza Marcus, "Asia Minority," *Tablet*, October 21, 2010, http://www.
     tabletmag.com/jewish-news-and-politics/47397/asia-minority.

2    Jon Gorvett, "Release of Kurdish Politician Leyla Zana Ends Awkward
     Episode for Ankara," *Washington Report on Middle East Affairs*,
     September 2004, http://www.wrmea.org/2004-september/talking-turkey-
     release-of-kurdish-parliamentarian-leyla-zana-ends-awkward-episode-
     for-ankara.html.

3    Ahmet Hamdi Akkaya and Joost Jongerden, "Reassembling the Political:
     The PKK and the Project of Radical Democracy," *European Journal of
     Turkish Studies*, January 18, 2013, http://ejts.revues.org/index4615.html.

4    Akkaya and Jongerden, "Reassembling the Political," 2013.

5    TATORT Kurdistan, *Democratic Autonomy in North Kurdistan*, trans.
     Janet Biehl (Hamburg: New Compass Press, 2013), 26.

6    Marcus, "Asia Minority," 2010.

7    TATORT, *Democratic Autonomy*, 49.

8    "Travel ban on mayor poses risk to his life," *Hurriyet Daily News*, October 18, 2011, http://www.hurriyetdailynews.com/default. aspx?pageid=438&n=travel-ban-on-mayor-poses-risk-for-his-life-2011-10-18.

9    Raffi Khatchadourian, "A Century of Silence," *The New Yorker*, January 5, 2015, http://www.newyorker.com/magazine/2015/01/05/century-silence.

10   Meline Toumani, "Minority Rules," *The New York Times*, February 17, 2008, http://www.nytimes.com/2008/02/17/magazine/17turkey-t. html?pagewanted=all&_r=0. Demirbas was arrested once more in September 2015, after the election, and released into medical care in October.

11   TATORT, *Democratic Autonomy*, 21.

12   TATORT, *Democratic Autonomy*, 31. Note that a dual legal system based on community control does not necessarily have a positive outcome for women—that depends on politics. In a conservative setting where fundamentalists or traditionalist elders are in control, it can mean the imposition of religious or customary law through special courts or informal processes.

13   TATORT, *Democratic Autonomy*, 118.

14   TATORT, *Democratic Autonomy*, 187, 173.

15   Aliza Marcus, "The Kurds' Evolving Strategy: The Struggle Goes Political in Turkey," *World Affairs*, November–December 2012, http://www. worldaffairsjournal.org/article/kurds'-evolving-strategy-struggle-goes-political-turkey.

16   Hamit Bozarslan, "The Kurds and Middle Eastern 'State of Violence': the 1980s and 2010s," *Kurdish Studies*, May 2014, 9, http://tplondon.com/ journal/index.php/ks/article/view/349.

17   Marcus, "Kurds' Evolving Strategy," 2012.

18   Marcus, "Kurds' Evolving Strategy," 2012.

19   Eyup Can, "PKK Changes Leadership," *Al-Monitor*, July 14, 2013, http:// www.al-monitor.com/pulse/politics/2013/07/structural-leadership-changes-pkk-turkey-kurds.html.

20   White, *The PKK*, 147–8; Stephen Smellie, "Self-Organisation of Kurdish Women: Delegation Report," *Left Project*, September 2015, http:// leftproject.scot/2015/self-organisation-of-kurdish-women-delegation-report/.

21   Sedat Yilmaz, "Efrin Economy Minister: Rojava Challenging Norms of Class, Gender, Power," *Rojava Report*, December 22, 2014, http://www.

rojavareport.wordpress.com/2014/12/22/efrin-economy-minister-rojava-challenging-norms-of-class-gender-and-power/.

22    David McDowall, *A Modern History of the Kurds* (London: I.B.Tauris & Co., 2004), 478.

23    Amed Dicle, "Rojava's Political Structure," *Jadaliyya,* September 23, 2013, http://www.jadaliyya.com/pages/index/14272/rojavas-political-structure.

24    Orla Guerin, "Crisis in Syria Boosts Kurdish Hopes," *BBC News,* August 18, 2012, http://www.bbc.com/news/world-middle-east-19301543.

25    International Crisis Group, "Syria's Kurds: A Struggle Within a Struggle," *Middle East Report N°136,* January 22, 2013, 2–3, http://www.crisisgroup. org/en/regions/middle-east-north-africa/syria-lebanon/syria/136-syrias-kurds-a-struggle-within-a-struggle.aspx.

26    Kamran Matin, "Kobani: What's In a Name," *The Disorder of Things,* October 15, 2014, http://thedisorderofthings.com/2014/10/15/kobani-whats-in-a-name/.

27    Carnegie Endowment for International Peace, "Syria in Crisis; The Syrian National Council," n.d., http://carnegieendowment.org/ syriaincrisis/?fa=48334; Kinda Kanbar, "Does the Muslim Brotherhood Dominate the Opposition?" *Syria Deeply,* April 25, 2013, http://www. syriadeeply.org/articles/2013/04/2326/muslim-brotherhood-dominate-opposition/; Hassan Hassan, "How the Muslim Brotherhood Hijacked Syria's Revolution," *Foreign Policy,* March 13, 2013, http://foreignpolicy. com/2013/03/13/how-the-muslim-brotherhood-hijacked-syrias-revolution/.

28    Joris Leverink, "The Revolution Behind the Headlines," *Telesur,* February 22, 2015, http://www.telesurtv.net/english/opinion/The-Revolution-Behind-the-Headlines-Autonomy-in-Northern-Syria-20150222-0011. html.

29    Yassin al-Haj Saleh, "Syria is a unique example of apathy, injustice, and amnesia," *The Chronikler,* January 20, 2016, http://chronikler.com/ middle-east/iraq-and-the-levant/yassin-al-haj-saleh/.

30    Robin Yassin-Kassab, "Peace or Pacification," *Qunfuz,* February 8, 2016, http://qunfuz.com/2016/02/07/peace-or-pacification/. He criticizes the PYD much more strongly in a subsequent essay, "'Democratic Confederalism' or Counter-Revolution," *Qunfuz,* February 22, 2016, http://qunfuz.com/2016/02/22/ democraticconfederalismorcounterrevolution/.

31    "Interview: Salih Muslim, Chairman of the PYD," *Kurdwatch,* October 20, 2011, http://kurdwatch.org/html/en/interview6.html.

32  Benjamin Hiller, "Syria's Kurds Quietly Consolidating" *Warscapes*, August 13, 2012, http://www.warscapes.com/reportage/syrias-kurds-quietly-consolidating.

33  Hiller, "Quietly Consolidating," 2012.

34  Yilmaz, "Efrin Economy Minister," 2014; Khedar Khaddour, 'The Assad Regime's Hold on the Syrian State," *Carnegie Middle East Center,* July 8, 2015, http://carnegie-mec.org/2015/07/08/assad-regime-s-hold-on-syrian-state/id3k.

35  Salih Muslim, as quoted in Ahmet Hamdi Akkaya and Joost Jongerden, "Democratic Confederalism as a Kurdish Spring: The PKK and the quest for radical democracy," in *The Kurdish Spring: Geopolitical Changes and the Kurds*, eds. Mohammad M.A. Ahmed and Michael M. Gunter (Costa Mesa: Mazda Publishers. 2013), 174.

36  Akkaya and Jongerden, "Democratic Confederalism," 2012.

37  Leverink, "Revolution Behind Headlines," 2015.

38  Hiller, "Quietly Consolidating," 2012.

39  Members of the delegation were Oktay Ay, researcher, Istanbul Bogazici University, Turkey; Janet Biehl, independent writer, USA; Devris Cimen, journalist, Kurdish Office for Public Affairs, Germany; Rebecca Coles, researcher, University of Nottingham, UK; Antonia Davidovic, lecturer of ethnology, University of Kiel, Germany; Dilar Dirik, PhD student, Cambridge University, UK; Eirik Eiglad, editor, New Compass Press, Norway; David Graeber, professor of anthropology, London School of Economics, UK; Lokman Turgut, journalist and researcher, *Kurd-Akad*, editor at StudiaKurdica journal, Germany; Thomas Jeffrey Miley, lecturer in sociology, Cambridge University, UK; Johanna Riha, PhD student, Cambridge University, UK; Naszan Ustundag, professor of sociology, Istanbul Bogazici University, Turkey; Christian Zeller, professor of economic geography, University of Salzburg, Austria. Julius Gavroche, "Testimonials from a Revolution in Rojava," *Autonomies*, January 19, 2015, http://autonomies.org/en/2015/01/testimonials-from-a-revolution-in-rojava/.

40  Janet Biehl, "Rojava's Communes and Councils," *New Compass*, January 31, 2015, http://new-compass.net/articles/rojavas-communes-and-councils.

41  Biehl, "Rojava's Communes," 2015.

42  Jonas Staal, "A Revolution of Life—Interview with Saleh Muslim," *TENK*, November 10, 2014, http://tenk.cc/2014/11/a-revolution-of-life/.

43  "Charter of the Social Contract," January 29, 2014, *Peace in Kurdistan*, https://peaceinkurdistancampaign.com/charter-of-the-social-contract/.

44   Nazan Ustundag, "Self-defense as a Revolutionary Practice in Rojava, or How to Unmake the State," *South Atlantic Quarterly,* January 2016, http://saq.dukejournals.org/content/115/1/197.full.pdf+html.

45   Janet Biehl, "My Impressions of Rojava," *Kurdish Question*, December 15, 2014, http://www.kurdishquestion.com/kurdistan/west-kurdistan/my-impressions-of-rojava.html.

46   Yilmaz, "Efrin Economy Minister," 2014.

47   "To the United Nations' General Secretariat," February 3, 2016, *ANHA,* Hawar News Agency, http://en.hawarnews.com/to-the-united-nations-general-secretariat/.

48   Yilmaz, "Efrin Economy Minister," 2014.

49   Michael Knapp, "Rojava—the formation of an economic alternative: Private property in the service of all," *Peace in Kurdistan,* February 6, 2015, http://www.peaceinkurdistancampaign.com/2015/02/06/rojava-the-formation-of-an-economic-alternative-private-property-in-the-service-of-all/.

50   Yahya M. Madra, "Democratic Economy Conference: An Introductory Note," *South Atlantic Quarterly,* January 2016, http://saq.dukejournals.org/content/115/1/211.full.pdf+html.

51   "Rojava: the women who wove a revolution," JINHA, July 17, 2015, http://jinha.com.tr/en/ALL-NEWS/content/view/26719.

52   Ruken Deri and Sosun Xane, "Rojava women organize peacekeeping through self-defense," JINHA, June 25, 2015, http://jinha.com.tr/en/ALL-NEWS/content/view/25436.

53   "YDG-K punishes man who abused wife," JINHA, September 19, 2015, http://www.jinha.com.tr/en/ALL-NEWS/content/view/31937

54   Ustundag, "Self-defense as a Revolutionary Practice," 2016.

## Chapter 7: The Battle of Kobane and Its Backlash

1    "How Kurdish women soldiers are confronting ISIS on the front lines," *PBS Newshour,* May 3, 2015, http://www.pbs.org/newshour/bb/kurdish-women-soldiers-confronting-fears-isis/; Dilar Dirik, "Western fascination with 'badass" Kurdish women," *Al Jazeera,* October 14, 2014, http://www.aljazeera.com/indepth/opinion/2014/10/western-fascination-with-badas-2014102112410527736.html; "Kurdish revolutionary: We are showing the strength of women," [interview with Nesrin Abdullah by Giuliana Sgrena], *Green Left,* October 26, 2015, https://www.greenleft.org.au/node/60457.

2    "The Course And Development Of The Fighting In Kobanê," *Harvest,* July 12, 2014, http://turkeyharvest.blogspot.co.uk/2014/07/this-article-comes-from-rojava-report.html.

3    Fehim Taştekin, "Islamic State moves to capture another Turkish border crossing," *Al-Monitor*, July 10, 2014, http://www.al-monitor.com/pulse/originals/2014/07/tastekin-rojava-strangle--kurdish-syria-isis-ypg-sunni.html.

4    The Soufan Group, "Turkey Weighs Action in Syria," *TSG IntelBrief*, July 9, 2015, http://soufangroup.com/tsg-intelbrief-turkey-weighs-action-in-syria/.

5    "Assault on Kobane," *A closer look on Syria*, September 2015, http://acloserlookonsyria.shoutwiki.com/wiki/Main_Page; "Building Unity In The Face Of The ISIS Counter-Revolution," *Harvest*, July 8, 2015, http://turkeyharvest.blogspot.co.uk/2014/07/building-unity-in-face-of-isis-counter.html.

6    David Axe, "Why arming U.S. allies can be like sending weapons straight to the enemy," *Reuters*, March 25, 2015, http://blogs.reuters.com/great-debate/2015/03/24/arming-americas-allies-is-risky-any-way-you-do-it/; "Kobane in Rojava Is Facing A Serious Threat from ISIS—A Call for Mass Solidarity and Resistance," *Harvest*, July 6, 2014, http://turkeyharvest.blogspot.co.uk/2014/07/kobane-in-rojava-is-facing-serious.html; Dexter Filkins, "The Fight of Their Lives," *The New Yorker*, September 29, 2014, http://www.newyorker.com/magazine/2014/09/29/fight-lives.

7    Michael Stephens, "YPG—The Islamic State's Worst Enemy," *IHS Jane's Defense Weekly*, September 11, 2014, http://www.janes.com/article/43030/analysis-ypg-the-islamic-state-s-worst-enemy; "The People's Defense Unit's Self-Made Tanks Are Protecting The Revolution," *Harvest*, August 21, 2014, http://turkeyharvest.blogspot.co.uk/2014/08/the-peoples-defense-units-self-made.html.

8    "Rojava's Kobane Canton Is Defeating The Embargo And Attacks Through Communal Production," *Harvest*, August 26, 2014, http://turkeyharvest.blogspot.co.uk/2014/08/rojavas-kobane-canton-is-defeating.html.

9    "The People Unite Against ISIS As Rojava's Revolution Moves Forward," *Harvest*, July 26, 2014, http://turkeyharvest.blogspot.co.uk/2014/07/the-people-unite-against-isis-as.html.

10    "Defeating the Embargo," *Harvest*, August 26, 2014.

11    Sedat Sur, "21st Century Epic of Resistance: Kobane," *ANF News*, September 18, 2015, http://anfenglish.com/kurdistan/21st-century-epic-of-resistance-kobane; "Thirty-Six Hours In Rojava's Revolution, *Harvest*, July 10, 2014,http://turkeyharvest.blogspot.co.uk/2014/07/thirty-six-hours-in-rojavas-revolution.html.

12    "Assault on Kobane," 2015.

13    "An Interview With A Women's Defense Forces (YPJ) Commander in Rojava," *Harvest,* August 1, 2014, http://turkeyharvest.blogspot. co.uk/2014/08/an-interview-with-womens-defense-forces.html.

14    "Assault on Kobane," 2015.

15    "Nurse says she's tired of treating ISIL terrorists," *Today's Zaman,* September 17, 2014, https://mobile.todayszaman.com/national_nurse-says-shes-tired-of-treating-isil-terrorists_358992.html; "Turkish President's daughter heads a covert medical corps to bring help ISIS injured members, reveals a disgruntled nurse," *AWD news,* July 15, 2015, http://awdnews.com/top-news/turkish-president's-daughter-heads-a-covert-medical-corps-to-help-isis-injured-members,-reveals-a-disgruntled-nurse; "Interview with Kurdish YPG Leader, Polat Can," *The Kurdish Project,* August 12, 2015, http://thekurdishproject.org/latest-news/rojava/interview-with-kurdish-ypg-leader-polat-can/. It is also rumored that Erdogan's son Bilal is in charge of Turkey's oil deals with ISIS. Bilal, named in a major corruption case and nervous about being prosecuted, moved his family to Italy after the AKP lost its majority in the June 2015 election. "Report: President Erdogan's son has settled in Italy with his family," *Today's Zaman*, October 6, 2015, http://www.todayszaman.com/anasayfa_report-president-erdogans-son-has-settled-in-italy-with-his-family_400738.html.

16    Thomas L. Friedman, "Obama on the World," *The New York Times,* August 8, 2014, http://www.nytimes.com/2014/08/09/opinion/president-obama-thomas-l-friedman-iraq-and-world-affairs.html?action=click&contentCollection=Middle East&module=RelatedCoverage&region=Marginalia&pgtype=article&_r=0.

17    David Romano, "The Dilemma of the Kurds in Syria," *Rudaw,* July 24, 2014, http://rudaw.net/english/opinion/240720141.

18    "Women on the frontlines of Kurdish struggles: An interview with JINHA news agency," *Corporate Watch*, January 21, 2016, https://corporatewatch.org/news/2016/jan/21/women-frontlines-kurdish-struggles-interview-jinha-womens-news-agency.

19    "The IS is hundreds of meters away from Ein al-Arab 'Kobane'," *Syrian Observatory for Human Rights,* October 2, 2014, http://www.syriahr.com/en/2014/10/the-is-is-hundreds-of-meters-away-from-ein-al-arabkobane/; Hannah Lucinda Smith, "Fears of massacre as Isis tanks lead assault on Kurdish bastion," *The Times*, October 4, 2014, http://www.thetimes.co.uk/tto/news/world/middleeast/article4226717.ece?shareToken=f900945 18fabc34e4ca7f4a59e7a3990.

20    Nick Tattersall and Selin Bucak, "Turkey vows support for besieged Syrian town, but no military pledge," *Reuters*, October 3, 2014, http://www.reuters.com/article/us-mideast-crisis-turkey-

idUSKCN0HS0ET20141003; "PKK, ISIL are the same, says Erdogan," *Today's Zaman,* October 4, 2014, http://www.todayszaman.com/national_pkk-isil-are-the-same-says-erdogan_360766.html.

21  Joost Jongerden and Bahar Simsek, "Turkey, the Islamic State, and the Kurdistan Liberation Movement," *E-International Relations,* November 24, 2014, http://www.e-ir.info/2014/11/24/turkey-the-islamic-state-and-the-kurdistan-liberation-movement/.

22  Michael Weiss, "How I Escaped from ISIS," *The Daily Beast,* November 18, 2015, http://www.thedailybeast.com/articles/2015/11/18/how-i-escaped-from-isis.htm.

23  Isabel Hunter, "John Kerry says preventing the fall of the town is 'not a strategic objective,'" *The Independent,* October 9, 2014, http://www.independent.co.uk/news/world/middle-east/isis-in-kobani-still-no-sign-of-turkey-reacting-to-threat-on-its-border-as-john-kerry-says-9783372.html.

24  "Turkish President Erdogan says airstrikes not enough to save Kobane," *Hurriyet Daily News,* October 7, 2014, http://www.hurriyetdailynews.com/turkish-president-erdogan-says-airstrikes-not-enough-to-save-kobane.aspx?PageID=238&NID=72650&NewsCatID=510.

25  "US meets with Syrian Kurds linked to terror group," *Associated Press,* October 16, 2015, http://www.salon.com/2014/10/16/us_meets_with_syrian_kurds_linked_to_terror_group/; "Biden apologizes to Turkish President Erdogan," *Deutsche Welle,* October 4, 2014, http://www.dw.com/en/biden-apologizes-to-turkish-president-erdogan/a-17974144. For more on Turkey's relationship with Daesh, see Martin Chulov, "Turkey sends in jets as Syria's agony spills over every border," *The Guardian,* July 25, 2015, http://www.theguardian.com/world/2015/jul/26/isis-syria-turkey-us?CMP=share_btn_tw; Nick Paton Walsh, "The secret jihadi smuggling route through Turkey," *CNN,* November 5, 2013, http://edition.cnn.com/2013/11/04/world/europe/isis-gaining-strength-on-syria-turkey-border/; Alexander Christie-Miller, "Kurds Accuse Turkish Government of Supporting ISIS," *Newsweek,* October 22, 2014, http://www.newsweek.com/2014/10/31/kurds-accuse-turkish-government-supporting-isis-278776.html; "Turkish Government's Support for ISIS Documented by Court," *ANF,* May 13, 2015, http://kurdishquestion.com/index.php/kurdistan/north-kurdistan/turkish-government-s-support-for-isis-documented-by-court.html; Nafeez Mosaddeq Ahmed, "ISIS wants to destroy the 'grey zone'. Here's how we defend it," *openDemocracy,* November 16, 2015, https://www.opendemocracy.net/nafeez-ahmed/isis-wants-destroy-greyzone-how-we-defend.

26  "Turkey will not cooperate in US support for Kurds in Syria, says Erdogan," *The Guardian,* October 19, 2014, http://www.theguardian.com/world/2014/oct/19/turkey-will-not-cooperate-us-support-kurds-erdogan.

27  Namo Abdulla, "US Takes Different Stance From Turkey on Syrian Kurds," *Rudaw,* October 21, 2014, http://rudaw.net/english/blog-21102014054359.

28  Constanze Letsch, Catherine James, Paul Lewis, and Nicholas Watt, "Syrian Kurds say airstrikes against ISIS are not working," *The Guardian,* October 6, 2014, http://www.theguardian.com/world/2014/oct/05/air-strikes-isis-not-working-syrian-kurds.

29  Meysa Abdo, "A Town Shouldn't Fight the Islamic State Alone," *The New York Times,* October 28, 2014,http://www.nytimes.com/2014/10/29/opinion/turkeys-obstruction-of-kobanis-battle-against-isis.html?_r=1.

30  "Assault on Kobane," 2015.

31  YPG fighters advance in Kobani, and IS militants shocked by the YPG resistance," *Syrian Observatory for Human Rights,* November 11, 2015, http://www.syriahr.com/en/2014/11/ypg-fighters-advance-in-kobani-and-is-militants-shocked-by-the-ypg-resistance/.

32  "Assault on Kobane," 2015; "The Turkish government is trying not to upset ISIS," *Harvest,* December 1, 2014, http://turkeyharvest.blogspot.com/2014/12/the-turkish-government-is-trying-not-to.html.

33  "We reproduce below a very informative Ask May Anything (AMA) from Reddit with a verified PKK fighter active in Kobane, Cizre, Bakur (Turkey) and Bashur (Iraq)," *Workers Solidarity Movement (Ireland), Facebook,* July 20, 2015, https://www.facebook.com/WorkersSolidarityMovement/photos/a.974071899285290.1073741894.132000150159140/1175786155780529/.

34  Weiss, "Confessions of an ISIS Spy," 2015.

35  Yvo Fitzherbert, "Rebuilding Kobani: call for help from a city in ruins," *Roar Magazine,* February 18, 2015, http://roarmag.org/2015/02/rebuilding-kobani-ypg-pyd/?utm_source=feedburner&utm_medium=feed&utm_campaign=Feed%3A+roarmag+%28ROAR+Magazine%29&utm_content=FeedBurner.

36  Joey Lawrence, " Guerrilla Fighters of Kurdistan," *Joey L. blog,* June 6, 2015, http://www.joeyl.com/blog/all/post/guerrilla-fighters-of-kurdistan.

37  Ben Hubbard, "Mass Killings by ISIS Fighters in Syrian Kurdish Town," *The New York Times,* June 26, 2015, http://www.nytimes.com/2015/06/27/world/middleeast/mass-killings-by-isis-fighters-in-syrian-kurdish-town.html?_r=0.

38  Tom Perry, "Syrian Kurds now say they now control territory the size of Qatar and Kuwait combined," *Reuters,* August 14, 2015, http://www.businessinsider.com.au/syrian-kurds-now-say-they-now-control-territory-the-size-of-qatar-and-kuwait-combined-2015-8.

39  Author's discussions with Sinam Mohamad, European Representative of Rojava and Co-Chair of TEV-DEM, November 2, 4, 5, 2015, in New York City.

40  Tom Anderson and Eliza Egret, "Rebuilding Kobane," *Red Pepper,* January 2016, http://www.redpepper.org.uk/rebuilding-kobane/.

41  "Congress Approving $721 Million for Syrian Rebels," *Roll Call,* December 12, 2014, http://www.rollcall.com/news/congress_approving_721_million_for_syrian_rebels-238703-1.html; Samuel Osborne, "US supplies Syrian rebels with 50 tonnes of weapons in airdrop," *The Independent,* October 13, 2015, http://www.independent.co.uk/news/world/middle-east/us-airdrops-50-tonnes-of-weapons-to-new-syrian-rebel-coalition-a6692126.html.

42  Michael R. Gordon and Rukmini Callimachi, "Kurdish Fighters Retake Iraqi City of Sinjar from ISIS," *The New York Times,* November 13, 2015, http://www.nytimes.com/2015/11/14/world/middleeast/sinjar-iraq-islamic-state.html.

43  Fehim Tastekin, "Kurdish rivalry delays victory in Sinjar," *Al-Monitor,* February 3, 2015, http://www.al-monitor.com/pulse/originals/2015/02/turkey-syria-iraq-kurdish-rivalry-yezidi-lan.html; Mahmut Bozarslan, "Kurdish infighting complicates Sinjar offensive," *Al-Monitor,* November 12, 2015, http://www.al-monitor.com/pulse/originals/2015/11/turkey-iraq-krg-sinjar-pkk-yazidis-town-kurds-cannot-share.html.

44  Tastekin, "Kurdish rivalry," 2015.

45  Jake Hess, "Washington's Secret Back-Channel Talks with Syria's Kurdish 'Terrorists,'" *Foreign Policy,* October 7, 2014, http://foreignpolicy.com/2014/10/07/washingtons-secret-back-channel-talks-with-syrias-kurdish-terrorists/.

46  International Crisis Group, "Syria's Kurds: A Struggle Within a Struggle," *Middle East Report No. 136,* January 22, 2013, footnote 59, http://www.crisisgroup.org/en/publication-type/media-releases/2013/mena/syrias-kurds-a-struggle-within-a-struggle.aspx.

47  Harut Sassounian, "Turkey Pays Former CIA Director and Lobbyists to Misrepresent Attacks on Kurds and ISIS," *Huffington Post,* August 19, 2015, http://www.huffingtonpost.com/harut-sassounian/turkeys-pays-former-cia-d_b_8002534.html.

48  Mutlu Civiroglu, "PYD's Salih Muslim: We Are Awaiting an Invitation for Talks with Washington," *Rudaw,* August 16, 2013, http://rudaw.net/

english/interview/16082013; Asli Aydintasbas, "PYD Leader holds Turkey responsible for fate of Kobani," *Al-Monitor*, September 23, 2014, http://www.al-monitor.com/pulse/security/2014/09/turkey-syria-kobani-isis-kurds-salih-muslim.html; Paul Richter, "U.S. denies Kurdish ally Salih Muslim's request to visit," *The Los Angeles Times*, January 30, 2015, http://www.latimes.com/world/middleeast/la-fg-us-denies-visa-request-from-ally-20150130-story.html.

49  Robert Ellis, "Turkey heads in the wrong direction—and Europe helps it on the way," *The Independent*, November 2, 2015, http://www.independent.co.uk/voices/turkey-heads-in-the-wrong-direction-and-europe-helps-it-on-the-way-a6718131.html.

50  "Journalist Spotlight, Khaled Yacoub Oweis Reveals How He Scored Exclusive on Syrian Army Moving Missiles to Avoid Strike," *Reuters*, September 5, 2013, http://www.reutersbest.com/articles/view/2449/journalist-spotlight-khaled-yacoub-oweis-reveals-how-he-scored-exclusive-on-syrian-army-moving-missiles-to-avoid-strike.

51  Khaled Yacoub Oweis, "The West's Darling in Syria," *SWP*, October 2015, 1, http://www.swp-berlin.org/en/publications/swp-comments-en/swp-aktuelle-details/article/the_wests_darling_in_syria.html.

52  Anthony Shadid, "Killing of Opposition Leader in Syria Provokes Kurds," *The New York Times*, October 8, 2011, http://www.nytimes.com/2011/10/09/world/middleeast/killing-of-opposition-leader-in-syria-provokes-kurds.html; "Assad ordered killing of Kurdish activist Mashaal Tammo: Leaked Files," *Al-Arabiya*, October 10, 2012, http://english.alarabiya.net/articles/2012/10/10/242928.html.

53  Oweis, "The West's Darling," 8.

54  "Syria: US ally's razing of villages amounts to war crimes," *Amnesty International*, October 13, 2015, https://www.amnesty.org/en/latest/news/2015/10/syria-us-allys-razing-of-villages-amounts-to-war-crimes/; *"We Had Nowhere Else To Go": Forced Displacement and Demolitions in Northern Syria*, http://www.amnesty.org.au/images/uploads/crisis/Syria_Nowhere_to_go_Amnesty_report.pdf.

55  "YPG General Commander Hemo on Syrian Democratic Force, US Weapons & Amnesty Report," *Personal Website of Mutlu Civiroglu*, October 15, 2015, http://civiroglu.net/2015/10/15/ypg-general-commander-hemo-on-syrian-democratic-force-us-weapons-amnesty-report/.

56  "YPG General Hemo," 2015.

57  "Syria: Arbitrary detentions and blatantly unfair trials mar PYD fight against terrorism," *Amnesty International*, September 7, 2015, https://www.amnesty.org/en/latest/news/2015/09/syria-abuses-mar-pyd-fight-against-terrorism/.

58   Gita Sahgal, email message to author, October 15, 2015. For an account of
     Sahgal's 2010 dispute with Amnesty, see Meredith Tax, "Gitagate, Two
     Years After," *Dissent*, June 27, 2012, https://www.dissentmagazine.org/
     blog/gitagate-two-years-after.

59   Badirkan Ali, "The Reality of Ethnic Cleansing and Kurdish State in
     Syria," *Jadaliyya*, August 25, 2015, http://www.jadaliyya.com/pages/
     index/22468/the-reality-of-ethnic-cleansing-and-kurdish-state- 1/.

60   "There's no 'ethnic cleaning' in Til Abyad against the Turkmen and Arabic
     population," Interview with Rami Abdulrahman, head of the "Syrian
     Observatory for Human Rights (SOHR)," London, *Gesellshaft fur bedrohte
     volker*, June 24, 2015, https://www.gfbv.de/en/news/theres-no-ethnic-
     cleansing-in-til-abyad-against-the-turkmen-and-arabic-population-7568/.

61   John R. Bolton, "To Defeat ISIS, Create a Sunni State," *The New York
     Times*, November 24, 2015, http://www.nytimes.com/2015/11/25/opinion/
     john-bolton-to-defeat-isis-create-a-sunni-state.html?_r=o.

62   Yerevan Saeed, "YPG dismisses Amnesty report accusing Kurds of
     ethnic cleansing," *Rudaw*, October 19, 2015, http://rudaw.net/english/
     kurdistan/191020152.

63   "We reproduce below a very informative Ask May Anything
     (AMA) from Reddit with a verified PKK fighter active in
     Kobane, Cizre, Bakur (Turkey) and Bashur (Iraq)," *Workers
     Solidarity Movement (Ireland), Facebook,* July 20, 2015, https://
     www.facebook.com/WorkersSolidarityMovement/photos
     /a.974071899285290.1073741894.132000150159140/1175786155780529/.

64   Staal, "Saleh Muslim Interview," 2014.

65   Hawzhin Azeez, *Facebook*, January 23, 2016, https://www.facebook.com/
     hawzhin.azeez/posts/1051483404914555?fref=nf.

## Chapter 8: The Birth of Daesh

1    Lawrence Wright, *The Looming Tower: Al-Qaeda and the Road to 9/11*
     (New York: Alfred A. Knopf, 2006), 48.

2    AWAAZ-South Asia Watch, "The Islamic Right—Key Tendencies,"
     June 2006, http://freethoughtblogs.com/maryamnamazie/files/2013/03/
     Islamic-Right-Key-Tendencies.pdf.

3    Meredith Tax, *Double Bind: The Muslim Right, the Anglo-American Left,
     and Universal Human Rights* (New York and London: Centre for Secular
     Space, 2012), 18–20.

4    "Interview Vali Nasr," *Frontline*, October 25, 2001, http://www.pbs.org/
     wgbh/pages/frontline/shows/saudi/interviews/nasr.html.

5    "Wikileaks: Saudis 'chief funders of Sunni militants,'" *BBC News*,
     December 5, 2010, http://www.bbc.com/news/world-middle-east-11923176.

6    A. Azzam, "Defence of the Muslim Lands: The First Obligation after Ima[n]," *Religioscope,* n.d., http://www.religioscope.com/info/doc/jihad/azzam_defence_1_table.htm.

7    Dilip Hiro, "The Cost of an Afghan 'victory,'" *The Nation,* January 28, 1999, http://www.thenation.com/article/cost-afghan-victory.

8    Wright, *Looming Tower,* 133; Yassin Musharbash, "The Future of Terrorism: What al-Qaida Really Wants," *Der Spiegel,* August 12, 2005, http://www.spiegel.de/international/the-future-of-terrorism-what-al-qaida-really-wants-a-369448.html.

9    Hiro, "Cost," 1999.

10   Michael Weiss and Hassan Hassan, *ISIS: Inside the Army of Terror* (New York: Regan Arts, 2015), 29.

11   Syed Saleem Shahzad, "Takfirism: a messianic ideology," *Le Monde Diplomatique,* July 3, 2007, http://mondediplo.com/2007/07/03takfirism. Syed Saleem Shahzad was a crusading Pakistani journalist, known for his exposures of links between the Pakistani secret intelligence agency the ISI, and jihadis; after receiving many death threats and being arrested by the ISI, he was found dead in a ditch in 2007.

12   David Ignatius, "How ISIS Spread in the Middle East—and how to stop it," *The Atlantic,* October 29, 2015, http://www.theatlantic.com/international/archive/2015/10/how-isis-started-syria-iraq/.

13   Dexter Filkins, "Did George W. Bush Create ISIS?," *The New Yorker,* May 15, 2015, http://www.newyorker.com/news/news-desk/did-george-w-bush-create-isis.

14   Yifat Susskind, "Promising Democracy, Imposing Theocracy: Gender-Based Violence and the US War on Iraq," *MADRE,* March 9, 2007, 3, http://www.madre.org/uploads/misc/1268922752_iraqreport.pdf.

15   Liz Sly, "The hidden hand behind the Islamic State militants? Saddam Hussein's," *The Washington Post,* April 4, 2015, https://www.washingtonpost.com/world/middle_east/the-hidden-hand-behind-the-islamic-state-militants-saddam-husseins/2015/04/04/aa97676c-cc32-11e4-8730-4f473416e759_story.html.

16   Huda Ahmed, "Women in Iraq," *Women's Rights in the Middle East and North Africa: Progress Amid Resistance,* ed. Sanja Kelly and Julia Breslin (New York: Freedom House/ Rowman & Littlefield, 2010), 2–3.

17   Susskind, 2007, 1.

18   Susskind, 2007, 7.

19   Quoted in Charles Lister, "Jihadi Rivalry: The Islamic State Challenges al-Qaida," *Brookings Doha Center Analysis,* 16, January 2016, 4, http://www.brookings.edu/research/papers/2016/01/27-islamic-state-challenges-alqaida-lister; Susan B. Glasser and Walter Pincus, "Seized Letter

Outlines Al Qaeda Goals in Iraq," *The Washington Post*, October 12, 2005, http://www.washingtonpost.com/wp-dyn/content/article/2005/10/11/AR2005101101353.html.

20  Weiss and Hassan, *ISIS* 18, 29, 59.

21  Weiss and Hassan, *ISIS*, 68–71.

22  Houzan Mahmoud, "A symptom of Iraq's tragedy," *The Guardian*, June 12, 2006, http://www.theguardian.com/commentisfree/2006/jun/12/theendofzarqawitheusmade.

23  Terri Judd, "For the Women of Iraq, the War is Just Beginning," *The Independent*, June 8, 2006, http://www.independent.co.uk/news/world/middle-east/for-the-women-of-iraq-the-war-is-just-beginning-481497.html.

24  Nadje al-Ali, "Iraq: gendering authoritarianism," *openDemocracy 5050*, July 15, 2013, https://www.opendemocracy.net/5050/nadje-al-ali/iraq-gendering-authoritarianism.

25  Rania Abouzeid, "Out of Sight; A former prostitute tries to rescue Iraq's most vulnerable women," *The New Yorker*, October 5, 2015, http://www.newyorker.com/magazine/2015/10/05/out-of-sight-letter-from-baghdad-rania-abouzeid.

26  Martin Chulov, "ISIS: the Inside Story," *The Guardian*, December 11, 2014, http://www.theguardian.com/world/2014/dec/11/-sp-isis-the-inside-story.

27  Christoph Reuter, "The Terror Strategist: Secret Files Reveal the Structure of Islamic State," *Der Speigel*, April 18, 2015, http://www.spiegel.de/international/world/islamic-state-files-show-structure-of-islamist-terror-group-a-1029274.html.

28  Chulov, "Inside Story," 2014; Weiss and Hassan, *ISIS*, 120–123; Tim Arango, "Top Qaeda Leaders in Iraq Reported Killed in Raid," *The New York Times*, April 19, 2010, http://www.nytimes.com/2010/04/20/world/middleeast/20baghdad.html?_r=0.

29  Chulov, "Inside Story," 2014; Reuter, "Terror Strategist," 2015.

30  Rania Abouzeid, "The Jihad Next Door," *Politico*, June 23, 2014, http://www.politico.com/magazine/story/2014/06/al-qaeda-iraq-syria-108214_full.html.

31  Weiss and Hassan, *ISIS*, p. 144; Abouzeid, "Jihad Next Door," 2014.

32  Abouzeid, "Jihad Next Door," 2014.

33  Abouzeid, "Jihad Next Door," 2014.

34  Naharnet Newsdesk, "Al-Nusra Commits to al-Qaida, Deny Iraq Branch 'Merger'," *Naharnet.com*, April 10, 2013, http://www.naharnet.

com/stories/en/78961-al-nusra-commits-to-al-qaida-deny-iraq-branch-merger/.

35    Thomas Joscelyn, "Analysis: Zawahiri's letter to al Qaeda branches in Syria, Iraq," *The Long War Journal,* June 10, 2013, http://www. longwarjournal.org/archives/2013/06/analysis_alleged_let.php. Although Zawahiri's decision and the feud in general were not made public until June, when Al Jazeera broadcast a letter from him dated May 23, it is likely that the parties involved were given the message privately much earlier.

36    "Iraqi al-Qaeda chief rejects Zawahiri orders," *Al Jazeera,* June 14, 2013, http://www.aljazeera.com/news/middleeast/2013/06/2013615172217827810. html.

37    Hussein Jemmo, Al-Qaeda's Internal Divide Grows in Syria," *Al-Monitor,* Aug. 19, 2013, http://www.al-monitor.com/pulse/security/2013/08/al-qaeda-internal-divide-syria-islamic-state-jabhat-nusra.html.

38    Reuter, "Terror Strategist," 2015.

39    Kendal Nizan, "When our 'friend' Saddam was gassing the Kurds," *Le Monde Diplomatique,* March 1998, http://mondediplo. com/1998/03/04iraqkn.

40    Christoph Reuter has been reporting for decades from the Middle East, and has written a book on suicide bombers (2002) and another on daily life in Iraq (2002). In April 2015, the Der Speigel publishing house brought out his most recent book, *Die schwarze Macht: Der »Islamische Staat« und die Strategen des Terrors (The Black Power: The "Islamic State" and the Strategists of Terror).*

41    Reuter, "Terror Strategist," 2015.

42    Sarah Birke, "How ISIS Rules," *The New York Review of Books,* February 5, 2015, http://www.nybooks.com/articles/archives/2015/feb/05/how-isis-rules/.

43    Aron Lund, "Who and What was Abu Khalid al-Suri? Part 1," *Syria in Crisis,* February 24, 2014, Carnegie Endowment for International Peace; Mohammed Al Attar, "Al Raqqa: The realities of the military brigades, the administration of the liberated city and the revolution to come," *Heinrich Böll Stiftung Middle East,* September 18, 2013, http://lb.boell.org/en/2013/09/18/raqqa-reality-military-brigades-administration-liberated-city-and-revolutions-come.

44    Matthew Barber, "The Raqqa Story: Rebel Structure, Planning, and Possible War Crimes," *Syria Comment,* April 3, 2013, http://www. joshualandis.com/blog/the-raqqa-story-rebel-structure-planning-and-possible-war-crimes/.

45  Firas al-Hakkar, "The Mysterious Fall of Raqqa, Syria's Kandahar," *Al Akhbar*, November 8, 2013, http://english.al-akhbar.com/node/17550.

46  Barber, "Raqqa Story," 2013.

47  "ISIS (Islamic State in Iraq and Sham): An enemy of the revolution and an ally of the Assad regime," *Comment Middle East*, March 19, 2014, http://www.commentmideast.com/2014/03/isis-islamic-state-in-iraq-and-sham-an-enemy-of-the-revolution-and-an-ally-of-the-assad-regime/; "How Did Raqqa Fall to the Islamic State of Iraq and Syria?" *Syria Untold*, January 13, 2014, http://www.syriauntold.com/en/2014/01/how-did-raqqa-fall-to-the-islamic-state-of-iraq-and-syria/.

48  Alison Tahmizian Meuse, "Raqqa's RSA Brigades Join Jabhat al-Nusra," *Syria Deeply*, September 20, 2013, http://www.syriadeeply.org/articles/2013/09/2493/raqqas-fsa-brigades-join-jabhat-al-nusra/.

49  Al-Hakkar, "Myserious Fall," 2013. See also Chapter 7, pp. 196–7

50  Al-Hakkar, "Mysterious Fall," 2013. Because Assad is an Alawite, this accusation is frequently made against Alawites and other Shia.

51  Al-Hakkar, "Mysterious Fall," 2013.

52  Al Attar, "Al Raqqa," 2013.

53  Mona Hamdan, "Father Paolo: The 'Icon' of the Syrian Revolution," *Al-Monitor*, August 13, 2013, http://www.al-monitor.com/pulse/politics/2013/08/syria-italian-priest-abducted-raqqa.html; Al Attar, "Al Raqqa." 2013.

54  Michael Weiss, "The schoolteacher versus al Qaeda," *NOW Media*, November 13, 2013, https://now.mmedia.me/lb/en/commentaryanalysis/520562-520562-facing-down-the-devil.

55  "The Raqqa woman who faced the Islamic State of Iraq and Syria," *Syria Untold*, October 17, 2013, http://www.syriauntold.com/en/2013/10/the-raqqa-woman-who-faced-the-islamic-state-of-iraq-and-syria/; Weiss and Hassan, *ISIS*, 187–189.

56  Doha Hassan, "ISIS is the child of the regime," *NOW Media*, November 11, 2013, https://now.mmedia.me/lb/en/reportsfeatures/520161-isis-is-the-child-of-the-regime.

57  "The Woman in Pants," https://www.facebook.com/photo.php?v=10151674274772016&set=vb.262595243783140&type=2&theater.

58  "The Woman in Pants," author's transcript of video interview.

59  Its name is translated as Descendants, Offspring, or Grandsons of the Prophet.

60  Reuter, "Terror Strategist," 2015; al-Hakkar, "Mysterious Fall," 2013.

61  Meuse, "Raqqa's RSA Brigades," *Syria Deeply*, September 20, 2013.

62  Al-Hakkar, "Mysterious Fall," 2013.

63   Sarah Birke, "How al-Qaeda Changed the Syrian War," *The New York Review of Books*, December 27, 2013, http://www.nybooks.com/blogs/nyrblog/2013/dec/27/how-al-qaeda-changed-syrian-war/; Reuter, "Terror Strategist," 2015.

64   Liz Sly, "Al-Qaeda disavows any ties with radical Islamist ISIS group in Syria, Iraq," *Washington Post*, February 3, 2014, https://www.washingtonpost.com/world/middle_east/al-qaeda-disavows-any-ties-with-radical-islamist-isis-group-in-syria-iraq/2014/02/03/2c9afc3a-8cef-11e3-98ab-fe5228217bd1_story.html.

65   Homa Khaleeli, Aisha Gani, and Mais al-Bayaa, "Ruqia Hassan: the woman who was killed for telling the truth about ISIS," *The Guardian*, January 13, 2016, http://www.theguardian.com/world/2016/jan/13/ruqia-hassan-killed-for-telling-truth-about-isis-facebook.

66   Weiss, "Schoolteacher vs. al Qaeda," 2013.

67   "Activists in Raqqa face daily threats," *Institute for War and Peace Reporting*, December 12, 2013, https://iwpr.net/global-voices/activists-raqqa-face-daily-threats.

68   "How Did Raqqa Fall," *Syria Untold*, 2014; Renee Montagne, "Secret Papers Reveal Islamic State's Structure," *NPR*, April 23, 2015, http://www.npr.org/2015/04/23/401655832/secret-papers-reveal-islamic-states-structure; "Activists in Raqqa," *IWPR*, 2013; Reuter, "Terror Strategist," 2015.

69   Weiss, "Schoolteacher vs. al Qaeda," 2013.

70   "If Assad falls the terrorists will fall too—Souad Nafal accepts the Homo Homini Award," *One World*, March 8, 2015, http://oneworld.cz/2015/news/712-if-assad-falls-the-terrorists-will-fall-too-souad-nawfal-accepts-the-homo-homini-award.htm.

71   "Sunni rebels declare new 'Islamic caliphate,'" *Al Jazeera*, June 30, 2014, http://www.aljazeera.com/news/middleeast/2014/06/isil-declares-new-islamic-caliphate-201462917326669749.html.

72   Adam Withnall, "Iraq crisis: Isis declares its territories a new Islamic state with 'restoration of caliphate' in Middle East," *The Independent*, June 30, 2014, http://www.independent.co.uk/news/world/middle-east/isis-declares-new-islamic-state-in-middle-east-with-abu-bakr-albaghdadi-as-emir-removing-iraq-and-syria-from-its-name-9571374.html.

73   Spencer Ackerman, Shiv Malik, Ali Younes and Mustafa Khalili, "Al-Qaida 'cut off and ripped apart by Isis'," *The Guardian*, June 10, 2015, http://www.theguardian.com/world/2015/jun/10/isis-onslaught-has-broken-al-qaida-its-spiritual-leaders-admit.

74   David Remnick, "The Death of Two Syrian Journalists," *The New Yorker,* October 30, 2015, http://www.newyorker.com/news/news-desk/the-death-of-two-syrian-journalists.

75   "Raqqa Is Being Slaughtered Silently, Syria," *Committee to Protect Journalists,* 2015, https://www.cpj.org/awards/2015/raqqa-is-being-slaughtered-silently-syria.php.

76   "Raqqa is Being Slaughtered," *CPJ,* 2015.

77   Remnick, "The Death of Two Syrian Journalists," 2015.

78   Rengin Arslan, "The death of Naji Jerf and the battle facing Syria's citizen journalists," *BBC,* January 13, 2016, http://www.bbc.com/news/world-europe-35295206.

79   "Syrian journalist Naji Jerf shot dead in Gazientep, Turkey," *Committee to Protect Journalists,* December 27, 2015, https://cpj.org/2015/12/syrian-journalist-naji-jerf-shot-dead-in-gaziantep.php.

80   Khaleeli, Gani, and Bayaa, "Ruqia Hassan," 2016.

## Chapter 9: Daesh vs. Kobane

1    Ishan Tharoor, "Islamic State burned a woman for not engaging in an 'extreme' sex act, U.N. official says," *The Washington Post,* May 22, 2015, http://www.washingtonpost.com/blogs/worldviews/wp/2015/05/22/islamic-state-burned-a-woman-alive-for-not-engaging-in-an-extreme-sex-act-u-n-official-says/?postshare=4031432347480556.

2    Flora Drury, "Islamic State's most wanted women: The fearless Yazidi sisters fighting to save ISIS sex slaves," *The Daily Mail,* December 22, 2015, http://www.dailymail.co.uk/news/article-3339837/ISIS-wanted-women-remarkable-Yazidi-sisters-fighting-beasts-Daesh-raping-girls-murdering-people.html.

3    Adam Withnall, "Isis releases 'abhorrent' sex slaves pamphlet with 27 tips for militants on taking, punishing and raping female captives," *The Independent,* December 10, 2014, http://www.independent.co.uk/news/world/middle-east/isis-releases-abhorrent-sex-slaves-pamphlet-with-27-tips-for-militants-on-taking-punishing-and-raping-female-captives-9915913.html; ISIL Committee of Research and Fatwas, "Fatwa Number: 64," January 29, 2015, http://graphics.thomsonreuters.com/doc/slaves_fatwa.pdf.

4    Kathy Gilsinan, "The ISIS Crackdown on Women, by Women," *The Atlantic,* July 25, 2014, http://www.theatlantic.com/international/archive/2014/07/the-women-of-isis/375047/.

5    "ISIS Women Kill 17-Year Old for Looking at Clothes in Store," *The Clarion Project,* July 12, 2015, http://www.clarionproject.org/news/islamic-state-beats-mosul-woman-death-lifting-niqab.

6    The manual is called "Women of the Islamic State: A manifesto on women by the Al-Khanssa Brigade," *Quilliam Foundation*, February 2015, https://www.quilliamfoundation.org/wp/wp-content/uploads/publications/free/women-of-the-islamic-state3.pdf.

7    "Women of the Islamic State," *Quilliam*, 21.

8    Kinda Jayoush, "Prisoners in Their Own City: ISIS Bans Women Under 45 From Leaving Raqqa," *Syria Deeply*, January 19, 2015, http://www.syriadeeply.org/articles/2015/01/6660/prisoners-city-isis-bans-women-45-leaving-raqqa/.

9    "ISIS Women Kill 17-Year Old," 2015.

10   Jayoush, "Prisoners in Their Own City," 2015.

11   Azadeh Moaveni, "ISIS Women and Enforcers in Syria Recount Collaboration, Anguish and Escape," *The New York Times*, November 21, 2015, http://www.nytimes.com/2015/11/22/world/middleeast/isis-wives-and-enforcers-in-syr.

12   Jayoush, "Prisoners," 2015.

13   Rania Abouzeid, "The Jihad Next Door," *Politico*, June 23, 2014, http://www.politico.com/magazine/story/2014/06/al-qaeda-iraq-syria-108214_full.html.

14   "Women of the Islamic State," *Quilliam*, 13.

15   "Women of the Islamic State," *Quilliam*, 19.

16   "Women of the Islamic State," *Quilliam*, 21, 24.

17   Olivia Goldhill, "This man risks his life every day to rescue kidnapped women from ISIS," *The Telegraph*, July 8, 2015, http://www.telegraph.co.uk/women/womens-life/11723360/Islamic-State-Meet-the-man-who-helps-kidnapped-women-escape-horrors.html.

18   Priya Joshi, "British Medical Student Turned Isis Jihadist Holds Severed Head in Twitter Image," *International Business Times*, September 14, 2014, http://www.ibtimes.co.uk/british-medical-student-turned-isis-jihadist-holds-severed-head-twitter-image-1465422.

19   Umm Layth, "Diary of a Muhajira-3," September 11, 2014, http://fatubalilghuraba.tumblr.com/post/97208872879/diary-of-a-muhajirah-3.

20   Graeme Wood, "What ISIS Really Wants," *The Atlantic*, March 2015, http://www.theatlantic.com/features/archive/2015/02/what-isis-really-wants/384980); Jack Jenkins, "What the Atlantic Gets Wrong About ISIS," *Think Progress*, February 18, 2015, http://thinkprogress.org/world/2015/02/18/3624121/atlantic-gets-dangerously-wrong-isis-islam; Haroon Moghul, "The Atlantic's big Islam lie: What Muslims really believe about ISIS," *Salon*, February 19, 2015, http://www.salon.com/2015/02/19/the_atlantics_big_islam_lie_what_muslims_really_

believe_about_isis/; Robert Wright, "The Clash of Civilizations That Isn't," *The New Yorker*, February 25, 2015, http://www.newyorker.com/news/news-desk/clash-civilizations-isnt.

21  For a feminist discussion of fundamentalism in many religions, see Ayesha Imam, Jenny Morgan, and Nira Yuval-Davis, eds., *Warning Signs of Fundamentalism* (Women Living Under Muslim Laws: London, 2004), http://www.wluml.org/node/224.

22  Mouin Rabbani, "The Un-Islamic State," *Jadaliyya*, September 9, 2014, http://www.jadaliyya.com/pages/index/19181/the-un-islamic-state.

23  Aymenn Jawad Al-Tamimi and Amarnath Amarasingam, "Is ISIS Islamic, and Other 'Foolish" Debates," *Jihadology*, April 3, 2015, http://www.aymennjawad.org/16383/is-isis-islamic-and-other-foolish-debates.

24  Amal Ghazal and Larbi Sadiki, "ISIS: The 'Islamic State' Between Orientalism and the Interiority of MENA's Intellectuals," *Jadaliyya*, Jan. 19, 2016, http://www.jadaliyya.com/pages/index/23616/isis_the-islamic-state-between-orientalism-and-the.

25  Al-Tamimi and Amarasingam, "Is ISIS Islamic," 2015.

26  "The Isis papers: a masterplan for consolidating power," *The Guardian*, December 7, 2015, http://www.theguardian.com/world/2015/dec/07/islamic-state-document-masterplan-for-power.

27  "The Isis papers," *The Guardian*, 2015.

28  Edward Delman, "Understanding Hitler's Anti-Semitism," [interview with Timothy Snyder], *The Atlantic*, September 9, 2015, http://www.theatlantic.com/international/archive/2015/09/hitler-holocaust-antisemitism-timothy-snyder/404260/.

29  "The Isis papers," *The Guardian*, 2015.

30  Charles Tripp, "IS: the rentier caliphate with no new ideas," *The New Arab*, February 8, 2015, http://www.alaraby.co.uk/english/politics/2015/2/8/is-the-rentier-caliphate-with-no-new-ideas.

31  Bill Spindle and Summer Said, "Oil's Drop Puts the Spotlight on Saudi Arabia," *The Wall Street Journal*, August 24, 2015, http://www.wsj.com/articles/oils-drop-puts-spotlight-on-saudi-arabia-1440459727; Clifford Krauss, "Oil Prices: What's Behind the Drop? Simple Economics," *The New York Times*, January 21, 2016, http://www.nytimes.com/interactive/2016/business/energy-environment/oil-prices.html.

32  Matthew Rosenberg, "U.S. Drops Bombs Not Just on ISIS, but Its Cash, Too," *The New York Times*, January 20, 2016, http://www.nytimes.com/2016/01/21/us/politics/us-drops-bombs-not-just-on-isis-but-on-its-cash-too.html.

33  Liz Sly, "The hidden hand behind the Islamic State militants? Saddam Hussein's," *The Washington Post*, April 4, 2015, https://www.

washingtonpost.com/world/middle_east/the-hidden-hand-behind-the-islamic-state-militants-saddam-husseins/2015/04/04/aa97676c-cc32-11e4-8730-4f473416e759_story.html.

34   Hanin Ghaddar, "ISIS's strategy of terror: interview with Christoph Reuter," *NOW Media*, July 15, 2015, https://now.mmedia.me/lb/en/10questions/565586-isiss-strategy-of-terror.

35   Ghaddar, "ISIS's strategy of terror," 2015.

36   Ghaddar, "ISIS's strategy of terror," 2015; Michael Weiss, "Confessions of an ISIS Spy," *The Daily Beast,* November 15, 2015, http://www.thedailybeast.com/articles/2015/11/15/confessions-of-an-isis-spy.html.

37   Jessica Stern and J.M. Berger, "ISIS and the Foreign-Fighter Phenomena," *The Atlantic*, March 8, 2015, http://www.theatlantic.com/international/archive/2015/03/isis-and-the-foreign-fighter-problem/387166/.

38   Olivier Roy, "What is the driving force behind jihadist terrorism? A scientific perspective on the causes/circumstances of joining the scene," speech at the BKS Autumn Conference, November 18–19, 2015, https://life.eui.eu/wp-content/uploads/2015/11/OLIVIER-ROY-what-is-a-radical-islamist.pdf.

39   Ben Taub, "Paris Attacks: The Belgium Connection," *The New Yorker,* November 16, 2015, http://www.newyorker.com/news/news-desk/the-belgian-connection.

40   Steven Mufson, "A decade ago, she warned of radical Islam in Belgium's Molenbeek," *The Washington Post*, November 18, 2015, https://www.washingtonpost.com/world/europe/a-decade-ago-she-warned-of-radical-islam-in-belgiums-molenbeek/2015/11/18/433c8ce4-8d54-11e5-934c-a369c80822c2_story.html?tid=magnet.

41   Lydia Wilson, "What I Discovered From Interviewing Imprisoned ISIS Fighters," *The Nation*, October 21, 2015, http://www.thenation.com/article/what-i-discovered-from-interviewing-isis-prisoners/.

42   Stefanie Marsh, "'I can't wait to have my own jihadi baby': the British women joining ISIS," *The Times,* December 4, 2014, http://www.thetimes.co.uk/tto/life/article4284138.ece

43   Lauren Williams, "In IS-ruled Raqqa, new class divides create tensions with local Syrians," July 10, 2015, *Middle East Eye*, http://www.middleeasteye.net/news/ruled-raqqa-new-class-divide-creates-tensions-local-syrians-1335876517SANLIURFA, Turkey -; Abouzeid, "Jihad Next Door," 2014.

44   Williams, "In IS-Ruled Raqqa," 2015.

45   Christoph Reuter, "The Terror Strategist: Secret Files Reveal the Structure of Islamic State," *Der Speigel*, April 18, 2015, http://www.spiegel.de/

international/world/islamic-state-files-show-structure-of-islamist-terror-group-a-1029274.html.

46    "Islamic State's Caliphate Shrinks by 14 Percent in 2015," *IHS*, December 21, 2015, http://press.ihs.com/press-release/aerospace-defense-security/islamic-states-caliphate-shrinks-14-percent-2015.

47    Jessica Hartogs, "ISIS cuts fighters' salaries due to 'exceptional circumstances'," *CNBC*, January 20, 2016, http://www.cnbc.com/2016/01/20/isis-cuts-fighters-salaries-due-to-exceptional-circumstances.html.

48    Karen Yourish, Derek Watkins, and Tom Giratikanon, "Where ISIS Has Directed and Inspired Attacks Around the World," *The New York Times*, updated March 22, 2016, http://www.nytimes.com/interactive/2015/06/17/world/middleeast/map-isis-attacks-around-the-world.html?_r=0; Ray Sanchez, Tom Lister, Mark Bixler, Sean O'Key, Michael Hogenmiller, and Mohammed Tawfeeq, *CNN*, updated April 12, 2016, http://www.cnn.com/2015/12/17/world/mapping-isis-attacks-around-the-world.

49    Sarah Almukhtar, "How Boko Haram Courted and Joined the Islamic State," *The New York Times*, June 10, 2015, http://www.nytimes.com/interactive/2015/06/11/world/africa/boko-haram-isis-propaganda-video-nigeria.html; Dionne Searcey and Marc Santora, "Boko Haram Ranked Ahead of ISIS for Deadliest Terror Group," *The New York Times*, November 18, 2015, http://www.nytimes.com/2015/11/19/world/africa/boko-haram-ranked-ahead-of-isis-for-deadliest-terror-group.html.

50    Nancy LeTourneau, "President Obama's Containment Strategy Against ISIS," *Washington Monthly*, November 23, 2015, http://www.washingtonmonthly.com/political-animal-a/2015_11/president_obamas_containment_s058747.php.

51    Callum Paton, "Libya's Raqqa: Is Isis Sirte stronghold the next target for coalition air strikes?" *International Business Times*, December 5, 2015, http://www.ibtimes.co.uk/libyas-raqqa-isis-sirte-stronghold-next-target-coalition-air-strikes-1531903.

52    "Islamic State's Caliphate Shrinks," *IHS*, 2015.

53    "Interview with Kurdish YPG Leader, Polat Can," *The Kurdish Project*, August 12, 2015, http://thekurdishproject.org/latest-news/rojava/interview-with-kurdish-ypg-leader-polat-can/.

## Chapter 10: War and Peace in Turkey

1    "Profile: Fethullah Gulen's Hizmat movement," *BBC*, December 18, 2013, http://www.bbc.com/news/world-13503361.

2    Shazdeh Omari, "China is world's worst jailor of the press, global tally second worst on record," *Committee to Protect Journalists*, December 17,

2014, https://www.cpj.org/reports/2014/12/journalists-in-prison-china-is-worlds-worst-jailer.php.

3    "Turkey's charismatic pro-Islamic leader," *BBC News*, November 4, 2002, http://news.bbc.co.uk/2/hi/europe/2270642.stm.

4    Martin Childs, "Necmettin Erbakan: Politician who served as Turkey's first Islamist prime minister," *The Independent*, October 22, 2011, http://www.independent.co.uk/news/obituaries/necmettin-erbakan-politician-who-served-as-turkeys-first-islamist-prime-minister-2231569.html.

5    Deborah Sontag, "The Erdogan Experiment," *The New York Times*, May 11, 2003, http://www.nytimes.com/2003/05/11/magazine/the-erdogan-experiment.html?pagewanted=all&src=pm.

6    "Terrorist PKK condemns TAK for Taksim attack," *Today's Zaman*, November 6, 2010, http://www.todayszaman.com/national_terrorist-pkk-condemns-tak-for-taksim-attack_226499.html; White, *The PKK*, 45–46.

7    "Peace be unto you," *The Economist*, August 18, 2005, http://www.economist.com/node/4300168.

8    James Brandon, "The Kurdistan Freedom Falcons Emerge as a Rival to the PKK," *Terrorism Focus*, 3, 40, October 17, 2006, The Jamestown Foundation; Nick Birch and Steven Morris, "Tourists warned to stay away as bomb attacks rock Turkey," *The Guardian*, August 28, 2006, http://www.theguardian.com/world/2006/aug/29/topstories3.turkey.

9    "Turkey blames Kurdish suicide bomber for Ankara attack," *Ekurd Daily*, May 23, 2007, http://ekurd.net/mismas/articles/misc2007/5/turkeykurdistan1185.htm.

10   "Kurdish fighters show support for Turkish plans to expand Kurdish rights," *Deutsche Welle*, October 19, 2009, http://www.dw.com/en/kurdish-fighters-show-support-for-turkish-plans-to-expand-kurdish-rights/a-4807619.

11   White, *The PKK*, 43.

12   Omer Taspinar, "Turkey: The New Model?" *Brookings*, April 2012, http://www.brookings.edu/research/papers/2012/04/24-turkey-new-model-taspinar; David Olopade, "Is Turkey the Key to a New Middle East Approach?" *The American Prospect*, April 6, 2009, http://prospect.org/article/turkey-key-new-middle-east-approach; Thomas Patrick Carroll, "Turkey's Justice and Development Party: A Model for Democratic Islam?" *Middle East Intelligence Bulletin*, June/July 2004, https://www.meforum.org/meib/articles/0407_t1.htm.

13   Meredith Tax, "Fundamentalists and Businessmen: the Battle for Secular Space," *Dissent*, June 12, 2013, https://www.dissentmagazine.org/blog/fundamentalists-and-businessmen-the-battle-for-secular-space; Deniz Kandiyoti, "A tangled web: the politics of gender in Turkey,"

*openDemocracy 5050*, January 5, 2011, https://www.opendemocracy.net/5050/deniz-kandiyoti/tangled-web-politics-of-gender-in-turkey.

14    Nazan Ustundag, "The AKP and the Peace Process," *Jadaliyya*, Dec. 1, 2013, http://www.jadaliyya.com/pages/index/15412/the-akp-and-the-peace-process.

15    Harut Sassonian, "Turkish Deputy Prime Minister Tells Women not to Laugh in Public," *The Huffington Post*, August 8, 2014, http://www.huffingtonpost.com/harut-sassounian/turkish-deputy-prime-mini_b_5656807.html; Pinar Tremblay, "Forget online dating, now the Turkish government will find you a spouse," *Al-Monitor*, November 1, 2015, http://www.al-monitor.com/pulse/originals/2015/10/turkey-election-pledges-davutoglu-offers-matchmaking.html#ixzz3riYc3S1P.

16    "Turkey moves down five places in global gender gap ratings," *Hurriyet Daily News*, November 22, 2015, http://www.hurriyetdailynews.com/Default.aspx?pageID=238&nID=91474&NewsCatID=339.

17    Dorian Jones, "Turkey's Murder Rate of Women Skyrockets," *Voice of America*, February 27, 2011, http://www.voanews.com/content/turkeys-murder-rate-of-women-skyrockets-117093538/170517.html.

18    Aliza Marcus, "Asia Minority," *Tablet*, October 21, 2010, http://www.tabletmag.com/jewish-news-and-politics/47397/asia-minority.

19    Human Rights Watch, "Turkey: Party Case Shows Need for Reform," July 30, 2008, https://www.hrw.org/news/2008/07/30/turkey-party-case-shows-need-reform.

20    "Turkey's Descent Into Paranoia," *The New York Times*, December 19, 2014, http://www.nytimes.com/2014/12/20/opinion/turkeys-descent-into-paranoia.html.

21    Ian Traynor and Constanze Letsch, "Turkey at a crossroads as Erdogan bulldozes his way to lasting legacy," *The Guardian*, June 2, 2015, http://www.theguardian.com/world/2015/jun/02/turkish-election-recep-tayyip-erdogan-legacy.

22    Adam Barnett, "Rojava Spirit Spreads," *Dissent*, February 25, 2015, http://www.dissentmagazine.org/online_articles/turkey-erdogan-putin-rojava-kurdish-democracy; Aliza Marcus, "The Kurdish Surge in Turkey's Election: A Boost in Backing for the PKK," *The Turkey Analyst*, June 17, 2015, 8,12, http://www.turkeyanalyst.org/publications/turkey-analyst-articles/item/405-the-kurdish-surge-in-turkey's-election-a-boost-in-backing-for-the-pkk.html.

23    "Critics castigate gov't security failure after Suruc explosion," *Today's Zaman*, July 20, 2015, http://www.todayszaman.com/anasayfa_critics-castigate-govt-security-failure-after-suruc-explosion_394119.html.

24  Agence France-Presse, "HDP co-chair Demirtas calls on PKK to halt violence 'without ifs or buts'," *Hurriyet Daily News,* August 23, 2015, http://www.hurriyetdailynews.com/hdp-co-chair-demirtas-calls-on-pkk-to-halt-violence-without-ifs-or-buts-.aspx?PageID=238&NID=87365&NewsCatID=338.

25  Hasnain Kazim, "Turkey's Demirtas: Érdogan Is Capable of Setting Country on Fire," *Der Spiegel,* July 31, 2015, http://www.spiegel.de/international/world/kurdish-leader-demirtas-calls-for-ceasefire-with-turkey-a-1046263.html.

26  ANF, "PKK's Duran Kalkan: Attacking the PKK Means Defending ISIS," *Kurdish Question,* August 6, 2015, http://kurdishquestion.com/index.php/kurdistan/north-kurdistan/pkk-s-duran-kalkan-attacking-the-pkk-means-defending-isis.html.

27  Nicole F. Watts, "Activists in Office: Pro-Kurdish Contentious Politics in Turkey," *Ethnopolitics,* 5.2, June 2006, https://www.academia.edu/1533711/Activists_in_office_Pro-Kurdish_contentious_politics_in_Turkey.

28  "Kurdish group claims 'revenge murder' on Turkish police," *Al Jazeera,* July 22, 2015, http://www.aljazeera.com/news/2015/07/kurdish-group-claims-revenge-murder-turkish-police-150722132945249.html; Sener Cagaptay, "Turkey Is in Serious Trouble," *The Atlantic,* October 5, 2015, http://www.theatlantic.com/international/archive/2015/10/turkey-isis-russia-pkk/408988/; Hasnain Kazim, Maximilian Popp, and Samiha Shafy, "To Progress and Back: The Rise and Fall of Erdogan's Turkey," *Der Spiegel,* September 24, 2015, http://www.spiegel.de/international/europe/turkey-under-erdogan-is-becoming-politically-riven-a-1054359.html; "1464 HDP/BDP Members Detained, 220 Imprisoned Since General Election," *Kurdish Question,* August 25, 2015,http://www.kurdishquestion.com/index.php/kurdistan/north-kurdistan/1464-hdp-dbp-members-detained-220-imprisoned-since-turkey-general-elections/1085-1464-hdp-dbp-members-detained-220-imprisoned-since-turkey-general-elections.html; TATORT, *Democratic Autonomy,* 109.

29  Margaret Owen, "Margaret Owen Reports on 9 Days of Curfew in Cizre," *Kurdish Question,* September 22, 2015, http://kurdishquestion.com/index.php/kurdistan/north-kurdistan/margaret-owen-report-on-the-9-days-of-curfew-in-cizre.html; Justus Links, "'You are all Armenians!'—The Place of Cizre in the Terror Wars," *CriticAtac,* September 15, 2015, http://www.criticatac.ro/lefteast/the-place-of-cizre-in-the-terror-wars/; Fehim Tastekin, "The revival of Turkey's 'lynching culture,'" *Al-Monitor,* September 22, 2015, http://www.al-monitor.com/pulse/originals/2015/09/turkey-revival-of-lynching-culture-against-kurds.html; Cagaptay, "Turkey Is in Serious Trouble," 2015.

30  Anonymous, "Understanding the Kurdish Resistance: Historical Overview & Eyewitness Report," n.d. [2015], http://www.crimethinc. com/texts/r/kurdish/; Laura Pitel, "Turkey in crisis: The Kurdish teenagers fighting-and dying—in urban clashes with security forces," *The Independent*, January 18, 2016, http://www.independent.co.uk/news/ world/middle-east/turkey-in-crisis-the-kurdish-teenagers-fighting-and-dying-in-urban-clashes-with-security-forces-a6820201.html.

31  Metin Gurcan, "Turkey, PKK clashes continue, but will there be a winner?" *Al-Monitor*, September 14, 2015; http://www.al-monitor.com/pulse/ originals/2015/09/turkey-pkk-clashes-worsening-balance-sheet.html.

32  Constanze Letsch, ""Kurdish civilians hit by snipers as Turkey cracks down on militants," *The Guardian*, September 8, 2015, http://www. theguardian.com/world/2015/sep/08/kurdish-civilians-killed-snipers-turkey-cracks-down-militants; "Turkey: Mounting Security Operations Deaths," *Human Rights Watch*, December 22, 2015, https://www.hrw.org/ news/2015/12/22/turkey-mounting-security-operation-deaths.

33  Sehahattin Dermitas and Figen Yusekdag, "HDP: Call to the International Community Following the Ankara Massacre," *Kurdistan Tribune*, October 12, 2015, http://kurdistantribune.com/2015/hdp-call-to-the-international-community-following-the-ankara-massacre/; Aydin Albayrak, "Paris attacks may increase pressure on Turkey over ISIL," *Today's Zaman*, November 22, 2015, http://www.todayszaman. com/diplomacy_paris-attacks-may-increase-pressure-on-turkey-over-isil_404814.html; Noah Blaser and Aaron Stein, "The Islamic State's Network in Turkey," *Turkey Wonk*, October 30, 2015, https://turkeywonk. wordpress.com/.

34  Christopher de Bellaigue, "The Sultan of Turkey," *The New York Review of Books*, December 17, 2015, http://www.nybooks.com/articles/2015/12/17/ erdogan-sultan-turkey/.

35  "Save Kobane: HDP Co-Chair Statements on Election Results," *Facebook*, Nov. 1, 2015. https://www.facebook.com/297459630456872/photos/a.298110 823725086.1073741829.297459630456872/481798745356292/?type=3&fref=nf.

36  Uzay Bulut, "Turkey's Murderous Assault on Kurds," *Gatestone Institute*, December 29, 2015, http://www.gatestoneinstitute.org/7122/turkey-assault-kurds.

37  Rosa Burc, "Turkey's Future? State Authoritarianism or Democratic Autonomy," *Telesur*, November 17, 2015, http://www.telesurtv.net/english/ opinion/Turkeys-Future-State-Authoritarianism-or-Democratic-Autonomy-20151117-0020.html.

38  "Diyarbakir Becoming Kobane," *Rojava Report*, November 13, 2015, https://rojavareport.wordpress.com/2015/11/13/diyarbakir-becoming-kobane/.

39    "Kurds Decide on Self-Rule in North Kurdistan (Turkey)," *Kurdish Question,* December 28, 2015, http://kurdishquestion.com/index. php/kurdistan/north-kurdistan/kurds-decide-on-self-rule-in-north-kurdistan-turkey.html; "Kurdish opposition believes autonomy the only way for peace," *Today's Zaman,* December 27, 2015, http://www. todayszaman.com/anasayfa_kurdish-opposition-believes-autonomy-the-only-way-for-peace_408077.html.

40    Asim Murat Okur, "Urgent Call from Turkey's Human Rights Organizations to the International Community," *Coalition Against Impunity,* January 11, 2016, http://en.ihd.org.tr/index.php/2016/01/11/urgent-call-from-turkeys-human-rights-organizations-to-the-international-community/.

41    "More than 1000 Academics Call for Peace Talks to Resume Between Turkey and PKK," *Kurdish Question,* January 11, 2016, http://www. kurdishquestion.com/index.php/kurdistan/north-kurdistan/more-than-1000-academics-call-for-peace-talks-between-turkey-and-pkk-to-resume.html.

42    "Briefing: End abusive operations under indefinite curfews in Turkey," *Amnesty International,* January 21, 2016, http://www.amnestyusa.org/news/news-item/briefing-end-abusive-operations-under-indefinite-curfews-in-turkey.

43    Abdullah Demirbas, "Undoing Years of Progress in Turkey," *The New York Times,* January 26, 2016, http://www.nytimes.com/2016/01/25/.

44    Selahattin Demirtas, "Free Speech Isn't the Only Casulty of Erdogan's Repression," *The New York Times,* April 13, 2016, http://www.nytimes. com/2016/04/14/opinion/free-speech-isnt-the-onlycasualty-of-erdogans-repression.html?_r=1. opinion/undoing-years-of-progress-in-turkey. html?_r=0.

45    CIA, "The Kurdish Minority Problem," December 8, 1948, http://www.foia.cia.gov/sites/default/files/document_conversions/89801/DOC_0000258376.pdf.

46    James Rosen, "Kurdish militia proving to be reliable partner against Islamic State in Syria," *McClatchyDC,* July 6, 2015, http://www. mcclatchydc.com/news/nationworld/national/article26598160.html; Gunay Aksoy Zana Kaya, "TEV-DEM: 'There Can Be No Democratic Syria Without Rojava,'" *The Rojava Report,* October 27, 2015, https://rojavareport.wordpress.com/2015/10/27/tev-dem-there-can-be-no-democratic-syria-without-rojava/.

47    ANF, "Geneva III Talks Postponed Once Again," *Kurdish Question,* January 28, 2016, http://kurdishquestion.com/index.php/kurdistan/west-kurdistan/geneva-iii-talks-postponed-once-again.html.

48  "Government Response to the House of Commons Foreign Affairs
    Committee Report: UK Government policy on the Kurdistan Region
    of Iraq," March 2015, https://www.gov.uk/government/uploads/system/
    uploads/attachment_data/file/415796/48533_Cm_9029_Accessible.pdf.

49  Aliza Marcus and Andrew Apostolou, "Why It's Time for a Free
    Kurdistan," *The Daily Beast*, November 27, 2015, http://www.
    thedailybeast.com/articles/2015/11/27/the-kurds-already-have-
    independence.html.

## Coda: Some Questions Remain

1   Janet Biehl, "Paradoxes of a Liberatory Ideology," *Biehl on Bookchin*,
    November 22, 2015, http://www.biehlonbookchin.com/paradoxes-
    liberatory-ideology.

2   David Graeber, "No. This is a Genuine Revolution," *Kurdish Question*,
    December 27, 2014, http://kurdishquestion.com/kurdistan/west-
    kurdistan/david-graeber-no-this-is-a-genuine-revolution.html.

3   Dave Johnson, "Now We Know Why Huge TPP Trade Deal Is Kept
    Secret From the Public," *Huffington Post*, March 27, 2015, http://
    www.huffingtonpost.com/dave-johnson/now-we-know-why-huge-
    tpp_b_6956540.html.

# Suggestions for Further Reading

*Most of the information in this book was drawn from articles online and resource websites. These references can be found in the footnotes. The following list is of books I found useful.*

In der Maur, Renée and Jonas Staal, eds., *New World Academy Reader #5, Stateless Democracy,* in dialogue with the Kurdish Women's Movement. BAK: Utrecht, Netherlands, 2015.

Marcus, Aliza, *Blood and Belief: The PKK and the Kurdish Fight for Independence.* New York: New York University Press, 2007.

McDowall, David, *A Modern History of the Kurds.* London: I.B.Tauris & Co., 2004.

Mojab, Shahrzad, ed., *Women of a Non-State Nation: The Kurds.* Costa Mesa: Mazda Publishers, 2001.

Ocalan, Abdullah, *Democratic Confederalism.* Cologne: International Initiative Edition, 2011..

_____, *Liberating Life: Woman's Revolution.* Cologne: International Initiative Edition, 2014.

_____, *Prison Writings: The Roots of Civilisation,* trans. Klaus Happel. London: Pluto Press, 2007.

_____, *Prison Writings: The PKK and the Kurdish Question in the 21st Century,* trans. and ed. Klaus Happel. London: Transmedia Publishing Ltd., 2011.

_____, *Prison Writings III: The Road Map to Negotiations,* trans. Havin Guneser. Cologne: International Initiative Edition, 2012.

_____, *War and Peace in Kurdistan.* Cologne: International Initiative Edition, 2009.

Ozcan, Ali Kemal, *Turkey's Kurds: A Theoretical Analysis of the PKK and Abdullah Ocalan.* London: Routledge, 2006.

Phillips, David L., *The Kurdish Spring: A New Map of the Middle East.* New Brunswick: Transaction Publishers, 2015.

Strangers in a Tangled Wilderness, eds., *A Small Key Can Open a Large Door.* New York: Combustion Press, 2015.

TATORT Kurdistan, *Democratic Autonomy in North Kurdistan*, trans. Janet Biehl. Hamburg: New Compass Press, 2013.

van Bruinessen, Martin, *Agha, Shaikh and State: The Social and Political Structures of Kurdistan* (Zed Books: London, 1992).

Weiss, Michael, and Hassan Hassan, *ISIS: Inside the Army of Terror*. New York: Regan Arts, 2015.

White, Paul, *Primitive Rebels or Revolutionary Modernizers? The Kurdish National Movement in Turkey*. London: Zed Books, 2000.

_____, *The PKK: Coming Down From the Mountains*. London: Zed Books, 2015.

Wright, Lawrence, *The Looming Tower: Al-Qaeda and the Road to 9/11*. New York: Alfred A. Knopf, 2006.

# Acknowledgments

MY DEEPEST GRATITUDE to:

Aliza Marcus for her research help and support, and her careful reading of the manuscript;

Gita Sahgal and Ariane Brunet, my closest collaborators—Gita, for her thoughtful and critical examination of the book; Ariane, for sharing her experiences in Syria; and both for many discussions of the political context;

Kevin Anderson, for taking the trouble to read and comment on work by someone he didn't even know;

and Nadje al-Ali, for taking time from a very hectic schedule to look at the book.

Many thanks to Miriam Frank for translating two German sources; to Sharzad Mojab for research advice; and to Dilar Dirik for responding to questions at a time when she was busy doing her own research; she is in no way responsible for any conclusions I have drawn. Thanks to Sinam Mohamed, European representative of the Rojava Cantons, for allowing me to follow her around New York for a few days; to Andrew Apostolou for his help understanding US policy; and to Choman Hardi, for an interview on Skype.

More thanks than I can say to Joey Lawrence, whose beautiful pictures illuminate this book, for the work he does and for sharing it with this audience.

As will be evident to those who read footnotes, I also owe an enormous debt to the work of Joost Jongerden and Ahmet Hamdi Akkaya, David McDowall, Aliza Marcus, and Martin van Bruinessen, as well as many other scholars and researchers. Various websites, including *Harvest, Jinha, Kurdish Question*, and *Rojava Report*, were invaluable sources of information.

*A Road Unforeseen* would not exist were it not for Bellevue Literary Press, whose publisher and editorial director, Erika Goldman, came up with the idea. Other members of the BLP team—Joe Gannon, Molly Mikolowski, Crystal Sikma, and board member Gloria Jacobs—have been indefatigably and unfailingly supportive. And thank you to the editors of *Dissent* magazine, who published the essay that led to this book.

For their emotional support and patience during the months I worked obsessively on this book, and frequently withdrew from their company, thanks and hugs to my family Elijah Tax-Berman, Jamillah Richards, and Augustus Jamil; my daughter-by-choice, Reem Abdel-Razek; and my friends Ynestra King, Marissa Piesman, Myra Malkin, and Ann Snitow.

To all those working to build, understand, support, and spread the word about the Rojava revolution: Thank you and I hope this book will be of some use.

# Index

Abdo, Meysa, 186
Abdullah, Asya, 44
Abdullah, Nesrin, 139
Abdullah, Shenah, 101
Abdulrahman, Rami, 197
Abouzeid, Rania, 212, 228
Abu Khaled, 184, 188
Aburish, Said, 64–65, 79–80, 83
academies, in grassroots democratic
     autonomy, 161
Acik, Necla, 55
al-Adnani, Abu Mohammed, 214, 221
Afghanistan, 21, 25, 204–5
Afrin canton, 53
     economy, 173–75
     underdeveloped, 164
*aghas* (village chiefs), 45, 59–61, 64
Ahrar al Sham militia, 215–16, 218
Akkaya, Ahmet Hamdi, 87, 149, 157
AKP (Justice and Development Party),
     158, 202
     founding of, 243–44
     "moderate Islamism" and, 246–57
Aksoy, Memed, 20
Alevi, 45, 51–52
Ali, Badirkan, 196–97
Al-Ali, Nadje, 29–30, 210
Alwany, Raheb, 219
Amnesty International, 194–96
Analyses by the Leadership (*Onderlik
     Çözümlemeler*) (Ocalan, A.),
     125–26
Anderson, Benedict, 55, 149, 151
Anfal, 81–85
Apostolou, Andrew, 257
Arab Belt, 164
Arab nationalism, 50–51, 196–97

Arab Spring, 23, 51, 56, 100–101, 169
Archimedes, 31–32
Arif, Abd el-Salam, 63–64
Armenian genocide, 52, 68, 159
asayish (local police force largely made up
     of women), 172, 176–77
Assad, Bashar al
     Daesh and, 211–12
     opposition to, 53, 165–68, 215
     as Syria's president, 50, 53, 165–68,
        211–12, 215
Association of Communities in Kurdistan.
     *See* KCK
Ataturk, Mustapha Kemal, 51, 67, 69, 113,
     148
Athena, 33
Aybola, Ercan, 150–51
Aydin, Vedat, 111
Azeez, Hawzhin, 199
Azzam, Abdullah, 203–4

Baath Party, 48, 50, 62–65, 211
Baghdadi, Abu Bakr al-, 211, 213–14, 221
al-Bakr, Ahmed Hassan, 64
Bangura, Zainab, 225
Baran, Sari, 87, 107–8
Barber, Matthew, 40, 215–16
Barnett, Adam, 53
Barzani, Masoud
     British colonialism and, 60
     corruption of, 99
     feminism and, 102
     KDP led by, 13, 38–39, 43–44, 80, 94,
        98, 189–91
     KNC and, 191
     KRG and, 19, 38, 43–45
     PKK and, 114–15, 190–91

Barzani, Mullah Mustafa, 60–66, 70–71, 256

Bayak, Cemil, 88, 152, 260

BDP (Kurdish Peace and Democracy Party), 14, 53, 249

Beijing Conference on Women, 26, 28, 30

Biden, Joe, 185

Biehl, Janet, 146, 150, 173

bin Laden, Osama, 204–6

Bookchin, Murray, 18, 150

Bozarslan, Hamit, 49–50, 89, 162

Bremer, Paul, 206–8

British colonialism, 60

Bucak, Mehmet Celal, 72–73

Bush, George H.W., 83–84, 95

Bush, George W., 96, 205–6

Caglayan, Handan, 23, 143–44

caliphate, 14, 37, 221, 232–33, 262–63

Camp Bucca, 210–11

Camp Zeli, 115, 128–29

Can, Polat, 241

Cansiz, Sakine
    assassination of, 152–53
    in PKK, 130, 133–36, 152–53

capitalism, 71–72, 128, 151, 260, 263
    modern, 34, 261
    narrative of, 21–23

Carter, Ash, 256

ceasefires, PKK, 114, 116–17, 146, 152, 244, 249–50

celibacy, 142–45

chemical warfare, 79–82, 92

Cheney, Dick, 95–96

China, 137–38, 260

Christian Coalition, 25

CIA, 111, 146

citizen journalists, 221–23

civil war, Syrian, 165–68, 211

Cizire canton, 53, 170, 178, 181
    economy, 173
    Kurdish women in, 41–42, 139–40, 154, 176

Clinton, Hillary, 203

Cockburn, Cynthia, 140

Cold War, 20–21, 61, 64, 255–56

colonialism, 60, 123–24, 128, 226

commune, 159, 170–71

community economy, 173–77

Constitution, KRG, 97–98

corruption, 99, 246, 248

crisis of masculinity, 24, 28

cultural revolution, 103

Curukkaya, Selim, 148

Daesh
    Assad and, 211–12
    beliefs of, 230–35
    birth of, 201, 210–15
    caliphate, 14, 37, 221, 232–33, 262–63
    defeat of, 35, 78, 241
    flag, 200
    genealogy, 14
    Islamism, 34, 180, 201, 203, 216–19, 231
    Jabhat al-Nusra and, 14, 212–14, 219, 221
    Kirkuk and, 38–39, 43–44
    Kobane battle and, 17, 38–39, 43, 141, 179–91, 239–41, 248
    KRG's non-aggression pact with, 43
    leaders, 236–41
    media, 237
    oil and, 234–35
    al Qaeda and, 14, 203, 210–14, 216, 218–19, 221
    rape by, 41, 225
    in Raqqa, 215–23
    recruits, 237–39
    revolution of, 56–57
    Rojava liberated from, 17–19, 34–35, 54
    at Sinjar Mountain, 36, 37–45, 56, 58, 182, 190
    suicide bombers, 104, 240, 251
    Sunni Muslims and, 56, 230, 232–33, 239
    in Syria, 14, 42, 211, 215–23
    in three-way struggle, 37
    Turkey and, 180, 182–87, 222, 248–49
    US and, 17, 42, 182–83, 185–86, 194–95

Daesh (cont'd)
    women and, 20, 28, 34, 141, 201,
        218–19, 225–30, 238–39
Dakhil, Deelan, 225
Dall'Oglio, Paolo, 217
Davutoglu, Ahmet, 184, 193, 247, 249,
    251–52
DDKO. *See* Revolutionary Eastern
    Cultural Hearths
"Declaration of Democratic
    Confederalism in Kurdistan"
    (Ocalan, A.), 157
DEHAP, 14, 156
Demirbas, Abdullah, 158–59, 254–55
Demirel, Suleyman, 111, 116–17
Demirtas, Selahattin, 187, 249, 252–53,
    255
democracy
    Ocalan, Abdullah, and, 124, 126, 150,
        157
    in Syria and Turkey, 35
democratic autonomy
    grassroots, 159–64
    Kurdish women and, 160–61
    PKK and, 155–58, 161–63, 261
    PYD and, 53–54, 164–73, 175, 194,
        256
    in Rojava cantons, 164–73, 259–63
    of Syrian Kurds, 164–73
    of Turkish Kurds, 153, 155–64,
        252–53
democratic confederalism, 56, 150, 157
democratic economy, in Rojava cantons,
    173–77
Democratic Front for the Liberation of
    Palestine. *See* DFLP
Democratic Labor Party. *See* DEP
Democratic Society Congress. *See* DTK
Democratic Society Movement. *See* TEV-
    DEM
Democratic Society Party. *See* DTP
Democratic Union Party. *See* PYD
DEP (Democratic Labor Party), 14, 118
Dersim, 68–69
DFLP (Democratic Front for the
    Liberation of Palestine), 73

diaspora, Kurdish, 92, 106
Dicle, Hatip, 113, 116
Dirik, Dilar, 141
district people's council, 170–71
Diyarbakir prison, 107–8, 134–35
Dogan, Fidan, 152
Dohuk, 85
Dostar, Heval, 189–90
"draining the swamp" strategy, 118
dress code, Daesh, 226–27
DTK (Democratic Society Congress), 14,
    157, 253
DTP (Democratic Society Party), 14,
    156–58, 245
Dundar, Komaran, 108–9

Eastern Kurdistan Protection Units and
    Women's Protection Units. *See*
    YRK-HPJ
economy
    democratic, in Rojava cantons,
        173–77
    women and, 175–76
Egypt, 23
Ehmed, Ilham, 256
Ellis, Robert, 193
Engels, Friedrich, 32
equality, Kurdish women and, 47, 102,
    142, 150, 198, 260
Erbil, 85, 98, 100–101
Erdogan, Recep Tayyip
    Islamism of, 243–44, 246
    support for, 193
    as Turkey's president, 52, 149, 152,
        161, 180, 182–85, 193,
        243–46, 247–52, 254
    Turkish Kurds and, 149, 152, 161,
        180, 182–85, 244–45,
        247–52, 254
    women and, 247
Ertas, Mehmet Ali, 135
EU. *See* European Union
Euphrates Volcano, 186
European Union (EU), 106, 119, 149, 193,
    246, 256

Fakih, Lama, 194–95
Falk, Richard, 18
Fanon, Frantz, 70, 72, 87, 89
Faris, Naima, 39–40
female genital mutilation (FGM), 26, 28,
        47, 98, 102
female labor, 28–29, 32
feminism
    Barzani, Masoud, and, 102
    fundamentalism and, 30–31
    in Gorran, 101–2
    in Iraq, 97–98
    militarism and, 140
    of Rojava cantons, 54, 56
    Western, strategic thinking by, 31–32
FGM. See female genital mutilation
Fidan, Hakan, 152
Filkins, Dexter, 43, 206–7
Fitzherbert, Yvo, 188
Flynn, Elizabeth Gurley, 20
Ford, Robert, 191–92
Fraihi, Hind, 238
France, 152–53
Fraser, Susan, 152
Freedom Falcons. See TAK
Free Syrian Army. See FSA
Free Women's Movement of Kurdistan.
        See TAJK
Free World narrative, 20–21
Freire, Paolo, 125
Freud, Sigmund, 144–45
Friedman, Thomas L., 182
FSA (Free Syrian Army)
    Daesh and, 216–18
    Syria and, 168, 180, 188, 196, 198,
        213, 216–18
fundamentalism. See also Islamism
    dangers of, 30–31
    rise of, 24–26, 28–29

Galbraith, Peter, 92
Gandhi, Mahatma, 142
gas reserves, 98–99
gender relations
    PKK, 136, 138–39, 145
    PYD and, 171

    in war, 140
Geneva Convention, 105
genocide
    Armenian, 52, 68, 159
    of Iraqi Kurds, 48–49, 81–83
    of Turkish Kurds, 68–69, 92
    of Yazidi, 40, 44
Germany, 193
global financial institutions, 262
globalization, 22–23, 25, 28–29
Gorran (Movement for Change), 13, 49,
        99–102
Goss, Porter, 192–93
Graeber, David, 18–19, 33, 260
grassroots democratic autonomy, 159–64
Grojean, Olivier, 90, 126–27
Gulf War, 49, 83
Guney, Omer, 152–53
Gungor, Cetin, 88

HADEP, 14
Haig, Alexander, 65
Haji Bakr, 211, 214–16, 239
Hajo, Siamend, 192
al-Hamz, Abdel Aziz, 221
Hardi, Choman, 85, 97, 100, 102
Hassan, Kawa, 100
Hassan, Ruqia, 222
HDP (People's Democratic Party), 14, 53,
        163, 181, 184, 249–52
Helms, Richard, 65
Helsinki Watch, 106–7, 111
Hemo, Sipan, 195
HEP (People's Labor Party), 14, 52,
        110–13, 116, 118
Hiller, Benjamin, 168
Hilterman, Joost, 97
Hitler, Adolf, 234
homosexuality, 145
honor killings, 102
HPG-YJA-Star (People's Defense Forces
        and Free Women's Forces),
        14, 163
human rights
    false accusations about, 194–98
    PKK and, 116–17, 147–49, 153

human rights (cont'd)
    violations, 47, 67, 81–84, 106, 111,
        114
    women and, 26–28
Human Rights Watch, 84, 106
Hussein, Saddam
    in Iraq, 48–49, 64–66, 79–85, 92–93,
        95–96, 102–3, 207, 234
    Iraqi Kurds and, 48–49, 64–66,
        79–85, 92–93
    women and, 102–3

Ignatius, David, 206
*Imagined Communities* (Anderson), 151
Imset, Ismet G., 85, 117, 119
India, 142
individual consciousness, transformation
    of, 120–21, 124–25
Industrial Workers of the World (IWW),
    20
intellectual class, 162
International Women's Day, *154*
*In These Times* panel, 18
Iran
    geography of, 13
    Iraq at war with, 48–49, 79–80, 83,
        102
    Iraqi Kurds and, 65–66
    Kurds in, 48, 79
    revolution in, 79
    Shah of, 65–66, 71, 79
    US and, 79–80
Iraq
    army, 37–38
    chemical warfare in, 79–82, 92
    feminism in, 97–98
    geography of, 13
    Iran at war with, 48–49, 79–80, 83,
        102
    Islamism in, 207–9
    Kurdistan in, 49–50, 60–63, 81, 85,
        92–103, 107, 190
    land reform in, 62
    1979 as turning point in, 79
    oil in, 64, 98–99
    al Qaeda in, 14, 206, 209–10

    resistance in, 29–30
    Saddam Hussein in, 48–49, 64–66,
        79–85, 92–93, 95–96,
        102–3, 207, 234
    US and, 49, 79–80, 83, 95–97, 107,
        205–10
    women in, 102–3, 207–10
Iraqi Kurdish militia. *See peshmerga*
Iraqi Kurdish parties, 13. *See also* Gorran;
    KDP; KRG; PUK
Iraqi Kurds
    autonomy of, 19, 43, 92–103, 151
    equality and, 47, 102
    genocide of, 48–49, 81–83
    history of, 48–50, 59–66
    Iran and, 65–66
    Islamism and, 97, 102
    Kirkuk and, 63, 65, 84–85, 96
    Kurdistan of, 49–50, 60–63, 81, 85,
        92–103, 107, 190
    paradigm of, 57
    PKK and, 114–15, 151–52, 190–91
    Saddam Hussein and, 48–49, 64–66,
        79–85, 92–93
    at Sinjar Mountain, 36, 37–45
    Syrian Kurds and, 39
    Turkish Kurds and, 59–61, 114–15
    as US allies, 38, 96–97
IS. *See* Islamic State
Ishtar, 32–33
ISIL (Islamic State in Iraq and the
    Levant), 14. *See also* Daesh
ISIS (Islamic State in Iraq and Syria/Iraq
    and al-Sham), 14, 210. *See also*
    Daesh
"The ISIS Papers," 232–34
Islam. *See also* Sunni Muslims
    patriarchal belt and, 23–24
    PKK and, 161–62
    Rojava backlash and, 198
    Shia, 83–84, 204–7, 209
Islamic State (IS), 14. *See also* Daesh
Islamic State in Iraq and Syria/Iraq and
    al-Sham. *See* ISIS
Islamic State in Iraq and the Levant. *See*
    ISIL

Islamism
  of Daesh, 34, 180, 201, 203, 216–19,
      231
  of Erdogan, 243–44, 246
  in Iraq, 207–9
  Iraqi Kurds and, 97, 102
  moderate, 246–57
  of al Qaeda, 201–6, 209
Italy, 146–47
IWW. *See* Industrial Workers of the
      World

Jabhat al-Nusra
  Afrin under attack by, 174–75
  Daesh and, 14, 212–14, 219, 221
  in Raqqa, 215–16, 218–19
  Turkey and, 180, 185
Jamaat e Islami, 25
*jash* (children of donkeys), 63, 80, 84,
      93–94
Jensen, Robert, 118
Jerf, Naji, 222
jihadis, 202–3, 237–38
Jineology, 33–34
Jongerden, Joost, 71, 87, 149, 157
journalists, 182–84, 188–90, 221–23
Julani, Abu Mohammad al-, 212–14
Justice and Development Party. *See* AKP

Kalkan, Duran, 250
Kandiyoti, Deniz, 24, 28
Kaya, Gonul, 33–34
KCK (Association of Communities in
      Kurdistan), 13, 54, 88, 155,
      163, 181
KDP (Kurdistan Democratic Party)
  Barzani, Masoud, leading, 13, 38–39,
      43–44, 80, 94, 98, 189–91
  Barzani, Mullah Mustafa, and, 61–66
  Gulf War and, 83
  history of, 49
  KNC and, 191
  in KRG, 38, 93–94, 98
  McDowall on, 63–64, 84, 93–94
  PKK and, 86, 94, 189–91
  protests against, 101

PUK fighting, 80, 94–95
Saddam Hussein and, 48–49
Sinjar Mountain and, 38–39, 41
split, 63–64, 80
Talabani and, 62–64
tribalism of, 93, 99
KDP-S, 164–65
Kemalism, 51–52, 67–76, 243
Kenya, 147–48
Kerry, John, 185
Keskin, Eren, 135–36
KH. *See* Kurdish Hezbollah
al-Khanssa Brigade, 226–30
Khomeini, Ayatollah, 79
Kirkuk
  Daesh and, 38–39, 43–44
  Iraqi Kurds and, 63, 65, 84–85, 96
Kisanak, Gultan, 134–35
Kissinger, Henry, 65–66
KJK (Kurdistan Women's Liberation
      Movement), 13
KNC (Kurdish National Council), 191–92
Kobane, Meryam, 182
Kobane canton
  backlash, 191–99
  battle of, 17, 38–39, 43, 141, 179–91,
      239–41, 248, 259
  importance of, 179–80
  in media, 182–84, 188
  Obama administration and, 182–83,
      185
  PYD in, 17–18, 38, 168, 183, 185–87
  refugees, 183, 189
  setting up of, 53
  YPG-YPJ and, 38–39, 41, 180–82,
      184–88
Korean War, 140–41
Korn, David A., 124
KRG (Kurdistan Regional Government),
      13
  Barzani, Masoud, and, 19, 38, 43–45
  capitalist modernity of, 34
  Constitution, 97–98
  Daesh's non-aggression pact with, 43
  demonstrations against, 100–101
  economy of, 175

KRG (cont'd)
  history of, 49–50, 93–99
  KDP in, 38, 93–94, 98
  PKK and, 151–52
  PUK and, 38, 93–94, 98
  Turkey and, 38–39, 45
Kurdaxi, Dara, 175
Kurdish Hezbollah (KH), 112
Kurdish National Council. *See* KNC
Kurdish Peace and Democracy Party. *See*
    BDP
Kurdish women
  in Cizire, 41–42, 139–40, 154, 176
  democratic autonomy and, 160–61
  equality and, 47, 102, 142, 150, 198,
      260
  fighters, 20, 28, 41–42, 47, 56,
      128–29, 132, 136–46,
      137–38, 149
  history of, 46–47
  imprisoned, 134–35
  in Iraqi Kurdistan, 94–95
  movement of, 31, 33–34, 141–42, 259
  Ocalan, Abdullah, and, 127–30,
      135–36, 142–43, 149–50
  in *peshmerga*, 138–39
  in PKK, 34, 37, 54–56, 108, 128–30,
      132, 133–36, 138–46, 258
  at Rojava's center, 54, 56, 260–62
Kurdistan
  geography, 13, 19, 37, 48, 85
  Iraqi, 49–50, 60–63, 81, 85, 92–103,
      107, 190
  Ocalan's dream for, 34–35, 123–24
Kurdistan Democratic Party. *See* KDP
Kurdistan National Front, 80
Kurdistan Regional Government. *See*
    KRG
Kurdistan Revolutionaries, 71–72
Kurdistan Women's Liberation
    Movement. *See* KJK
Kurdistan Workers Party. *See* PKK
Kurds. *See also* Iraqi Kurds; Kurdish
    women; Syrian Kurds; Turkish
    Kurds
  Cold War and, 61

  Daesh defeated by, 35, *78*, 241
  diaspora, 92, 106
  future of, 37
  history of, 45–53, 59–61
  independent state desired by, 151
  Iranian, 48, 79
  nationalism of, 55–56, 60–61, 69, 164
  refugees, 49, 66, 82, 84, 182
  religions of, 45, 194
  revolution of, 53–57, 59, 71–72
  tribalism of, 45–46, 60–61, 63–66,
      87–88, 93, 99
  uniting of, 44–45
  in WWI, 46
Kutschera, Chris, 122, 148
Kuwait, 49, 83

Lawrence, Joey, 188, 264
Lawrence textile strike of 1912, 20
Leverink, Joris, 169–70
*Liberating Life: Woman's Revolution*
    (Ocalan), 56
Libya, 241
Local Coordination Committees, 165–66
local councils, 168–69
local police force largely made up of
    women (asayish), 172, 176–77
*The Looming Tower* (Wright), 201–2
*The Lord of the Rings* (Tolkien), 19, 35
Lorraine, Percy, 68–69
Lubbock, Eric, 114

Mahajan, Rahul, 118
Mahmood, Aqsa, 230
Mahmoud, Houzan, 96–98, 141, 209–10
Mahsum Korkmaz Academy, 89–90, 125,
    135
al Majid, Ali Hasan "Chemical Ali," 81
Makhmour, 78
Malay, Mustafa, 114
Mao Zedong, 72, 118
Marcus, Aliza, 247
  on Kurdish autonomy, 257
  on PKK, 115, 122, 129–30, 136, 155,
      158, 161–63
marriage, PKK and, 142–44

Marxism, 32–33, 56, 70–72, 125, 151
masculinity, crisis of, 24, 28
Matin, Kamran, 165
matriarchy, 33
McDowall, David
    on KDP, 63–64, 84, 93–94
    on Turkey, 52, 68, 110, 117
media
    backlash in, 195
    Daesh, 237
    journalists, 182–84, 188–90, 221–23
    Kobane canton in, 182–84, 188
Mehta, Hansa, 27
Mesopotamia, 32, 123–24
militarism, 140–42
military conscription, 91, 119
Milosevic, Slobodan, 25
MIT (Turkish military intelligence),
    152–53
mixed-sex military units, 137–38
Mojab, Shahrzad, 47, 102
Molyneux, Maxine, 138
Monroe, Derek, 98
Mosul, 38, 43, 220
Movement for Change. *See* Gorran
Muslim, Enver, 181
Muslim, Salih
    excluded from peace talks, 256
    PYD and, 50–51, 164–65, 167, 169,
        171, 193, 198
Muslim Brotherhood, 165, 192, 198

Nasr, Vali, 203
nationalism, 25, 161, 234, 243
    Arab, 50–51, 196–97
    Kurdish, 55–56, 60–61, 69, 164
    Ocalan and, 55–56, 123, 157, 262
    tribalism and, 45–46
    Turkish, 52, 123
nation-state
    model, 19, 45, 55, 122–23, 145, 151,
        157, 262–63
    Rojava and, 172
Nawfal, Souad, 217–18, 220
neighborhood councils, 159–60
neoliberalism, 22–23, 28

Nezan, Kendal, 92
NGOs, 102, 190

Obama administration, 17, 42, 182–83,
    185–86, 240
Ocalan, Abdullah
    ceasefire offered by, 114, 116–17, 146
    "Declaration of Democratic
        Confederalism in
        Kurdistan," 157
    democracy and, 124, 126, 150, 157
    dream of, for Kurdistan, 34–35,
        123–24
    in exile, 50, 73, 122, 146–47
    imprisoned, 52, 54–55, 70, 147–48,
        155, 261
    influences on, 55, 149–51
    Kurdish women and, 127–30,
        135–36, 142–43, 149–50
    *Liberating Life: Woman's Revolution*,
        56
    Mahsum Korkmaz Academy and,
        89–90, 125
    nationalism and, 55–56, 123, 157, 262
    *Onderlik Çözümlemeler*, 125–26
    PKK led by, 18, 31–35, 50, 52–55, 72,
        78, 88–90, 107–8, 113–17,
        120–27, 129–30, 133–35,
        148–52, 155, 163, 259
    *Prison Writing I*, 149
    as radical student, 70–72
    trial of, 148–49
Ocalan, Osman, 115, 122, 129, 152
oil
    Daesh and, 234–35
    Iraqi, 64, 98–99
    in Rojava, 175
*Onderlik Çözümlemeler* (Analyses by
    the Leadership) (Ocalan, A.),
    125–26
One Voice, 101–2
Operation Anfal, 81–85
Operation Desert Storm, 95–96
Organization for Women's Rights in Iraq
    (OWFI), 96, 210

*Origin of the Family, Private Property and the State* (Engels), 32
Ottoman Empire, 45–46
Oweis, Khaled Yacoub, 193–94
OWFI. *See* Organization for Women's Rights in Iraq
Ozcan, Ali Kemal, 46–47, 110, 125
Ozul, Turgut, 116–17

PAJK (Party of Free Women of Kurdistan), 139
Palestine, 109
Paris attacks, 238
parliamentary parties. *See* Turkish Kurds, parliamentary parties of
Party for a Free Life in Kurdistan. *See* PJAK
Party of Free Women of Kurdistan. *See* PAJK
patriarchal belt, 23–24
Patriotic Revolutionary Youth Movement. *See* YDG-H
Patriotic Union of Kurdistan. *See* PUK
peace movement, women's, 140–41
peace process, 245–46
*The Pedagogy of the Oppressed* (Freire), 125
Pell, Claiborne, 92
People's Defense Forces and Free Women's Forces. *See* HPG-YJA-Star
People's Democratic Party. *See* HDP
People's Labor Party. *See* HEP
People's Protection Units and Women's Protection Units. *See* YPG-YPJ
*peshmerga* (Iraqi Kurdish militia)
    female members of, 138–39
    founding of, 63
    *jash* and, 63, 80, 84
    in Kirkuk, 38
    Sinjar Mountain and, 39–44
    struggle of, 17, 37
    united, 80–81
    US and, 65–66
PJAK (Party for a Free Life in Kurdistan), 13
PKK (Kurdistan Workers Party), 242, 258
    armed struggle by, 86–92, 148–49, 255

Barzani, Masoud, and, 114–15, 190–91
    ceasefires, 114, 116–17, 146, 152, 244, 249–50
    celibacy and, 142–45
    collective leadership of, 155
    democratic autonomy and, 155–58, 161–63, 261
    development of, 107–11
    DTP and, 158
    founding of, 72–73
    gender relations in, 136, 138–39, 145
    human rights and, 116–17, 147–49, 153
    ideological transformation of, 54–55
    Iraqi Kurds and, 114–15, 151–52, 190–91
    Islam and, 161–62
    KDP and, 86, 94, 189–91
    KH's blood feud with, 112
    KRG and, 151–52
    Kurdish women in, 34, 37, 54–56, 108, 128–30, *132*, 133–36, 138–46, *258*
    Marcus on, 115, 122, 129–30, 136, 155, 158, 161–63
    marriage and, 142–44
    military conscription by, 91
    network, 13–14
    Ocalan, Abdullah, leading, 18, 31–35, 50, 52–55, 72, *78*, 88–90, 107–8, 113–17, 120–27, 129–30, 133–35, 148–52, 155, 163, 259
    organizational culture of, 122
    organizational structure of, 163
    PAJK in, 139
    personal sacrifice in, 126–27
    PUK and, 94
    Rojava cantons and, 54
    Sakine Cansiz in, 130, 133–36, 152–53
    Sinjar Mountain and, 42–43
    in "Special War," 113–21
    strategy change of, 103, 105, 119–30, 146–53, 260

Syrian Kurds in, 50
TAK and, 244–45
Talabani, Jalal and, 114–15
as terrorists, 18, 106, 152
training program, 125–26
transition of, 146–53
van Bruinessen on, 87–90, 105–6, 112
PKK-Vejin (Revival), 108
*The Power of the Word: Culture,
Censorship and Voice*
(Women's WORLD), 30–31
*Prison Writing I* (Ocalan, A.), 149
PUK (Patriotic Union of Kurdistan)
Gorran split from, 99–101
Gulf War and, 83
history of, 49
KDP fighting, 80, 94–95
KRG and, 38, 93–94, 98
PKK and, 94
Talabani leading, 13, 38, 66, 80, 94, 98
Putin, Vladimir, 22
PYD (Democratic Union Party)
Abdullah, Asya, co-president of, 44
democratic autonomy and, 53–54,
164–73, 175, 194, 256
founding of, 50–51, 165
gender relations and, 171
KNC and, 191–92
in Kobane canton, 17–18, 38, 168,
183, 185–87
Muslim, Salih, and, 50–51, 164–65,
167, 169, 171, 193, 198
in PKK network, 13
in revolution, 53–54, 164–68
US and, 185–86, 194–95

al Qaeda
Daesh and, 14, 203, 210–14, 216,
218–19, 221
in Iraq, 14, 206, 209–10
Islamism of, 201–6, 209
struggle of, 37
Qasim, Abdal Karim, 62–63

Rabbani, Mouin, 43, 231

rape, 24, 27, 40–41, 67, 94, 98, 101, 141,
144, 209, 225, 228
Raqqa
Daesh in, 215–23
Jabhat al-Nusra in, 215–16, 218–19
women in, 226–30
Raqqa is Being Slaughtered Silently
(RBSS), 221–23
recruits
Daesh, 237–39
YPG-YPJ, 189, 259
refugees
EU and, 193, 199
from Kobane, 183, 189
Kurdish, 49, 66, 82, 84, 182
Rojava, 183, 189, 198
Syrian, 225
Yazidi, 42
Reich, Robert, 45
Reich, Wilhelm, 144–45
Remnick, David, 221
Resettlement Law, 68
Resolution 1325, UN, 140
Reuter, Christoph, 44, 215, 236
Revival. *See* PKK-Vejin
revolution
from bottom up, 53–57
cultural, 103
of Daesh, 56–57
Iranian, 79
Kurdish, 53–57, 59, 71–72
PYD in, 53–54, 164–68
of Rojava cantons, 56–57, 103,
164–68, 260–62
strategies, 71–72
Revolutionary Eastern Cultural Hearths
(DDKO), 69–70
right-wing identity movements, 24–26
Robertson, Pat, 25
Rojava cantons. *See also* Afrin canton;
Cizire canton; Kobane canton
backlash, 191–99
democratic autonomy in, 164–73,
259–63
democratic economy in, 173–77
experiment of, 35

Rojava cantons (cont'd)
  feminism of, 54, 56
  growth of, 241
  liberated, from Daesh, 17–19, 34–35,
    54
  nation-state and, 172
  oil in, 175
  questions remaining about, 259–63
  refugees, 183, 189, 198
  revolution of, 56–57, 103, 164–68,
    260–62
  Russia and, 257
  Social Contract or Charter, 171–72
  struggle of, 37
  stumbling blocks, 259–60
  women at center of, 54, 56, 260–62
  Women's Council, 176
Romano, David, 183
Roy, Olivier, 237
Rumsfeld, Donald, 96
Rushdie, Salman, 25
Russia, 22, 257. *See also* Soviet Union

Sahgal, Gita, 24–25, 144, 196–97
Sakik, Semdin, 117
salafis, 202–3, 206–7, 211, 226, 231, 262
Saleh, Najat Ali, 43
Saleh, Yassin al-Haj, 166
Salih, Cinar, 170
Sartre, Jean-Paul, 72, 87
Sarukhanyan, Seval, 99
Sassounian, Harut, 192–93
*The Satanic Verses* (Rushdie), 25
Saudi Arabia, 203–5, 226
SDF (Syrian Democratic Forces), 190, 241
Sednaya Prison, 211–12
Sener, Mehmet Cahit, 107–8, 129, 135
*Serhildan* (uprising), 108–10, 114
Seroxan, Newroz, 139–40
Sexo, Ehmed, 168
sex slavery, 40–41
sexuality, 142–46
Shah of Iran, 65–66, 71, 79
shaikhs, 45, 59–61, 64
sharia law, 25, 97, 141, 201–3, 208, 215,
  219, 229, 231, 238, 262

Shia Muslims, 83–84, 204–7, 209
Shiv Sena, 25
SHP. *See* Turkish Social Democratic Party
single-sex military units, 137–38
Sinjar Mountain
  battle of, 36, 37–45, 56, 58, 182, 190
  investigation of, 43–45
  Yazidi and, 36, 39–44, 58
Snyder, Timothy, 234
Social Contract or Charter, 171–72, 198
socialism, Soviet approach to, 119–20
Socialist Camp narrative, 20–21
Soviet Union, 20–22, 25, 119–20, 204, 255
Soylemez, Leyla, 152
"Special War," Turkey's on Kurds, 113–21
Stalinism, 64–65
Steinem, Gloria, 140–41
strategic thinking, 31–32
structural adjustment, 22
suicide bombers, 104, 186–87, 240, 251
Sukru, Siddik Hasan, 191
Suleimaniya, 85, 95, 100–101
sultanism, 99
Sumer, 123
Sunni Muslims, 207, 209
  Daesh and, 56, 230, 232–33, 239
  Kurds as, 45, 194
  salafis, 202–3
Sykes-Picot treaty, 233
Syria
  Arab Belt in, 164
  Assad president of, 50, 53, 165–68,
    211–12, 215
  civil war in, 165–68, 211
  Daesh in, 14, 42, 211, 215–23
  democracy in, 35
  FSA and, 168, 180, 188, 196, 198, 213,
    216–18
  geography of, 13
  jihadis in, 53
  opposition in, 165–66, 194, 198, 257
  refugees from, 225
  US and, 182–83, 185–86, 190, 211
Syrian Democratic Forces. *See* SDF
Syrian Kurds. *See also* PYD; Rojava
  cantons; YPG-YPJ

democratic autonomy of, 164–73
history of, 50–51, 164
Iraqi Kurds and, 39
in PKK, 50
Syrian civil war and, 165–68
terminology, 19
in three-way struggle, 37
Syrian Observatory for Human Rights, 184

TAJK (Free Women's Movement of
    Kurdistan), 13, 137
TAK (Freedom Falcons), 244–45
Talabani, Jalal
    corruption of, 99
    KDP and, 62–64
    PKK and, 114–15
    PUK led by, 13, 38, 66, 80, 94, 98
Taliban, 25, 204–5
Al-Tamimi, Aymenn Jawad, 231–32
Tammo, Mashaal, 194
Tas, Nizamettin, 152
Taussig, Michael, 144–45
Tekin, Asya, 183–84
terrorism
    attacks, 205
    logic of, 236–41
    PKK and, 18, 106, 152
    war on, 46, 205
TEV-DEM (Democratic Society
    Movement), 13, 53–54
    democratic autonomy and, 169–72
    KNC and, 192
Tolkien, J.R.R., 19, 35
tribalism
    of KDP, 93, 99
    Kurdish, 45–46, 60–61, 63–66, 87–88,
        93, 99
    nationalism and, 45–46
Tribunal on Violence Against Women,
    1993, 27–28
Tripp, Charles, 235
Truman Doctrine, 51
Tuncel, Sebahat, 133
Turkey
    armed struggle in, 85–92
    backlash and, 191–93

battle of Kobane and, 179–80,
    182–87, 191
Daesh and, 180, 182–87, 222, 248–49
democracy in, 35
Erdogan as president of, 52, 149, 152,
    161, 180, 182–85, 193,
    243–46, 247–52, 254
EU and, 106, 119, 149, 193, 246
geography of, 13
Jabhat al-Nusra and, 180, 185
Kemalism in, 51–52, 67–76, 243
KRG and, 38–39, 45
Kurdish refugees and, 84
lobbyists in Washington, 192–3
mass democratic movement in, 105,
    110, 126
McDowall on, 52, 68, 110, 117
minorities in, 51–52
"moderate Islamism" in, 246–57
nationalism in, 52, 123
Resettlement Law, 68
in "Special War," 113–21
US and, 111–12, 146–47, 193, 248,
    255–57
in WWI, 46
Turkish Kurds. *See also* PKK
    democratic autonomy of, 153,
        155–64, 252–53
    Erdogan and, 149, 152, 161, 180,
        182–85, 244–45, 247–52,
        254
    genocide of, 68–69, 92
    history of, 51–53, 59–61, 67–76
    Iraqi Kurds and, 59–61, 114–15
    terminology, 19
    tribalism of, 87–88
Turkish Kurds, parliamentary parties of
    BDP, 14, 53, 249
    DEHAP, 14, 156
    DEP, 14, 118
    DTP, 14, 156–58, 245
    genealogy, 14
    HDP, 14, 53, 163, 181, 184, 249–52
    HEP, 14, 52, 110–13, 116, 118
Turkish military intelligence. *See* MIT

Turkish Social Democratic Party (SHP), 110–13

UDHR. *See* Universal Declaration of Human Rights
UN. *See* United Nations
Union of Patriotic Revolutionary Young Women. *See* YDG-K
United Nations (UN)
    conferences, 26–28, 30
    Resolution 1325, 140
    sanctions, 49, 93–94
United States (US)
    capitalist narrative of, 21–22
    Christian fundamentalism in, 25–26
    CIA, 111, 146
    Daesh and, 17, 42, 182–83, 185–86, 194–95
    female labor in, 28
    Free World narrative of, 20–21
    Gulf War, 49, 83
    Iran and, 79–80
    Iraq and, 49, 79–80, 83, 95–97, 107, 205–10
    Iraqi Kurds as allies of, 38, 96–97
    KNC and, 191–92
    military interventions by, 18, 25, 42
    Obama administration, 17, 42, 182–83, 185–86, 240
    Operation Desert Storm and, 95–96
    *peshmerga* and, 65–66
    PYD and, 185–86, 194–95
    Syria and, 182–83, 185–86, 190, 211
    Truman Doctrine of, 51
    Turkey and, 111–12, 146–47, 193, 248, 255–57
    "war on terror" by, 46, 205
Universal Declaration of Human Rights (UDHR), 26–27
uprising (*Serhildan*), 108–10, 114
US. *See* United States
Ustundag, Nazan, 129–30, 172–73, 177, 246

van Bruinessen, Martin, 47, 59–60, 63

Kurdistan's geography described by, 37
on PKK, 87–90, 105–6, 112
village chiefs (*aghas*), 45, 59–61, 64
village guards, 87–88, 91
violence
    asayish and, 176–77
    against women, 23–24, 27–28, 101–2, 176–77, 207–9, 225

Waltz, Susan, 26–27
war, gender relations in, 140
"war on terror," 46, 205
Watts, Nicole, 250
Weiner, Tim, 147
Weiss, Michael, 184, 188
Western feminists, strategic thinking by, 31–32
"The West's Darling in Syria" (Oweis), 193–94
White, Paul, 122, 245
Whitman, Lois, 106
Wilson, Lydia, 238
Wobblies. *See* Industrial Workers of the World
Wolf, Christa, 33
women. *See also* gender relations; Kurdish women; women's movement
    in Arab Spring, 23
    asayish, 172, 176–77
    Beijing Conference on, 26, 28, 30
    in China, 137–38
    councils of, 171
    Daesh and, 20, 28, 34, 141, 201, 218–19, 225–30, 238–39
    economy and, 175–76
    Erdogan and, 247
    in Iraq, 102–3, 207–10
    labor by, 28–29, 32
    in patriarchal belt, 23–24
    peace movement of, 140–41
    in Raqqa, 226–30
    violence against, 23–24, 27–28, 101–2, 176–77, 207–9, 225
Women Living Under Muslim Laws, 29

*Women of the Islamic State: A Manifesto by the Al-Khanssa Brigade*, 228–29
women's movement. *See also* feminism
   fundamentalism and, 25–26
   global, 25–28
   human rights and, 26–28
   Kurdish, 31, 33–34, 141–42, 259
Women's WORLD (Women's World Organization for Rights, Literature and Development), 30–31
Wood, Graeme, 231
World Social Forums, 29
World War I (WWI), 46, 233
*The Wretched of the Earth* (Fanon), 72, 87
Wright, Lawrence, 201–2
WWI. *See* World War I

Yassin-Kassab, Robin, 166–67
Yazidi
   genocide, 40, 44
   Kurds as, 45
   militias, 190–91
   Sinjar Mountain and, 36, 39–44, 58
YDG-H (Patriotic Revolutionary Youth Movement), 14, 184, 250
YDG-K (Union of Patriotic Revolutionary Young Women), 14, 177
Yildirim, Kesire, 108, 130, 135
YJA-Star, 42, 136–37, 142

Yoruk, Erdem, 69
Yousef, Amaad, 164, 173–74
YPG-YPJ (People's Protection Units and Women's Protection Units), 53, 104, 165, 178, 224, 256, 264
   celibacy and, 142–45
   false accusations against, 194–98
   Kobane canton and, 38–39, 41, 180–82, 184–88
   patrol truck, 224
   in PKK network, 13
   recruits, 189, 259
   Sinjar Mountain and, 38–39, 41–43, 182, 190
   trials, 196
YPJ. *See* YPG-YPJ
YRK-HPJ (Eastern Kurdistan Protection Units and Women's Protection Units), 13
Yugoslavia, 25
Yuksekdag, Figen, 252

Zana, Leyla, 73–76, 103, 156, 250
   in HEP, 113, 116
   imprisoned, 91–92, 118–19
Zana, Mehdi, 74–76, 91
al Zarqawi, Abu Musab, 205–6, 209–10
al-Zawahiri, Ayman, 206, 209, 213–14, 216, 219
Zelin, Aaron, 219
Zumrut, Zubeyde, 163

BELLEVUE LITERARY PRESS is devoted to publishing
literary fiction and nonfiction at the intersection of
the arts and sciences because we believe that science and the
humanities are natural companions for understanding the human
experience. With each book we publish, our goal is to foster a rich,
interdisciplinary dialogue that will forge new tools for thinking and
engaging with the world.

To support our press and its mission, and for our full catalogue of
published titles, please visit us at blpress.org.

BELLEVUE LITERARY PRESS
New York